LESSONS FROM THE PAST

LESSONS FROM THE PAST

An Introductory Reader in Archaeology

Kenneth L. Feder

Central Connecticut State University

Mayfield Publishing Company
Mountain View, California
London • Toronto

Library of Congress Cataloging-in-Publication Data

Lessons from the past : an introductory reader in archaeology /
    Kenneth L. Feder.
        p.   cm.
    Includes index.
    ISBN 0-7674-0453-X
    1. Archaeology.   2. Archaeology — Methodology.   I. Feder, Kenneth L.
CC165.L44   1998
930. 1 — dc21   98-44708
                                                                CIP

Manufactured in the United States of America
10   9   8   7   6   5   4   3   2   1

Sponsoring editor, Janet M. Beatty; production editor, Melissa Kreischer; manuscript editor, Kay Mikel; design manager, Susan Breitbard; cover designer, Diana Coe; art editor, Amy Folden; illustrator, Joan Carol; cover photo, © Nicholas DeVore III- Photographers/Aspen, Inc./RNI; back cover photo, National Park Service, Little Bighorn Battlefield National Monument; manufacturing manager, Randy Hurst. The text was set in 10/12 Palatino by ColorType and printed on acid-free 45# Optimatte by Banta Book Group, Harrisonburg.

This book is printed on recycled paper.

Preface

Most introductory archaeology texts focus on the methods used by archaeologists to reveal the human past. These books do an admirable job of describing how we know what we know about the past through the study of the material remains of human behavior.

Exposure to method alone, however, may not be enough to provide beginning students with a full appreciation for the field of archaeology. Students want to see archaeology in action—to learn how archaeology is *applied*. In this sense, they share a sentiment with Socrates, who criticized purely hypothetical or technical discussion, saying:

I might compare myself to a person who, on beholding beautiful animals either created by the painter's art or, better still, alive but at rest, is seized with a desire of seeing them in motion or engaged in some struggle or conflict to which their forms appear suited. (1952:443)

This reader offers a series of articles in which archaeologists are engaged in the "struggles" that suit them best: to explain the present, serve the needs of modern communities, contribute to the solution of a contemporary problem, decipher a historical mystery, approach the present from an archaeological perspective, or even to solve a crime.

The articles in this thematic reader are divided into six parts:

The Past Is the Key to the Present looks at insights gained from the study of past societies and how they can be used to explain the modern world.

Serving Communities through Archaeology provides a historical voice for people who might otherwise remain voiceless.

A Useful Past: Archaeology in the Modern World demonstrates how the methodology of archaeology is applied to modern problems.

Helping History: Setting the Record Straight and Solving the Mysteries describes how archaeology is used to attempt to solve historical puzzles.

If the Present Were an Archaeological Site contains articles that—sometimes humorously—get at the question "How can archaeologists tell what they're looking at?"

Forensic Archaeology examines how the methodology of field archaeology has been used to solve

crimes and provide some closure to the issue of Vietnam MIAs.

Between these parts the reader will find seven autobiographical sketches, written specifically for this book, of a diverse group of working archaeologists. Accompanied by photos of the archaeologists, these moving personal stories reveal how individuals with very different backgrounds came to devote their lives to the study of the human past—in very different ways.

Archaeology is not simply an esoteric enterprise involving arcane knowledge of pots, points, and pyramids. I hope the selection of articles in this book will reveal archaeology for what it truly is—a dynamic and exciting field that can provide valuable insights, meaningful solutions, and just plain fascinating information about the past that can contribute to a better understanding of the present.

PEDAGOGICAL AIDS

To help students better understand what they read, I've provided the following:

- an annotated table of contents, which provides just a hint about each article's subject
- a brief description that prefaces each article and places its importance within the context of the lesson from the past that it conveys
- a series of issues and questions to think about that precedes each article
- a glossary

To help busy instructors, I've prepared an Instructor's Manual that summarizes the message of each article and provides a series of test questions for each article.

ACKNOWLEDGMENTS

Any published compendium of articles relies absolutely on the generosity of colleagues, and this book is no exception. I want to thank the authors, editors, and publishers who granted permission to reprint their articles in this volume. Though other compilers of similar volumes warned me in advance of uncooperative colleagues, recalcitrant journal editors, and greedy publishers (who would require most of my royalties along with my first-born child for the privilege of reprinting their article or chapter), I encountered no such beasts. Everyone I dealt with was extremely cooperative and remarkably accommodating. It was a genuine pleasure working with them all.

I would like to thank especially those who prepared new pieces for this volume. In particular, I owe an enormous debt to the seven archaeologists who produced splendid accounts of their personal journeys and varied pathways to archaeology. Thank you for sharing your lives with us here: Meg Conkey, Frank McManamon, Tim Pauketat, Warren Perry, Cece Saunders, Lynne Sebastian, and Bob Stewart. Thanks also to Michael Park, Tom King and Ric Gillespie, and Al Harper for preparing new articles for this book. I needed to provide no special inducement to these terrific people to encourage their participation in this project; all I had to do was ask.

Thanks also are due to the many colleagues who helped out directly in obtaining the requisite permissions for the use of their work and for providing artwork to accompany their articles. In particular, I would like to thank Mel Adams, Nick Bellantoni, Heather Devine, Brian Fagan, Don Hardesty, Tom Holland, Maureen Kaplan, Dorothy Lippert, Kevin McBride, Ivor Noël Hume, Warren Perry, and Doug Scott. Also, many thanks to Jessica Saraceni, Associate Editor at *Archaeology* for helping obtain permission to reprint articles from the magazine; Jodie O'Gorman at the Center for American Archaeology Press for her help with the articles from the late and lamented magazine *Early Man*; Merle Okada at *Natural History*; and Glen Gibbons at *GPS World*.

I'm grateful for the incisive comments of the reviewers of the manuscript: Christopher DeCorse, Syracuse University; René Péron, Santa Rosa Junior College; Barbara Roth, Oregon State University; David Small, Lehigh University; and James Skibo, Illinois State University. Their suggestions and encouragement are greatly appreciated.

I first discussed my idea for a theme-driven reader for introductory archaeology with sponsoring editor Jan Beatty in 1992. Over the next few years, other projects diverted my attention from the reader, but Jan never let me forget our earlier discussion. This book's publication is a testament to her persistence. I also must thank my production editor, Melissa Kreischer; this is the third project I have worked on with Melissa, who must have done something awful in a previous life to have been so afflicted. She is incredibly good at what she does. Also, she is just too cool.

I live a charmed existence. I am able to share my life and work with three of the nicest people and two of the silliest cats I know or can imagine: my wife Melissa, our two boys Josh and Jacob, and the kitties Randolph and Harpo. Without their understanding and picking up the slack when I am in the middle of a book project, the entire process would not have been possible. Okay, okay: I promise to clean the litter box more regularly now.

Contents

PART 2 *Serving Communities through Archaeology*   29

Families become separated by distance, disagreements, and time. In the case of the Walton family of Griswold, Connecticut, archaeologists have been able to reunite living members of the family with their ancestors whose remains were nearly lost by time's amnesia.

PART 3   *A Useful Past: Archaeology in the Modern World   87*

PART 4   *Helping History: Setting the Record Straight and Solving the Mysteries   121*

Lessons from the Past:
The Search for a "Relevant" Archaeology

To many, **archaeology** is the very essence of esoterica, one in a list of utterly useless scientific pursuits much like those practiced and perfected by the Modern Major-General in Gilbert and Sullivan's operetta, *The Pirates of Penzance*. Though William Gilbert's lyrics do not include archaeology, it would have been entirely in character had the Major-General listed "things archaeological" among the "matters vegetable, animal, and mineral" that he claimed as his accomplishments.

Archaeology may seem innocent enough and vaguely interesting on its surface in the popular imagination, but it is thought to be of no significant use in the real world. An interesting hobby, perhaps, but a grown person surely would not devote much of his or her time to it. After all, archaeology focuses—or so it would seem—largely on the unknowable minutiae of past worlds whose significance in and import for the present are tenuous at best. Isn't archaeology just another in a line of academic disciplines that do little more than provide jobs for its practitioners? Aren't most (all?) archaeologists eccentric, white-bearded old gentlemen who argue animatedly over the weighty details of **potsherds, spear points,** and the crumbling splinters of ancient bones? Certainly, it might be interesting to learn about past times and past lives, but of what practical consequence or relevance are archaeological data and theory to our modern world? We face far more immediate and manifold problems.

Such caricatures of archaeology are common, but these are wrong-headed in the extreme. Indeed, at the core of this book is the categorical rejection of the notion that archaeology represents the foolish and ultimately doomed pursuit of some ephemeral and unreachable past. The articles contained in this reader belie this libel and show how archaeological research can make important contributions to the modern human dialogue about ourselves.

Archaeology is a subdiscipline within the broader field of **anthropology,** the study of humanity. The focus of much of archaeology is **material culture**—the things people made and used and then discarded, lost, or abandoned, as well as the fortuitously preserved bones of the people themselves. For the vast majority of humanity's tenure on this planet, these physical remains are all we have to illuminate the lives of past peoples. For this **prehistoric** period—literally the period before the invention of writing—there is little choice, short of the invention of time travel, but to conduct archaeology if we want to know about the lives of our distant human ancestors. Their stories are not written in words on a page but in bits of pottery and seeds, in stone spear point tips and the bones of their prey, in pyramids and tombs, in their tools and items of personal adornment, as well as in their own skeletal remains.

Furthermore, archaeology does not end with the beginning of the written record. Written history is neither complete nor inclusive; the lives of the vast majority of people who have ever lived were simply ignored by the history writers of their own time. Officially recorded history isn't even always truthful. An old cliché states that "history is written by the winners," who may play fast and loose with the facts so that their own people, as well as history, may look more kindly on them.

Especially in the centuries before our own, most people were not literate. History was written by those who worked for, and reflected the interests and views of, the rich and powerful. Pharaohs, kings, and emperors were wealthy and powerful enough to support a coterie of specialist scribes whose job it was to memorialize on clay tablets, papyrus sheets, or stone monuments the accomplishments of their bosses. The vast numbers of individuals whose labor and sweat filled the granaries, manned the armies, baked the bread, and built the temples and pyramids that characterize ancient civilizations could not write, and few who could thought enough of their stories to record them. Peasants, farmers, soldiers, and workers are, at least as individuals, largely invisible in history, but as archaeological remains, the tools they used, the ruins of their houses, the trash they disposed of, and even their skeletons may yet tell their stories.

Archaeology does not end even here, with the early literate civilizations. Even in recent times, many people have been ignored by or misrepresented in the written record. In our own nation, little more than 130 years ago, an entire race of people was held in bondage. Kidnapped from their ancestral homelands in Africa, stacked in ships like cargo, and then transported to America, they labored in the cotton fields and "big houses" of southern plantations and, yes, the farmsteads of the rural north and the cities of New York, Boston, and Philadelphia. In some states it was illegal to teach slaves to read or write. Even if slaves were literate, it is unlikely that they would have been afforded the opportunity to write and distribute the stories of their lives. But archaeology is not silent about their plight; the homes where they were kept, the caches in which they stored the cultural treasures they kept hidden from their overseers, and the remains of the food they foraged to supplement what was provided by the slave owners still survive to answer our questions and to provide us with a narrative of their lives. Even their bones have, in some cases, survived and can be read by specialists, revealing the physical deprivation and pain wrought by slavery.

It is a little different for others in the modern period, yet archaeology can still teach us much about their life experiences. For example, though literacy may have been more widespread among those of European descent living in North America, most rural farmers and urban factory workers in the seventeenth, eighteenth, nineteenth, and even the twentieth century still had little inclination and even less free time to tell us their stories in their own words. Without access to printing presses, those who could put their personal sagas in words did so in diaries or in the opening pages of family Bibles, and we are enormously lucky and privileged to have such records. These written histories, as well as the official government and church records kept of births, marriages, deaths, taxes, and land transactions, are used together with the material record by **historical archaeologists.** In historical archaeology, the written records that do exist are examined together with the physical remains of farmsteads, urban tenements, outcast villages, pioneer forts, copper mines, woolen mills, Indian reservations, and so forth to enable us to fill in the gaps left by written history and official records, to correct the biases and inaccuracies of those who in the past wrote about their own times with imperfect knowledge, and simply to provide a new, fresh, unbiased perspective on the recent history of our own society.

The purpose of this reader, finally, is to bring together a wide variety of articles and essays in which archaeologists—and other scientists using the data produced by the archaeological study of the human past—have attempted to apply the unique perspective garnered from our discipline with its distinctive focus on material culture to issues and puzzles facing modern humanity. Specifically, the articles in this compendium exemplify how, working in the present and thinking about our future, we can apply valuable lessons derived from the study of the past.

I AM AN ARCHAEOLOGIST

Far too often in science we forget that the work is done, not by cold, dispassionate, unemotional drones but by thinking, feeling, imperfect human beings. It is not surprising that scientists often play down the role of personality, ego, and emotion in science. "After all," many scientists would assert, "*We* are not the story. It is the results of our research that are important." As a consequence, scientists often do all they can to eliminate their personal sentiments—both their disappointments and their sense of exhilaration—from their written work. Many scientific publications avoid discussions of the personal intellectual voyage taken by the scientist, and some even go to the extreme of avoiding the use of personal pronouns, as if an "I" or a "me" might somehow compromise the purity and objectivity of the research.

Although it is reasonable to eschew ego and to focus on data and the results of experiments in scientific writing, that contradicts my purpose here. Who we are very much affects—and has always had an effect on—the kinds of archaeology we choose to do and the perspectives we bring to that task. For example, there was a time in archaeology when it would have been fair to characterize its practitioners as mostly male, mostly white, and mostly upper class. It is also fair to suggest that the kind of research people thought was important and worthy of funding when this was the case was greatly affected by the fairly narrow population of intellectuals afforded the opportunity to explore the past. It should not surprise us, for example, that in the early twentieth century Lord Carnarvon, a member of the British nobility, was interested in funding archaeological research that might result in the discovery of the magnificent tombs of ancient Egyptian nobility. It likely did not even occur to him that the lives of Egyptian commoners might have been every bit as interesting and important in our attempt to understand the society over which the nobility ruled. Certainly, we must thank Lord Carnarvon for funding the work of archaeologist Howard Carter. His generosity led to the discovery and preservation of the tomb of the boy king, Tut-ankh-amun, perhaps the most famous archaeological **excavation** ever conducted. But to understand the workings of ancient Egypt, it is as important to understand the lives of those whose toil built the pyramids as it is to comprehend the lives of those who spent eternity within them.

The stereotypic archaeologist of the nineteenth and early twentieth centuries no longer exists. Today the people engaged in the science of archaeology are a fascinating and far more diverse group. They are men and women—more than 50% of students in graduate archaeology programs in the United States are women—of various ethnic and social backgrounds. This far greater demographic diversity renders our interests more eclectic and, in a sense, more democratic. Lord Carnarvon may have identified with King Tut and the Egyptian nobility and wished to illuminate their lives. Many entering the field today can identify better with the peasants who built the pyramids and find the process of revealing their lives to be at least as rewarding.

It is also true that archaeology attracts people at different points along their life trajectory. Some of us became captivated by the past at an early age; archaeology is all I and many of my colleagues can remember ever wanting to do. Others came late to the discipline, bringing with them a lifetime of experience doing something else. Their varied experiences often provide this group of archaeologists with unique insights about human behavior.

People are attracted to archaeology for many different reasons. Some are drawn to the field because of an enormous, ecumenical fascination for the times and lives that characterize human antiquity. For them, it makes little difference whether the subject is ancient America, the first settlers of Australia, the **Neandertals,** Egypt of the pharaohs, **Stonehenge,** or any other time or place. If the discussion is about the human past, they are fascinated. Others feel a special and personal connection to and reverence for the past of particular groups of peoples, often because those past peoples are these archaeologists' direct ancestors (see the articles in Part 2, "Serving Communities through Archaeology").

I am going to introduce you to a small group of working archaeologists and allow them to tell their very personal stories. None of these folks are unique; I chose them idiosyncratically. These are people whose work I find most interesting, and I use them here, in a sense, as symbols or emblems of modern archaeologists. A different group of my colleagues would have resulted in stories varying greatly in their particulars but conveying the same fundamental message. Archaeologists bring to their work an intense and passionate curiosity about how things happened in the past and why. They are focused on discovering, explaining, understanding, protecting, and preserving the human past. Starting with Meg Conkey and then following each section of this reader, you will find the short autobiographies of seven of my colleagues. They will explain how and why they became archaeologists. If archaeologists enjoy any aspect of the job as much as the research itself, it is explaining to laypersons what they do and why it is important work. Let us proceed and find out just who is an archaeologist.

I AM AN ARCHAEOLOGIST

Margaret W. Conkey

(Courtesy of Meg Conkey)

My mother always thought I should be a librarian, and maybe an archaeologist is just one kind of librarian. We, too, are interested in systematic information, in preservation and storage of "texts" that we can try to read, "texts" in many forms that can be used, especially if organized and classified, to make inferences, in this case, about the lives of past humans. Archaeologists are well known for their love and care of material culture (we never break things at our convention hotels). Archaeologists are well known for their attention to detail and for their ability to recognize patterns (my children could never understand how I knew they had been snitching cookies, as even a few crumbs could not escape my attention as a clue to past behavior). Archaeologists are well known for their ability to classify things (we only have archaeologists as house sitters because they keep everything more or less in place). And, of course, archaeology is much more than these useful quirks.

In any event, I became an archaeologist instead of a librarian, and my mother does not seem to mind. I was clearly headed in this direction as an undergraduate. Although I never took an anthropology course, I eventually declared a joint major in ancient history and art history. The really significant event for me was the fluke opportunity to join an archaeological excavation in the summer between my junior and senior years. The full story of how this happened is too long to tell here. However, it all started as a dorm room joke and a letter of inquiry to an archaeologist: "Did he need an extra person?" The next thing I knew—thanks to funds from a family friend and my undergraduate student government association—I was spending a long summer in a very hot Middle East country where our limited water supply went first to washing potsherds and only occasionally to us for showers. I couldn't believe that I could learn to accept that I would not wash my hair for weeks at a time!

That experience directed me first toward the University of Chicago's famous Oriental Institute for graduate studies. However, by the time I arrived on campus, I had unexpectedly been exposed to anthropology, which, for me, was like an infectious disease. In that last summer before graduate school, I found myself working at the Wenner-Gren Foundation for Anthropological Research—yes, as a librarian! What a job; there I was in bustling New York City, reading and organizing books, articles, and other publications about all sorts of anthropology. At Chicago, I went to work for the foundation's international journal, *Current Anthropology,* and despite my interest in the courses I took in the archaeology of the Middle East, I soon transferred into the anthropology Ph.D. program. This was a time of enormous excitement in anthropological archaeology; the late 1960s and the veritable fever of what was called the **"New Archaeology"** was not just in the air but had its locus at Chicago. Some of my peers were central figures in a self-styled "revolution" in archaeology. I was also drawn into the climate of excitement over the archaeology of the European Paleolithic (or **Old Stone Age**). At the time of both the M.A. and Ph.D. theses, I was convinced that we could learn a lot about the ancient **hunter-gatherer** peoples from their cave art and the engraved pieces of bone and antler that were made in the **Upper Paleolithic,** especially between 15,000 and 11,000 years ago in southwestern Europe (what is today France and Spain).

I guess I did my wandering early on. After a few fieldwork experiences in other places—the chinampas of the Valley of Mexico and a historic fort in Michlimackinac, Michigan—almost all of my archaeology has been in southwestern Europe. I am still very interested in why many Upper Paleolithic peoples produced and reproduced what appears to us to be an intensely material and visual culture. They used pigments to draw on cave walls, to "color in" engraved animals and designs on bone and antler, and to augment shapes and forms on stone slabs. They carved thousands of items out of bone, antler, and ivory, including now celebrated human figurines and hundreds of perforated items that look like "beads." They placed geometric designs on implements that appear to have been for everyday use. From a detailed analysis of some 1,200 engraved bones from sites in Cantabrian, Spain (for my Ph.D. dissertation), to our current project in the French Midi-Pyrénées, much of my work has been directed toward understanding the why of this visual and material **culture** that has been so fortuitously well preserved for us.

Although I began Paleolithic archaeology firmly committed to trying to "say" something about these people of the past without getting deeply involved in the study of their ubiquitous **stone tools,** I now find myself in the greatest irony of all. Our survey project, which is seeking to find traces of Upper Paleolithic people across a regional landscape in the areas "between the caves," is completely dependent on our finding the **stone tools** that were left behind, which we can today recover from plowed fields. It is through these "lithic landscapes," the differential distribution of artifacts, that we will infer the pathways of the people, discover how they used their resources, and perhaps learn how and why certain places in the open air, as well as certain caves, became focal points for human activities and for the material practices, including "art."

Because my work has been as much about issues of "art" and human symbolic and social behavior, including the study of gender, as about the systematic and scientific recovery of archaeological information, I have been able (as are many archaeologists) to garner research support from both humanistic and scientific funding agencies. Our current survey project is funded by the National Science Foundation but is in collaboration with French scientists studying the **paleo-environment,** and for that work we have funds from the France-Berkeley fund. Indeed, international as well as interdisciplinary collaboration has long been an important feature of most archaeological research.

Archaeologists must work in teams, and we all learn to live together to do our fieldwork, often in less than glamorous field camps! Our work is a puzzle in the human sciences; we have to think about societies whose people probably lived lives that are really alien to us today. We have to use every shred of evidence in a very careful way, and we have to learn to live with ambiguity. Archaeology is the best way to develop critical thinking about anything, so even if you do not choose to become an archaeologist—an archivist and interpreter of past human lives—questioning "how we know what we know" is an important lesson for all of us.

PART 1

The Past Is the Key to the Present

Humanity's roots can be traced back some 4 million years or more, yet the **historical record** illuminates barely the last 5,000 years of our story—less than one-eighth of one percent of the tenure of upright **hominids** (the taxonomic family that includes humans and our direct ancestors) on this planet.

From this fact alone, it can be argued reasonably that much of what makes us human is rooted in **prehistory,** wherein more than 99% of the human story resides. It is not difficult to conclude that to understand the modern human condition we need to understand the enormous proportion of the human past that is literally prehistoric—that is, the time before the invention of writing and before people could self-consciously tell us their stories. Human existence on this planet that dates to more than 5,000 years ago, therefore, is the exclusive purview of prehistoric archaeologists and **paleoanthropologists.** With a focus precisely on this segment of the human past, the science of archaeology is in a unique position to contribute to our understanding of ourselves.

Put another way, because the historical record represents only a small fraction of our story, it follows that much of what makes us human is rooted in prehistoric antiquity. As an analogy, imagine that the story of humanity was written as an actual book of 400 pages, with events reported in that book at a point proportional to when they actually happened in the past. Written history would be represented only on the bottom half of the final page of this book. The first 399-and-a-half pages of the human story would be devoted to the human saga before our ancestors developed the tools to write about their lives and experiences. In fact, of course, there is no such book. The only way to "read" those first 399-and-a-half pages of the human story is by doing archaeology.

The argument can and has been made (to the point of cliché) that one cannot understand the present human condition without reference to the vast proportion of our existence that predates recorded history. In a sense, archaeologists turn nineteenth-century geologist Charles Lyell's guiding principle—"The present is the key to the past"—on its head. For Lyell, only by studying modern processes of weathering and erosion acting in the present can we comprehend how ancient landforms were produced. For archaeologists, the reverse is true—the past is the key to the present. This is not to say that the archaeological study of the past can, by itself, resolve all or even some of the major problems facing the world today. Not even the most ardent of archaeology's supporters believe that it can. However, archaeologists do provide a vital perspective on the human condition because we often focus on the vast segment of the human story that predates the invention of writing—and, further, we do not rely on the self-conscious attempts of people to tell their own story from their own perspective. Therefore, at least in an *implicit* way, archaeological data and interpretation illuminate the human story and the human condition.

Archaeologists, however, do not often use the material record of the past in an *explicit* way to examine the modern human condition. Although archaeological data and the unique perspective archaeologists bring to their data could and should provide important insights about our species, most of us have tended to shy away from using our data in this way. Happily, however, a few, sometimes courageous, attempts have been made to use archaeology to illuminate modern philosophical, economic, ideological, or even practical issues.

Topics such as the energy crisis, pollution, urban decay, discrimination, war, overpopulation, and so on are all major issues facing humanity today. In one form or another all of these issues have been faced by people in the centuries and even millennia preceding our own. Archaeology can show us how people reacted to some of these challenges in the past, providing models of response to these recurrent issues. Important lessons can be learned by studying the past, and these insights may help us respond to similar challenges in the present. The underlying theme of Part 1—and the reason for its inclusion—is that archaeology can provide crucial insights into these issues because, in one form or another, they all are rooted in antiquity.

Part 1 includes articles that show how archaeologists and other thinkers have used archaeological data derived from prehistoric and more recent records either to elucidate a specific issue challenging modern humanity or to generalize about the modern human condition.

1

The Original Energy Crisis

Fred Plog

The late Fred Plog was an eloquent spokesperson for a new brand of archaeology that emerged in the 1960s. Here he applies the lessons of the past to our thinking about modern issues in a terrific example of what the "New Archaeology" was about.

Points to consider when reading this article:

1. On what basis do some archaeologists propose that there was an energy shortage in the ancient American Southwest?

2. What impact might the hypothesized wood shortage have had on the ancient cultures of the American Southwest?

3. What lessons can we learn by studying how the inhabitants of the ancient Southwest responded to the prehistoric energy crisis?

4. In what fundamental way does a wood shortage differ from an oil or coal shortage?

Without thinking much about it, we turn on our furnaces in the morning to take the chill off and make enough hot water for a shower. We plug in the coffeemaker, slip a couple of slices of bread into the toaster, retrieve butter and eggs from the refrigerator, and turn on the stove to cook a hearty breakfast. We then slip behind the wheel of our SUV or minivan and head off to work or school.

In each of these actions, we have used up just a little more of the finite energy resources this planet has to offer us. We have used up just a little more oil, a little more gas, or we have burned a little more coal. And there is just that little bit less for future generations. The prices of these fuels remain high, and those who control the gas, oil, or coal fields—people not always on friendly terms with us—accrue more and more wealth and, with it, greater power.

Is ours the first society to have to deal with a finite and diminishing source of energy? Are there any historical, or prehistoric, examples of how societies have responded when the fuel they relied on became scarce and expensive? Our society is certainly not the first to be faced with an energy crisis; history—and prehistory—is filled with examples of how energy shortages affected ancient societies. Here, archaeologist Fred Plog examines a prehistoric energy crisis in the American Southwest. This is a splendid example of how the study of the past can provide insights into problems facing us in the present.

F or decades, archaeologists working in the American Southwest have sought to understand why many major prehistoric centers in Arizona, New Mexico, Colorado and Utah were suddenly abandoned between about A.D. 1100 and 1400. This exodus happened at different times and in different areas, but it was a dramatic event in every case. At one moment full of large towns, small villages, farmsteads, homesteads, agricul-

tural fields, and in some cases elaborate road systems, area after area—Chaco Canyon, Mesa Verde, Hovenweep, Wupatki—suddenly became empty. Archaeologists have considered many possible causes for the phenomenon: a major epidemic, warfare, invasion by Athabascan ancestors of the Navajo and Apache, and drought. Recently, a new possibility has come under scrutiny, one that is all too familiar to us today: a shortage of fuel.

No, the Anasazi, Hohokam and Mogollon who lived in the Southwest did not fall victim to a prehistoric ayatollah, an oil cartel, or a new geopolitical reality. The fuel that became scarce was not oil, but

From *Early Man*, Spring 1982. Reprinted here courtesy of the Center for American Archaeology, Kampsville, IL.

wood. Throughout the human past, wood shortages have been a major factor in the relocation of villages and the migrations of thousands — in some cases millions — of people.

Graduate student Don Dove at Arizona State University, reviewing historic evidence of fuelwood problems, discovered that during the 17th and 18th centuries England experienced a wood shortage so severe that Napoleon restricted the export of wood from continental Europe. A visitor to Scotland during that time is reported to have commented: "If Judas had chosen this country in which to repent, he would not have found a tree from which to hang himself."

Even today, as heavy an impact as oil problems have on our lives, wood shortages are affecting fully three-quarters of the people on the globe who depend on wood for heating and cooking. During the last 30 years, more than half of the forests on our planet have been stripped for fuel and construction. In the meantime, the population has been expanding.

Most of us are conditioned to thinking of wood as a relatively free resource. Fireplaces typically serve decorative purposes, rather than functional ones. True, with our oil and gas shortage, more and more Americans are turning to the use of stoves and fireplaces for heating. However, while the cost of a cord of wood has increased, it remains relatively inexpensive — even less so for hearty souls willing to endure a trek into the woods and an afternoon of strenuous work to cut their own.

Given the vast forested areas on our continent, how is it reasonable to even entertain the possibility that prehistoric Americans might have experienced fuel shortages? Three factors must be considered. First, there were times in some areas of prehistoric North America when human numbers were very high. Second, for many of these people, wood was not only used for fuel and cooking, but was also a primary material in construction. Finally, there were no pickup trucks, no beasts of burden, to carry wood. The area from which wood could be obtained was limited by the number of humans available to transport the resource economically.

My own curiosity about the possibility of prehistoric wood shortages began with the reading of two comments by William Sanders of Pennsylvania State University concerning his research in the Valley of Mexico. Sanders observed that some of the existing peasant villages there were forced to purchase charcoal for fuel from villages in closer proximity to sources of wood. He also mentioned the problems encountered by archaeologists attempting to reconstruct the natural vegetation of the area: at those altitudes where farming has been especially heavy, the natural vegetation has been removed during 4,000 years of cultivation.

Certainly, the Valley of Mexico is an extreme case; it is unique in the length and intensity of human exploitation of the land. But what is the likelihood that similar problems, perhaps of a lesser magnitude, occurred elsewhere in North America? Is there a possibility that in less heavily forested areas the impact of human activity on the natural landscape may have had even more dire consequences?

At best, the information available to archaeologists for estimating the magnitude of the problem prehistoric people might have faced in acquiring wood is indirect. Since hearths are continually cleaned, and ash is dispersed into middens and then further scattered by the wind, it is virtually impossible to obtain a record of changing fuelwood use at a single site. Nor do archaeologists typically find woodpiles in prehistoric deposits. If any wood was left at a camp or village, it would have been found and used by later groups. However, at least for some areas, information does exist on the quantity of fuelwood available. Similarly, a few studies have been done on the rate at which preindustrial peoples today use fuelwood.

I was fortunate enough to be able to obtain such figures for the Mogollon Rim area of Arizona. In order to aid in planning fuelwood use by our own society, the U.S. Forest Service has carried out studies to estimate the availability of fuelwood in the Apache-Sitgreaves Forest. Scott Russell, a graduate student at Arizona State University working on a doctoral dissertation dealing with the Navajo, had collected information on fuelwood use among this modern group. While the Navajo do not provide an exact analog to the behavior of prehistoric peoples, differences between the two groups would generally be offsetting. For example, the Navajo do not make extensive use of wood for firing pottery. On the other hand, they use wood stoves that are more efficient than the open hearths common among prehistoric groups.

Using average figures for the availability of fuelwood in the Mogollon Rim area (3.4 cords per acre) and average rates of per capita consumption (2.7 cords per person), it is possible to project that, with an average population density of 20 people per square mile, trees would have been depleted over an entire square mile before there was any chance for them to grow back. Thus, where population density reached this average — a frequent occurrence in many areas of the northern Southwest by A.D. 1100 — prehistoric peoples would be competing with one another for scarce fuel resources.

In the case of larger sites, those with populations of about 1,000 people, a 3.5-mile radius from the village would have been cleared of trees within a single generation. The radius would increase to six miles before any meaningful regeneration of the woodlands occurred,

FIGURE 1   Nestled in a naturally occurring hollow in the cliff face, Square Tower House is one of the many impressive dwellings built by the ancient Anasazi Indians at Mesa Verde and elsewhere in the Four Corners region of the American Southwest. It is the opinion of Fred Plog that the archaeology of the Anasazi shows that they experienced an "energy crisis" long before our modern culture was threatened by a cutoff of our oil supply. (K. L. Feder; not in the original article)

thus impinging on the fuelwood resources of the inhabitants of smaller nearby sites. If, as seems likely, the forests had already been depleted by millennia of fuelwood use, a population density as low as 10 people per square mile would have created significant competition for fuel within a 75-year period.

Thus a reasonable case can be made that a scarcity of fuelwood could have caused severe problems in areas with far fewer people than there were in the Valley of Mexico—assuming the use of wood for fuel alone. Steadman Upham of New Mexico State University, in his studies of the village ruins of Nuvaqwewtaqa south of Winslow, Arizona, has shown that the need for construction timbers at large sites such as this one would have aggravated the problem considerably.

A more sophisticated approach to questions about wood availability has been taken by Don Dove in his study of the Agua Fria River Valley north of Phoenix. Compared with nearby areas, this one was occupied for only a relatively brief period between A.D. 700 and 1250. In attempting to understand the hazards of living in his valley, Dove took into account the practice of agriculture there and the availability of fuelwood from

the mesquite forests that once covered river bottoms throughout the Phoenix area.

The technique Dove used is known as computer simulation, in which factors are identified that are critical to understanding a particular problem. To understand agriculture, for example, we would want to know the number of people to be fed, the availability of good agricultural land, the likelihood of sufficient rainfall to produce crops, and the ability of the soil to retain moisture. The computer is then given a set of minimum, average and maximum possible values for each of the factors. In addition, random factors to simulate floods and other catastrophes may be used. For each year, over a period of centuries or even millennia, the computer can then come up with the likelihood of a successful crop.

Applying this technique to the fuelwood issue, Dove concluded that fuelwood was likely to have become a source of competition between nearby population clusters within a few hundred years of the initial occupation of the area.

Looking back on some of his earlier work there, Dove observed: "At the Calderwood ruin, two fire hearths contained only remains of tiny burned twigs. At the time, I thought the material was creosote. I didn't connect the situation with a firewood shortage . . . what I found would have been an inefficient fuel and not likely used if a more favorable alternative was available."

Dove also explores the possibility that a major architectural change—from wood and mud single-family residences to large adobe and stone apartment complexes—may in part have been the result of less and less readily available construction timbers.

It is probably through the careful examination of charcoal recovered in hearths that archaeologists will eventually resolve the fuelwood issue. Hearths with large quantities of identifiable charcoal can be rare.

Furthermore, such features have not always been given careful archaeological study. However, if prehistoric people in the Southwest did experience a fuelwood crisis leading to the abandonment of population centers, this should be reflected in the use of less and less desirable fuels.

Another avenue for exploring the question is through environmental change. Archaeologists have been prone to assume that climate was the major factor in environmental fluctuations that we see reflected in prehistoric pollen records and other data. But could these changes have been the product of human impacts? Are the environments of *today* in the Southwest and other parts of North America more an inheritance from our prehistoric predecessors than from nature?

2

A Lesson in Humility

Kenneth L. Feder

Ken Feder is an archaeologist and author at Central Connecticut State University.
Any similarity between him and the editor of this volume is entirely coincidental.

Points to consider when reading this article:

1. What do ancient technological achievements like Stonehenge or Montezuma's Castle show us?
2. What do modern technological disasters like the Hartford Civic Center roof collapse or the collapse of the Mianus River bridge show us?
3. Are there other examples you can think of where ancient technology has withstood the ravages of time better than some of our modern projects?
4. Why is this article titled "A Lesson in Humility"?

The inspiration for this paper came from a conversation I had with a very nice person I know—a friend—who can be fairly characterized as a "technodweeb." The guy is an engineer with an overall far too cheery acceptance of the human ability to "control all the variables" through the application of increasingly sophisticated technologies. My friend is the polar opposite of the Jeff Goldblum character in *Jurassic Park* for whom, no matter how careful the application of complex technologies, chaos is always hiding in the bushes.

Several years ago my engineer friend and I had a conversation about modern technology. He held fast to his position that as complex as the task may become, technology can get it right, and I held equally steadfastly to my far more pessimistic view of the imperfection of human works. He accused me of spending too much time with my mind in the past. "Sure," he pointed out, "ancient technologies were far less sophisticated than our own, so, of course, the archaeological record that so fascinates you is characterized by trial-and-error screwups. But modern technology is so much more advanced, so much more sophisticated, we just don't see that anymore." This conversation occurred not more than two weeks before a modern and highly sophisticated roof design failed under the weight of an accumulation of wet snow and collapsed onto the seats and arena of the Hartford Civic Center colosseum. The colosseum had been filled for an event that evening, but the roof fell in the dead of night. No one was hurt. The same cannot be said for our pride in modern technology.

W̲e archaeologists are admittedly a strange lot, with one foot in the present and one in the clutter of arrow points, potsherds and pyramids that constitutes the remains of the past. To some, our field is esoteric. Our discoveries, it is recognized, make little contribution to the Gross National Product. However, our pursuit of the past provides us with nothing if not a unique perspective of the present.

We inhabitants of the 20th century tend to view ourselves as the culmination of all that has come

before—the zenith of human endeavors stretching back across the millennia. We are afflicted by what might be called a kind of temporal chauvinism. Our society, we are certain, is what it was all leading up to from the very beginning.

Archaeology, however, places our civilization in a more realistic—sometimes humbling—context. Our culture is only the latest in a long string of cultures, all of whom had beginnings, reached ascendancy, withered and then died. Our material accomplishments are indeed great, but so were those of various groups of ancient people who have long since slipped into the amnesia of time. The rule of prehistory teaches us that all is temporary. The Egyptians, the Mesopotamians, the Harappans (of Pakistan), the Inca, and the Aztecs

From *The Hartford Courant,* September 1983. Reprinted here courtesy of the author.

FIGURE 1   Using tools made of wood and stone, without animal power or any mechanical device or machine, ancient Native Americans built the cliff dwelling that came to be called Montezuma's Castle. The structure looks much the same today as when it was built 800 years ago. (K. L. Feder)

all had their "moments" of glory and then succumbed to the relentless flow of time.

So, it is likely, will the glory of the 20th-century civilization also fade into oblivion. We have no good reason to believe that we are somehow the exception to the rule.

When the Mianus River bridge collapsed, national commentators made overblown generalizations about how we live in an era of no personal responsibility, and about how pride and quality no longer exist in the things we create. An archaeologist's reaction was different: the incident could prove to be a tragic but valuable lesson in cultural and temporal humility.

The bridge over the Mianus River, built in 1958, was a scant 25 years old when it fell. All of our 20th-century engineering skills, construction techniques, structural theory and stress-testing technology could not keep this major transportation artery intact and could not keep alive three human beings performing one of the most common functions of life in the second half of the 20th century—driving a motor vehicle.

As a humbling contrast, consider that more than 800 years ago a group of Indians living in a canyon in what we now call the state of Arizona were faced with

a dilemma. Cultivatable land that could support their families was scarce, and relations with neighbors were hostile. To build their village on the canyon floor would have wasted precious farmland and left them vulnerable to attack. To build their homes on the rim of the canyon would have made them no safer and placed them too far from their fields.

There was, however, a shallow declivity, a tall, broad depression in the face of a sheer cliff, overlooking the valley floor. There they could and did build, wasting no land and protecting themselves from the depredations of marauding enemies. In the side of that cliff, almost 100 feet above the valley floor (coincidentally at about the same height as the Mianus River bridge), with no cranes or derricks, with no architects or blueprints, without even metal tools, these prehistoric, so-called primitive people built their small village—a five story, 20 room apartment house made of mud, rock, and logs.

There they lived, quite successfully, as the richness of the archaeological record attests, for close to 200 years. Then, for reasons as yet unclear, they left their cliffside castle. Perhaps drought forced them to abandon their protected bastion. Their home, made of mud

FIGURE 2   Begun more than 5,000 years ago, much of Stonehenge still stands today, a literal and figurative monument to the architectural and engineering skills of the ancient inhabitants of Great Britain. Stonehenge has lasted far longer than many modern engineering marvels that have graced our landscape. (K. L. Feder)

and rock, built with no heavy machinery or state inspectors or high technology, still stands today, over 600 years after their departure. Called "Montezuma's Castle," the site is now a National Monument and is but one of literally thousands of similar, spectacular prehistoric architectural and engineering feats that still stand in testimony to the genius of ancient cultures.

There are many other examples. The Great Pyramid at Cheops in Egypt is, by volume, one of the largest structures ever made. Built of over two million precisely fashioned stone blocks, it covers an area of over 13 acres and rises to a height of nearly 500 feet. It is over 5,000 years old, and it, too, still stands.

Each of the so-called "capstones" or lintels at Stonehenge in England weigh close to 14,000 pounds. They were cut to exact dimensions without the use of iron or steel, and each was fitted precisely in position atop upright stones standing some 15 feet in height. And Stonehenge has lasted 4,000 years. (The ruin that you can see today is largely the result of fairly recent stone robbing.)

Lest we miss the point and praise ancient technologies too strongly, note that there were problems. While building an early pyramid at Meidum, in Egypt, the angle was too steep and the entire stone facing of the structure collapsed, killing probably thousands of workers. Errors in the positioning of some of the 50,000-pound uprights or "sarsens" at Stonehenge necessitated some fancy, last-minute stone cutting. The technological accomplishments of ancient people were great, but sometimes, they made great mistakes. Just like us.

We are not the first civilization, probably not the last, and, in some respects, we are not the greatest. Pride in the material accomplishments of our culture is certainly warranted, but so too is modesty. Our feeling of technological superiority and our assumption that we are the culmination of human history bears some sober reconsideration and reflection when our bridges fall down after 25 years and our civic center roofs collapse after just a few.

3

Braniff's Ruin

William L. Rathje

William Rathje is an archaeologist whose fieldwork includes major contributions to our understanding of the Maya civilization of Mesoamerica and the material culture of the more recent people of the North American civilization called the United States through the analysis of their trash (see articles 16 and 17).

Points to consider when reading this article:

1. In Rathje's argument, what did the ancient Maya and Braniff Airways have in common?

2. What is a **potlatch**? How does this term apply to the Maya and the board of directors of Braniff?

3. There's a take-off on an old cliché, "When the going gets tough, the tough go shopping." How does this apply in Rathje's argument?

4. Do potlatches make sense?

It is hard to imagine. Today, new "bargain" airlines spring up, each one trying to provide fewer services than its competitors, all on the name of lower ticket prices. Even in established carriers, meals are rarely served anymore, and when they are provided, they are often little more than the equivalent of bag lunches. There are fewer attendants, planes are full and often overbooked, and the seats are smaller.

Yet, little more than thirty years ago, an airline attempted to carve out a niche for itself in the air travel market by being ostentatious and offering luxurious

services to all of its customers. Fancy paint jobs on their planes, fancy meals, fancy seats, and fancy outfits on the flight attendants did not come cheap, and ticket prices eventually could not keep up with the increasing costs incurred in running an airline that had as its motto, "when you got it—flaunt it." Braniff flaunted it until it simply didn't have *it* anymore (the "it" being cash to pay for mundane things like jet fuel and pilots). Bankruptcy was the ultimate result.

The archaeological and historical records are replete with examples of entire societies using the Braniff approach. They followed the practice of "living large" only to be deflated in the end when their expenditure of energy for image outstripped their ability to pay for the mundane but hardly trivial needs of their people for food, housing, and protection from enemies. Archaeologist Bill Rathje suggests here that the ancient and impressive Native American civilization called the Maya succumbed to the same temptation that befell Braniff. The irony is this—had they not practiced wasteful and spendthrift policies in building fabulous temples and pyramids, few of us would even have heard of them.

Between A.D. 700 and 800, the lowland rain-forests of today's Guatemala were alive with Maya dedicating sumptuous new temples, palaces, tombs and monuments. Suddenly, in the midst of this lavish celebration of itself, Classic Maya civilization collapsed.

All civilizations rise and fall. Most go through predictable stages, usually including a long, drawn-out de-

From *Early Man,* Autumn 1982. Reprinted here courtesy of the Center for American Archaeology, Kampsville, IL.

cline. What makes the Maya case so mysterious is that this culture went bust in the middle of a boom. Oddly, the Maya—the epitome of unexpected demise—were joined last spring by a prominent airline.

"When you got it—flaunt it" was the ad slogan for Braniff International Airways, which flaunted "it" again and again. There were designer uniforms by Pucci in 1965 and Halston in 1977, genuine leather seats in 1977 (even in coach) and planes painted by modern artist Alexander Calder (in 1973 and 1975) at more than $100,000 each. Its corporate headquarters, completed in 1979, included racquetball courts, a nine-hole golf course, and according to rumor, a private elevator to lift the president's car directly into his office.

Like the Classic Maya, the airline dripped with the trappings of success. Then, suddenly, on May 12 just after a grandiose expansion of its routes, Braniff announced that it was broke.

Both the Classic Maya and Braniff fell apart without the usual warning signs of decay. Since the false signs of success were the artifacts both left behind—roof-combed temples and pastel airplanes—studying them falls within the province of archaeology. From this perspective, there is an artifact pattern which explains these and like cases—the "potlatch syndrome."

At traditional potlatches among natives of the Northwest Coast, such as the Kwakiutl, "bigmen" would give away food, blankets and valuables to enhance their status and to put others in their debt. After European-introduced smallpox decimated the local population, wealth per capita increased, and for the first few decades after contact, food and valuables were both given away and destroyed by burning.

For a bigman in the Northwest Coast, potlatching had its practical side. Other bigmen who received "gifts" were expected to reciprocate within a few years with goods worth two or three times the original presents. Sometimes the payback happened, sometimes not, and an over-extended potlatcher could quickly find himself tapped-out. Economically, potlatching was a big gamble.

This is the sense in which I use the term "potlatch"—the flaunting or conspicuous consumption of status-marking goods to perpetuate or regain success. We all do it. It can be the reason for designer jeans, limousines with wet bars, penthouses and the costly monuments nations are forever building to their greatness. In fact, the potlatch syndrome is a driving force in the American economy—anyone, no matter how lowly, can put on a show of status through the acquisition and display of intrinsically frivolous things.

Whole societies potlatch by pumping resources into flashy public ceremonies and monuments. In theory, such potlatching has economic benefits—building the morale and productivity of insiders, drawing the attention of outsiders to local goods and services, and offering customers the opportunity to identify themselves with "success."

The Knoxville World's Fair is a modern city's potlatch, just as the Colossus of Rhodes in the Mediterranean and the Olmec stone heads at San Lorenzo in Mexico were ancient ones. Venice is another example; an examination of its potlatch (in the 15th and 16th centuries) explains its immense contributions to the Renaissance as well as some of the factors behind the Maya and Braniff splurges.

By the early 1400s, merchant princes had made Venice the busiest port of entry to the lucrative markets of Europe. The city's annual revenues from import-export taxes amounted to about $30 million in present-day terms. The backbone of the trade were spices carried overland from the Far East, and with the proceeds, Venice assembled an empire. Beginning in the 1450s, however, Venice suffered severe losses on two fronts. In the eastern Mediterranean, a number of disastrous conflicts stripped away most of its outposts. Worse yet, in 1500, a successful expedition to India by 13 Portuguese ships established Lisbon as the chief entryway for oriental goods into Europe.

How did the Venetians respond to these portents of economic disaster? By sea exploration? In fact, one of the best explorers was a Venetian; unfortunately he was employed by the Portuguese. The route to India had not simply been stumbled on, but was won by a century of expeditions financed by Portugal, beginning with Henry the Navigator, who pioneered a systematic exploration—not unlike our NASA program of space probes.

But by 1450, the Venetians were already 50 years behind the Portuguese, and, given geographic and political handicaps, did not have much chance of catching up. Heavier investments in military preparedness might have worked, but here also the Venetians were far behind and preferred a strategy of appeasement and slow withdrawals.

The merchants of Venice, not oblivious to their predicament, took action by replacing outmoded ships and diversifying with lucrative publishing and glass-making ventures. However, even more ducats poured into potlatches.

Oddly enough, during the good times, Venice had remained rather plain. There was, of course, St. Mark's, the haphazard monument of cosmopolitan influence, and the Palace of the Doges. But mostly, money was reinvested where it brought immediate results—in ships, trading outposts and expeditions. As one historian has observed, "Venice, despite her wealth, unique domestic security and sophistication of wide travel, long stood aside from the main currents of the Renaissance." That is, until her empire faltered.

By 1481, the Renaissance had arrived, one example being the Palazzo Vendramini. The Piazza of St. Mark's was paved for the first time in 1495. And beginning in 1450, a torrent of famous artists—Titian, Tintoretto, Giorgione and the brothers Bellini—flooded the walls of their patrons' marble palaces with paintings. Thus, the more the economy was threatened the more Venetian merchants gussied up their city.

"Venice is still alive and well, bigger and better than ever," they were saying with their version of the potlatch.

FIGURE 1   The ancient city of Uxmal is just one of many spectacular ceremonial centers constructed by the ancient Maya. William Rathje suggests that the desire to build ever more impressive palaces, temples, and pyramids at such centers may have contributed to the downfall of the Maya economy. (K. L. Feder; not in the original article)

Contemporary observers believed them. The French ambassador described Venice in 1495 as "the most triumphant city I have ever seen," and many other foreigners concurred. In hindsight, we know that this same Venice of marvelous cultural achievements was in the middle of the 100-year period when her commerce suffered its most serious setbacks. Nevertheless, a combination of pragmatic moves and fancy floorshows succeeded in reviving the Venetian economy — at least for a time.

Every society potlatches, but clearly, some societies succumb to the potlatch syndrome more than others. Venice was aloof to it when the city was economically viable. The merchant princes bought the gewgaws of a large-scale potlatch only in the face of rapid economic decline. For most societies, such an all-out potlatch is a last desperate attempt to revive itself by propping up its flagging image. Such gambles are usually taken only after safer investments have failed. Thus, the grandest potlatches are often false fronts without substance, the omens of imminent collapse — recall the shah's extravagant party for Iran in 1971 at ancient and opulent Persepolis.

Although potlatching did not destroy Venice, potlatching beyond its means can quickly kill an ailing society. This seems to have been the fate of the Late Classic Maya — demonstrated at Tikal in lowland Guatemala, for example — who became extreme potlatchers for some of the same reasons as the Venetians. By one view, the Maya economy was suffering due to a decline in revenues from exports, mainly because many one-time importers began to make their own goods locally. By another view, the economy ran into the problem of too many people and too little food at a point when adding more laborers brought proportionately less to eat. Regardless of which view is accepted — both may be correct — the grip of the Maya elite was failing.

In response, manpower and materials which once flowed out to bring back trade goods or expand intensive agriculture were potlatched at home in feats of conspicuous consumption, which were orchestrated to whip up local support for the crumbling power structure.

Tikal's grandest architecture and burials (Temple IV was as high as a 20-story building and Ruler A's tomb was furnished with unprecedented jade and shell offerings) all date to Tepeu 2, a time when locally-made fancy pottery found its way into even the most humble households. These material signs of success were Tikal's last hurrah.

Braniff International Airways may represent an even greater extreme of potlatching, for the airline was not out merely to forestall its fall. To its heart, Braniff was flamboyant and devil-may-care. Once government deregulation gave the airlines free rein in 1978, Braniff plunged into national and international route expansions like the front line of the Dallas Cowboys. Rather than pursue gradual growth, Braniff management believed that by making a splashy grab they could muscle in on all of the company's competition at once. The result was mismanagement of over-committed resources and a long-term debt Atlas couldn't have carried.

Thus, instead of taking safer avenues for investment, which were always available, Braniff acted out its own public relations gimmick — if it looks successful, it will be successful — until it was, as has been said, "consumed by the very flair that had propelled it to greatness."

The danger for potlatchers is clear: Those who — like the Classic Maya and Braniff — use the most ostentatious trappings of success to fool others may end in fooling themselves.

4

The Worst Mistake in the History of the Human Race

Jared Diamond

Jared Diamond is not an archaeologist; he is a biologist whose specialty is ornithology. But Diamond is also a polymath and a generalist, who sees the connections between all the disciplines of science. Using that ability, Diamond makes a provocative argument here that the economic strategy that has made modern life possible is, as the title maintains, "the worst mistake" our species has ever made.

Points to consider when reading this article:

1. What is the "progressivist" view of the agricultural revolution?

2. Is agriculture easier than a hunting and gathering **mode of subsistence**? Is it safer? more secure? more productive?

3. As Diamond sees it, what were the negative consequences of the adoption of agriculture?

4. If agriculture caused so many problems, why did it fairly quickly (8,000 years is a relatively short period of human history) become the dominant mode of subsistence across almost the entire world?

Most of us take it for granted that our agricultural economy is the most sensible, economic, efficient, and secure subsistence system any human group has yet devised. No living hand-to-mouth for us, no having to traipse through the jungle to fill our larders. Food is produced in prodigious quantities by specialist farmers, enabling the rest of us to engage in more interesting pursuits, like, say, archaeology.

Certainly, agriculture—developed by our species a little more than 10,000 years ago and now the dominant subsistence mode on the planet—provides us with more food than the hunting and gathering that characterized the first 99.9% of human antiquity ever could. But, Jared Diamond asks, at what cost? He sees an agricultural way of life as the root of many of the ills that afflict the modern world.

Diamond makes a good point, but it is a tough call. Agriculture may be at the root of many diseases, deficiencies, and even war, but without a system that allows the production of huge quantities of food, far fewer human beings could survive on this planet. Though we may be justifiably ambivalent about the size of the world's human population and the impacts that population has had on the Earth's many ecosystems, we should not forget this important point. Each one of us is a part of that population. Without agriculture, there might never have been avaricious nation-states, war, poverty, racism, or heart disease. Then again, there likely would have been no me, no you, and, I imagine, no Jared Diamond.

To science we owe dramatic changes in our smug self-image. Astronomy taught us that our earth isn't the center of the universe but merely one of billions of heavenly bodies. From biology we learned that we weren't specially created by God but evolved along with millions of other species. Now archaeology is demolishing another sacred belief: that human history over the past million years has been a long tale of progress. In particular, recent discoveries suggest that the adoption of agriculture, supposedly our most decisive step toward a better life, was in many ways a catastrophe from which we have never recovered. With agriculture came the gross social and sexual inequality, the disease and despotism, that curse our existence.

At first, the evidence against this revisionist interpretation will strike twentieth century Americans as irrefutable. We're better off in almost every respect than the people of the Middle Ages, who in turn had it easier than cavemen, who in turn were better off than apes. Just count our advantages. We enjoy the most abundant and varied foods, the best tools and material goods, some of the longest and healthiest lives, in history. Most of us are safe from starvation and predators. We get our energy from oil and machines, not from our sweat. What neo-Luddite among us would trade his life for that of a medieval peasant, a caveman, or an ape?

For most of our history we supported ourselves by hunting and gathering: we hunted wild animals and foraged for wild plants. It's a life that philosophers have traditionally regarded as nasty, brutish, and short. Since no food is grown and little is stored, there is (in this view) no respite from the struggle that starts anew each day to find wild foods and avoid starving. Our escape from this misery was facilitated only 10,000 years ago, when in different parts of the world people began to domesticate plants and animals. The agricultural revolution gradually spread until today it's nearly universal and few tribes of hunter-gatherers survive.

From the progressivist perspective on which I was brought up, to ask "Why did almost all our hunter-gatherer ancestors adopt agriculture?" is silly. Of course they adopted it because agriculture is an efficient way to get more food for less work. Planted crops yield far more tons per acre than roots and berries. Just imagine a band of savages, exhausted from searching for nuts or chasing wild animals, suddenly gazing for the first time at a fruit-laden orchard or a pasture full of sheep. How many milliseconds do you think it would take them to appreciate the advantages of agriculture?

The progressivist party line sometimes even goes so far as to credit agriculture with the remarkable flowering of art that has taken place over the past few thousand years. Since crops can be stored, and since it takes less time to pick food from a garden than to find it in the wild, agriculture gave us free time that hunter-gatherers never had. Thus it was agriculture that enabled us to build the Parthenon and compose the B-minor Mass.

While the case for the progressivist view seems overwhelming, it's hard to prove. How do you show that the lives of people 10,000 years ago got better when they abandoned hunting and gathering for farming? Until recently, archaeologists had to resort to indirect tests, whose results (surprisingly) failed to support the progressivist view. Here's one example of an indirect test: Are twentieth century hunter-gatherers really worse off than farmers? Scattered throughout the world, several dozen groups of so-called primitive people, like the Kalahari Bushmen, continue to support themselves that way. It turns out that these people have plenty of leisure time, sleep a good deal, and work less hard than their farming neighbors. For instance, the average time devoted each week to obtaining food is only 12 to 19 hours for one group of Bushmen, 14 hours or less for the Hadza nomads of Tanzania. One Bushman, when asked why he hadn't emulated neighboring tribes by adopting agriculture, replied, "Why should we, when there are so many mongongo nuts in the world?"

While farmers concentrate on high-carbohydrate crops like rice and potatoes, the mix of wild plants and animals in the diets of surviving hunter-gatherers provides more protein and a better balance of other nutrients. In one study, the Bushmen's average daily food intake (during a month when food was plentiful) was 2,140 calories and 93 grams of protein, considerably greater than the recommended daily allowance for people of their size. It's almost inconceivable that Bushmen, who eat 75 or so wild plants, could die of starvation the way hundreds of thousands of Irish farmers and their families did during the potato famine of the 1840s.

So the lives of at least the surviving hunter-gatherers aren't nasty and brutish, even though farmers have pushed them into some of the world's worst real estate. But modern hunter-gatherer societies that have rubbed shoulders with farming societies for thousands of years don't tell us about conditions before the agricultural revolution. The progressivist view is really making a claim about the distant past: that the lives of primitive people improved when they switched from gathering to farming. Archaeologists can date that switch by distinguishing remains of wild plants and animals from those of domesticated ones in prehistoric garbage dumps.

How can one deduce the health of the prehistoric garbage makers, and thereby directly test the progressivist view? That question has become answerable only in recent years, in part through the newly emerging techniques of **paleopathology,** the study of signs of disease in the remains of ancient peoples.

In some lucky situations, the paleopathologist has almost as much material to study as a pathologist today. For example, archaeologists in the Chilean deserts found well preserved mummies whose medical conditions at time of death could be determined by autopsy. And feces of long-dead Indians who lived in dry caves in Nevada remain sufficiently well preserved to be examined for hookworm and other parasites.

Usually the only human remains available for study are skeletons, but they permit a surprising number of deductions. To begin with, a skeleton reveals its owner's sex, weight, and approximate age. In the few cases where there are many skeletons, one can construct mortality tables like the ones life insurance companies use to calculate expected life span and risk of death at any given age. Paleopathologists can also calculate growth rates by measuring bones of people of different ages, examine teeth for enamel defects (signs of childhood malnutrition), and recognize scars left on bones by anemia, tuberculosis, leprosy, and other diseases.

One straightforward example of what paleopathologists have learned from skeletons concerns historical changes in height. Skeletons from Greece and Turkey show that the average height of hunter-gatherers toward the end of the ice ages was a generous 5'9'' for men, 5'5'' for women. With the adoption of agriculture, height crashed, and by 3000 B.C. had reached a low of only 5'3'' for men, 5' for women. By classical times heights were very slowly on the rise again, but modern Greeks and Turks have still not regained the average height of their distant ancestors.

Another example of paleopathology at work is the study of Indian skeletons from burial mounds in the Illinois and Ohio river valleys. At Dickson Mounds, located near the confluence of the Spoon and Illinois rivers, archaeologists have excavated some 800 skeletons that paint a picture of the health changes that occurred when a hunter-gatherer culture gave way to intensive maize farming around A.D. 1150. Studies by George Armelagos and his colleagues then at the University of Massachusetts show these early farmers paid a price for their new-found livelihood. Compared to the hunter-gatherers who preceded them, the farmers had a nearly 50 per cent increase in enamel defects indicative of malnutrition, a fourfold increase in iron-deficiency anemia (evidenced by a bone condition called porotic hyperostosis), a threefold rise in bone lesions reflecting infectious disease in general, and an increase in degenerative conditions of the spine, probably reflecting a lot of hard physical labor. "Life expectancy at birth in the pre-agricultural community was about twenty-six years," says Armelagos, "but in the post-agricultural community it was nineteen years. So these episodes of nutritional stress and infectious disease were seriously affecting their ability to survive."

The evidence suggests that the Indians at Dickson Mounds, like many other primitive peoples, took up farming not by choice but from necessity in order to feed their constantly growing numbers. "I don't think most hunter-gatherers farmed until they had to, and when they switched to farming they traded quality for quantity," says Mark Cohen of the State University of New York at Plattsburgh, co-editor, with Armelagos, of one of the seminal books in the field, *Paleopathology at the Origins of Agriculture.* "When I first started making that argument ten years ago, not many people agreed with me. Now it's become a respectable, albeit controversial, side of the debate."

There are at least three sets of reasons to explain the findings that agriculture was bad for health. First, hunter-gatherers enjoyed a varied diet, while early farmers obtained most of their food from one or a few starchy crops. The farmers gained cheap calories at the cost of poor nutrition. (Today just three high-carbohydrate plants — wheat, rice, and corn — provide the bulk of the calories consumed by the human species, yet each one is deficient in certain vitamins or amino acids essential to life.) Second, because of dependence on a limited number of crops, farmers ran the risk of starvation if one crop failed. Finally, the mere fact that agriculture encouraged people to clump together in crowded societies, many of which then carried on trade with other crowded societies, led to the spread of parasites and infectious disease. (Some archaeologists think it was crowding, rather than agriculture, that promoted disease, but this is a chicken-and-egg argument, because crowding encourages agriculture and vice versa.) Epidemics couldn't take hold when populations were scattered in small bands that constantly shifted camp. Tuberculosis and diarrheal disease had to await the rise of farming, measles and bubonic plague the appearance of large cities.

Besides malnutrition, starvation, and epidemic diseases, farming helped bring another curse upon humanity: deep class divisions. Hunter-gatherers have little or no stored food, and no concentrated food sources, like an orchard or a herd of cows: they live off the wild plants and animals they obtain each day. Therefore, there can be no kings, no class of social parasites who grow fat on food seized from others. Only in farming populations could a healthy, nonproducing elite set itself above the disease-ridden masses. Skeletons from Greek tombs at Mycenae *c.* 1500 B.C. suggest that royals enjoyed a better diet than commoners, since the royal skeletons were two or three inches taller and had better teeth (on the average, one instead of six cavities or missing teeth). Among Chilean mummies from *c.* A.D. 1000, the élite were distinguished not only by ornaments and gold hair clips but also by a fourfold lower rate of bone lesions caused by disease.

Similar contrasts in nutrition and health persist on a global scale today. To people in rich countries like the U.S., it sounds ridiculous to extol the virtues of hunting and gathering. But Americans are an élite, dependent on oil and minerals that must often be imported from countries with poorer health and nutrition. If one could choose between being a peasant farmer in Ethiopia or a Bushman gatherer in the Kalahari, which do you think would be the better choice?

Farming may have encouraged inequality between the sexes, as well. Freed from the need to transport their babies during a nomadic existence, and under pressure to produce more hands to till the fields, farming women tended to have more frequent pregnancies than their hunter-gatherer counterparts—with consequent drains on their health. Among the Chilean mummies, for example, more women than men had bone lesions from infectious disease.

Women in agricultural societies were sometimes made beasts of burden. In New Guinea farming communities today I often see women staggering under loads of vegetables and firewood while the men walk empty-handed. Once while on a field trip there studying birds, I offered to pay some villagers to carry supplies from an airstrip to my mountain camp. The heaviest item was a 110-pound bag of rice, which I lashed to a pole and assigned to a team of four men to shoulder together. When I eventually caught up with the villagers, the men were carrying light loads, while one small woman weighing less than the bag of rice was bent under it, supporting its weight by a cord across her temples.

As for the claim that agriculture encouraged the flowering of art by providing us with leisure time, modern hunter-gatherers have at least as much free time as do farmers. The whole emphasis on leisure time as a critical factor seems to be misguided. Gorillas have had ample free time to build their own Parthenon, had they wanted to. While post-agricultural technological advances did make new art forms possible and preservation of art easier, great paintings and sculptures were already being produced by hunter-gatherers 15,000 years ago, and were still being produced as recently as the last century by such hunter-gatherers as some Eskimos and the Indians of the Pacific Northwest.

Thus with the advent of agriculture an élite became better off, but most people became worse off. Instead of swallowing the progressivist party line that we chose agriculture because it was good for us, we must ask how we got trapped by it despite its pitfalls.

One answer boils down to the adage "Might makes right." Farming could support many more people than hunting, albeit with a poorer quality of life. (Population densities of hunter-gatherers are rarely over one person per ten square miles, while farmers average 100 times that.) Partly, this is because a field planted entirely in edible crops lets one feed far more mouths than a forest with scattered edible plants. Partly, too, it's because nomadic hunter-gatherers have to keep their children spaced at four-year intervals by infanticide and other means, since a mother must carry her toddler until it's old enough to keep up with the adults. Because farm women don't have that burden, they can and often do bear a child every two years.

As population densities of hunter-gatherers slowly rose at the end of the ice ages, bands had to choose between feeding more mouths by taking the first steps toward agriculture, or else finding ways to limit growth. Some bands chose the former solution, unable to anticipate the evils of farming, and seduced by the transient abundance they enjoyed until population growth caught up with increased food production. Such bands outbred and then drove off or killed the bands that chose to remain hunter-gatherers, because a hundred malnourished farmers can still outfight one healthy hunter. It's not that hunter-gatherers abandoned their life style, but that those sensible enough not to abandon it were forced out of all areas except the ones farmers didn't want.

At this point it's instructive to recall the common complaint that archaeology is a luxury, concerned with the remote past, and offering no lessons for the present. Archaeologists studying the rise of farming have reconstructed a crucial stage at which we made the worst mistake in human history. Forced to choose between limiting population or trying to increase food production, we chose the latter and ended up with starvation, warfare, and tyranny.

Hunter-gatherers practiced the most successful and longest-lasting life style in human history. In contrast, we're still struggling with the mess into which agriculture has tumbled us, and it's unclear whether we can solve it. Suppose that an archaeologist who had visited us from outer space were trying to explain human history to his fellow spacelings. He might illustrate the results of his digs by a 24-hour clock on which one hour represents 100,000 years of real past time. If the history of the human race began at midnight, then we would now be almost at the end of our first day. We lived as hunter-gatherers for nearly the whole of that day, from midnight through dawn, noon, and sunset. Finally, at 11:54 P.M., we adopted agriculture. As our second midnight approaches, will the plight of famine-stricken peasants gradually spread to engulf us all? Or will we somehow achieve those seductive blessings that we imagine behind agriculture's glittering façade, and that have so far eluded us?

5

The Psyche of Saddam Hussein

Brian Fagan

Brian Fagan is an archaeologist at the University of California at Santa Barbara. Brian is, without doubt, the most prolific archaeologist/writer the discipline has ever seen. This article shows the ever-articulate—and provocative—Brian Fagan at his best.

Points to consider when reading this article:

1. What is Fagan's point in this essay?
2. What precious resources were the ancient Mesopotamian's fighting over?
3. In what sense are the reasons for war in Mesopotamia more than 4,500 years ago the same as just a few years ago in the Persian Gulf War?
4. How does it help to understand the possible historical roots of Saddam Hussein's behavior on the world stage?

The threats never cease. The bravado never diminishes. We virtually destroyed his army and infrastructure in a short war where we lost dozens and he lost thousands. Yet he continues to thumb his nose at us. His military technology is outdated, an embargo prevents him from re-equipping his devastated military, and his people suffer tremendously as a result of his intransigence. What is it with this guy? Is he nuts? Is he suicidal? Is he diabolically clever? Or is he all of the above?

Saddam Hussein can be understood only within the historical context of the land that forged him. Ironically, perhaps, in this arguably most volatile place on Earth, the world's first civilization developed more than 4,500 years ago with true cities, a written language, mathematics, and astronomy. Great rulers emerged here in "Mesopotamia," literally "the land between the two rivers," the Tigris and the Euphrates. Before the Greeks appeared on the world stage, before the pharaohs began to build their pyramids, and before Stonehenge, powerful cities evolved in Mesopotamia and held sway over the Middle East for hundreds, sometimes for thousands of years. And almost immediately upon their evolution, disputes between them erupted into lengthy wars. Archaeologist Brian Fagan maintains that Saddam Hussein knows his history well and sees himself as the bearer of the torch of a civilization that was the world's first and is destined to emerge from the shadows once again.

Be it known that your city will be completely destroyed! Surrender!" In the Middle East the rhetoric of aggression was as loud in 2600 B.C. as it is today. Sumerian rulers were just as adept as Saddam Hussein at border disputes and at annexing their neighbors' lands without warning. Their clay tablets and cuneiform inscriptions boast of their diplomatic triumphs, wars, and dirty dealings with idioms that seem startlingly familiar.

In 2600 B.C., Sumeria, a harsh land of violent storms and unpredictable floods, consisted of myriad small city-states that bickered constantly over land, water rights, trade, and political power. Mesalim, king of the northern Babylonian city of Kish, controlled a large part of the fertile land between the Tigris and the Euphrates. He was a powerful monarch and warlord who commanded great respect, so much so that he was remembered in local lore for more than two centuries. His influence extended to the two city-states of the south—Umma and Lagash. An able diplomat, he settled for a time a long-simmering border dispute between them. The Umma-Lagash conflict centered around an area called the Gu'edena ("Edge of the

From *Archaeology*, vol. 44, no. 1, 1991. Reprinted courtesy of Brian Fagan.

Plain"), a strip of land that was the "beloved field" of the god Ningirsu, the chief deity of Lagash. Mesalim was able to divide Gu'edena between the rival city-states. With impeccable religious protocol, Mesalim, we are told, was able to negotiate a deal between Shara, the supreme deity of Umma, and Ningirsu of Lagash. According to the agreement, "Enlil, king of all lands, father of all gods . . . demarcated the border between [Umma] and [Lagash]. Mesalim, king of Kish . . . measured it off and erected a monument there." The terms were as follows: Lagash leased the land to Umma for "grain-rent," a portion of the annual crop yield. Nigirsu's grain would be cultivated by another city, but part of the yield came back to the god as a lease payment.

In the long term, this was a high-risk arrangement, which gave Umma and Lagash plenty of ready excuses to attack each other. If Umma was strong and Lagash in a period of decline, payment would not be forthcoming and there was nothing the latter could do about it. When Lagash was strong, it could demand payment of grain-rent with impunity. Sometime after Mesalim's brilliant diplomatic coup (the date is disputed), Umma's armies crossed the border and were thrown back by Lagash. The god Ningirsu was so incensed by Umma's incursions, we are told, that he engendered a mighty ruler for Lagash named Eanatum. Eanatum went to war against Umma, defeated the invader, and reestablished the boundary. After another invasion by Umma, Lagash prevailed again. Only this time Eanatum deprived Umma of previously available farmland by extending "the [boundary] channel . . . leaving 215 *nindan* (ca. 4,000 feet) of . . . land . . . and establishing a no-man's-land there. He inscribed monuments at that channel and restored the monument of Mesalim."

The border dispute continued to fester—over agriculture, over payments for land, and over the improper use of irrigation canals. The rulers of Umma and Lagash and their successors looked for excuses to quarrel, at the same time quietly raising levies and as-

sembling mercenaries. Then the armies would descend without warning, setting fire to shrines and cities, diverting irrigation canals, and "bundling off precious metals and lapis-lazuli." The conflict not only pitted monarch against monarch but also patron god against patron god. And in time the routine of rhetoric, sudden attack, and bloody battle became a familiar one, complete with its own vocabulary.

This remote, and long forgotten, border dispute between two powerful cities is a fascinating mirror of the 1990s rhetoric coming out of Iraq. We can only glimpse at the events that took place on that obscure Sumerian frontier, but the oratory is chillingly familiar, and the saber-rattling eerily reminiscent of some of the fiery speeches emanating from both Baghdad and Washington.

The ebb and flow of ancient events along the border is much fragmented and telescoped in the clay cones, tablets, and inscriptions that have come down to us. We have a one-sided picture, too, for most of the surviving tablets come from Lagash. But the long-term pattern of the boundary dispute repeats again and again. And, all of it was justified in the name of the gods, much like Hussein's jihad, or holy war, and trumpeted forth with a barrage of propaganda that would make the present-day leader of Iraq proud. And, at the end, there was always a quiet deal that restored at least a semblance of status quo.

We tend to think of Saddam Hussein as a crazy megalomaniac. I suspect that he sees himself as a latter-day "fierce-headed noble of Sumer," destined to set right perceived historical injustices by divine fiat. As such, he seeks to achieve his goals with brutal methods that have an ancient and notorious ancestry. What is frightening is that he seems to believe that Sumerian brutality and rhetoric will work in the late twentieth century. Perhaps those who study Saddam Hussein's psyche from afar should ponder some of the lessons learned from Sumerian archaeology. One of those lessons is that the Sumerians respected little else than might, power, and violence.

I AM AN ARCHAEOLOGIST

Timothy R. Pauketat

The path I followed to archaeology began near a creek bed, where slowmoving pools of water trickled over fossil-studded limestone covered in the falling leaves from oaks and hickories. I had a youthful interest in all things natural and historical—animals, fossils, trees, and genealogy. I collected everything collectible, including historical relics of my parents and grandparents and the Indian artifacts that I soon discovered were everywhere around my home. I enjoyed photography, sketching, and creative writing. I became a self-appointed junior paleontologist, artist, photographer, writer, and, later, archaeologist. I discovered then what I still find to be true: I could do everything I enjoyed! I rarely questioned the idea of graduate school and a professional career; they were inevitabilities (ignoring the year or two that I seriously considered life as a musician).

There were other experiences along the way that led me to become most interested in wanting to know why people allow themselves to be "dominated" by others. Growing up on the uphill side of an obviously segregated social and racial landscape was one. A father subject to a seemingly heartless employer was another. A summer in the field working near sharecroppers was still another. All in all, I came to appreciate a fundamental process of concern to archaeology—the development of social inequality and the exercise of political power as a force that shapes history.

In the New World, such processes were part of the early civilizations of Native Americans. I was enamored with the pre-Columbian people along the Mississippi. These "Mississippians" built impressive central capitals of earth, wood, and thatch. They grew crops and paid homage to particular individuals of powerful clans. Why? I am seeking the answers to that question at and around the granddaddy of such Mississippian chiefdoms, Cahokia. Moreover, I have found that there are answers, and these answers are not simply because of the environment or some innate tendency summed up as the "if-you-build-it-they-will-come" theory of civilization. Instead, we discover a history of social give and take, involving the negotiation of power, gender, and kinship, that had uncertain outcomes.

Well over nine-tenths of all human history is accessible only through archaeology. Yet we use that fraction of history that we think we know to explain who we are and where we are going in the future. If all the archaeology ever done tells us any one thing, it is that other times and places were different, despite certain shared human qualities. I think, then, that we had better heed the lessons of archaeology, allowing them to influence our contemporary philosophical and moral positions. Despite my high regard for the cultural icons of the centuries, Plato, Tacitus, Locke, Jefferson, Marx, and Einstein were men who did not know what we, as archaeologists, can

(Courtesy of Timothy Pauketat)

know. They could not contribute what we, as archaeologists, can contribute to both historical and evolutionary understandings of the human experience. My own interests are certainly more specialized than the breadth of Jefferson's interests, and less encompassing than Einstein's theory of relativity. But my interest in the struggles over identity and power in Native American chiefdoms such as Cahokia are nonetheless relevant to social science and to social history.

I am actively conducting field and laboratory research to understand this instance of the human struggle. Every summer for the past five years has found me in the field, with funding from sources like the National Science Foundation, the National Geographic Society, the Wenner-Gren Foundation, the Cahokia Mounds Museum Society, and my own university. I locate sites, map sites in three dimensions (now using **laser transits** and **global positioning** technology), and, finally, excavate sites. Of all, the last is the most thrilling because the answers to research questions appear out of the ground and out of the past. The days are long, hot, and sometimes trying, but these strains add to the satisfaction and the sheer enjoyment of doing it. To see a pot smashed on a house floor and to know that there rests a moment of history—a convergence of the past with the present—is a powerful experience.

My own fieldwork takes place along the Mississippi River in the American Midwest and upper Midsouth. It takes me from the middle of Cahokia's "Grand Plaza" to the earthen pyramids of outlying towns and to the marginal settlements of relatively impoverished pre-Columbian farmers. I visit the fascinating archaeological sites of other lands, but my fascination still finds a home in the American heartland. Not that I spend most of my time in the field. No, the life of an academic professor requires working in a lab, writing at a computer, teaching in classrooms, public speaking, and travel to distant sites and professional conferences. Part of the time I act like a detective, using the artifacts, maps, and notes from the field to solve a particular case in my laboratory. I specialize in the study of pottery, and this entails repe-

titious, sometimes mind-numbing forms of data recording. Part of this time, I function either as a teacher or an author. Teaching and writing, as I do for well over half of the year, allows me to share my revelations with others. Knowing that my finds are directly influencing the thoughts of students in class, and colleagues through journals and books, completes the cycle of archaeological research that began in the field.

Taken together, the tasks I face daily make archaeology a challenging career. There is always another article to write, another collection to analyze, another excavation to fund, and another academic or resource-management issue to resolve. "You won't see want ads for archaeologists in the evening papers," said a particularly annoying biology teacher in a failed attempt to sway me away from such a career. I held my tongue, but I was undaunted. Nonetheless, archaeology is not a career to take lightly. Addressing the larger scientific and historical questions of concern to us all requires commitment. It is a career to go into full throttle. I live it, breathe it, and sleep it. Because of this, I enjoy it wholeheartedly.

PART 2

Serving Communities through Archaeology

Most archaeologists serve at least two constituencies. The first of these is the community of other professional archaeologists. Archaeological researchers and teachers need to be up to date on the latest discoveries, techniques, and theories in their field. Colleagues regularly report on these in professional journals. For example, most professional American archaeologists who conduct research in North America belong to the Society for American Archaeology whose major publication is the periodical *American Antiquity*. In Great Britain, the journal *Antiquity*, and in Latin America, the journal *Latin American Antiquity* serve a similar function. In the United States archaeologists who focus on sites dating to the period beginning with European colonial settlement of the Western Hemisphere subscribe to the journal *Historical Archaeology*, the periodical published by the professional organization the Society for Historical Archaeology.

Essentially, the pages of these professional journals are filled with detailed, usually highly technical, and often quite theoretically focused articles written by archaeologists for other archaeologists. They cannot be characterized as light reading, but anyone who works in the field of archaeology is obliged to keep abreast of recent developments—and researchers are similarly obliged to report their work in these publications. Whether or not the work relates to one's own particular scholarly or research focus, if it is about the human past, the community of archaeologists is interested and desires—and needs—to know more. These professional journals, along with professional conferences, represent important ways in which archaeologists share their work with each other.

This brings us to the second constituency that professional archaeologists serve, the archaeologically curious public. Archaeology attracts a great deal of media attention. Many people are drawn to the human past and are curious about the work done by archaeologists. Some archaeologists eschew popular publishing, opting to write only for their colleagues in archaeology. But many others take quite seriously the view that without a public interested in the human past and willing to pay for the research that illuminates that past there would be no archaeology. As a result, along with writing for professional journals, many archaeologists also

29

write less technical summaries of their work or present speeches about their research for the general reading and listening public.

The glossy magazines *Archaeology* and *American Archaeology,* for example, are wholly devoted to disseminating archaeological information to this public constituency. Also, it is almost impossible to find an issue of the popular science magazines *Discover, Natural History,* or *National Geographic* that do not have a substantial article about archaeology. All of these publications serve the admirable purpose of keeping an interested public informed about the research and results of modern archaeology.

Along with professional archaeologists and the public, there also is another more specific constituency served by archaeologists. This group (actually, there are many groups) represents a subset of the broader, archaeologically aware public. My friend and colleague, archaeologist Warren Perry, refers to the archaeology he conducts as a kind of "community service," referring specifically to communities of nonarchaeologists who feel a special tie or bond to a particular province of the archaeological record. In most cases, this special attachment is perceived by people who represent the directly descendant communities of those who produced the archaeological record in question. In other words, not surprisingly, many people, whether they are generally interested in the past or not, have a particular curiosity about and reverence for the archaeological remains left behind by their own ancestors. The intellectual as well as the emotional relationship that exists between Native Americans and the sites of their ancestors in the Western Hemisphere, between African Americans and the sites of their ancestors in North America, between contemporary aboriginal Australians and the archaeological record of native Australia, between modern Jews and the archaeology of the ancient Hebrews in Israel all represent a unique connection, a cultural and biological tie that transcends time. In some cases, for example, in Israel, the archaeologists themselves are members of these communities, researching the ancestors of their own people, but this is not a prerequisite. In fact, most prehistoric archaeologists in North America are not Indian, most historical archaeologists researching the lives of slaves and slave descendants are not African American, and most Australian archaeologists are not aboriginal Australians.

Regardless of their own specific backgrounds, however, most archaeologists recognize that descendant communities have invaluable and unique insights concerning the ancient people we all study — after all, they are members of the same cultural continuum. Although the work we do serves the broad purpose of informing a world community interested in the past of all people, most archaeologists recognize their special obligation to the living descendants of the people who produced the particular archaeological remains so painstakingly recovered and so carefully analyzed.

Each article presented in Part 2 reflects the concept of archaeologists serving this public constituency — the community of descendants of those who left the archaeological record being studied.

6

Great Zimbabwe

Webber Ndoro

Webber Ndoro is a historian at the University of Zimbabwe. He was the coordinator of the nation of Zimbabwe's Monuments Program and conservator of Great Zimbabwe National Monument from 1988 to 1994.

Points to consider when reading this article:

1. Why was there so much controversy over the question of who built Great Zimbabwe?

2. What cultures have been credited with constructing the spectacular stonework structures of Great Zimbabwe?

3. Who do we now know was responsible for the construction of Great Zimbabwe?

4. What features might we infer about a culture with the technological ability to construct a monument like Great Zimbabwe?

Racial stereotypes know no temporal boundaries. Many people subconsciously project their biases into the past and thereby deny the remarkable histories of those against whom they harbor prejudices in the present.

Sometimes, however, those histories are impossible to ignore. For the Europeans who first encountered its ruins in southern Africa in the late nineteenth cen-

tury, Great Zimbabwe was an enigma. The people who had built the great walls and enclosures of Zimbabwe had been a technologically sophisticated people. Many of the first Europeans to investigate Zimbabwe found it inconceivable that local Africans had been responsible for building the site. Their assumption was that indigenous Africans were incapable of such a complex undertaking. Some went so far as to suggest that Zimbabwe had been built not by native Africans but by interlopers from the Middle East.

Even into the 1960s and 1970s, attempts were made by some commentators to deny ancient Zimbabwe its African heritage. But the archaeological record is quite clear on this point: the builders of Great Zimbabwe and a large number of smaller sites of the same cultural tradition were the ancestors of the contemporary people of south-central Africa. Archaeologist Webber Ndoro describes how the people of Great Zimbabwe produced their own indigenous complex society.

On the southern edge of the Zimbabwe plateau in the watershed between the Zambezi and the Limpopo rivers sits the largest and loveliest archaeological site in sub-Saharan Africa. With its high conical tower, its long, curved stone walls and its cosmopolitan artifacts, Great Zimbabwe attests to the existence of a thriving city that may have dominated trade and culture throughout southern Africa sometime between the 12th and 17th centuries. Its unique architecture and sculpture—particularly the enigmatic birds carved from soapstone—bespeak a rich history, one that archaeologists continue to piece together today. The

country of Zimbabwe—formerly Rhodesia, until its independence from England in 1980—was named for this site.

Like many ancient cities, Great Zimbabwe has been shrouded by legend. In the 1500s Portuguese traders visiting Angola and Mozambique—where they established colonies—wrote of a kingdom in the interior of Africa. Their descriptions offered many Europeans the promise of King Solomon's mines, for according to the Bible, Solomon would send to Ophir for his gold. In *Paradise Lost*, John Milton situates Ophir somewhere near the Congo and Angola. This powerful myth of the city of Ophir, populated by Semitic people, shaped the later cultural and historical interpretations of Great Zimbabwe. The fable is, in large part, the reason so many archaeological mysteries remain about the site. Because whereas the story of Great Zimbabwe

From *Scientific American*, November 1997. Reprinted here courtesy of *Scientific American*.

FIGURE 1   Map showing the location of Great Zimbabwe in the modern nation Zimbabwe named for the ancient site in southern Africa.

is ultimately that of early Shona culture and the African **Iron Age,** it is also a tale of colonialism and of often shoddy, politically motivated archaeology.

MASTERFUL STONEWORK

Constructed between A.D. 1100 and 1600, Great Zimbabwe seems not to have been designed around a central plan but rather to have been altered to fit its changing role and population. Its scale is far larger than that of similar regional sites—including Dana-mombe, Khami, Naletale, Domboshava (in northern Botswana), Manikweni (in Mosambique) and Thu-lamela (in northern South Africa)—suggesting that Great Zimbabwe was the area's economic and political center. Because it is situated on the shortest route between the northern gold fields, where inland rivers were panned for the precious metal, and the Indian Ocean, the rulers of Great Zimbabwe most likely regulated the thriving medieval gold trade.

Great Zimbabwe covers 1,779 acres and comprises three main structures: the Hill Complex, the Great Enclosure and the smaller Valley Ruins. The Hill Complex, dubbed the Acropolis by Europeans, forms the oldest part of the site; evidence hints that farmers or hunters may have encamped there as early as the fifth century. From its position on the rocky, 262-foot-

high hill, the oval enclosure—about 328 feet long and 148 feet wide—would have allowed its inhabitants to see potential invaders. The outer wall, which stands nearly 37 feet high, would also have afforded good protection. Inside the walls, as inside all the other enclosures, stand *daga* houses, curved, hutlike structures made of Africa's most common building material: dried earth, mud and gravel.

Below the Hill Complex sits the most stunning of Great Zimbabwe's structures, the Great Enclosure, or Elliptical Building. Called *Imbahuru,* meaning "the house of the great woman" or "the great house," by the Karanga-speaking people who lived there during the 19th century, the Great Enclosure was built at the height of Great Zimbabwe's power. (Karanga is the most common dialect of Shona and is spoken by the inhabitants of south-central Zimbabwe.) The enclosing wall is 800 feet long and stands 32 feet high at some places; an estimated one million blocks were used in its construction. An inner wall runs along part of the outer wall, creating a narrow, 180-foot-long passageway.

The function of the Great Enclosure is not known, although it is thought to have served as a royal palace. Because of the presence of grooves in the walls (perhaps representing the female anatomy) and of phallic structures, some historians have postulated that the compound was used for adolescent initiation rites or for other important ceremonies. It may have also housed the many wives of the ruler. The great conical tower, which stands 30 feet high and is 18 feet in diameter at the base, appears not to have been used for any particular purpose and may have served a merely symbolic function.

In addition to the Hill Complex and the Great Enclosure, Great Zimbabwe is made up of the smaller Valley Ruins. This series of compounds stands in the valley between the two larger structures. The walls seem to be youngest here, suggesting that these structures were built as the population expanded and Great Zimbabwe needed more residential space.

Great Zimbabwe is unusual not only in its size but in its stonework. Many of the structures are made of rectangular blocks cut from nearby granite outcroppings. The city's name derives from the Shona term *dzimbabwe,* meaning "houses of stone." The blocks, set in layers without mortar, form stable free-standing, curved walls that are often about twice as high as they are wide. Although round, buttresslike structures rest along the base of many walls, they have no supportive role. Some archaeologists speculate that these curved extensions may have served to soften the approach to a doorway, or to have made passageways more complicated to navigate or perhaps even to have hidden rooms from direct view. They also may have served to control access to some areas, be-

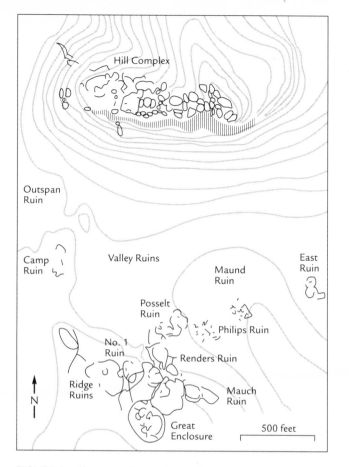

FIGURE 2   Site map of Great Zimbabwe.

cause people could have moved into the area in single file only.

The stonework is, in certain places, astonishingly sophisticated: rounded steps grace some of the entrances, and chevron designs decorate some of the walls. The walls are also punctuated by drains and occasionally by four-foot-wide doorways, some of which had wood lintels.

A MYSTERIOUS CULTURE

Although we know very little about the people of Great Zimbabwe, we can guess something about them from our knowledge of Mapungubwe sites, which appear to have been the center of Shona civilization around A.D. 1000. The largest Mapungubwe settlements, found in the Shashi-Limpopo area, are very similar to Great Zimbabwe. Wealth was apparently based on cattle production, ivory trade and gold. The Mapungubwe culture spread into western parts of Zimbabwe as the presence of Leopard's Kopje pottery (in Mapungubwe style) attests. With the rise of Great Zimbabwe, it ap-

pears that trade shifted and Mapungubwe declined as an important center, becoming abandoned just as Great Zimbabwe prospered.

Artifacts unearthed at Great Zimbabwe have not clarified the social and cultural organization of the settlement, but they have distinguished it from other Iron Age sites. In particular, a group of soapstone birds, many of them 14 inches high and sitting atop three-foot-tall columns, is unlike any sculpture found elsewhere. Each bird has a different pattern or marking; none is identifiable as a local creature. Because of the regard contemporary Shona people hold for their dead and because some Shona tribes use iron rods to mark tallies of their dead, some archaeologists have speculated that the avian icons indicate aggregates of ancestors used in rituals.

Other artifacts indicate that Great Zimbabwe was well established as a trading community by the 14th century. Objects from distant lands made their way to Great Zimbabwe: Syrian glass, Chinese celadon dishes (mostly from the Ming Dynasty, A.D. 1368 to 1644), Persian faience bowls, coral, bronze bells and an iron spoon—a utensil not used by the Shona. There is no blue-and-white Chinese porcelain, which became widespread during the mid-15th century; its absence suggests that Great Zimbabwe's economic importance was less by that time. Indeed, it does appear that the site was largely empty by 1700.

There are several reasons Great Zimbabwe may have been abandoned. By the late 1600s the northern rivers had been panned clean, and the gold trade began to move west. No longer centrally located, the city may not have been able to thrive when revenue and trade dried up. Another possibility is that the population became unsustainable. By some estimates, Great Zimbabwe had between 10,000 and 17,000 residents at its peak—a population equivalent to that of medieval London. (Other estimates are more conservative, placing the populace at a maximum of 2,000.) The area may have become devegetated as huge herds of cattle grazed it or as it was extensively farmed; recent environmental data suggest that a succession of severe droughts caused people to disperse. Or there may have been some other impetus, such as war, although there is no evidence besides minimal weaponry to support this argument. More archaeological clues, further digs at Great Zimbabwe and excavations at other Iron Age sites are needed to resolve the question of decline.

PLUNDER AND MISAPPROPRIATION

Empty for 200 years or so, Great Zimbabwe was probably used only irregularly for religious ceremonies—as it is today—until the late 1800s. It was then that

Europeans arrived, lured by visions of gold from King Solomon's mines, and it was then that the archaeological record became so damaged as to become largely indecipherable.

A German explorer, Karl Mauch, was first to arrive, in 1871. He befriended another German, Adam Render, who was living in the tribe of Chief Pika, a Karanga leader, and who led him to Great Zimbabwe. (Had he known the outcome, Render, who was married to two tribeswomen and well integrated, might have steered Mauch into the Zambezi River.) On seeing the ruins, Mauch concluded very quickly that Great Zimbabwe, whether or not it was Ophir, was most certainly not the handiwork of Africans. The stonework was too sophisticated, the culture too advanced. It looked to Mauch to be the result of Phoenician or Israelite settlers. A sample of wood from a lintel bolstered Mauch's rapid assessment: it smelled like his pencil, therefore it was cedar and must have come from Lebanon.

Mauch's visit was followed by one from Willi Posselt, a looter, who lugged off a carved soapstone bird and hid others so he could return for them later. Posselt was followed by a series of visitors, some of whom worked for W. G. Neal of the Ancient Ruins Company, which had been created in 1895. Cecil Rhodes, founder of the British South Africa Company, gave Neal a commission to exploit all Rhodesian ruins. Neal and his rogues pillaged Great Zimbabwe, and other Iron Age sites, taking gold and everything of value, tearing down structures and throwing away whatever was not valuable to them (**pottery shards,** pots, clay figurines).

The first official archaeologist to visit the site, James Theodore Bent from Britain, had added to the confusion in 1891 by digging around the conical tower in the Great Enclosure—thereby completely destroying the **stratigraphy** and making it impossible for later archaeologists to make sense of its age. Bent also threw away clay and metal artifacts, including Persian and Arab trade beads, as insignificant. The archaeologist concluded that Great Zimbabwe had been built by a local "bastard" race—bastards because their fathers must have been white invaders from the north—since, as Rhodes and most European settlers maintained, native Africans could never have constructed Great Zimbabwe themselves.

A 1902 report written by Neal and a journalist named Richard N. Hall reiterated Bent's conclusions: the architecture was clearly Phoenician or Arabian. This attitude was pervasive in colonialist Africa: the continent had no history, no sophistication; its people and tribes were unchanging, unable to develop, culturally barren.

Archaeologists who suggested otherwise were not well received. In 1905 David Randall-MacIver, an Egyptologist who had studied under the famous William Matthew Flinders Petrie, excavated at the site and uncovered artifacts very similar to the ones being used by Shona, or Karanga, people living in the vicinity. By turning to indigenous people for cultural clues and interpretation rather than just for labor, Randall-MacIver was indeed doing something unprecedented. Had any other investigators of the time drawn on the lore or knowledge of the local people, many of the questions about Great Zimbabwe might well have been answered.

The continuity of artifacts suggested to Randall-MacIver that the site had been built by people whose culture was similar. He also demonstrated that the Arab and Persian beads were no older than 14th or 15th century and thus did not date back to biblical times and King Solomon. And he argued that the stonework was not at all Arabic, because it was curved and not arranged in geometric or symmetrical patterns. Randall-MacIver concluded that native Africans had built Great Zimbabwe.

Two subsequent researchers held the same opinion. In 1926 J. F. Schofield reiterated Randall-MacIver's conclusions, and in 1929 Gertrude Caton-Thompson did the same. Her excavations of the undisturbed Maund Ruin—which lies at the opposite end of the valley from the Great Enclosure—again supported the theory of indigenous construction. Caton-Thompson's detailed drawings and careful stratigraphy have been crucial in piecing together what little is known about Great Zimbabwe.

Despite the mounting evidence and archaeological testimony, most European settlers in Rhodesia rejected the record. From 1965 until independence in 1980, the Rhodesian Front censored all books and other materials available on Great Zimbabwe. This party, established by then prime minister Ian Smith to prevent Africans from gaining power, was based on a system of apartheid. Archaeologists, such as the noted Peter S. Garlake, who were vocal about the native origin of Great Zimbabwe were imprisoned and eventually deported. Africans who took the same view lost their jobs. Displays at the site itself were censored as well, although it hardly mattered because they were in English, and locals were not allowed to use the premises for any ceremonies.

RECLAIMING THE PAST

Today Great Zimbabwe is a symbol of African cultural development. Popular books have made the monument somewhat more accessible to the people of Zimbabwe. Yet, at the same time, Great Zimbabwe remains largely inaccessible. Because of past archaeological mistakes, much of the history of the site is elusive. Given the condition of contemporary archaeology in southern Africa, there is little chance this will change soon.

The two archaeologists currently stationed at the site are responsible not only for the preservation of the decaying monument but for dealing with visitors and maintenance—and the 5,000 other sites under their jurisdiction as well (out of a total of 35,000 recorded sites in Zimbabwe). Although the ruins are protected by the National Museums and Monuments of Zimbabwe and were designated a World Heritage Site by UNESCO, only two conservators and fewer than 10 archaeologists are available in Zimbabwe to study and look after all the archaeological sites, including Great Zimbabwe.

The situation in other sub-Saharan countries is no better. According to Pierre de Maret of the Free University of Brussels, less than $150,000 is spent annually on archaeology in 10 sub-Saharan countries—and there are a mere 20 professional archaeologists among them. The sale of African objects abroad however, reaches into the millions of dollars every year.

It is clear that cultural legacies are being lost as monuments decay and artifacts are taken out of the various countries. If contemporary cultures, fragmented and ruptured by centuries of colonialism, are going to be able to piece together and to reconnect with their severed past, archaeology needs to assume a more important place in African society. Great Zimbabwe is so important not simply because of its masterful masonry but because it is a cultural clue that survived and that has been reclaimed. Now it needs to be fully interpreted and placed within the larger context of sub-Saharan history, a context that still lies hidden.

7

Prologue to *Uncommon Ground*

Leland Ferguson

Leland Ferguson is an archaeologist at the University of South Carolina. He is a leading researcher in the historical archaeology of plantation life in the American South and the author of Uncommon Ground: Archaeology and Early African America *(Smithsonian Institution Press).*

....

Points to consider when reading this article:

1. How did Ferguson find the slave quarters on the Middleburg Plantation?

2. What work did slaves do on plantations?

3. When conducting plantation archaeology, what can archaeologists do in addition to digging to illuminate the lives of slaves?

4. Isn't there plenty written about slavery? Why do we need to do archaeology to understand slave life on southern plantations?

It is remarkable to note that just a bit more than 130 years ago that "peculiar institution," slavery, was legal in parts of the United States. Kidnapping human beings was sanctioned; separating husband from wife and children from parents was rationalized; and buying and selling people, imprisoning them, and forcing them to work with no legal recourse was an accepted part of the American economy. It was not so very long ago. There are people alive today in the United States whose grandparents were born into slavery and whose great-grandparents were born in Africa.

Africans were brought to the United States in the bowels of ships as depicted in the recent Steven Spielberg movie *Amistad.* Many did not survive this "middle passage," and those who did were thrust into an alien world where they were considered little more than property that could be bought or sold, whipped, or worked to death.

But these people had something to hold onto— something to give them strength and hope. The overseer's chains and the foreman's whip could deny these Africans their freedom, but they could not deny them their culture. Their gods and spirits, beliefs and philosophies also survived the middle passage, and they survived imprisonment and the slaves' diaspora as well. Archaeologists like Leland Ferguson are recovering the hidden story of cultural resistance by African slaves in the southern United States. In the objects these people left behind we see a reflection of their dignity, a dignity that never succumbed to the shackles or whips.

....

AFRICAN AMERICAN PIONEERS

In 1740 blacks in South Carolina outnumbered whites by almost two to one, and one half of that majority had been born in Africa. As slaves, they cleared trees to build plantations, and in some of those clearings they built their settlements. Research in history and folklore combined with recent archaeological finds help us imagine what those early homes were like:

. . . Linked by sandy yards, three small, two-room houses stand in the smoky shadows of tall pines and moss-draped live oaks. No little white cottages from "Gone with the Wind," these are more like African houses than the "slave cabins" we know preserved from the middle nineteenth century. Roofs of split planks and palmetto thatching top clay walls without windows.

In a sunny clearing behind the houses, saplings and stumps, the debris from clearing land, surround a garden; they keep the cattle out of the okra, corn, and sweet potatoes. Posts and poles, for this purpose and that, stand like sentinels in the well-swept yards. Near each house are two or three large holes. First dug for clay to build house walls, they now receive sweepings from the yard. These pits contain mostly sand and bark, wood shavings, and pine cones. Yet here also are fragments of broken pots, discarded bones, pieces of glass, metal, buttons, and other little things.

In front of one house a young mother goes about her late morning chores. They call her Benah, an African name for a girl-child born on Tuesday. She stoops to move the old basket holding her baby into the warm sunlight. The baby coughs and Benah quickly touches the single blue glass bead tied with a string around the baby's neck. Then she turns to stir a clay pot simmering on the hearth fashioned from three big bricks. Standing upright on legs bowed from childhood malnutrition, Benah deftly adjusts the skirt wrapped about her waist with one hand and slips the stem of her white clay tobacco pipe into the waistband. Beneath her bare feet lies the charcoal of hundreds of cooking fires kindled on this very spot since her mother and other black pioneers first built temporary thatched houses and began transforming forests and swamps into productive rice fields.

Scattered about are her cookwares. Three more pots sit near the fire—an iron one issued by Ben, the white planter's son, and two others of clay handbuilt by Benah. Clay pots are best for savory sauces. Although Benah uses the iron pot, her mother—one of the Africans with scars on her breast—never would. She always complained that the iron legs stuck into the ground and that the metal pot cooked too hot and fast. She preferred the slow cooking of her earthenware.

Benah's mother, now a spirit living near her grave in the pine woods, dug clay in the rice field ditch and taught her daughters to build pots and make spicy African sauces. Serving bowls for sauces are stacked on a split log. Two of these bowls, glazed and colored brown and yellow, were also given to her by Ben. Unknown to her, they were made by working women in Staffordshire, England. The others, like the cooking pots, were made right here in the sandy yard.

Benah's family usually eats morning and evening meals in front of the house beside the fire. Her family sits on the ground or planks while she serves rice or corn meal mush on large palmetto leaves. They dip handfuls of the stiff starch into piquant sauces made from okra leaves and other greens gathered from the woods and fields.

The small houses both have two rooms with separate entries. One room of Benah's house is reserved for her mother's brother, another African—a man who talks to spirits. Inside the other room Benah, her sister, brother, and three small children sleep. Benah's husband, a cooper and woodcarver who digs out cypress canoes, lives on a plantation across the river. Often on Sunday and sometimes at night he paddles the short distance between the banks to visit.

In the center of the earthen house-floor, an open hearth holds fires that fight the cold of winter and the devilish mosquitoes of the long hot months. In rainy weather Benah moves her cooking inside to this small fire. On the wall beyond the hearth, a leather bag and fishing net hang from a wrought-iron nail. Cow hides and woolen blankets that serve as beds are rolled up and piled in a corner. An empty wine bottle and a wooden bucket made by her husband and filled with water stand just beside the door. Outside, the young woman empties the pot of corn meal mush into a large gourd bowl, covering it with leaves to keep it warm. Then, gathering up her ailing baby, she balances the bowl on her head and walks off toward the place her relatives are clearing for new rice fields.

For thirty more years, Benah and her family and neighbors live in this settlement. In the last decade of the century, not long after the Revolutionary War, they move to some new houses closer to the rice fields along the river. The old settlement slowly settles into the ground. The heart pine posts reinforcing the clay walls rot in place but, hidden beneath the dark humus, the stains of these posts remain in the yellow sand of the subsoil. Wrought-iron nails used to hold the rafters together fall to the ground and begin to rust. The charred wood in the hearths is covered with blowing sand. Unless moved by some human or natural action, this charcoal will remain, preserved, in just this spot for thousands of years. The clay pits continue to fill with washings from frequent rains—broken pieces of pottery, buttons, fragments of glass and bone concealed within. Once a small village of pioneering African Americans, this eighteenth-century homeplace is now an archaeological site holding a retrievable story of early American life.

FINDING THE "NEGRO HOUSES"

In the summer of 1986, students in my archaeological field class and I set out to find an eighteenth-century African American village. We were searching on Middleburg Plantation in an old rice-growing district about 25 miles north of Charleston, South Carolina. This district lies near the center of the South Carolina lowcountry, the region of the largest black majority in colonial America. Our excavations were part of a bigger survey project aimed at learning more about early slave communities by finding the geographical pattern of settlements on the East Branch of Cooper River. Our summer research provides an example of the methods and techniques used in African American archaeology.

While the location of the slave quarters at Middleburg was not obvious we could easily see other features of this antebellum rice plantation. The shining white "big house" of Middleburg still stands where it stood since at least 1699, nearly three hundred years. Here and there, other reminders of the plantation days remain. The avenue of oaks was established by the wealthy planter Jonathan Lucas sometime before 1831. Although Lucas is credited with "planting" the trees, they probably were uprooted, transported, set out, and cared for by slaves. The wide, nicely crowned road bed of the avenue certainly was graded with hoes and shovels in black hands. Behind the house a kitchen and decaying servants' quarters flank a formal garden, which is now more lawn than garden, and two nineteenth-century Gothic-revival style barns stand about one hundred yards away in a grassy field. A picture postcard of the scene might bear the caption: "The Simple Grace of the Old South is Well-Preserved at Middleburg Plantation. Middleburg is Located on the Cooper River in South Carolina's Lowcountry." Missing from the picture are the people in servitude who built this and other plantations and who left an abundant archaeological record underground.

Down the path behind the house lie the river, marsh, and rice fields. Now grown up in aquatic weeds, these fields are surrounded by more than a mile of earthen dikes or "banks" as they were called. Built by slaves, these banks are severely eroded now. Originally they were taller than a person and up to 15 feet wide. By the turn of the eighteenth century, rice banks on the 12½-mile stretch of the East Branch of Cooper River measured more than 55 miles long and contained more than 6.4 million cubic feet of earth. This means that within approximately fifty years of tidal rice agriculture, Middleburg slaves, working in the water and muck with no more than shovels, hoes, and baskets, had built an earthwork approximately one-half the size of Monks Mound, the largest prehistoric Indian mound in North America. By 1850 Carolina slaves working on plantations like Middleburg throughout the rice growing district had built a system of banks and canals greater in volume than the Egyptian pyramid at Cheops.

Near the Middleburg rice fields a brick smoke stack, almost 100 feet tall, stands amid the pines and live oaks like an ancient Mayan temple. At its base, slowly sinking into the junglelike growth, are the ghostly remains of a nineteenth-century steam engine and the brick foundation of a rice pounding mill. Although we have yet to find the proof, local legend claims that ships left the Middleburg wharf loaded with rice, bound for England.

From early in the eighteenth century until 1861, Middleburg was a thriving rice plantation. A tour around the estate reveals much of the original layout, and the informed eye sees the skill and handiwork of African Americans everywhere—in the house, the roads, the fields, the mill. From probate records we know that fifty-nine slaves lived at Middleburg in 1772 and ninety in 1790. In fact, the majority of people who have ever lived at Middleburg were black. African American slaves built this plantation—they sawed the boards, drove the nails, laid the bricks, built the banks, and worked the crops. Yet there is no obvious evidence of their homes; the evidence is hidden within the soil.

Our archaeological strategy for finding the missing slave quarters was simple. We would search in the most likely places. The trick to this strategy was determining where the "most likely places" might be.

First we studied maps and talked to people. The land contours of the modern United States Geodetic Surveys and the sites of surviving plantation structures suggested to us that the quarters probably were situated on the same ridge as the "big house," overlooking the river or else adjacent to the marsh and near the rice fields. We thought these conjectures were good, but we wanted as much locational information as possible to minimize the amount of digging required to find foundations and floors. So we also looked for maps from the period when the plantation was operating. We knew from notes on early twentieth-century plats that there had been at least one plantation map made in the late eighteenth century and another in the middle of the nineteenth century. We even found a book, *Charleston Gardens,* which referred to an earlier map and described the "twelve cabins for the Negroes." We searched archives and libraries as well as the personal collections of family and friends of the owners, but still we could not find the map or maps we thought existed. We had to be content with the written account.

In questioning local people we seemed to have more success. Mr. John Gibbs, a member of the white family that recently owned the plantation, thought he knew roughly where some quarters had stood until they were torn down early in the twentieth century. Black informants from the community remembered when people lived in the servants' quarters adjacent to the "big house," and they remembered some houses "across the hard road" about a mile from the plantation, but they could not recall old slave quarters on what is now Middleburg. Reasoning that quarters in the early twentieth century might well be in the same location as those two hundred years earlier, and that an eyewitness description should provide the most reliable information, we began our test excavations where Mr. Gibbs had thought some cabins should be, and we found nothing.

From this we went to Briggs's description in *Charleston Gardens* of a very old map of Middleburg: "This drawing . . . shows a forecourt with a square formal garden on each side. Beyond one garden are twelve cabins for the Negroes and beyond the other, a barn and machine house with other accessory buildings." This description was pretty clear. The quarters were obviously located on one of two sides of the forecourt and garden, but what was the front of the house?

Eighteenth-century houses on important waterways such as the Cooper River often faced the water, and the present garden at Middleburg is on the river side of the house. The house now fronts the oak avenue away from the river, but it is one of those buildings that could be seen as "fronting" in either of two directions. We finally decided on the front as the side with the oak avenue, and we put in small **test excavations** on the western side of the yard. Here, we found a few artifacts—some glass, a few nails, and a brick footing—and concluded that we were in the vicinity of the barns. We moved our attention to the eastern side of the front yard, where we laid out a scattered pattern of eight 1 by 1 meter squares for our test excavations.

Cutting through the sod, we excavated with shovels in layers approximately 10 centimeters thick. We threw dirt into our mechanical sifters and collected everything larger than the quarter-inch mesh of the screens. As we watched the artifacts showing up in the screen baskets, there was the debris from the slave village! It wasn't spectacular—we didn't expect spectacular artifacts in our **test pits**—but it was there and it was substantial. The dark brown, almost black earth gave up hundreds of things; just the kinds of things we had hoped and expected to find around the quarters. There was the slave-made pottery we call Colono Ware, imported English ceramics from the late eighteenth century, food bones of various kinds including birds and mammals, fragments of brick, hundreds of nails, pieces of glass, and other little things like buttons and fragments of imported white-kaolin tobacco pipes as well as locally made earth-colored pipes. Rich with artifacts, the dark, charcoal and grease-stained soil looked like the sort commonly found around old houses. And this scatter of refuse—or **midden** as archaeologists would call it—was where we expected the slave quarters to be located. We had found it! Tens of thousands of the everyday things of slaves were still there, waiting to be excavated.

On the very weekend after we found the Middleburg quarters, we came upon a copy of the eighteenth-century map verifying our find. That Saturday evening, graduate student David W. Babson visited Mr. and Mrs. Thomas Huguenin at adjacent Halidon Hill to copy a nineteenth-century map of their plantation. Halidon Hill had been part of Middleburg in the eighteenth century, and we hoped this later map would provide clues to earlier features. This was the fourth time we had visited the Huguenins inquiring about maps and other historical sources, and they had willingly combed through drawer after drawer of maps and papers accumulated through the years. That evening David set up his drawing board and Mrs. Huguenin, as usual, searched for more things. Going through a drawer filled with modern maps she found a copy of the old Middleburg map hidden between some larger United States Geodetic Survey sheets. Drawn in 1786 by the well-known Charleston mapmaker Joseph Purcell, the map showed the entire Middleburg plantation: road, fences, rice fields, barns, the "big house," and there, just where we had been digging, were twelve small squares labeled "Negro Houses."

The next week we continued our excavations in the dark earth around the "Negro Houses." Digging in one test pit, Elaine Nichols, another graduate student, noticed a disturbance in the soil—yellow sand mottled in the darker **matrix** stretched across the center of the square. After carefully cleaning the surface, Elaine photographed and drew this feature, then continued taking out another layer of soil. When she had come to the bottom of the midden, more than 50 centimeters below the ground surface, Elaine cleaned the top of the yellow, sandy subsoil. Here a band of dark earth about 25 centimeters wide crossed the bottom level of the excavation. Looking more closely we saw that the parallel edges of the **feature** were composed of the blurred arcs left by posts that had been set side-by-side and rotted in place in the ground.

In 1710 Thomas Nairne advised prospective settlers that one of the first jobs on a new plantation was to "cutt down a few Trees, to split Palissades, or clapboards, and therewith make small houses or Huts to shelter the slaves." Our excavation showed the bottom portion of a palisadelike wall, a wall set in the ground by slaves more than one hundred and fifty years ago. We would only have to follow the wall to find the outline of the entire structure.

As is often the case in archaeology, our first hypothesis wasn't supported. This palisade was apparently an early fence and not a house wall; however, these particular excavations led to the discovery of a late eighteenth-century house built by slaves. Although we know African Americans occupied this village in the early eighteenth century, we are still looking for the earliest houses.

8

The Earth Is Their Witness

Larry McKee

Larry McKee is an archaeologist at Vanderbilt University in Nashville, Tennessee. He is staff archaeologist at the Hermitage, the estate of Andrew Jackson, seventh president of the United States.

Points to consider when reading this article:

1. How did some people in the mid-nineteenth century justify slavery—or at least maintain that it wasn't so bad?

2. It is sometimes said that at least slaves were well fed by their owners. How does the archaeological record call this into dispute?

3. Is the material culture of slaves at the Hermitage universally limited and poor? What does archaeology tell us of the "wealth" of at least some of the slaves?

4. How does archaeology show that slaves maintained some of their African spiritual beliefs?

Many of us have taken tours of the beautiful and stately historic mansions that grace the landscape of our nation. Mount Vernon, the family home of George Washington, Thomas Jefferson's Monticello, and the Hermitage estate of Andrew Jackson are three of the best known and most often visited, but there are literally hundreds of others. In the typical tour, a docent (tour guide) walks us through the estate, pointing out the lovely marble fireplace imported from an ancient castle in Italy, the ornately carved wood paneling in the study, the dining room chandelier made by French craftsmen, and so on. The rooms where children played, were nursed, and where they sometimes, sadly, died can be seen with some of their original furnishings.

Usually, the tour will take us through the kitchen where we are treated to glimpses of fine imported china, crystal goblets, and brilliantly polished silverware. Reference may be made to "cooks" or "servants" or "help," as if these people were hired laborers whose good work allowed for the smooth operation of the estate.

But there is a darker side to the opulent life lived by some of our American presidents and heroes, the people we read about in textbooks and for whom holiday celebrations are held. Washington, Jefferson, and Jackson were slave owners; the lovely homes in which they lived, the beautiful estates they oversaw and that we now marvel at, were made possible and depended absolutely on the work of a people who were imprisoned and subjugated. Tour guides and history books may attempt to ignore this fact, but we must not—and the archaeological record will not allow us to forget. Larry McKee's work at the Hermitage is an excellent example of how archaeology forces us to confront this truth.

In the spring of 1835, as Andrew Jackson approached his last year in the White House, his mind was already back at the Hermitage, the cotton plantation near Nashville where he would die ten years later. In a letter to Andrew Jackson Jr., his adopted son and temporary master of the Hermitage, the president tried to pass on some of what he had learned about plantation management. "One willing hand is really worth two who only does what labour he is forcibly compelled to perform," he wrote, after praising the plantation overseer, who had "reduced the hands to good subordination, and in doing this [had] obtained their confidence and attachment."

Jackson's "hands" were, of course, slaves. In the first half of the nineteenth century the Hermitage was home to more than 130 slaves and one of the largest plantations in the fertile central basin of Tennessee. In contrast to Thomas Jefferson, who compared his own slave ownership to holding a "wolf by the ears,"

From *The Sciences*, March/April 1995. Reprinted here courtesy of the New York Academy of Sciences.

Jackson never questioned his right to own other human beings. Fervently populist yet racist to his bones, pragmatic yet prone to furious rages that often ended in fisticuffs and in one case a formal duel, Jackson was a great champion of the southern status quo. Slave ownership was a purely practical matter to him, an organizational problem no more anguishing than the weather or the price of cotton.

In an earlier letter to his son, Jackson had declared without irony that slaves "will complain often, without cause." To a modern reader, taught to think of slavery as a nightmare of backbreaking labor and unrelenting brutality, that statement seems shockingly insensitive. If Jackson seems to have been blind to the psychological horror of slavery, however, the modern understanding of plantation life too often translates that horror into physical terms. Slaves were the most valuable assets on any plantation: common sense required planters to provide them with adequate food, clothing and shelter, and to keep workloads moderate, and brutal, corporal punishments to a minimum. Plantation life, however demeaning, must have also fostered at least a fragile consensus between blacks and whites. Why else would the great majority of slaves never have run away or directly revolted against their oppressors? How else could a handful of white owners and overseers have controlled hundreds of slaves twenty-four hours a day?

Making sense of Jackson's offhand comments requires a calm, nuanced assessment of slavery, one that moves beyond the inflammatory rhetoric that has always surrounded the subject. From the start, studies of slavery have been hampered by a dearth of hard data or reasonably objective accounts by contemporary observers. In delivering speeches, writing letters or even filling out the pages of diaries, participants in the slavery debate seem to have been always conscious of the eyes of history upon them, of the need to record for posterity their most extreme—and often, therefore, their least objective—arguments.

Those in the pro-slavery camp stressed the humane paternalism of plantation owners and their role in "civilizing" a "savage" people. As one planter wrote in 1846:

> Our slaves will bear a favorable contrast with that of any other laboring population in the world, so far as comfort and happiness is concerned, and will not fall below them in any other point of view than that of mere abstract notions of human rights, about which, it is true, there has been much nonsensical prating in this as well as in other countries.

Abolitionists, for their part, usually matched their opponents' rhetorical excesses. Frances Anne Kemble, author of *Journal of a Residence on a Georgian Plantation in 1838–1839* put it this way:

> Though the Negroes are fed, clothed, and housed, and though the Irish peasant is starved, naked, and roofless, the bare name of freemen . . . are blessings beyond food, raiment, or shelter; possessing which, the want of every comfort of life is yet more tolerable than their fullest enjoyment without them.

To withstand the buffeting winds of such rhetoric, an understanding of slavery needs to be anchored in simple facts about day-to-day plantation life. Because the historical documents are nearly devoid of such facts, one has to examine the actual remains of slave life—the bones, potsherds, bottle glass and broken trinkets buried on plantation grounds throughout the South. Paltry, as they seem, such remains, together with information gathered from documents, folklore, anthropological theory and whatever else may be of use, can help build (to use a term coined by the anthropologist Clifford Geertz of the Institute for Advanced Study in Princeton, New Jersey) "thick descriptions" of the world that slave and master made and occupied together.

The archaeological study of slavery began in the late 1960s, with the pioneering work of the late Charles H. Fairbanks along the southeastern coastal lowlands. In the quarter-century since that time, the study has spread through all former slaveholding regions of the United States and the Caribbean, as well as parts of Central and South America. Archaeologists have excavated the remains of dozens of slave quarters and have pieced together an understanding of power structures, trade networks and social relations within slave communities.

In the 1980s, excavations of slave dwellings at Monticello, by William M. Kelso of the Association for the Preservation of Virginia Antiquities, added a new dimension to the understanding of Thomas Jefferson. More recently, excavations at the colonial-period African Burial Ground site in lower Manhattan provided a sobering reminder that slavery was not confined to the South. Poor interdisciplinary communication and the usual scholarly turf wars have kept mainstream historians from appreciating the significance of such discoveries, much less incorporating them into their work. It now seems, however, that in the next decade archaeology will be firmly accepted as an indispensable tool in the study of slavery.

My own work, as staff archaeologist at the Hermitage since 1988, has uncovered dramatic evidence of initiative and autonomy among Hermitage slaves. In hunting for wild meat after work, surreptitiously bartering for goods or observing their ancestors' beliefs, Hermitage slaves refused to accept their dispossession, and they strove to improve their lives rather than submit passively to their owner's orders. If Jackson's overseer did indeed reduce Hermitage slaves to "good subordination," the slaves' remains show that he often did so by subordinating his own wishes to their needs.

A visitor taking the current public tour at the Hermitage gets little sense that 130 slaves once lived on the property. Most of the tour is devoted to the Jackson family's Greek Revival mansion, set within a bucolic landscape. Gone are the rutted roads, squealing hogs and crowds of slaves toiling in the fields to make the planters' high life possible. A log cabin behind the mansion provides the only hint of slavery on the tour. Signs describe it as the home of Alfred Jackson, a Hermitage slave who stayed on after emancipation until his death in 1901. His gravestone, in the garden near the family tomb, commemorates him as "Uncle Alfred, faithful servant of Andrew Jackson."

No other African-Americans are buried in the garden, and the slave burial ground has never been found. Lacking any antebellum maps of the Hermitage slave quarters, or any diaries or letters written by the slaves themselves, historians have been largely at a loss to recover the slaves' side of the plantation's history. But archaeologists, by locating the remains of the slave quarters, have begun to clarify Jackson's intentions toward his slaves.

Like many planters, Jackson divided his slaves into two groups: those assigned to household duties lived in cabins set up near the mansion; those assigned to farming lived in cabins in the fields, clustered in two subgroups, one 250 yards and the other 600 yards from the mansion. In designing the cabins, Jackson almost certainly consulted southern farm journals in the Hermitage library. Constructed of brick and, in plan, nearly always a square twenty feet on a side, the cabins bespeak an effort at "social engineering" of the kind advocated by essays in those journals.

"The ends aimed at in building negro cabins should be: First, the health and comfort of the occupants," one planter wrote in 1856. "Secondly, the convenience of nursing, surveillance, discipline, and the supply of wood and water; and Thirdly, economy of construction." Like plain, sturdy stables built to shelter valuable livestock, such housing kept slaves literally and figuratively in their place, implying that the contrast between shabby slave quarters and the grand mansion was part of an immutable natural order.

In Jackson's time each slave family at the Hermitage occupied a single 400-square-foot room with a wooden floor, an attic loft, one door and one window. Larger Hermitage families, which had as many as ten children, according to the 1850 farm census, must have found life in such cramped quarters chaotic. Yet the cabin design Jackson chose was a product of more than a century of give-and-take between owner and slave. As late as 1820, our excavations show slaves on the Hermitage (as elsewhere in the South) were crammed together in hut-like log buildings that offered families little or no privacy.

The permanent, family-based slave quarters built later in the nineteenth century, like many other improvements in slave life, were a result of complicated, mostly indirect negotiations. Surly behavior, work slowdowns, theft, sabotage or flight were the slaves' only weapons in this cold war. The owners might have retaliated with whippings or worse, but more often they tried gentler methods. Coaxing was preferable to coercing, three planters wrote in 1846, in "promoting [the slaves'] happiness, and consequently their usefulness to us." Compliant slaves might be allowed to travel off the property when not at work, or to take extra time off following the harvest or during holidays. They might get cash bonuses for chopping extra firewood or for producing crafts. Such noblesse oblige was meant to win the slaves' "confidence and attachment" while demonstrating the owner's self-confident authority and managerial savvy.

Like military barracks, the rows of identical slave cabins at the Hermitage seem to suggest lives shaped and dictated by a local authority. But beneath their façades, the cabins hid evidence of less regimented lives, conducted in near secret. The most direct gateways to those secret lives were found under each cabin floor: small squared-off pits dug into the stiff clay soil and sometimes lined with brick. Such pits served primarily as cool, dry root cellars, but they were often also used as places for items (and, on occasion, people) that had to be kept hidden from master and overseer.

Jackson and many other plantation owners allowed slaves to dig the pits for food storage, although they probably knew that the "hidey holes" could also be used for clandestine activities and stolen goods. One planter, writing in 1851, cautioned that houses should have "no place to stow away anything." Another, writing the year before, recommended that slave dwellings be placed on piers: "When thus elevated, if there should be any filth under them, the master or overseer, in passing, can see it and have it removed."

Small game and baskets of root crops were among the most common items stored in the pits, and their remains are among the most revealing to the archaeologist. Food was always a major point of contention on any plantation. Planters disagreed with slaves as well as with one another about what constituted adequate rations and how those rations ought to be distributed. Some thought it best to distribute a week's worth of raw rations at a time, whereas others favored a central kitchen where slaves could go for their meals. Although it appears that many planters believed, in the words of one essayist, that "A negro slave is so constituted that he is dependent in a great measure for happiness on his food," the rations provided hardly seem to bear out that dictum. Research into plantation records from all over the South shows that between thirty-two and forty-eight cups of cornmeal and three and a half pounds of meat a week was all a slave could expect to receive from his owner.

Contrary to popular belief, however, few slaves were content to eat only their rations. Of the more than 100,000 animal bones we have excavated so far, most came from pigs. Moreover, in some years, according to Hermitage records, more than nine tons of pork was processed on the property. Those numbers imply that every household at the site, including the Jackson family itself, chose pork for 70 to 80 percent of its meals. Mutton and beef were about equally favored as alternatives. Each slave family rounded out those provisions with foods as varied as family members were resourceful. Depending on which cabin site we excavated, we found bones from chickens; geese, ducks and other wild birds; opossums, raccoons, groundhogs and other small mammals; and turtles, fish, shellfish and other aquatic animals.

By allowing slaves to hunt and collect wild foods and to raise garden crops and livestock, the planters saved the cost of providing truly sufficient rations and, perhaps, promoted a sense of self-satisfaction within the plantation community. Keeping rations to a minimum also enabled planters to reward good behavior and added effort with extra rations. "If occasionally a little molasses be added to the allowance," an essayist wrote in 1850, "the cost will be but a trifle, while the negro will esteem it a great luxury."

Such rewards may have helped fulfill Jackson's goal of creating "willing hands," but at a cost of some loss of authority and control. Slaves often chose to sell their personal produce rather than consume it themselves. As one planter from Alabama put it:

> A privilege to work in their patches until 9 or 10 o'clock at night is often construed into a privilege to visit a neighbor's hen house or pig yard; or perhaps to get a mule and take a turn of corn to some market and barter it for a jug of whiskey, or something of little more value.

If slaves stashed important items beneath cabin floors, one might assume the cabins themselves held little of value. But excavations at the Hermitage have revealed an astonishing wealth of artifacts among cabin remains, and in one slave cabin at Monticello archaeologists unearthed fragments of fifteen matching porcelain dinner plates from China. Jackson and Jefferson were particularly wealthy planters, able to offer their slaves gifts of chipped or outmoded objects along with a few basic furnishings. But mansion castoffs alone cannot account for all the Hermitage artifacts, including coins, bone-handled cutlery and combs, a brass thermometer backing plate, glass beads in a variety of styles and colors, and 1,190 ceramic shards, mostly from refined white earthenware vessels made in England.

Some of those items might have made their way to Tennessee with new slaves from Florida or New Orleans. Given their diverse origins, however, many items probably arrived through surreptitious trade networks run by the slaves themselves. Passing from hand to hand, coat lining to coat lining, in a continual yet ephemeral system of barter and trade, goods reached slaves all over the South from ports as distant as Europe and the Caribbean. Cities such as Nashville, Memphis and New Orleans, linked by land and river, were key nodes in the trade network.

Among the Hermitage slaves, as among their white owners, success at trade would have been regarded as one sign of social rank. Given the conventional wisdom that house slaves were better treated and generally more comfortable than field slaves, one would expect their material remains to be richer. At the Hermitage, however, cabins belonging to house slaves and cabins belonging to field slaves yielded equally impressive artifacts. Such evidence seems to suggest that class structure at the Hermitage had less to do with the social order Jackson tried to impose than with the slaves' own reckoning of their talents and achievements. Field slaves might have received fewer castoffs from the mansion, but living further from the overseers' eyes gave them more freedom to hunt and trade.

Such discoveries serve as reminders that plantation slaves, against all odds, formed true communities, complete with social mobility, scandal, gossip and ceremony. Bones and trade goods document the daily struggle for food and minor liberties, but the most intriguing artifacts offer a window on those parts of slave life that made bondage bearable. In the course of three excavating sessions, for instance, our teams have uncovered three beautifully wrought brass amulets shaped like human fists. Only one similar charm has been recovered by archaeologists—on the grounds of a house in Annapolis, Maryland, occupied by white families and their slave attendants during the eighteenth and nineteenth centuries. Elsewhere in the world, however, hand images are common and are often believed to confer spiritual power.

In Islamic folklore, the "Hand of Fatima" is used to ward off the evil eye. In Brazil and elsewhere in Latin America, hand-shaped charms and votive items, known as *figas* and *milagros,* respectively, are still widely used to confer good luck and fertility, as defenses against witchcraft and as religious offerings. The meaning that Hermitage slaves probably bestowed on their charms is clearly linked to the use of the word *hand* in African-American folklore as a generic term for any item intended to bring good luck or to ward off evil.

Hundreds of other items uncovered at the Hermitage and at other southern plantations were probably thought to have similar spiritual powers: quartz crystals, medicine vials, lumps of sulfur, cut silver coins and a pierced coin-like medallion, glass beads used to protect slaves from witchcraft, gaming pieces made from shards of European pottery, prehistoric projectile points, and a smoothed and polished raccoon penis bone. More than any other artifacts, such spiritual items show how slaves created an independent world within the bounds of their bondage—a culture within a culture, defined by its own beliefs concerning supernatural powers.

Slave owners usually dismissed slave superstitions as primitive and childlike, forbidding them to be openly observed for fear they might disrupt plantation discipline. That slaves almost uniformly ignored such orders demonstrates how spirituality helped build solidarity in the slave community and thus provided a moral compass in a world that must have seemed largely senseless and evil.

To nurture a culture in the heart of oppression, slaves had to become masters of disguise, shielding their inner lives from prying eyes, hiding or even burying their most precious belongings, assuming the trappings of obedience while secretly subverting their role. Archaeologists can sometimes get to the truth behind those disguises, but not without getting fooled themselves from time to time. Am I right in thinking the odd smooth stones sometimes found at the Hermitage are spiritual items—akin to similar stones found in medicine bundles used by African curers—or are they just leftovers from a child's collection of curios? If Hermitage slaves managed to conduct trade networks and forbidden rituals beneath their owners' noses, might they not easily deceive me a century later? I often imagine the slaves themselves watching me at work, listening to the tales I spin based on their garbage and ruins. Do they feel exposed—violated, even—watching me piece together the remains of their secrets? Or do they just laugh, shaking their heads at the persistence of delusion?

After spending more than a decade digging up slave quarters in Virginia and Tennessee, I realize that the "truth" of slavery will always remain elusive. As long as race, oppression and inequality remain burning, contemporary issues, the scholars of every generation will reinterpret slavery for their own time. In Tennessee today the world of plantation slavery seems simultaneously familiar and unthinkable. Blacks and whites live in relative harmony, yet they are only three or four generations removed from slaves and slave owners. Slavery may not be a constant topic of discussion, but a confederate flag, a hymn to old Dixie, or a hiring based on affirmative action can still stir up a fight.

When the issue of race so deeply divides society, common sense about slave life has a hard time escaping the distorting gravity of myth. On the one hand, a minister for Louis Farrakhan's Nation of Islam describes slavery as the worst crime "in the history of humanity. . . . The Holocaust did not equal it." On the other hand, some southern whites call slavery a necessary step in our national development. In comparison, the conclusions my colleagues and I have reached about life at the Hermitage may seem self-evident: anyone who has read a line of Faulkner knows that slaves and masters endlessly negotiated the details of daily life. For all its apparent mundanity, however, archaeology can help prepare new ground for such sensible old ideas, extinguishing the fires of ideology with a rain of specific detail.

To their credit, some plantation museums in the U.S. are evolving from shrines for southern myths into places where visitors can confront facts about the past. At the Hermitage, on a busy day in the summer, more than a thousand people stop by to watch the excavations behind the mansion. Some move on quickly; others stop just long enough to crack jokes about finding gold; a few pace along the edge of the excavation pit, asking questions that they have never had answered. Most of the truths they take away are only partial, but one is complete: that the Hermitage was a home to slaves as well as slave owners—elegance as well as injustice—although the mansion stands unblemished and the cabins are survived by holes in the ground.

9

Archaeology as Community Service: The African Burial Ground Project in New York City

Warren Perry and Michael Blakey

Warren Perry is an archaeologist at Central Connecticut State University. He is the associate director of the Laboratory of Archaeology for the African Burial Ground Project. He is featured in one of the archaeological biographies presented in this book.

Michael Blakey is a biological anthropologist at Howard University. He is the director of the African Burial Ground Project and is conducting the forensic analysis of the skeletons of the 420 individuals whose remains have been recovered.

Points to consider when reading this article:

1. How did the existence of the African Burial Ground come to light?

2. Do you feel that the descendant community's reaction to the initial treatment of the African Burial Ground was justified?

3. What can the study of the bones of slaves tell us about their lives that the historical record does not already tell us?

4. What are the goals of the African Burial Ground Project?

The debate has been ongoing in the press for at least a couple of years: Should the U.S. government offer an official apology for slavery? Some view such an apology as a simple act of contrition long overdue. Others complain, "Hey, I never owned slaves, so why should I apologize? Besides, that was a long time ago." The view of still others is more conspiratorial, interpreting an official governmental apology as a ploy, a foot in the door for modern African Americans to sue the U.S. government for reparations in the billions of dollars—or, perhaps, just for that "forty acres and a mule" they were promised long ago.

Whatever the result of this debate, it is yet another indication that as we approach the twenty-first century, the United States is still attempting to confront its historical shame in having been a nation built, at least in part, on the enslavement of an entire class of human beings.

Confronting the historical realities of slavery is facilitated by African American archaeology wherever it is practiced, even in New York City. But wait, wasn't slavery confined to the South? Were there slaves in the North? The answer is yes, absolutely. Though the practice was abandoned before the Civil War, slavery was legal throughout most of the North. Here again, what history has glossed over archaeology forces us to face. The more than four hundred skeletons of African slaves and slave descendants revealed in the African Burial Ground of New York City speak to us of the violence, indignity, and terror of slavery in a way that history has refused to and, in all likelihood, simply cannot.

. . . it is our past, our culture and heritage, and forms part of our present life. As such it is ours to control and it is ours to share on our own terms. (Rosalind Langford 1983)

The past is contested terrain over which archaeologists among others struggle. How the past is conceptualized shapes our perceptions of the present and what is possible in the future. (Thomas Patterson 1993)

From *North American Dialogue*, vol. 2, no. 1, 1997. Reprinted here courtesy of Michael Blakey and Warren Perry.

INTRODUCTION

Since its discovery in 1991, the African Burial Ground (ABG) in New York City has been the subject of discussion in a variety of scholarly and popular media (Wilson 1996). Its significance ranges from the fact that its discovery gives voice to a marginalized African historiography in the United States, to the window it provides into African captivity in the north. The ABG experience has inspired public curiosity about both the African diaspora and the practice of archaeological science. Through its public education programs it continues to teach the descendant community to recognize and combat improper research techniques and to identify cultural resources in the cities and towns where they live. Finally, the ABG project has provided the descendant community with political awareness through concrete historical experiences that afford opportunities to make alternative history and inclusion in the production of knowledge.

Recently, there has been some attention paid to the social relations involved in the archaeological production of knowledge and the movement of indigenous communities in demanding control of their own past. These studies suggest that it is within the cultural sphere that most struggles for identity and knowledge production take place (Blakey 1983, 1991, 1996; Gero and Conkey 1993a and b; Gathercole and Lowenthal 1994; LaRoche and Blakey 1996; Schmidt and Patterson 1995; Perry 1996, 1997, in press; Perry and Paynter in press). All scholars produce knowledge in specific sociocultural and historical contexts. In this essay, the ABG will be situated within the continuity of the African struggle that envisions a shared past, empowering African descendants to challenge injustice and to demand justice, dignity and power. The deeply sacred and symbolic role played by the ABG in both past and present has spawned descendant community outrage and unmasked institutionalized racism as excavations commenced with callous indifference to the wishes of the African community, both living and dead (Blakey 1996).

Here I will describe the racial tensions emanating from the African Burial Ground from its 18th century inception to the present, paying close attention to the conflicting relations among the General Services Administration (GSA), archaeological consultants and the ethical client, the African descendant community. Chronicling these events and documenting these relations is significant for evaluating claims to knowledge in order to reveal the conditions under which that knowledge is produced (Schmidt and Patterson 1995). The struggle around the ABG requires coequal relationships and symmetrical exchanges of ideas and actions between the scientific community and the African descendant community. Only in this way can authority be established over the ABG to create knowledge in the service of the community. The goal of this essay is to show how public and scholarly engagement, part of a legacy of African descendant activist scholarship, has become a source of important insights into understanding and representing the past and in contributing to the African descendant community's understanding of itself.

THE AFRICAN BURIAL GROUND: LEGACY OF STRUGGLE

Early Resistance

The first African captives arrived in Dutch New Amsterdam in 1626 from West and Central Africa and later from Caribbean plantations. Due to constant conflicts with Native Americans, the Dutch created a buffer zone for themselves by granting Africans "half-freedoms" and small parcels of farmland outside the city walls about 1643. Since the ABG is located in this area, Africans may have begun burying their dead there soon thereafter, although as yet there is no conclusive documentary evidence of this. The marginal spatial location and the respective marginal social positions of Natives and Africans meant that their settlements were likely locales for intercultural social and economic relations (Foote et al. 1993; Taylor 1992).

When the British colonized New Amsterdam in 1664, the 700-plus Africans constituted 40 percent of the population. This percentage was greater than in any other English settlement except Charleston, South Carolina, and more than was found in any northern settlement. The British revoked African half-freedoms, instituted harsher laws, confiscated African lands and imported more Africans for sale to the south. There were a number of insurrections by Africans in this area during the 18th century, and the highest proportion of escapees with a greater likelihood of success than elsewhere on the continent (White 1988). Indeed, individuals allegedly involved in these revolts were executed at the ABG (Barto 1991; Will 1991). New York gradually emancipated Africans from 1799 to 1827, but census and court records indicate that slavery continued at least until the 1860s (Jaffe 1995).

The ABG is the oldest (late 1600s to 1796) and largest (five to six acres) African descendant cemetery excavated in North America to date. Situated near the banks of the Collect Pond, the ABG not only provided privacy but its location near water was in keeping with the common central African practice of associating cemeteries and bodies of water (Foote et al. 1993; Thompson 1984). After 1750, several noxious chemical industries desecrated the ABG by disposing of their wastes there; medical students at New York Hospital also stole corpses for dissection. During the ABG occupation, Africans seem to have controlled their own funerals, mortuary and burial practices, but not without resistance (Blakey 1997; Foote et al. 1993; Harrington 1993; Jamieson 1995). Furthermore, only during funerals were Africans permitted outside after sunset and to gather in unsupervised groups larger than three persons. In 1731 the British sought to curb African subversive activity by passing laws requiring daytime burials with limited attendance. Pawls (the cloth used to cover a casket during the funeral and procession to the grave site) and pall bearers were also banned at African funerals (Epperson 1997). These laws suggest that the British suspected that African funerals were used to mask insurgent activity.

Recent Struggles

Today the ABG is located under some of the most valuable real estate in the world. It is estimated that from 10,000 to 20,000 first-generation African Americans were buried in the ABG. Since only 14,000 square feet were excavated, most of those interred remain beneath the city.

In 1989 the GSA sought to purchase a block of land from New York City. The plan was to erect a $276-million federal office building in lower Manhattan. Documentary research conducted for the GSA by the Advisory Council on Historic Preservation (ACHP) and NYC Landmarks Preservation Commission (LPC) indicated the presence of a "Negroes Burying Ground" on the proposed building site. In 1991 GSA, as mandated by the National Historic Preservation Act of 1966, contracted Historic Conservation and Interpretation (HCI), an archaeology consultant firm, to begin fieldwork. The study of the human remains was contracted to the Metropolitan Forensic Team (MFAT) from Lehman College. As more human remains were uncovered, GSA pressured HCI and MFAT to comply with the original one-year construction schedule (Epperson 1997; Harrington 1993, 1996). Meanwhile, the descendant community held meetings, religious observances, vigils and protests at the ABG (Blakey 1997). Since the excavations began without any significant community consultation or participation as to the treatment of the cemetery—as required by the mandate of scientific requirements for the preservation of the site's history—there was immediate and often volatile reaction to the excavations by the African descendant community (see the Kutz video series for an account of these events).

In 1991 burials were disturbed by construction workers, further alarming the African descendant community. Community persons who were monitoring the excavations and had seen the remains at Lehman College complained about the way the skeletons were being conserved. Problems included remains wrapped in newspaper under improper environmental conditions and inadequately stored on top of each other (La Roche and Blakey 1996). The descendant community condemned this behavior as disrespectful, arrogant and insensitive. Their encounter with contract archaeology made it clear that the few African American archaeologists who exist were never consulted or involved in the ABG research in any substantive way. It also became clear that consulting firms reap huge profits from studying African Americans and strongly influence how African Americans are historically defined. These were major issues of concern and contention for the African descendant community (La Roche and Blakey 1996).

Since MFAT and HCI failed to produce a timely and comprehensive research design, and had treated the remains unscientifically and disrespectfully, the descendant community demanded that the remains be placed under the care of Michael Blakey, one of the few African American biological anthropologists in the United States. Blakey, who is a professor of anthropology at Howard University in Washington, DC, was concerned that HCI and MFAT had no experience in African or African American history, cultures or skeletal biology. He was also aware that when archaeologists used construction equipment to remove the earth down to the burial outline, they had already destroyed artifacts that Africans customarily placed atop their graves and coffins (Satchel 1997).

The descendant community, cognizant of the ignorant portrayals of African diasporic history, recognized that archaeological interpretation is an active and subjective struggle between contending versions of history that demands political engagement (Gathercole and Lowenthal 1994; Schmidt and Patterson 1995). To insure that the spiritual, cultural and inspirational significance of the site and its contents were subject to African-centered paradigms and scholarship, they demanded incorporation of African descendant voices and histories (La Roche and Blakey 1996). They insisted that those working on the project have a knowledge of and respect for African diasporic studies and a commitment to their struggle to reclaim their past. For the descendant community, the skeletal remains and the ancestral possessions are the only concrete material evidence of the lives of this first generation of African Americans in New York City. As such, they constitute powerful links to a shared African past.

In 1992 David Dinkins, New York City's first African American mayor, and U.S. Rep. Gus Savage of Illinois, who chaired the House Committee for Building

QUANTITATIVE STUDIES: TWO EXAMPLES

Two skeletal indicators, one involving teeth and the other involving bone, serve to demonstrate the kinds of basic statistics currently being derived. Each involves samples of the African Burial Ground population. This information is not as certain to reflect trends that we will be shown from a study of the entire population of skeletons. It should nonetheless, provide a reasonable approximation of what we can expect to find at the end of our study.

The first indicator of interest is dental **enamel hypoplasia,** a developmental defect of dental enamel that results from childhood malnutrition and disease. Our laboratory at Howard has been conducting research on these defects in enslaved and free black populations since 1985. As a result, we can compare the New York population to those who were enslaved in Virginia and Maryland in the 18th and 19th centuries, as well as to a mixed group of free and enslaved African Americans who died in Philadelphia during the first half of the 19th century. Another 19th century South Carolina plantation studied by Dr. Ted Rathbun will also be used for comparisons. Those interested in a full description of those earlier studies, should consult our article available in any university library.

As we all know from experience, "baby teeth" (primary or deciduous dentition) first grow below the gums and then erupt and appear over time to produce a full set of small, children's teeth. Hypoplasia in these teeth occur before they appear in the mouth, and represent nutritional and disease problems that interrupted dental growth during the first year of the child's life.

. . . [A] little over 60% of the New York African Burial Ground and Philadelphia children had health problems that would cause dental hypoplasia during their infancies. These are among the highest frequencies shown for baby teeth in any human population. (Data from baby teeth are not yet available from the southern plantation studies.) The fact that the health of these children had been stressed as early as infancy probably has some relationship to the fact that they died in childhood.

Now, let us turn to the information derived for adult men and women. Let's begin with what we all know to be true, and that is that adult teeth (called secondary or permanent teeth) begin to erupt and replace the baby teeth as a person matures. These adult skeletons were persons who had lived long enough to have a full set of adult teeth by the time of death. Although they were all more than 17 years of age when they died, their dental enamel had developed under the gums during childhood. So, the developmental defects in their tooth enamel had occurred during their childhoods, providing a record of health problems during the first years of life.

Alright, this gets to be a little complicated (even for professional researchers). Just bear in mind that all defect frequencies represent nutritional and disease problems of childhood. Of those in the African burial Ground sample who survived into adulthood, about 50% had had at least one bout of health problems during their childhoods that resulted in enamel hypoplasia in their adult teeth. Compared with the other populations, those who died as adults in New York experienced childhoods that were about ½ as stressful (½ the frequency) of dental defects as in South Carolina, Virginia, Maryland, and Philadelphia.

Funds, were able to establish an advisory committee on the project, halt the excavation and close down the site. At the request of the African descendant community, New York State Senator David Patterson, who is also African American, formed an oversight task force for organizing various forms of political activity around the ABG (Howson 1992). The descendant community continued to press for the involvement of African American scholars in directing the research, analysis and interpretation.

In 1993 Howard University gained control over the research project and, along with John Milner Associates (JMA), another contract archaeology firm, submitted a more comprehensive research design to ACHP that incorporated the concerns and desires of the descendant community. The archaeological materials were placed in the Foley Square Lab under JMA, while the 400-plus human remains were transferred to the Cobb Biological Anthropology Laboratory at Howard University. Pageantry and celebration accompanied the caravan of remains from New York to Washington, DC, with stops at historically significant African American churches in several cities along the way. The transfer culminated in a ceremony entitled "The Ties that Bind" at Howard University. The descendant community and its allies were in evidence throughout the transfer celebration. Representatives from the African American community, the U.S. Muslim community, the Native American community, and from the Akan in Ghana were all in attendance at Howard. In 1994 African chiefs from Ghana returned to Howard on a tour of *fihankra,* a movement of unity that involves prayers and rituals for forgiveness to the ancestors to atone for colonial-era involvement in the trade of African captives.

Although I have spoken of the descendant community throughout, there is, of course, no homogeneous African descendant community; this entity is actually multi-dimensional and ideologically heterogeneous. Throughout the struggle around the ABG, how-

Do we conclude that life was better for Africans in colonial New York than at other sites? If the evidence from baby teeth also showed low frequencies of defects, we might reach just that conclusion. Those dying as children in New York City, however, seem to be just as stressed as the children in Philadelphia. Those dying as adults in Philadelphia have the very high frequencies of prior childhood stress shown for southern plantations. Our other data on childhood diseases and high death rates in New York also point to very poor health during the early years of life.

The dental record of relatively good health during the early lives of those who died as adults in New York, is inconsistent with the other findings. They are the "odd man out" in this analysis. It is as though those who died in New York City often had childhoods in some other healthier society and economic environment than their dead children.

Our best guess at this point in the study, is that those who died as adults are showing evidence of the lower stresses of life they experienced as children in various African societies where they had previously lived. Those who died while children in New York show evidence of poor health in New York. Evidence of poor health that is comparable to Philadelphia and, by extension, similar to the plantation south. Our historians already tell us that many of those buried in the African Burial Ground should have been children in Africa. The biological data should make us even more curious about what those African societies were like.

A second example of the physical quality of life contributes to the view of colonial New York as harsh for its African population. As earlier *Update* reports by Mark Mack and Cassandra Hill have shown, we are gathering very interesting information about the skeletal stresses of rigorous work and heavy load bearing and lifting in those who died as adults. Most muscles are attached to bony ridges. As strain on muscles persists for long periods of time, those bony attachments become enlarged in order to better adapt to the strain. When that strain is too great for the bony attachments to handle, the muscles will tear away along with plugs of bone, leaving large, often elongated bone lesions called "enthesopathies."

The evidence for these lesions on African Burial Ground sample is dramatic. About 75% of men and 65% of women had at least one enthesopathic lesion in the shoulders, arms, or legs. This is clear evidence of extreme work and load-bearing in *most* adults, which pressed them to the very limits of human work capacity. Although it is clearly true that their work experiences were very harsh, few studies record enthesopathies routinely. It might become necessary for us to examine other, comparative populations (such as the colonial English in New York City or contemporary Ashanti in Ghana) before we can get a handle on the relative severity of those harsh experiences. The historians will add much to our analysis by telling us the range of the types of work in which the Africans of colonial New York were involved. We are carrying on at The Cobb Laboratory with these and many other explorations. The examples given are meant to provide a sense of what the increasingly analytical phases of our work entail. I welcome everyone to think about these ideas and to write us in order to contribute their own possible explanations for what we are finding.

---

ever, all segments of the African descendant community and their allies were and continue to be involved. There continues to be a consensus that the site, the human remains, the artifacts and their interpretation must be controlled by the descendant community.

THE CURRENT RESEARCH PROJECT

The current scientific project constitutes yet another dimension of the struggle for control of the ABG. We seek to illuminate the impact of African captivity upon the lives of our ancestors and their living descendants, and to reconstruct knowledge of their origins and identities that were deliberately distorted in the effort to bolster the identity of Euroamericans at the expense of African Americans (Blakey 1997). As Scientific Director of the African Burial Ground Project, Michael Blakey has brought together a national and international research team of scholars from Africa and the U.S. who are concerned with creating alternative histories. The ABG Project has evolved into a multi-disciplinary scientific effort comprised of complementary natural and social science teams with expertise in the African diaspora. These include: molecular genetics, bone chemistry, skeletal biology, history and archaeology (African and African American), ethnology, conservation and African art history. This collaborative effort has global and universal implications, transcending any particular discipline or the interests of any one segment of the descendant community.

These organizational changes have resulted in the selection of four basic research questions to guide our scientific analyses. They are relevant both for activist scholars and the descendant community:

1. What are the cultural and geographical roots of the individuals interred in the African Burial Ground?

2. What was the physical quality of life for Africans enslaved in New York City during the colonial

period and how was it different from the quality of life in their African homeland?

3. What biological characteristics and cultural traditions remained unchanged and which were transformed during the creation of African American society and culture?

4. What were the modes of resistance and how were they creatively reconfigured and used to resist oppression and to forge a new African American culture?

In addition to the scientific teams, the ABG has an Office of Public Education and Interpretation of the African Burial Ground Project (OPEI), directed by Dr. Sherrill Wilson. OPEI's primary roles are to educate and inform the public of ABG project events, to assure public access to the site, the skeletal and artifactual remains, and to allow appropriate cultural ceremonies to commemorate the ancestors. It also provides community involvement/education activities such as educators' symposia, laboratory tours and two newsletters that update the public on the research and introduce archaeology, anthropology and conservation to children and adults.

CONCLUSION

New York City's ABG project is a case of archaeology as community service. It emerged from a protracted struggle over control of the ABG and its products between an organized descendant community and its allies, and the GSA and archaeology consulting firms. This struggle has resulted in an increased awareness of the disciplines of anthropology and archaeology within the African descendant community. It has produced a public education program that facilitates a reciprocal dialogue between researchers and the general public, maximizing the interpretative potential of the archaeological record and creating an historical consciousness that challenges the distortions of Eurocentric history (Singleton 1995). Through this struggle the descendant community and its allies have successfully achieved the incorporation of African American scholars in the creation and maintenance of research design and agenda that establish a prominent role for historically underrepresented African Americans in the analysis and interpretation of an internationally renowned archaeological site (Mathis 1997). By taking moral responsibility for the spiritual and physical control of the site, the descendant community seized intellectual power — forcing changes in the composition and direction of the professional leadership of the project (La Roche and Blakey 1996). The original ancestral ABG community

and the modern descendant community have used this sacred social space to resist and to honor their African heritage in spite of institutionalized racist disrespect. The struggle for the proper treatment of the ABG reaffirms its significance in the past and gives the site continued significance in the present; it is an important part in the legacy of struggle to control and interpret the African past (Blakey 1996).

REFERENCES

Barto, S. 1991. Chain of Title Block 154 (Principally) Northern Half. Unpublished Historical Research Reports for the African Burial Ground Project. Historic Conservation and Interpretation (HCI). On file with the African Burial Ground Project.

Blakey, M. L. 1997. The New York African Burial Ground Project: an examination of enslaved lives, a construction of ancestral ties. Briefing prepared for the Subcommission on Prevention of Discrimination and Protection of Minorities Commission on Human Rights, United Nations. Delivered at the Palais des Nations, Geneva, Switzerland, 19 August.

——. 1996. Howard University research reaches a new plateau. *Newsletter of the African Burial Ground and Five Points Archaeological Project.* 1 (10):3–7.

——. 1991. Man and nature, white and other. In Harrison, F., ed. *Decolonizing Anthropology.* pp. 15–23. Washington, DC: American Anthropological Association.

——. 1983. Socio-political bias and ideological production in historical archaeology. In Gero, J. M., D. M. Lacey and M. Blakey, eds. *The Socio-Politics of Archaeology.* Research Report #23, Department of Anthropology, U Mass, Amherst.

Epperson, T. W. 1997. The politics of "race" and cultural identity at the African Burial Ground excavations, New York City. *World Archaeological Bulletin.* 7:108–117.

Foote, T. W., M. Carey, J. Giesenberg-Haag, J. Grey, K. McKoy, and C. Todd. 1993. Report on Site-Specific History of Block 154. Written for the African Burial Ground Research Project. New York.

Gathercole, P. and D. Lowenthal, eds. 1994. *The Politics of the Past.* New York: Routledge.

Gero, J. and M. W. Conkey. 1993a. *Engendering Archaeology: Women and Prehistory.* Basil Blackwell.

——. 1993b. Tensions, pluralities and engendering archaeology. In Gero, J. and M. W. Conkey, eds. *Engendering Archaeology: Women and Prehistory.* pp. 3–31. Basil Blackwell.

Harrington, Spencer. 1993. New York's great cemetery imbroglio. *Archaeology.* March/April. pp. 30–38.

——. 1996. An African cemetery in Manhattan. In Fagan, B., ed. *Eyewitness to Discovery.* pp. 324–333. London: Oxford U Press.

Howson, J. E. 1992. The Foley Square Project: an 18th century cemetery in New York City. *African American Archaeology.* Newsletter No. 6, Spring. pp. 3–4.

Jaffe, S. H. 1995. "This Infernal Traffic": New York Port and the illegal slave trade. *Seaport: New York's History Magazine.* 29 (3):36–37.

Jamieson, R. W. 1995. Material culture and social death: African-American burial practices. *Historical Archaeology.* 29 (4):39–58.

Kutz Television, Inc. 1994. *The African Burial Ground: An American Discovery.* Parts I–IV. The National Technical Information Services. National Audio Visual Center, VA.

Langford, R. 1983. Our heritage—your playground. *Australian Archaeology.* 16, 1–6.

La Roche, C. J. and M. L. Blakey. 1996. Seizing Intellectual Power: the Dialogue at the New York African Burial Ground. Paper, pp. 1–48.

Mathis, R. 1997. The Harris Matrix as a useful method in the stratigraphic analysis of the African Burial Ground. Unpublished Draft Statement of Field, for the Department of Anthropology, U Mass, Amherst.

Patterson, T. C. 1993. *Archaeology: The Historical Development of Civilizations.* Prentice-Hall.

Perry, W. In Press. Dimensions of power in Swaziland research: coercion, reflexivity and resistance. In *Transforming Anthropology.* A Publication of the Association of Black Anthropologists, Arlington, VA.

——. 1997. Analysis of the African Burial Ground Archaeological Materials. *Update: Newsletter of the African Burial Ground and Five Points Archaeological Projects,* Vol. 2 #2:1–5 & 14.

——. 1996. The African Burial Ground Project. *African Update: African Studies Newsletter* Vol. IV, #4:1–5, CCSU, New Britain, CT.

Perry, W. and R. Paynter. In press. Epilogue: Artifacts, Ethnicity and the Archaeology of African Americans. In Singleton, T., ed. *We Too Are America: Essays in African American Archaeology.* Charlottesville, VA. University Press of Virginia.

Satchel, M. 1997. Only remember us: skeletons of slaves from a New York grave bear witness. *U.S. News and World Report.* July 28:51 and 54.

Schmidt, P. R. and T. C. Patterson. 1995. *Making Alternative Histories. The Practice of Archaeology and History in Non-Western Settings.* Santa Fe, NM: School of American Research Press.

Singleton, T. A. 1995. The Archaeology of Slavery in North America. In *Annual Review of Anthropology,* Vol. 24, pp. 119–140.

Taylor, R. 1992. Land of the blacks. *New York Newsday.* Thursday, February 6. p. 60.

Thompson, R. F. 1984. *Flash of the Spirit: African and Afro-American Art and Philosophy.* New York, Vintage.

White, S. 1988. We dwell in safety and pursue our honest callings: free blacks in New York City, 1783–1810. *The Journal of American History.* 75 (2):445–470.

Will, G. 1991. Salvage archaeology in Manhattan offers a perspective about America. *Hartford Courant.*

Wilson, S. 1996. *Citations on the New York African Burial Ground 1991–1996.* (3rd Ed.) Compiled by the Office of Public Education and Interpretation of the African Burial Ground. New York City.

10

Mighty Cahokia

William R. Iseminger

William Iseminger is an archaeologist and an accomplished artist. He also is curator at the Cahokia Mounds State Monument. The walls of the state-of-the-art museum at the site are graced by his wonderful mural reflecting his conception of Cahokia at its peak.

Points to consider when reading this article:

1. How does the archaeological record of Cahokia contradict commonly held stereotypes of Native Americans?

2. What evidence indicates that they may have possessed a socially stratified society?

3. Was Cahokia a true city?

4. What evidence does the author of this article cite to support his contention that Cahokia was the effective capital of a geographically broad ancient society?

The native people of North America are burdened by stereotypes, some clearly libelous whereas others are apparently positive. For some, Indians were blood-thirsty savages, primitive people who could only benefit from contact with the more "civilized" European colonizers of the New World. For others, especially more recently, Indians have been generalized as noble primitives, peaceful and egalitarian folks, natural ecologists in harmony with their environment.

Stereotypes—positive as well as negative—ignore the great complexity of human societies. The ancient culture of Cahokia provides an excellent case in point. Cahokia was an urban-like settlement of Native Americans at its peak 900 years ago—some 400 years before the arrival of Columbus. The enormity of the earthen mounds constructed by the inhabitants of Cahokia, the sophistication of the art and craftwork produced by its artisans, and the monumental log wall enclosing the sacred precinct of the community belie any notion of "primitive savages." At the same time, the burial of the young man in Mound 72, with its rich array of grave goods along with the dozens of human beings sacrificed, perhaps to accompany a prince of Cahokia to the afterlife, negate any stereotype of egalitarian perfection.

The people of Cahokia and their descendants deserve far more than tired stereotypes. They deserve the genuine history made possible by archaeology.

It is the time of the annual harvest festival celebrating the fall equinox. Traders from distant territories have brought precious offerings for the lords of Cahokia. Ramadas have been erected everywhere to shelter the merchants and their goods: beads and other ornaments shaped from native copper; drinking vessels and gorgets cut from large whelk and conch shells, many engraved with symbolic designs; baskets of tiny marginella shells; bangles cut from sheets of mica; quivers of arrows tipped with gemlike points; galena, hematite, and ocher from which to make pigments for pottery, clothing, and body paint; and salt from springs and seeps to the south. In exchange the Cahokians offer their own goods: feathered capes; freshwater pearls; finely woven fabrics; fur garments made from otter, mink, and beaver; chert hoes and axes; and corn, dried squash, pumpkin, and seeds from many other plants. These will be taken back to distant places, some in polished black ceramic vessels bearing incised designs of interlocking scrolls, forked eyes, and nested chevrons, symbols of power and prestige because of their place of origin—mighty Cahokia.

This fanciful yet fairly accurate description of Cahokia's harvest celebration is drawn from archaeological studies and early historical accounts of remnant Mississippian cultures in the Southeast. Eight miles

FIGURE 1 Monks Mound is one of the largest pyramid structures ever built by an ancient society. An enormous and coordinated labor force was necessary to produce this 100-foot-tall artificial mountain, covering sixteen acres at its base and containing 20 million cubic feet of earth (a standard, 2,000-square-foot house has a volume of less than 20,000 cubic feet). (Courtesy Cahokia Mounds State Historic Site)

east of St. Louis, Cahokia was in its day the largest and most influential settlement north of Mexico. Its merchants traded with cultures from the Gulf Coast to the Great Lakes, from the Atlantic coast to Oklahoma, and they helped spread Mississippian culture across much of that vast area. Some 120 earthen mounds supporting civic buildings and the residences of Cahokia's elite were spread over more than five square miles—perhaps six times as many earthen platforms as the great Mississippian site of Moundville, south of Tuscaloosa, Alabama. At its core, within a log stockade 10 to 12 feet tall, was the 200-acre Sacred Precinct where the ruling elite lived and were buried. Atop a massive earthen mound stood a pole-framed temple more than 100 feet long, its grass roof possibly decorated with carved wooden animal figures festooned with glimmering beads, feathers, and cloth. Here Cahokia's rulers performed the political and religious rituals that united the realm. Estimates of the city's population at its zenith, ca. A.D. 1050–1150, range from 8,000 to more than 40,000, though most fall between 10,000 and 20,000. Around A.D. 1200, perhaps having exhausted its natural resources, Cahokia went into a decline that left it virtually empty by 1400.

In 1810 the lawyer and journalist Henry Marie Brackenridge, while surveying the Mississippi and Missouri valleys, visited the site and marveled at the "stupendous pile of earth" at its center. At the time a colony of Trappist monks was growing wheat and fruit trees on the earthen structure, soon to be known as Monks Mound. Their plans to build a monastery atop it were

abandoned when fever and a shortage of money forced them to leave the site in 1813. The first archaeological excavations at Cahokia took place in the 1920s under the direction of Warren K. Moorehead of the R. S. Peabody Museum in Andover, Massachusetts. Moorehead's work confirmed that the mounds were neither natural hills nor the work of a mysterious race of Mound Builders or Precolumbian colonists from Europe—as imagined by nineteenth-century amateur historians—but had been built by American Indians. In the 1940s and 1950s archaeologists from the University of Michigan, the Illinois State Museum, the Gilcrease Institute of Tulsa, and elsewhere conducted scattered excavations at the site, but the most intensive work began in the early 1960s when Interstate 55–70 was routed through it. Over the years many of Cahokia's mounds have been lost to the bulldozer and the plow, to subdivisions, highways, and discount stores. Today fewer than 80 remain, 68 of which are preserved within the 2,200-acre Cahokia Mounds State Historic Site, managed by the Illinois Historic Preservation Agency.

Cahokia owed its existence to a floodplain 80 miles long at the confluence of the Mississippi and Missouri rivers. Known as the American Bottom, the plain was interlaced with creeks, sloughs, lakes, and marshes. With fertile soil, extensive forests, and plentiful fish and game, the region was an ideal place to settle. During the Palaeoindian (ca. 9500–8000 B.C.) and Archaic (ca. 8000–600 B.C.) periods transient hunter-gatherers set up temporary camps or seasonal villages here.

FIGURE 2   An artist's conception of the urban-like Cahokia at its peak more than 800 years ago. Monks Mound dominates the plaza, which appears to have been the central location of ancient Cahokia. Cahokia and the many other mound sites belie the commonly held stereotype of Native American culture. (William Iseminger; courtesy Cahokia Mounds State Historic Site)

During the Woodland period (ca. 600 B.C.–A.D. 800) the population grew, cultivation of native crops began, and larger and more settled communities, including Cahokia, were established. Settlements spread slowly and grew in size throughout the Emergent Mississippian period (ca. A.D. 800–1000), then expanded rapidly in the Mississippian (ca. A.D. 1000–1400) as more intense farming, especially of corn, made fast population growth possible. Cahokia reached its apex during this period, when it was surrounded by dozens of satellite settlements and scores of smaller villages.

In time, Cahokia's influence spread far beyond the American Bottom. Artifacts made there, including Ramey Incised pottery and hoes of Mill Creek chert from southern Illinois, have been found at sites as far north as Minnesota, as far west as eastern Kansas and Oklahoma, and as far south as the lower Ohio River Valley, Arkansas, and Mississippi. Local imitations of Cahokia's wares, especially pottery, have also been unearthed in these regions. At Cahokia itself we have found copper from the area of Lake Superior; mica from the southern Appalachian Mountains; shells from the Atlantic and Gulf coasts; and galena, ocher, hematite, chert, fluorite, and quartz from throughout the Midwest. Finely made ceramics from the lower Mississippi Valley, perhaps used to carry exotic commodities such as shells from that area, have also been discovered at Cahokia, along with local copies of many of these forms.

The most visible remains of the ancient city are its mounds. Most are rectangular with flat tops (platform mounds) that supported civic buildings and the homes of the elite. Somewhat rarer are conical mounds that may have contained elite burials, as they did in the earlier Woodland period. During the 1920s Moorehead excavated several such burials, but it is often difficult to tell from his records whether they were found in the mounds themselves or in earlier layers. Rarest of all are rectangular ridgetop mounds that may have marked important locations such as community boundaries or mortuary complexes. The destruction of one such mound by farmers in 1931 revealed mass burials laid upon platforms of shell beads and cedar bark.

Monks Mound stands at the center of the site, on the northern edge of the 40-acre Grand Plaza. Covering 14 acres at the base and rising in four terraces to a height of 100 feet, it is the largest prehistoric earthen structure in the New World. Some 19 million man-hours of labor would have been required to excavate, carry, and deposit the estimated 22 million cubic feet of earth needed for this project. Excavations and soil cores indicate that it was built in stages between ca. A.D. 900 and 1200, each possibly related to the accession of a new leader. Probes on the summit have revealed wall trenches for a wooden building 104 feet long and 48 feet wide. Here the leader of Cahokia governed his domain, performed ceremonies, consulted with the spirit world, and may have resided as well. The bones of deceased chiefs may also have been stored here, as was the custom among some historical tribes in the Southeast.

One of the most fascinating discoveries at Cahokia came during the 1967–1971 excavation of Mound 72, a ridgetop one-half mile south of Monks Mound. Measuring 140 feet long, 70 feet wide, and barely six feet high, Mound 72 is oriented along a northwest-southeast axis, one end pointing toward the winter solstice sunrise and the other toward the summer solstice sunset. Excavations revealed that it had originally been three separate, smaller mounds, two platforms and one conical. Around and beneath these three mounds were some 280 burials dating to Cahokia's initial development between ca. A.D. 1000 and 1050. Some of the dead had been borne to their graves on litters or wrapped in mats or blankets, while others had simply been tossed into pits, suggesting that people of different statuses were buried at the same place. Soon after the burials the three mounds were fused into a single ridgetop mound with a final mantle of earth.

In one opulent burial a man about 40 years old, perhaps one of Cahokia's early leaders, was laid upon a bird-shaped platform of nearly 20,000 marine-shell beads. Around him were several other bodies, perhaps of retainers or relatives, some interred for the first time and others reburied from elsewhere. Heaped atop six nearby burials were two caches of more than 800 newly made arrowheads, whose Midwestern cherts and hafting styles suggest possible origins in Wisconsin, Illinois, Missouri, Tennessee, Arkansas, and Oklahoma. One cache included 15 large concave ground-stone discs, sometimes known as "chunkey" stones, after a game played with similar stones by historical tribes in the Southeast. Also found were a large pile of unprocessed mica from the southern Appalachian Mountains, a three-foot-long roll of copper (possibly a ceremonial staff) hammered from Lake Superior nuggets, and more marine-shell beads.

Further excavations under Mound 72 revealed several mass burials, most of females between 15 and 25 years old, suggesting human sacrifice. The largest pit held more than 50 women laid out in two rows and stacked two and three deep; two others contained 22 and 24 women. A fourth pit, with 19 women, had been partially redug, and more than 36,000 marine-shell beads, another cache of unused arrowheads (more than 400 of chert and a few hundred more of bone and antler), and several broken ceramic vessels had been deposited there. Another burial, of four males whose heads and hands had been removed, may represent the ritual sacrifice of vassals or retainers, perhaps to accompany their leader in death. How and why these people were sacrificed remain mysteries, but there may be parallels with rituals performed by the Natchez Indians of seventeenth- and eighteenth-century Mississippi, where individuals often volunteered to be sacrificed upon a leader's death to raise their own or their family's status.

In the early 1960s archaeologists working in the remains of a residential area outside the stockade, to the west of Monks Mound, discovered a number of postholes at regular intervals along the circumferences of at least five circles of different diameters. Four of these constructions are thought to have been complete circles, with 24, 36, 48, and 60 posts, respectively. The fifth seems only to have had 12 posts standing along a portion of the circle; if complete it would have had 72. Why all five circles were formed of multiples of twelve posts is unknown, though some scholars have speculated that the number may have been related to lunar cycles. Because of their resemblance to the famous English megalithic monument of Stonehenge, Cahokia's circles of standing wooden posts became known as "woodhenges." One, with a large center post and 48 evenly spaced perimeter posts, was 410 feet in diameter and dates to just after A.D. 1100. It is the most completely excavated of the woodhenges and has been reconstructed in its original location. From a platform atop the central post a priest might have observed sunrises along the eastern horizon aligning with particular perimeter posts at the equinoxes and solstices. On the equinoxes the sun would have risen over the front of Monks Mound, perhaps symbolizing the bond between earthly ruler and solar deity. Other posts may have marked other important dates, such as harvest festivals or moon and star alignments.

Most of the work at Cahokia has dealt with the everyday life of its people, many of whom lived outside the stockade in small, rectangular one-family pole-and-thatch dwellings with walls covered with mats or sometimes daub. Compounds of these dwellings grouped around small courtyards may have housed kinfolk. Each compound also included buildings used for storage, food processing, and cooking. Excavation of refuse pits around the houses has revealed that the Cahokians ate mainly cultivated corn, squash, and pumpkin, as well as the seeds of cultivated sunflower, lambs' quarters, marsh elder, little barley, and may grass. This diet was supplemented by hundreds of different wild plants and mammals, birds, fish, reptiles, and amphibians.

Household groups were in turn arranged around larger communal plazas that may have defined neighborhoods. Other structures found in each neighborhood included small circular sweat lodges, where water sprinkled upon heated rocks produced steam for ritual cleansing of the body and spirit; community meeting lodges, granaries, and storage buildings; and possibly huts to which women would have been restricted during menstruation.

Ceremonial structures, special-use buildings, and the dwellings of the elite were generally larger versions of the basic house. Many of the elite must have lived within the stockade, but so far none of their residences has been excavated. Elite areas outside the wall include a plaza mound group to the west; another group to the east; Rattlesnake Mound (named for the snakes in the area) to the south; and the North Plaza and Kunnemann (named after a family that once owned the land) groups to the north. We do not know whether the elite living outside the stockade differed from those living inside, although relationship to the leader by lineage or clan affiliation may have been a factor.

Evidence for warfare at Cahokia remains largely circumstantial. A stockade was erected around the Sacred Precinct ca. A.D. 1150 and rebuilt at least three times during the next hundred years. The defensive nature of the wall is suggested by the regular spacing of bastions at 85-foot intervals along its length. From elevated platforms in these projections, warriors could launch arrows at attackers and protect the narrow L-shaped entryways between some bastions. The everyday function of the wall may have been more social, to isolate and protect the Sacred Precinct. Free access may have been limited to the elites who lived there, probably members of the ruling lineage, with the general population admitted only for ceremonial occasions or markets, or in times of war.

The stockade was a monumental construction, built at a great cost of time, labor, and materials. Much of my own fieldwork at Cahokia has involved excavations along the lines of the stockade east of Monks Mound. Based on that work I have estimated that builders would have used nearly 20,000 logs each time the wall was built, and conservatively 130,000 man-hours to fell, trim, debark, transport, and place the posts in excavated trenches. Construction of the stockade, itself designed to protect the city center, may have contributed to Cahokia's decline beginning ca. A.D. 1200. The demands for wood would have been staggering, even for such a renewable resource. Wood was also needed for fires and construction, and people from nearby communities would have been competing for the same resources. The forests around Cahokia, and the animals and plants living there, would have been affected. Soil eroding from deforested slopes may have clogged streams and lakes with silt, increasing localized flooding of valuable farmland.

Beginning in the thirteenth century, a cooling of the climate and concomitant floods, droughts, and early and late frosts may have led to more crop failures and reduced yields. As food and other natural resources became scarce, economic disruption and social unrest could have become problems, perhaps even leading to wars between Cahokia and its neighbors. Eventually its political and economic power base eroded as nearby groups became more autonomous. Although increases in contagious diseases and nutritional deficiencies caused by a heavily corn-based diet may have affected Cahokia's population, more data are needed to determine the role of such health problems in Cahokia's decline.

Where the people of Cahokia went is one of the site's many mysteries. There is no evidence that the city was destroyed in a single catastrophe. It appears that its people slowly dispersed, breaking up into smaller groups, some establishing new communities and perhaps new ways of life elsewhere. Many small Late Mississippian villages and hamlets have been found in the uplands surrounding the American Bottom and at higher elevations in the bottomlands themselves. Other people may have been absorbed into existing groups elsewhere, possibly where kinship ties already existed. In any event Cahokia was abandoned by 1400, and no positive ties have been established between the great city and any historical tribe.

Because of limited funding and the site's enormous size, only a small percentage of Cahokia has been excavated. Research continues through small field-school programs that include nondestructive remote-sensing projects using electromagnetic conductivity, electrical resistivity, and magnetometry, as well as soil coring. These efforts help locate man-made features underground, providing direction for future small-scale excavations. Detailed mapping projects, combined with soil-core studies, are helping identify the original forms of mounds that have suffered from heavy plowing or erosion. Unpublished data from earlier excavations are being analyzed or reexamined and the results published. In addition, salvage projects at contemporary sites in the American Bottom, such as East St. Louis, are providing insight into Cahokia's interactions with these outlying sites.

Though I have worked at Cahokia for 25 years, I still marvel at what I see. It is an awesome site, massive and mysterious, especially in the predawn hours as I drive past the dark shapes of mounds poking through ground-hugging mist on my way to greet modern-day solstice and equinox observers at the reconstructed woodhenge. Cahokia, the largest prehistoric community north of Mexico, was one of the crowning achievements of the American Indians. Here they established a complex social, political, religious, and economic system and influenced a large portion of the midcontinent. Today, as then, the climb to the top of Monks Mound is breathtaking, literally as well as figuratively, and looking out from the summit one can only imagine what this truly extraordinary place must have been like.

11

In Front of the Mirror: Native Americans and Academic Archaeology

Dorothy Lippert

Dorothy Lippert is a doctoral candidate in the Department of Anthropology at the University of Texas at Austin. She is an archaeologist with a particular interest in **bioarchaeology** *and the ethical issues surrounding the excavation analysis, and repatriation of Indian burials. Lippert is a member of the Choctaw Indian Tribe.*

Points to consider when reading this article:

1. Why do many Native Americans mistrust archaeologists?

2. How does Dorothy Lippert justify archaeology? Why does she think it can make an important contribution to Native Americans' understanding of their own past?

3. What does Lippert mean when she refers to a "voice made of bone"?

4. Do you think that non-Indian archaeologists have any right to excavate the Indian past?

The relationship between Native Americans and North American archaeologists has been rather tense in recent years. This is a sad irony. The vast majority of archaeologists in North America who focus on native sites are not, themselves, native people. However, they (me too) entered the field at least in part because of an abiding interest in and respect for the aboriginal cultures of the New World. However, as outsiders, too many of us (me too) have expended too little time trying to communicate the rationale or results of our work to the very people whose past we are studying.

For many Native Americans, archaeologists are intruders—just another group of outsiders who exploit Indians for their own purposes. The common and, unfortunately too often, reasonable view of many Indians is that archaeologists are scientists who study Indian ancestors but who have little interest in and no accountability to the descendants of the people who produced the cultures and sites upon which they focus.

Archaeology, nevertheless, can make an important and significant contribution to native communities, even if archaeologists have, with few exceptions, made little effort to help in this regard—at least until fairly recently. In fact, some Native Americans have recognized the potential of the archaeological study of their own people and have elected themselves to become archaeologists (or **cultural** or **biological anthropologists**). Dorothy Lippert relates the story of her journey to become an archaeologist of her own people.

The role of Native Americans within the world of academic archaeology is currently undergoing a great deal of change and revitalization. In part due to legally directed consultation, more and more Indians are becoming involved in archaeology. A growing number of us have chosen to pursue the discipline of archaeology as a career, and in this paper I would like to consider some of the many factors that affect us as we work at this vocation.

The pressures involved in becoming an archaeologist are somewhat different for a Native American than they are for nonnatives. In addition to expectations from within the profession, other, more personal stresses can be involved. Some of these are directly related to the history of archaeology in America, while others relate to current political activities. University education about the Native American past may also

From *Native Americans and Archaeologists: Stepping Stones to Common Ground*, 1996. Reprinted with permission. Published in cooperation with the Society for American Archaeology, Walnut Creek, CA: Altamira Press.

serve as a barrier to one's desire to study our history in an academic context, as a distressing personal example shows. A key to presenting archaeology as a profession open to Native American input is communication. This is a very simple thing to say, but it is more complex in its execution.

Finally, I would argue that archaeology as a discipline must realistically consider not only the roles of Native Americans within the discipline, but also Indian perspectives on the past. We can bring many views on the ancient people to our work, the most important being an impression of the ancients as ancestors. As Indian archaeologists we feel the heavy burden of telling their stories, not just for reasons of furthering academic knowledge, but also out of respect for our elders and those who were here before us.

HISTORY

The history of interaction between academic archaeologists and native peoples fuels much of the resentment many Indian people feel toward the discipline. Anthropologists from the early years of the discipline sought to study and record as much information as possible about various tribes out of a fear that cultural ways were fast disappearing (Trigger 1989). For many tribes this was indeed the case, and, in fact, there have been instances in which knowledge preserved by anthropologists has become an important source of information for continuing cultural practices (Hubert 1989b). However, in many more cases native peoples found anthropologists to be intrusive and annoying. Much of the information shared with ethnographers was published, and tribes came to resent the fact that local and sometimes sacred knowledge was taken and used improperly. Many Indians were made to feel like interesting specimens rather than people.

Archaeology might have seemed to escape this problem because of a focus on past or extinct cultural groups. However, this formulation of the discipline reflected a divergent concept of the ancient history of the North American continent from that implied by anthropology. Publications in both the popular and scholarly press reflected a bias against existing tribes, seeing Indian peoples as remnants of a once noble past. With the days of glory long gone, contemporary Indian life could hold no keys to understanding the mysteries of the past.

The seeds for the repatriation dispute were planted in this era. The idea had been formed that the ancient past could only be unlocked using scientific reasoning, which belonged to the archaeologists. Native perspectives on what became known as "prehistory" were defined as myth and folklore, neither of which was as powerful as science. Such an understanding of the past cut out the only peoples who are actually related to the ancient North Americans. The need to make this point clear factored into much of the determination Indian activists felt when trying to explain why it is necessary to see the modern tribes as historically, genetically, and emotionally linked to ancient peoples.

Again, with the collecting of skeletal material, Native Americans were made to feel like specimens. This imagery underlies much of the dialogue about repatriation today (Lippert 1992). In part because native peoples and native knowledge were not seen as vital to the discipline of archaeology, few Indians attempted to gain academic credentials and participate in the profession. In addition, other factors, notably economic and social, played into this situation. Then, as today, Native Americans fall below the poverty level in staggering numbers. For many Indians, higher education has never been a viable choice.

In the fall of 1990, Native Americans made up less than 1 percent of the total number of students enrolled in institutions of higher education (Reddy 1993)—a figure comparable to their representation within the general population. However, it is certain that a fraction of these students are not, in fact, related to the original inhabitants of this continent. At the University of Texas at Austin, ethnicity is self-determined, and judging from lists of Indian students obtained by the Native American Student Organization (NASO), it is apparent that the original ancestry of at least 5 percent of the individuals listed was in India!

Further up in the academic strata, the number of Native Americans becomes smaller. In 1988–1989, less than a quarter of 1 percent of students receiving doctorates were Native Americans (84 out of 35,692). This rate moves up to nearly a third of a percent when one considers the social sciences, but it is still somewhat less than admirable. In 1990, out of a total of 2,047 doctorates in the social sciences, American Indians received 6 (Reddy 1993).

ACADEMIA AND NATIVE AMERICANS

Many Native Americans who choose to study anthropology do so out of a desire to explore their ethnic background. It is not always easy to make or maintain this choice within the academic arena. At the University of Texas, I once enrolled in a course (not in the Anthropology Department) that promised to consider the ways in which the image of Indianness has been constructed using texts written by and about Native Americans. However, I found that the professor was so steeped in his own perspectives of the Indian as "Noble Savage" that he was somewhat less than knowledgeable or sympathetic to modern Indian concerns about identity.

Unable to escape the class after the drop deadline, I endured weeks of irritation. He compared the intellect of the painters of southwestern rock art with that of elementary school children because he thought the drawings looked similar to children's artwork. At one point, he seemed to regret that all of the Indians in Texas had either been killed or moved out of the state. Hearing a statement like this could indeed lead a Native American student to seriously question her presence at the university! In fact, according to the 1990 census, Texas ranks eighth in the country for numbers of Native American residents (Reddy 1993). I include this class description not merely to blow off some steam, but to point out that academia is not neutral in its approach to the study of Native American history: sometimes things can get downright hostile.

In addition, the opposite condition has begun to occur. In the wake of the quincentennial, it has become fashionable once again to mythologize Native American culture. Our history is sometimes transformed into an impossibly serene, all knowing, cooperative, gender-sensitive enterprise that is then held as a shining example for the rest of the world to follow. White culture, corrupted by civilization, could supposedly learn much from our heritage. This benevolent, though misguided, viewpoint again places Native Americans in a category other than human. At times it seems easier to contend with clear-cut ignorance rather than well-intentioned romanticization.

Archaeology classes are generally much better, but they often fail to make the connection between living Native American groups and the "prehistoric" past. In most of my archaeology classes, little or no mention has been made of the modern Indian tribes who are related to the various aspects, chiefdoms, and phases being studied. One gets the idea that living Indian people are irrelevant to the study of North American prehistory, and maybe within the current formulation of prehistory, we are. But I believe that this merely illustrates the need for a reconsideration of what we have defined as archaeology. Are we uncovering the past for its own sake or for reasons of our own? We may be trying to be objective and scientific, but isn't there a sense of wanting to connect with the ancient peoples that drew all of us into this profession? It seems to me to be dangerous to define a past that does not possess a human soul.

COMMUNICATION

Communication between archaeologists and Native American groups has increased over the years, especially after the passage of the **Native American Graves Protection and Repatriation Act.** However, this term—communication—may involve different actions and have different meanings. If discussions only take place within the boundaries of legally mandated sharing of information, a true dialogue may not result. Let us consider the various Indian communities and ways in which archaeologists can open less formal communication with them.

Information about archaeological research need not be distributed only in cases where excavations take place on Indian lands. Members of tribes who are culturally or spatially related may be fascinated by studies that seem commonplace in departments of anthropology. It is vital that archaeologists come to view sharing information with Indian groups as an integral part of conducting research.

The method of transmission of information is also important. Sending a copy of the published report may be useful, but many of those who are interested may find it difficult to interpret. While technical reports may be useful to members of tribes who are considering archaeology as a career, academic language may obscure information fascinating to the general Indian community.

One interesting report has been published by the U.S. Department of the Interior's Fish and Wildlife Service about burials found at the Stillwater National Wildlife Refuge (Raymond 1992). This report discusses the project and the information learned from the burials in nontechnical language. It even describes paleopathological research in a clear manner. Because of financial constraints, reports like this one may be rare, but similar efforts should be undertaken where possible.

Other approaches to consider are giving talks at community centers, or tribal meetings, or inviting people to visit labs or excavation sites. I once arranged the NASO to take a tour of the Texas Archaeological Research Laboratory. In an apparent long-standing tradition, members of the Caddo Tribe of Oklahoma regularly attend an annual conference on Caddo archaeology. The level of communication that takes place at the conference may be questioned, however; at the last meeting, a Native American student commented to me that "It all looks very interesting, but I didn't understand a word of it."

When considering a connection to the Indian community, archaeologists often overlook intertribal organizations. Texas has many organizations that enable Indian people of all backgrounds to come together to discuss common concerns. These groups should not be dismissed in attempts to educate the native public about archaeology just because they are composed of people from many different tribes. The majority of the 65,000 Indians in Texas don't live on tribal lands (Reddy 1993).

I have been privileged to be a speaker at the American Indian Resource and Education Coalition's annual conference on Indian education in Texas. At the 1995 conference, I gave a short talk on skeletal research, discussing what is actually done and the sorts of information that can be learned. I had been quite nervous about making that speech. On other occasions I have been made to feel like a traitor for studying human remains. In fact, the listeners seemed quite interested and asked thoughtful questions. It became clear to me that many had not known what could be learned from skeletal analysis. To me, this incident represents a clear breakdown in communication because this group has been one of the more active in Texas to push for repatriation.

I do not mean to state that with a little more education members of groups such as this would change their minds about reburial, rather I think that they should be fully informed about the nature of archaeology and about what can be learned. As Lynne Goldstein states, "Since Native Americans often have little idea of what we do, they may invent our culture for us, based on the limited information they have on hand" (Goldstein 1992:61).

NATIVE AMERICAN ARCHAEOLOGISTS

There have been many calls for an increase in the numbers of Native Americans in archaeology, and in fact our ranks have grown. However, the number of Indians who acquire a college education remains small, and the number of Indian graduate students remains even smaller. At the University of Texas at Austin, 182 students out of 48,000 are listed as American Indian or Alaska Native. Native Americans are not considered a minority group with regard to recruitment efforts (Office of Admissions, University of Texas at Austin, personal communication 1996). In Texas, Native Americans are not considered minorities when applying for state-regulated financial aid specifically available to minority students (Red Elk 1995). NASO has made efforts to recruit Native American graduate students, but it is nearly impossible to recruit undergraduates since we receive no support for this from the university.

Calls for an increase in the number of Native American archaeologists are easy to make, but can be much harder to answer. In stating a desire for more practicing native archaeologists, we must address what it is the discipline really expects of us. We are capable of bringing perspectives to our work that go against standard archaeological knowledge about the peoples of North America. Will these be accepted, or rejected as nonscientific?

For example, we know that at one time these lands were inhabited only by our ancestors. This country was Indian for at least 20 times as long as Europeans and their descendants have been here. This knowledge can provide modern Indian people with a feeling of kinship that transcends tribal boundaries. I have found that my own studies in archaeology reflect an emotional connection that is a result of being related somehow to the "prehistoric" peoples of North America.

I think the best way to explain this is to relate an experience I had as an undergraduate at Rice University. I was visiting the Houston Museum of Natural Science to study an exhibit of precolumbian Central American artifacts. I remember wandering happily through the exhibit, comfortable in the feeling of kinship with the ancient makers of the objects. When I examined a case of personal adornment items, I stared into a black obsidian mirror and was struck by a deeply satisfying thought: the owner of the mirror had probably seen a sight similar to the one I was seeing when he or she looked into the polished glass.

As Native Americans, when we study the past, we see our ancient selves, living and acting in a world not yet impacted by 504 years of colonial confusion. When we work at archaeology, we do so with a sometimes unspoken responsibility: we know why we need to preserve the memories of those who went before us. It might be argued that this can lead to unobjective results; how can one scientifically study prehistory if one is also reverent of the ancestors? This question points me toward another difficulty of belonging to both groups. Is it reverent to the ancient peoples to pursue one of my interests, the study of health conditions in a "prehistoric" community through examination of their skeletal remains?

SKELETAL RESEARCH

I believe that one can attempt to maintain appropriate reverence toward the ancients while continuing to learn from their material remains. For many of our ancestors, skeletal analysis is one of the only ways that they are able to tell us their stories. The forthcoming information may not be as clear as it is from other sources; it seems that it is difficult to speak with a voice made of bone. Nevertheless, while so much has been lost, these individuals have found one last way to speak to us about their lives.

While working on my dissertation research, I have observed many different people and their approaches toward skeletal analysis. Many appear to work quite casually, and I know that I have irritated some by insisting on following rules about working conditions to the letter. In doing so, I find that I am attempting to foster an awareness of the heavy responsibility of working with human remains. Bioarchaeological research is a privilege. It must not be taken lightly.

I could not conduct skeletal research against the wishes of a related Indian community. If possible, I would make known to concerned individuals the types of studies that could be done and what could be learned, as well as my willingness to follow procedures that address religious needs. In the end, however, I would be forced by my own ethics and humanity to comply with their wishes. One of the basic common beliefs among native peoples is respect for elders and their wisdom.

CONCLUSION

As a Choctaw and an archaeologist, I am often forced to defend my own work and my choice of archaeology as a profession to members of various Indian groups. This is one of the more difficult aspects of being a Native American archaeologist. As a member of both groups, I can't help getting drawn into various conflicts. Although this leaves me quite cynical at times, I still feel that more Native Americans are needed for the future of archaeology. It has been hard sometimes to clearly articulate why this is necessary, but I think it has something to do with the image I saw in the obsidian mirror.

When we study the people of the past, we do so with a frame of reference that is constructed in the present. However unknowingly, we carry our own perspectives and experiences into our studies, and this affects to various degrees our conclusions about the past. The next people to come along in the precolumbian exhibit I mentioned above were an older, white couple. They also stared appreciatively into the mirror, but I knew there was little chance that their images were comparable to the owner's. Yet there must be similarities; we share common, human characteristics.

I believe that Native American archaeologists can study the past in ways that are both divergent and complementary to the more traditional canon. For us, the past is strong. The precolumbian past of this continent is a powerful, almost mythic time that illustrates the accomplishments of native peoples: it serves as a source of strength when confronted with the struggles of the present. This is the perspective that influences my own attitudes and activities in archaeology.

In continuing my studies of the past, I do so gratefully, with the tools developed by generations of archaeologists, most of whom are not Indian. It is necessary, however, to recognize that Native American archaeologists may see some areas of the past more closely. We look through an emotional lens that is knowingly constructed through our blood, the genetic characteristics of which echo in the bones of our ancestors.

I do not think that it is impossible to know the American past without being related to the peoples being studied. In fact, if we consider the history of North America when we define our profession, we may recognize a justice of a sort. While so much of our native history was lost through the actions of European peoples, it is perhaps fair that so many of their descendants strive so hard to restore it. White archaeologists might try to consider their work as a sort of penance rather than a right.

We must reconsider what our purposes are when we conduct archaeological research. We must recognize that our actions do affect native peoples on many levels. Acknowledging this fact need not compromise a scientific study of the past, it should merely force one more step toward active communication. Archaeology must also consider what is implied in calls for an increase in the numbers of Native American archaeologists. How much of a native perspective is to be incorporated? How easy is it for a Native American to choose archaeology considering the social and economic pressures that may be involved? Increasing the numbers of Indians practicing archaeology is certainly desirable, but it should be just as necessary to educate tribes and intertribal groups.

Finally, I do not maintain that the Native American perspective on the past be privileged to the exclusion of any other approaches, merely that it be recognized as an existing canon. There should be room in this discipline for a variety of viewpoints. After all, we are all human. We all share genetic characteristics and fundamental concerns, and when we look in the mirror we all see basically the same thing: our very human selves.

REFERENCES

Goldstein, L. 1992. The potential for future relationships between archaeologists and Native Americans. In *Quandaries and Quests: Visions of Archaeology's Future*, edited by LuAnn Wandsnider, pp. 59–71. Center for Archaeological Investigations, Southern Illinois University at Carbondale.

Hubert, J. 1989. A proper place for the dead. In *Conflicts in the Archaeology of Living Traditions*, edited by R. Layton, pp. 131–266. Unwin Hyman, London.

Lippert, D. 1992. Skeletons in our closets: Archaeology and the issue of reburial. Unpublished M.A. thesis, Department of Anthropology, University of Texas, Austin.

Raymond, A. 1992. Who were the ancient people of Stillwater National Wildlife Refuge, Nevada? U.S. Department of the Interior, Fish and Wildlife Service, Stillwater Wildlife Refuge, Fallon, Nevada.

Reddy, M.A., editor. 1993. *Statistical Record of Native North Americans*. Gale, Detroit.

Red Elk Hardman, R. 1995. Presentation at the 1995 Conference on Indian Education in Texas, San Antonio.

Trigger, B. 1989. *A History of Archaeological Thought*. Cambridge University Press, Cambridge.

12

CRM and Native Americans: An Example from the Mashantucket Pequot Reservation

Kevin McBride

Kevin McBride is an archaeologist at the University of Connecticut. He is the chief archaeologist for the Mashantucket Pequot Tribe and has played a major role in the tribe's efforts to recapture its history.

Points to consider when reading this article:

1. Who are the Pequot?

2. Why does the relationship between the Pequot and archaeologists seem so much better than the relationship between other Indian groups and archaeologists investigating the native past?

3. What has archaeology contributed to Pequot history?

4. What is the Pequot's goal in supporting an active and ongoing archaeology program on their reservation?

It shouldn't be difficult to understand. Many Native Americans resent outsider archaeologists who are hired by other outsiders to illuminate native history. In this usual scenario, the archaeologists are in no way accountable to the people whose ancestors are being studied.

It has been quite a different situation for the Mashantucket Pequot in southeastern Connecticut. With the enormous wealth generated by their successful gambling casino, the Pequot are funding and controlling the investigation of their own past. Working together with archaeologists from the University of Connecticut, the Pequot have sponsored numerous archaeological surveys and excavations, uncovering supporting evidence for that part of their past for which **oral history** provides an outline. Archaeology has also enabled the Pequot to reconstruct the most ancient part of their history, a time that dates to before the stories passed down from parent to child.

Now, when Pequot tribal chairman Skip Haywood drives various foreign dignitaries or the politically powerful from Washington, D.C., by the old house in which the white reservation overseer lived in the eighteenth century, he can point to it and declare: "That's where one of our employees, our chief archaeologist, lives."

Kevin McBride is that chief archaeologist. Here he describes the enormously successful cooperative project he runs, recapturing the history of a tribe experiencing a renaissance.

The relationship between archeologists and Native Americans has often been based on conflict. Native groups throughout the Northeast have become increasingly vocal about the way in which archeological research is conducted on sites they believe to be associated with their culture and history. Although the goals of both groups are often compatible, rarely have long-term working relationships developed between them. This situation has changed in recent years, particularly in southern New England, as Native groups have become federally recognized, settled land claims, and begun to pursue economic and social developments on their respective reservations. In addition, as newly recognized tribes begin to initiate economic development projects on trust lands, they are faced with a variety of

From *CRM*, vol. 18, no. 3, 1995. Reprinted here courtesy of the author.

issues related to the identification, assessment, protection, and management of archeological resources. Archeologists have found themselves in a position of assisting groups such as the Narragansetts, Mashantucket Pequot, Gay Head Wampanoag, and Mohegan in identifying and assessing cultural resources on their reservations in anticipation of development projects. This situation is made more complex because many of the federally recognized tribes in southern New England reside on reservations that have been continuously occupied throughout the prehistoric and historic periods, constituting some of the most complex and significant resources in the eastern United States.[1] Although forced together initially out of necessity, solid relationships have been established between archeologists and native groups in the region.

Since 1980, the Mashantucket Pequot Tribe has worked with federal, state, and local agencies including the Connecticut Historical Commission, Bureau of Indian Affairs, National Park Service, Department of Anthropology at the University of Connecticut, the Public Archaeology Survey Team, Inc., and the Planning Commission of the Town of Ledyard to develop a comprehensive research and **cultural resource management** plan to study and protect **cultural resources** associated with their cultural heritage. Collectively, this effort is known as the Mashantucket Pequot Ethnohistory Project, with a blend of archeological and historic research and cultural resource management objectives.

Tribal regulations developed in accordance with this plan require that cultural resource management surveys be conducted prior to all construction actions undertaken within reservation boundaries as well as fee lands. All surveys, undertaken by qualified archeologists under contract with the tribe, are reviewed by the Connecticut State Historic Preservation Office to assure conformance with historic preservation regulations. All cultural materials located during tribal undertakings are curated in facilities located on Reservation grounds or in the archeological laboratory of the University of Connecticut.

The Mashantucket Pequot Tribal Council vigorously implements historic preservation policies and regulations. The Tribal Council also continues to support ongoing research. A recently published book, *The Pequots in Southern New England*, contains scholarly papers presented at a symposium on Mashantucket Pequot culture and history in October 1987. A second conference was organized in October 1993, with presented papers on **ethnohistory,** archeology, history and the federal recognition process. The federal government recognized these and other efforts by the Mashantucket Pequot Tribe with a National Historic Preservation award in 1988.

HISTORIC CONTEXT

The Mashantucket Pequot Reservation has been continuously used and occupied by the Pequots and their ancestors for the last 10,000 years. When the reservation was established in 1666, it was centered around a 500-acre wetland called the Great Cedar Swamp. **Archeological surveys** and excavations have documented sites dating from the Paleo-Period through the Late Woodland Period.[2] The nature of land use documented around the swamp is similar to prehistoric land use documented elsewhere in the region with a few significant differences.[3] The highest density of prehistoric archeological sites have been documented during the **Middle** and **Terminal Archaic Periods** (ca. 8,000–6,000 B.P.; 3,800–3,000 B.P.). The lowest frequency of archeological sites dates to the **Late Archaic Period** (6,000–4,000 B.P.). This pattern is in sharp contrast to other areas of southern New England, and probably reflects differences in the nature of the wetland over time. Paleo-environmental reconstructions of the swamp indicate a period of lowered water table and intermittent desiccation between 7,500–4,000 years ago. During the late prehistoric period and until the **Pequot War** (1637), the cedar swamp was used for hunting. This pattern is reflected in the archeological record by a number of small temporary or task specific sites.[4] Documents associated with the Pequot War (1636–1637) indicate that the swamp was also used as a place of refuge by the Pequots during periods of conflict.

When the reservation was established 30 years after the Pequot War, it became the focal point of Mashantucket land use and settlement throughout the historic period. In a region of the United States where the Native American archeological record is usually truncated by the middle of the 17th century, archeological sites at Mashantucket increase in density and complexity until the early-19th century. Archeological surveys and excavations have documented one of the richest historic period Native American archeological records in the region. The significance of this record resulted in the placement of the Mashantucket Pequot Reservation on the **National Register of Historic Places** in 1983, and the subsequent designation of the Mashantucket Pequot Reservation Archaeological District as a National Historic Landmark in 1993. Contributing resources include 17th-century cemeteries, camps and villages, 18th-century farmsteads and hunting camps, and an 18th-century village. Most recently, a late-17th-century Mashantucket fortified village (Monhantic Fort) was identified and is believed to have been constructed during King Philip's War (ca. 1675).

Following the abandonment of the reservation by one of the Mashantucket communities in the Brothertown

Indian Movement at the end of the 18th century, subsequent reductions in land base and population resulted in a dramatic decline in the frequency of archeological sites through the third quarter of the 20th century. By the middle of the 19th century the population on the reservation had declined to approximately 10 individuals, dropping from a high of 500 in the 17th century, 300 in the 18th century, and 50 by the mid-19th century. In 1993, 10 years after federal recognition, the population of the reservation exceeded 250.

Federal recognition has brought the Mashantucket Pequot an opportunity to pursue economic development on an unprecedented scale. Through the proceeds of the most successful Native American gaming enterprise in the country, the Mashantucket Pequot Tribe has engaged in an ambitious program of social and economic development. To date, this has included the construction of over 65 housing units, and the purchase of 65 more, five miles of new roadways, a community center, health center, office complex, and safety complex. The Mashantucket Pequots are currently designing a 300,000-square-foot museum and research center to be completed in 1997 [Editor's note: The museum actually opened in the summer of 1998].

MANAGEMENT SUMMARY

Four major goals have been identified by the Mashantucket Pequot Tribal Council for the Mashantucket Pequot Ethnohistory Project: (1) reconstruct Mashantucket Pequot tribal history; (2) use the archeological and ethnohistoric data to plan and construct exhibits for the planned museum on tribal history; (3) develop a cultural resources management program for the reservation; and (4) train tribal members in archeological field techniques and ethnohistoric methods.

The first objective, reconstruction of Mashantucket Pequot history, is an ongoing process. This effort consists of archeological surveys and excavations, document research, and compilation of oral histories. Archeological surveys have identified over 200 Native American and Euro-American components on the current 1,400 acre reservation (trust lands) and an adjacent 1,500 acres (fee lands). A number of prehistoric and historic period archeological sites have been or are in the process of being studied. These studies are complemented by an ambitious program of Paleo-environmental studies conducted by botanists and geologists from the University of Connecticut, Yale University, Connecticut College, and Brown University. A number of graduate students from the University of Connecticut's Department of Anthropology and Yale University's Forestry Department have also initiated dissertation research projects, including studies of a late Paleo-Indian camp, historic period agricultural practices and land use, and reconstruction of the Paleo-environmental history of the Great Cedar Swamp.

Document research has been an integral part of the ethnohistory project from the beginning. Over 7,000 documents, photographs, and other materials related to Pequot history and culture have been obtained. These records have been secured from repositories in the United States, Bermuda, New Zealand, England, and the Netherlands. All of this information will eventually be available in the Mashantucket's planned research center.

The second goal of the ethnohistory project is to provide the information necessary to construct exhibits on the tribe's history and culture for their museum and research center. Approximately 85,000 square feet of exhibits are planned for the Mashantucket Pequot Museum and Research Center. The information used in the content and design of the exhibits is based on data generated from the ethnohistory project. Tribal members, archeologists, and exhibit designers are all involved in the design process, incorporating a wide range of data and perspectives in the design effort. Planned exhibits will span the **Paleo-Indian** through late historic periods including a diorama of a caribou kill, reconstruction of a 16th-century village, a film on the Pequot War, and outdoor interpretive exhibits on an 18th-century farmstead. One of the more ambitious exhibits will be the reconstruction and interpretation of a 17th-century fortified village. This exhibit will not only interpret the lifeways of the period, but will be used to inform the public on archeological and ethnohistoric methods and techniques.

The third objective of the ethnohistory project, development of a cultural resource management plan, is ongoing and the tribe is in the process of reviewing and adopting regulations regarding the protection and management of its cultural resources. The commitment of the tribe to its history and culture is directly reflected in a high degree of interest and concern over the archeological resources on the reservation. These resources are viewed not only from the perspective of being associated with their immediate or distant ancestors, but as the most important means by which the tribe can reconstruct elements of their history. No construction project takes place on trust or fee lands unless an archeological survey has been completed and the significance of all resources is assessed. This process is initiated whenever additional properties are purchased by the Tribe. This is an active ongoing process as over 3,000 acres have been acquired by the Tribe over the last 10 years.

Tribal planners are furnished with locations of all inventoried sites in accordance with tribal regulations requiring consideration of project impacts on cultural resources. To date, tribal development actions have not adversely affected significant archeological resources located within the Mashantucket Pequot Archaeological District. Construction plans associated with several projects have been explicitly altered to avoid negative impacts on potentially significant cultural resources.

The Tribe's cultural resource management plan currently includes the following elements: (1) statement of the theoretical approach and research goals in the study of the reservation and tribal history; (2) summary of existing prehistoric and historic period cultural resources (both Native American and Euro-American) and a discussion of their significance and relationship to research goals; (3) determination of individual site boundaries, assessment of integrity, and statement of significance for each identified site on the reservation; (4) discussion of factors that may affect the long-term protection and management of identified resources such as development, erosion, gravel mining, etc.; (5) recommendations for additional surveys as well as ongoing evaluation and protection priorities for identified sites; and (6) development of a framework for using the plan to make management decisions concerning the preservation and or data recovery of sites threatened by development on the reservation or on properties owned by the Tribe.

The final goal is to train tribal members in archeological and ethnohistoric methods and techniques. One element of this training has been participation by tribal members in the University of Connecticut's Field School in Archaeology. The Tribe has recently received a grant from the Department of the Interior to aid in the excavation and interpretation of the Monhantic Fort. Tribal members have also been integral participants in the research and design of exhibits for the museum. The long-term goal is to train tribal members in key positions so that they can assume administrative and field positions in the museum and ethnohistory project.

NOTES

1. McBride, Kevin A.

1990 The Historical Archaeology of the Mashantucket Pequot. In *The Pequots in Southern New England: The Fall and Rise of an American Indian Nation,* eds. Laurence Hauptman & James Wherry. University of Oklahoma Press, Norman, pp. 96–116.

1992 Prehistoric and Historic Patterns of Wetland Use in Eastern Connecticut. *Man in the Northeast,* 43: 10–24.

1994 "'Ancient and Crazie': Pequot Lifeways During the Historic Period." In *Algonkians of New England: Past and Present.* Peter Benes, ed. pp. 63–67. Annual Proceedings of the 1991 Dublin Seminar: Boston University.

Glover, Suzanne and McBride, Kevin A.

1992 "Land Use Patterns and Community Structure Among the Gay Head (Aquinnah) Wampanoag." Paper presented at Gay Head (Aquinnah) History Conference, Gay Head, MA.

2. Jones, Brian

1992 The Power Plant Site: A Late Paleo-Indian Occupation. Preliminary Results of Phase I, II and III Investigations. Report prepared for the Mashantucket Pequot Tribe.

McBride, Kevin A.; 1994 "'Ancient and Crazie': . . .".

3. McBride, Kevin A.

1984 Prehistory of the Lower Connecticut River Valley. PhD Dissertation, University of Connecticut. University Microfilms, Ann Arbor, MI.

McBride, Kevin A. and Mary Soulsby

1989 Prehistory of Eastern Connecticut: Phase I, II and III Archaeological Surveys, Relocation of Route 6/I-84. Prepared for the Connecticut Department of Transportation. Public Archaeology Survey Team, Inc. (with Mary Soulsby), 485 pages.

4. McBride, Kevin A.; 1994 "'Ancient and Crazie': . . .".

13

Champion of Aboriginal Art

Denis D. Gray

Denis Gray is a writer, journalist, and Associated Press bureau chief in Bangkok, Thailand.

Points to consider when reading this article:

1. Why do some people consider Australian Aborigines to be a primitive people?

2. What do the paintings produced by Australian Aborigines imply about their intellectual abilities?

3. How old is the oldest native Australian art? How does this compare with the Upper Paleolithic cave paintings of ancient Europe?

4. What do you think the future holds in store for native Australian art?

It is interesting how we can dismiss an entire group of people—and their culture—with a single word, "primitive." Though there is a specific meaning of the word in anthropology with no pejorative intent (a tribal or nonindustrial people), the word carries so much baggage, is so charged with emotion and implications in its vernacular use, most anthropologists simply will not use it. The dictionary definition makes reference to "simplicity" or "crudity." There also is mention of a "lack of sophistication." Anthropologists know that these terms apply to no human group.

Though it is difficult, as an anthropologist, to conceive of an appropriate application of the common meaning of "primitive" to any human group, it is almost impossible to read a popular description of the native cultures of Australia without seeing this term, often repeatedly. Their technology is described as "primitive," their lifestyle is "primitive," their clothing, housing, tools, weapons, and politics are all "primitive."

But even those who view the material aspects of native Australian life through this lens recognize an enigma; this otherwise "primitive" people have an extremely complex, sophisticated, and richly textured social and artistic life. I would wager that a native Australian knows the precise way in which he or she is related to a broader cast of relatives than does anyone reading this book (once most of us get past our first cousins, we are virtually lost). At the same time, Australian Aborigines have created what may be the world's longest lived artistic tradition, and in this art they have recorded their history, worshipped their spirits, and left a legacy for us all to appreciate and ponder. The archaeological study of aboriginal art sites is providing us with a new perspective on these "primitive" people.

Yooo. . . . Yooo," he calls out in sharp, full-throated bursts as we near a snake-shaped outcrop deep in the Australian bush. "Politeness," explains Percy J. Trezise, "lets the spirits know we are coming. . . ."

The lean, 67-year-old Trezise pushes ahead with a vigorous stride, dressed in green shorts, a kepi, and leggings to protect against thorny undergrowth. He is at ease in this rugged land, already shimmering with heat and buzzing with insects although it is hardly past mid-morning.

Rainbow Serpent Shelter, which bears a remarkable resemblance to an overfed python, is sacred Aboriginal ground soaked in ancestral myths—and it's a very special place for Trezise. Here, in a shallow cave engraved with barely discernible geometric patterns, he is conducting research, convinced he will prove Aboriginal tribes lived and created art on the Australian continent longer than has generally been believed.

And this, he says with crusading ardor, will not only spur greater academic interest in the Aboriginal past but help restore pride to a people still maligned and once massacred by invading Europeans who regarded them as capable of little more than infantile scribblings on cave walls.

Rainbow Serpent Shelter is near the tiny town of Laura on the Cape York Peninsula, an England-sized area of trackless forests and untamed seacoasts that is Australia's last great wilderness. The shelter is just a single exhibit in what Trezise describes as one of the world's largest galleries of rock and prehistoric art. For 30 years he has explored this region, finding, cataloging, and analyzing hundreds of sites. Along the way, he has also championed Aboriginal causes and recorded tribal legends, many woven into 19 highly popular children's books he has written and illustrated. These, he believes, are helping to change attitudes toward the "first Australians."

Trezise dates his involvement in such matters to 1939, when he won a book about the Aborigines as a high school prize. Nineteen years later, a blinding rainstorm forced Trezise—then a professional pilot who had served in World War II—to land at Laura. It would become his second home and the focus of his life.

Aboriginal rock art had long been studied across Australia, from Arnhem Land in the Northern Territory to the Flinder's Ranges of South Australia, from the Kimberly and Pilbara areas of the west to Sydney in the southeast. But the first significant discovery in Cape York wasn't made until 1959 when road-construction crews near Laura came upon what was later to be called the Split Rock Galleries.

Trezise saw these galleries the same year, was overwhelmed by their richness and convinced they could not be the only site in the area. Fortunately, his flight routes took him over the area almost daily. He used the opportunity to conduct aerial surveys, swooping down low to the consternation of both passengers and wildlife on the ground, to pinpoint extensive sandstone escarpments that might enfold the art he sensed was spread out below.

At the same time, Trezise set out to befriend normally reticent Aboriginal elders who possessed knowledge of vanishing tribal lore and could thus help decode the art's meaning. Dick Roughsey, a talented artist of the Lardil Aboriginal group, became a close friend to whom Trezise was designated "brother" in the kinship system of the tribe. Proudly, Trezise recalls being given the name of Warrenby, a legendary Lardil leader.

With Roughsey and other mentors, like Caesar Le Choo, Willy Long, George Pegus, and Harry Mole, Trezise entered what he described in his 1969 book *Quinkan Country* as "a land where legend still overshadowed reality—a living land whose rocks and trees possessed spirits to murmur secrets to those who wished to hear them."

Viewed through the psyches of his guides, the Cape York bush became a continuum of the Dreamtime, when ancestral spirits came down from the sky and up from the earth to create the world and then assumed the shapes of trees and hills and pools. What was to Trezise a geologically and aesthetically interesting granite hilltop was to Roughsey and the others the terrifying spot where Gidja the Moon Man cooked and ate his two grandsons; the inconspicuous matchwood tree, the font of life and death whose trunks are inverted into graves so souls can slide up through the magic wood and onward to Woolunda, the Aboriginal heaven.

Blistering heat, venomous snakes, and stinging insects assaulted Trezise and his companions during their numerous expeditions. But Trezise's recollections are mostly happy ones: of days coming upon exciting rock-art discoveries; evening meals of wallabies, plain turkeys, and barramundi fish; and settling in around a campfire to tape legends of millennia past over rum and river water. At nighttime, Trezise's companions would nestle close to the fire for protection against the Quinkans, malevolent spirits said to haunt the Laura region and often portrayed in rock-art paintings as creatures with grotesquely outstretched legs and arms, bouncing across the land with the aid of their powerful penises.

During 15 years Trezise probably discovered more rock-art sites in the region than anyone else. He is a skilled artist and photographer. Thousands of his quarter-scale drawings, all produced on-site, now form an invaluable database at the Australian Institute of Aboriginal and Torres Strait Islander Studies in Canberra.

Sometimes his treks became family affairs with sons Matthew and Stephen, daughters Victoria and Anna, and Trezise's wife Beverly helping to scour the bush. In the early 1960s the family bought the quaint Laura Hotel, which Matthew runs, and paid out another 18,000 Australian dollars for 25 square miles of rock-art-rich land. On it they built a pleasantly ramshackle homestead and the Jowalbinna Bush Camp, a riverside camping ground from which Stephen guides small groups of tourists into the surrounding galleries. Adjacent to their land is the 400-square-mile Quinkan Reserve, established in 1977 after a Trezise-led campaign to place under protection as much of the Laura country as possible. The reserve is administered by the Ang-gnarra Aboriginal Corporation.

With Jowalbinna Bush Camp as our base and Steve as our guide, we dipped into forested gorges, hiked up escarpments, and clambered into overhanging shelters to a magnificent museum-in-the-wild. At Split

Rock: a female ancestral being of elongated shape, elaborate headdress and serene, Madonna-like expression. At Giant Wallaroo: hunting action as packs of dingoes track down mountain kangaroos. At Emu Dreaming Gallery: a row of equidistant oval-shaped pits in the cave wall.

Trezise is the acknowledged authority in explaining the forces that inspired Cape York rock art, its meanings, and the chronological sequence of art styles that span several thousand years. But inevitably his detective work has gaps and dead ends; the arrival of Europeans led to rapid detribalization of the Aborigines during which links with the past—earlier maintained through oral tradition—were severed. Trezise's old Aboriginal friends could identify or make reasonable deductions about some of what they saw on the cave walls: mythical heroes, totemic ancestors, and spirits; hunts, sorcery, and love magic. But many depictions drew a blank. Were the oval-shaped pits at Emu Dreaming eggs of the emu, or were they used for counting the seasons?

Such engravings belong to what Trezise categorizes as the earliest rock-art style, featuring geometric shapes, bird and animal tracks, and linear designs resembling mazes. From this presumably symbolic beginning evolved engravings of human beings, animals, and plants followed by stencils of hands and weapons, then simple linear drawings in monochrome. In time, the Aborigines drew large polychrome figurines in red and yellow ochres, decorated with white or cream pipeclay.

The last stage of what Trezise calls "one of the most continuous art forms in the world" was a tragic one. It came as gold was discovered on the Cape in the early 1870s, sparking a rush by tens of thousands of Europeans and Chinese. The Aborigines in their path were decimated by firepower and disease. The survivors retreated to their cave dwellings in the high country to hide from the bullets and to paint.

One of their works was of a horse, more than 17 feet long and ten feet high, in yellow red ochre with a white outline. Trezise surmises that at first the tribes must have been terrified of this animal import, never having seen any fauna bigger than a red kangaroo until they spotted the gun-wielding Europeans on horseback. The Aborigines tried to stem the incursion, and when their spears proved useless, they attempted to kill the invaders with black magic. In both the Emu Dreaming and Pig galleries a half dozen white men with rifles are depicted. In the Pig Gallery, birds are shown standing atop the bodies of two of the men, beaks thrust into their armpits.

"The Aborigines are bloody good blokes," says Trezise. He is sitting on the verandah of his homestead under a star-studded sky, sipping whiskey and water. His stories of vanished Aboriginal society are both graphic and sometimes idealized. He takes us on an imaginary hunt for kangaroo, imitating the stalking stance and calls of the trackers as they close in on a targeted animal with spears and boomerangs. Trezise describes the nomadic tribes as careful "land managers," never taking from the natural environment more than was needed to sustain them. He pictures them in their last strongholds, executing the large sorcery paintings and sensing that their race and way of life are doomed. "I am passionately committed to bringing justice to the Aborigines, to telling the world they have the world's oldest art," Trezise says. "Even today, there is an abysmal ignorance about them. Most white Australians haven't had a single conversation with an Aborigine in their lives."

The next morning, Trezise takes us by Landrover and foot to Rainbow Serpent Shelter. He and several archaeologists have worked there for years, excavating the cave floor and attempting to date the residues of human habitation. In 1960, when Trezise began his Laura treks, evidence for the earliest peopling of Australia was less than 10,000 years. Since then, he and others have steadily been pushing back this date. The research at Rainbow Serpent Shelter, he says, indicates it was a living site from some 13,000 years ago to early in this century. But the first visitors came here more than 40,000 years ago. Initially, Trezise exposed a boulder rising from the cave floor and found it was entirely covered with engravings, some overlaid with silica. Scientists at Australia's James Cook University who studied the samples said anything under the silica would be more than 18,000 years old. Excavations of the cave floor yielded occupational debris, stone tools, a stone ax, utilized quartz crystals, and charcoal. From this and associated data, Trezise has constructed a tentative profile of environmental and life-style changes in the Laura area over the millennia. He is certain that dating tests now in their final phase will confirm the great antiquity of Aboriginal culture in Australia.

Trezise hopes the last stage of his life will be a further refinement and synthesis of material gathered over the past three decades. He co-chaired the Second Australian Rock Art Association Congress last summer in the tropical resort of Cairns in northern Queensland. More than 350 delegates from around the world attended, making it the biggest rock-art congress ever held. The main item of news from the Congress was the announcement by the Ang-gnarra Aboriginal Corporation, custodians of many decorated sites around Laura, that an Australian geologist named Alan Watchman had dated paint on the wall of a shelter to 24,600 years ago, making it among the oldest dated painted sites in the world.

Meanwhile Trezise has written another book, titled *Dream Road*. "I made a promise to the last of the old initiated men," Trezise says. "I told them I would publish all their material in a book which will become available to their descendants when they again become interested in the ancient traditions and history."

Dick Roughsey and Caesar Le Choo and almost all his other companions have already made their way up the matchwood trees to Woolunda. And while professing non-belief in the hereafter, Trezise says that, somehow, he feels their spirits hovering around when he visits the sacred sites and galleries of Quinkan country.

14

Rescue, Research, and Reburial: Walton Family Cemetery, Griswold, Connecticut

Nicholas F. Bellantoni, Paul S. Sledzik,
and David A. Poirier

Nick Bellantoni is the state archaeologist of Connecticut and an expert in the analysis of bones found at archaeological sites.

Paul Sledzik is curator of anatomical collections at the National Museum of Health and Medicine at the Armed Forces Institute of Pathology in Washington, D.C.

Dave Poirier is a historical archaeologist specializing in sites of European colonists of the New World. He is staff archaeologist at the Connecticut Historic Commission, a state agency charged with the task of preserving historical landmarks in Connecticut.

Points to consider when reading this article:

1. Why did the editor of this book place an article about the rescue of a historic cemetery in a section labeled "serving communities through archaeology"?

2. Without tombstones indicating who the individuals were, how did the scientists involved in this project figure it out?

3. What diseases or conditions affected members of the Walton family?

4. How did the researchers interpret the grave that had been broken into, with the individual's bones rearranged?

When the Walton family laid their deceased loved ones to rest in their family cemetery in Griswold, Connecticut, in the nineteenth century, it was certainly their hope and expectation that this rest would be eternal. They likely believed that Waltons would always live and flourish in the lovely farming region marked by clapboard houses, red barns, and white-steepled Con-

gregational churches. Surely their descendants would tend to the graves, read the inscriptions on the tombstones, and reflect with reverence and love on the lives of their long dead ancestors. There would always be Waltons in Griswold, those nineteenth-century family members must have believed, to tend the plots, right the fallen grave markers, place flowers on the tombs, and simply to remember.

But one by one the Waltons moved away until there were none left in southeastern Connecticut. The tombstones fell into disrepair and soon were lost. Grass and weeds covered the graves in the little family plot, and soon the worst possible fate befell the final resting place of the Waltons—it was forgotten. Death had robbed these Waltons of their place in the world, and now time had stolen their memorial.

But a gravel quarry in just the right place (and children playing in a gravel quarry, as children do) resurrected at least the memory of the Walton clan. This article tells the poignant story of the archaeological "rescue, research, and reburial"—and, I might add, the reunion—of the Walton family.

INTRODUCTION

Emigrating from the Boston, Massachusetts, area with his wife Margaret, Lawrence Walton arrived in the

Town of Preston, Connecticut in 1690. He shortly thereafter purchased property near the Quinebaug River in the northeast portion of town and established a working farm in this rural eastern Connecticut community. Lawrence and Margaret had five children. Their first child, John, was born in 1694, and became a celebrated preacher in the Congregational Church. Four more children would be born into this colonial farming family, though none would obtain the notoriety of their eldest brother. The second son, Nathaniel, remained on the farm with his wife Jemima for the rest of their lives. In 1757, Nathaniel Walton purchased a plot of land (3 rods by 4 rods) for 12 shillings from his neighbor, sea captain Stephen Johnson, to be used as a family burial ground for Nathaniel and his descendants. Situated on the north end of a sandy knoll, northeast of the Johnson dwelling, the Walton family burying ground was originally bounded by 4 stakes surrounded by heaps of stones. Nathaniel and Jemima's descendants continued to be buried there until the turn of the nineteenth century, when the family began to disperse, eventually settling in Madison County, Ohio, to farm that much flatter, less stony soil. The cemetery has never appeared on subsequent land deeds.

The Walton Family Cemetery continued to be used for a short time into the nineteenth century by another unidentified family. Eventually abandoned and overgrown with vegetation, the cemetery was never listed in town records until David Phillips (1918) recorded and described 22 historic burial places in Griswold, Connecticut (incorporated from the Town of Preston in 1815), in the early twentieth century. Of the Walton Cemetery, Phillips (1918:205) notes that

> about 30 graves can still be made out marked by crude stone slabs gathered from the fields. For the most part these stones bear no marks of identification of those laid here; one however, reveals the grave of the wife of Nathaniel Walton, the brother of John the Scholar, for crudely hammered on the stone by an unskilled hand are made characters which spell out the following

> September ye 18 1759
> Then died thee
> Wife Nathaniel
> Walton Name
> Jemima.

In 1934, the *Hale Index*, a statewide Works Progress Administration inventory of gravestone inscriptions, described the cemetery as having only 7 unmarked fieldstones aligned in 2 rows and showed the cemetery location on a different hill east of the knoll and across a swift-flowing brook from where the cemetery was subsequently rediscovered. The historical narrative of the Walton family of Griswold, Connecticut, is sparse and primarily consists of Congregational Church records; Norwich, Preston, and Griswold town records; probate and census data; and newspaper accounts.

The Walton Family Cemetery is never mentioned again in any recorded sources, becoming lost and forgotten in the community's memory. That is, until November 1990, when a sand-and-gravel operation began mining the northwest end of the knoll to the rear of the historic Johnson homestead. Human skeletal remains and decomposed wooden coffin parts were encountered eroding out of the gravel embankment. The Walton Family Cemetery had been rediscovered in a most dramatic and unexpected way.

DISCOVERY

The Connecticut State Police and the Office of the State Chief Medical Examiner were notified in the late fall of 1990 that two human crania had been discovered by three preteenage boys playing in a privately operated sand-and-gravel mine in Griswold, Connecticut. Sliding down the slope of the gravel pit, the boys dislodged two skulls, which proceeded to tumble down the embankment with them. The chief medical examiner notified the state archaeologist as mandated by state statutes whenever "historic" human remains are uncovered that are not part of a modern criminal investigation. Local officials assumed that the remains might be Native American because legends note an early historic "battleground" in the area. However, laboratory analysis indicated a European biological affiliation for the two crania.

On-site inspection of the exposed side wall of the gravel quarry revealed six darkened soil stains extending 3 to 4 feet in depth from a disturbed ground surface. These distinctions in the soil profile were immediately interpreted as grave shafts; it became readily apparent that the gravel operation had encountered the first row of a historic cemetery. By law, the developer was only required to conduct title searches for the property dating back 40 years. No mention of a cemetery was discovered. However, he did have access to the *Hale Index* and suspected a historic cemetery on his property, but not in the area to be mined. The Office of State Archaeology was satisfied that the owner had no prior knowledge that the cemetery was located in his quarry site until human remains were accidentally exposed.

Emergency efforts were immediately undertaken by the Office of State Archaeology, the University of Connecticut, and the State Historic Preservation Office to rescue and recover human remains endangered by erosion. Unfortunately, the instability of the sand-and-gravel quarry precluded *in situ* preservation and necessitated total archaeological excavation of the remaining burials. Twenty-seven individuals were eventually excavated from the cemetery, including 5 adult males, 8 adult females, and 14 children ranging from infants through adolescents (Table 1). The property owner voluntarily assisted the rescue excavations in a number of ways including suspending his gravel removal activities, donating financial aid and labor from his work force, and constructing a temporary structure heated by propane to permit fieldwork through the winter season.

ARCHAEOLOGICAL RESCUE

Fieldwork at the Walton Family Cemetery began immediately upon our initial inspection of the site. A request for volunteer assistance resulted in students from the University of Connecticut and amateur archaeologists from the Albert Morgan Archaeological Society responding and participating in the rescue excavations. The Public Archaeological Survey Team, Inc., established a grid system as excavations began along the gravel cliff. The owner cooperated by stock-piling soils against the gravel bank in an effort to reduce erosional loss.

Archaeological field methods included the location and mapping of soil feature stains indicative of burial shafts that existed back from the vertical edge of the gravel bank. In previous years, the knoll had been prepared for the sand-and-gravel operation in phases that included deforestation and the stripping of topsoil to a depth of 2 feet. This resulted in the mechanical removal of fieldstones and other cemetery markers. Nonetheless, elimination of the topsoil permitted efficient use of shovel-scraping with flat-edged blades to locate grave shafts in the upper level of the B horizon. In addition, soil cores were systematically sampled across the knoll as a back-up approach to locating burial features by shovel-scraping.

Field methods also included mapping, illustrative and photographic recording at various stages of the excavation, and the systematic removal of each skeletal element within the burials. Excavation stages began within the soil stains, which eventually exposed a thin, dark brown, linear stain representing the sideboards of the wooden coffin. A series of rusted hardware coffin nails, usually with preserved wood attached, were located along the top and bottom of the sideboards. These two rows of coffin nails provided information on depth and coffin-making technology. Once coffin dimensions were recorded, excavation continued inside the vertical sideboards until human remains were encountered.

Upon exposure of the skeletal remains, the following descriptive information was recorded: orientation of the skeleton, positioning of the arms and legs, state of preservation, preliminary estimates of age and sex, artifacts associated with the burial, and inventories of each skeletal element recovered. In addition, whenever possible, samples of hair, wood, and soil were taken. Skeletal elements were placed in acid-free tissue and bubble wrap for transportation to the Archaeology Laboratory at the University of Connecticut. Once the skeletal remains were removed, excavations continued beneath the coffins and along the sideboards to recover any additional bone and/or hardware present.

The most persistent field problem was the rate of soil erosion off the gravel bank. In the first two weeks, the outermost edge of the embankment collapsed in over 7 feet in some areas, threatening the second row of the cemetery. Ironically, erosional rates were enhanced by the combined weights of the archaeologists working on the cliff edge. Although various stabilization efforts were employed, significant soil loss was not uncommon and required constant monitoring during field excavations.

WALTON FAMILY CEMETERY

The rescue excavations at the Walton Family Cemetery resulted in the recovery of 27 individuals in 28 graves. Burial 12 yielded a pattern of coffin nails but no organic preservation of wood or bone within it. The burials were placed in somewhat poorly defined rows, which were in a north-south alignment (Figure 1). Each burial was oriented east-west, with the head of the individual to the west, a standard mortuary practice for colonial period Christian burials. Three exceptions are Burials 10, 14, and 15, which have a southwest-northeast orientation. The configuration of the cemetery suggests clusters of burials as opposed to an orderly arrangement of rows. The 2 rows nearest the gravel bank exposure toward the west are discernible. However, toward the east, clusters of burials occur in the north and south portions of the cemetery. For example, the northern cluster is composed of 7 graves in close proximity that are the remains of small children and may represent a disease epidemic within the family or community.

All deceased family members were placed in wooden coffins, of which 12 were hexagonal and 11 were rectangular in shape, while 5 coffin shapes could not be discerned due to erosional collapse prior to rescue excavations. Nine of the 12 hexagonal and all of the unknown coffin shapes are associated with adult individuals, while all of the 11 rectangular coffins are associated with subadults. When preservation permitted, wood samples were taken from top, side, and bottom coffin boards and analyzed by Lucinda McWeeney

TABLE 1   Overview of the Walton Cemetery Skeletal Remains, Including Sex, Age, Stature, and Pathological Condition

Burial #	Sex	Age	Stature	Pathology
1	F	55–59	159.07	Vertebral and joint OA, Schmorl's nodes
2	M	60+	173.94	Joint OA
3	F	30–35	161.21	None
4	M	50–55	180.40	Vertebral and joint OA, healed fractures, periostitis, tuberculosis
4A	F	45–54	177.60	Vertebral and joint OA, temporomandibular joint OA
5	S	10–11	N/A	None
6	S	1–1.5	N/A	None
7	S	6–7	N/A	None
8	M	20–35	174.55	None
9	F	20–29	170.87	None
10	S	0.5–0.75	N/A	None
11	F	35–44	156.75	None
12	No Burial Remains			
13	S	8–9	N/A	None
14	F	50–65	N/A	Edentulous
15	M	60+	N/A	Vertebral and joint OA
16	S	1–1.5	N/A	None
17	S	1.5–2.5	N/A	None
18	F	60–75	N/A	Osteopenia, unhealed femoral neck fracture, vertebral OA
19	S	2–3	N/A	None
20	M	30–34	180.71	Heavy dental calculus
21	S	11–12	N/A	None
22	F	22–26	167.46	None
23	S	12–14	N/A	None
24	S	1–2	N/A	None
25	S	7–8	N/A	None
26	S	6–7	N/A	None
27	S	6–7	N/A	None

Note: Sex estimates are given for males, females, subadults; age numbers are in years; stature is recorded in centimeters; N/A means data not applicable; and OA abbreviates osteoarthritis.

(1992) for species identification. Identifications from 17 burials showed that white pine (*Pinus strobus*) was used predominately (11 coffins), while red and white oak were used to a lesser extent (6 coffins). In addition, McWeeney (1992) identified paint stains on the lids of two coffins: black paint associated with Burial 5, and red paint with Burial 4.

Coffin hardware, analyzed by Ross Harper (1992), was limited and consisted primarily of hand-wrought nails. While every coffin yielded a series of hand-wrought nails, only Burials 4, 4A, 5, and 18 had coffin screws and brass tacks as part of the coffin hardware material. In addition, Burials 4, 5, and 18 have copper dowel hinges on the lids of the coffin. According to Rumford (1965:78), hinged and divided coffin lids began to appear in the early nineteenth century. The lid of the coffin was divided in order to expose the head area to view the face of the deceased. Burials yielding

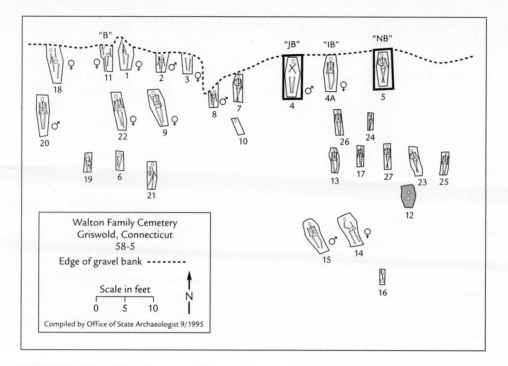

FIGURE 1 Map of burials excavated from Walton Family Cemetery.

no hinges are interpreted as having plain one-piece lids. Burial 15 produced a series of three nails located longitudinally along the axial skeleton and may suggest a gable-lidded coffin (Noel Hume 1982). However, for the most part, the cemetery consists of rather plain, undecorated hexagonal coffins for adults and rectangular coffins for children. We found no evidence of decorative butterfly hinges, handles, glass viewing plates, or lining tacks. No machine cut nails were recovered, suggesting that all the burials predate the 1830s.

Two burials (Nos. 4 and 5) were placed in stone and unmortared brick crypts. The hexagonal coffin in Burial 5, consisting of a two-piece lid with brass tacks arranged in the initials and number "NB 13," was located within several courses of unmortared bricks built on a single brick width and covered by slabs of fieldstones. "NB" are the initials of the deceased and "13" is the age of death. Sex could not be determined for this adolescent individual. The coffin in Burial 4 is similar; however, the crypt consists of stone slabs set vertically and horizontally along the sides and top, enclosing the coffin. A few bricks do appear along the sideboards of the coffin as structural supports. Brass tacks form the initials and number "JB 55." The corpse is an adult male. The appearance of crypts are more likely interpreted as changes in mortuary practices in the nineteenth century as well as socioeconomic factors.

No evidence of clothing, including boots, buttons, or buckles, was recovered from the burials. The only material culture associated with the skeletal remains was the presence of two-piece, copper-headed, brass and silver straight pins. Recovered from 11 burials, these pins were aligned to one side of the body and used to hold a burial shroud in place. Burial 14 yielded a small shard of a slipware bowl rim. However, this ceramic appears to have been introduced into the grave from backfilling the burial shaft rather than as a funerary object.

Burial depth from the original ground level was impossible to calculate due to the extensive activities of the sand and gravel mining. However, the graves of the children were encountered at the surface of the stripped knoll or within a foot of excavation. Adult burials were always recovered from deeper levels. We estimate that the children were buried around 3 feet in depth while adult graves were dug to an average of 5 to 6 feet.

OSTEOLOGICAL RESEARCH

Preliminary analysis of the skeletal remains from the Walton Family Cemetery was conducted at the University of Connecticut as each burial was processed in the laboratory upon field recovery. Extensive analysis was conducted by Paul S. Sledzik and Allison Webb Wilcox at the National Museum of Health and Medicine, Armed Forces Institute of Pathology, in Washington, D.C. Table 1 presents an overview of age, sex, and stature estimates and pathological conditions in the Walton Cemetery skeletal remains.

Demographic Discussion

The striking **demographic** statistic in the mortality distribution is the number of children represented in the cemetery. Fifty percent of the burials are preteenagers. Six individuals, almost one-fourth of the cemetery population, are infants under the age of 2 years. As the Walton Family Cemetery most likely represents a biological lineage, that is, a breeding population, the disproportionate number of children may reflect the hardships of survival in colonial New England. Seasons of low nutrition, unsanitary conditions, and overcrowded rural farmsteads may account for the spread of communicable diseases among New England farming families. Children were especially vulnerable to outbreaks of measles, colds, yellow fever, tuberculosis, smallpox, and other pathologies (Clark et al. 1987). Town of Norwich Death Records indicate a measles epidemic in 1759 and a smallpox epidemic in 1790. Either of these events could be represented in this cemetery population. Due to a child's limited resistance to these pathogens and subsequent expeditious death, the evidence for these diseases were not manifest on the **osteological** remains.

Striking also is the high percentage (23%) of individuals over 50 years of age. Age distribution frequencies are bimodal: children and older adults. Combined, these age groups represent almost 75% of the total cemetery population. The disproportionately low number of young and middle-aged adults is probably a result of developed immunities and stronger resistance to disease. The demographic pattern appears to reflect what we would expect in a historic cemetery population.

Pathology Discussion

Of the 8 individuals exhibiting signs of pathology, all are over the age of 30 years, with 6 individuals over 50 years old. The most prevalent ailment is vertebral and joint osteoarthritis, which appears on 5 of the 6 individuals over 50 years of age at death (Table 1).

Burial 1 is an elderly female who suffered from mild osteoarthritis in her neck and major joints. The presence of Schmorl's nodes, a neuromechanical deformity exhibited in the spinal column, indicates heavy and repetitive lifting with the back. The loss of nearly all teeth before death made it difficult for her to chew food.

Burial 2 is a partial skeleton of an elderly male showing evidence of mild to moderate osteoarthritis in most joints. The changes in the acetabulum and proximal femora indicate moderate osteoarthritis, with this individual experiencing pain in these joints.

Burial 4 is the most interesting individual from the entire sample in terms of pathology. Chronic dental disease, as evidenced by antemortem loss, severe carious lesions, and alveolar bone resorption, indicate that this person suffered from periodontal disease. Osteoarthritis and fractures would be expected, given his life as a farmer. A healed fracture of the right clavicle was probably the result of an insult to the front of the collarbone, which traveled toward the back of the body. The fracture was not set, resulting in the observed defect seen. A severe osteoarthritic lesion on the joint surface of the left knee may have caused him to walk with a limp, and most certainly with pain. Periostitis of the lower left tibia and fibula may be a result of the foot lesion or a separate entity. The lytic activity of the left foot has several possible diagnoses including blastomycosis (a fungal infection), tuberculosis, osteomyelitis, and maduramycosis (fungal). Although the lesion is similar in appearance to other cases of maduramycosis and blastomycosis, these fungi are not found in Connecticut. The possibility of tuberculosis is good, given the lesions on the upper left ribs. These lesions, which are similar to those described by Kelley and Micozzi (1984) and Roberts, Lucy, and Manchester (1994), have been ascribed to tuberculosis.

Burial 4A is an adult female who suffered from upper neck problems (arthritis) and had temporomandibular joint disorder, where the mandible hinges to the left temporal bone of the skull. This disorder resulted in pain and joint soreness, especially when chewing.

Burial 18 is the skeleton of an elderly female (60 to 75 years of age) exhibiting postcranial bones that are light and thin and give the appearance of generalized osteopenia. The left femur exhibits an unhealed fracture of the femoral neck. The bone has attempted to repair itself, resulting in a pseudoarthrosis type of appearance. Periostitis extends down the neck of the femur and proximal portion of the femur, where pitting and new bone development are present. This is a typical hip fracture seen in modern elderly women. The fracture can be attributed to the osteopenic nature of the entire skeleton.

Burial 20 is a nearly complete skeleton of an adult male, 30–40 years of age. The mandibular teeth exhibit an unusually heavy amount of dental calculus (tartar). The calculus is heavier on the incisors, canines, and premolars than on the molars. As a result of the calculus, the anterior mandibular and maxillary teeth do not occlude. The temporomandibular joints are unusually large and rounded in appearance, possibly due to compensation for the malocclusion. The calculus has also resulted in large spaces between adjacent teeth. The mandible also appears to be Hapsburg in shape, although this may also be due to the mechanical stresses in overcoming the malocclusion.

Pathological conditions seen in the Walton Cemetery sample are not unusual for a rural, nineteenth-century population. The prevalence of vertebral and joint osteoarthritis and Schmorl's nodes is not unexpected given the hard physical labor required of males and females to maintain New England farms. Healed fractures of various bones (e.g., clavicle, ribs) indicate strenuous activity and the ability of the person to continue to work after the insult occurred.

Stature Discussion

Walton family adult men within our sample have an average stature of 175.53 cm (5'10''), while the women stand at 165.49 cm (5'6''). Burials 4 and 20 are adult males having the tallest stature at 180 cm (6'), while Burial 8 represents the shortest male at 167 cm (5'6''). The range of variation is greater among females. Burial 4A represents the tallest adult female at 177 cm (5'10'') and Burial 11 is the shortest female at 156 cm (5'2'').

Comparisons of statures of groups contemporaneous with the Walton cemetery sample . . . show that the Walton males are as tall as the two military skeletal samples (Snake Hill and Fort William Henry) and taller than the pauper cemetery samples (Uxbridge and Highland Park). The stature of the Walton males is not exceptionally tall for the time period, given that the stature figures are estimates based on osteological measurements. The range of variation in the samples . . . is 7.6 cm (3''), so comparisons between the groups reflect very minor differences.

Dental Disease

Examination of dental caries, antemortem tooth loss, and alveolar abscess is provided. . . . In all cases, females exhibit nearly twice the frequency of males. The severity of caries in females is also greater than that observed in males. Since the sample dates from the mid-eighteenth to mid-nineteenth centuries, one explanation of the rates of caries frequency may be attributed to an increased intake of processed grains and sugars (Sledzik and Moore-Jansen 1991). Females in the Walton Cemetery sample may have had increased availability to these grains and sugars, perhaps in the making of food. The rate of antemortem loss in both males and females is remarkably high, perhaps as a result of tooth loss from severe caries.

BIOARCHAEOLOGICAL INTERPRETATIONS

In historical bioarchaeological research, investigators use historical information to interpret osteological and archaeological evidence. Such information allows re-

searchers to test the reliability of historical documents and interpretations and can lead to insights into unique cultural practices (Owsley 1990; Bell, this volume). The Walton Family Cemetery offered us insight into a distinctively New England folk practice.

Burial 4 contained the skeletal remains of "JB 55," a 50- to 55-year-old male interred in a stone-lined crypt. When the grave was opened, the skull-and-femora were found in a "skull-and-crossbones" orientation on top of the ribs and vertebrae, which were also found in disarray (Figure 2). Taphonomically, the physical arrangement of the skeletal remains in the grave indicates that no soft tissue was present at the time of rearrangement, which may have been 5 to 10 years after death. No other burial had been so desecrated at the cemetery. The coffin style and crypt suggest an early nineteenth-century temporal placement for the burial. Historic research to date has been unsuccessful in determining the *B* family surname. Griswold town and Congregational Church records show a series of families beginning with the letter *B* interacting with the Waltons and the community (e.g., Brown, Bishop, Bennett, Burnham, Bissell, Burton). Unfortunately, we have been unable to identify the appropriate family and their relationship to the Waltons. It appears that the *B* family may have utilized the burial ground after the Waltons' departure from Griswold. Although historical research into the family and colonial community had begun with the field rescue of the cemetery, this desecrated burial raised a new concern.

Historical research continued searching for a plausible explanation to what was observed in the archaeological context. An intriguing piece of evidence was found in a historic newspaper account:

> In the May 20, 1854, issue of the *Norwich [Connecticut] Courier,* there is the account of an incident that occurred at Jewett [City], a city in that vicinity. About eight years previously, Horace Ray of Griswold had died of consumption. Afterwards, two of his children—grown up sons—died of the same disease, the last one dying about 1852. Not long before the date of the newspaper the same fatal disease had seized another son, whereupon it was determined to exhume the bodies of the two brothers and burn them, because the dead were supposed to feed upon the living; and so long as the dead body in the grave remained undecomposed, either wholly or in part, the surviving members of the family must continue to furnish substance on which the dead body could feed. Acting under the influence of this strange superstition, the family and friends of the deceased proceeded to the burial ground on June 8, 1854, dug up the bodies of the deceased brothers, and burned them on the spot. (Wright 1973)

This account places a New England vampire folk belief in the Griswold area two miles from the Walton

Cemetery just a few years after the time span of the projected death of "JB."

The term "vampire" conjures up images of Dracula, Bram Stoker's fictional character. The reality behind the fiction and the popular cultural manifestations of the vampire are rooted in historic European and American folklore. In this folklore, the vampire was a dead person or spirit who acted in various ways to "drain" the life from the living. To stop these actions, the bodies of supposed vampires were exhumed to look for indications of "life," such as a bloated chest, long fingernails, and blood draining from the mouth. These changes are now known to be the result of postmortem decomposition (Barber 1988; Mann et al. 1990). Deaths resulting from disease epidemics were also blamed on vampires. To stop the epidemic, vampires were sought out and "killed" by various methods (Perkowski 1989).

In nineteenth-century New England, residents of rural areas of Rhode Island, Connecticut, Massachusetts, and Vermont held a belief similar to the European vampire folklore (Stetson 1898; Sledzik and Bellantoni 1994). These New Englanders believed that a deceased tuberculosis victim could return from the dead as a vampire, causing the surviving relatives to "waste away." The actions of the vampire were stopped by exhuming the body of the consumptive and disrupting the corpse in various ways. Numerous historic accounts of this activity indicate that the belief was not uncommon in nineteenth-century New England (see Sledzik and Bellantoni 1994, Table 1).

This interpretation of contagion is consistent with the etiology of tuberculosis. The historic accounts incorporate tuberculosis and examination of the body of the vampire for putative signs of life. Following the death of a family member from tuberculosis (also known as consumption), other family members who became infected began to show signs of tuberculosis infection. The "wasting away" of these family members was attributed to the deceased consumptive, who was returning from the dead to drain the lives of the surviving relatives. To kill the vampire, the corpse was exhumed, and if found undecomposed, the heart was removed and burned. In other circumstances, the corpse was turned face down, burned, or disrupted in other ways.

Based on the historical accounts, actual evidence of the New England vampire folklore should be found in New England cemeteries. The Walton Cemetery contains three pieces of evidence supporting the folklore: (1) the postmortem rearrangement of skeletal elements in Burial 4; (2) paleo-pathological evidence of tuberculosis in this burial; and (3) the historical account of the vampire folk belief from mid-nineteenth-century Griswold, Connecticut, discussed above. We hypothesize that, in the absence of a heart to be burned, the

FIGURE 2   Likely the most interesting discovery at the Walton Cemetery was the grave of this large male. Long before the archaeological salvaging of the grave, the femurs (thigh bones) had been removed from their correct anatomical position and placed crosswise across the deceased's chest. Researchers have solved this mystery through careful historical analysis. (Nick Bellantoni)

apotropaic remedy was to place the bones in a "skull-and-crossbones" arrangement. In support of this hypothesis, we note that decapitation was a common European method of dispatching a dead vampire, and that the Celts and Neolithic Egyptians were known to separate the head from the body, supposedly to prevent the dead from doing harm (Barber 1988).

Among the numerous pathological conditions observed in the skeleton of Burial 4 was evidence of tuberculosis in the second, third, and fourth left ribs. The whitish-gray, pitted lesions were observed on the visceral rib surface near the rib head adjacent to the pleura. The lesions, respectively 30 mm, 35 mm, and 25 mm in length, comprise an area of approximately 30 cm mediolaterally and 45 cm superiorly-inferiorly when considered in anatomical position. The lesions are similar to those described by Kelley and Micozzi

(1984) and Roberts, Lucy, and Manchester (1994) as being associated with primary pulmonary tuberculosis.

The New England vampire folklore is also consistent with modern knowledge of the transmission of tuberculosis. Many of the historic vampire accounts indicate that family members living in close association became infected with the disease before or soon after the death of the "vampire." Tuberculosis is notorious for being transmitted between individuals of different generations living under crowded conditions, a situation common in rural nineteenth-century New England farming communities (Hawke 1988). Seasonal periods of low nutrition and the unsanitary conditions of eighteenth- and nineteenth-century farming compounds increased the opportunity for the transmission of tuberculosis between family members (Clark et al. 1987; Kelley and Eisenberg 1987). Although there is no evidence of tuberculosis in the remaining Walton cemetery skeletons, an 1801 narrative of Griswold history indicates that during the 25 years preceding the account "consumptions have proved to be mortal to a number" (Phillips 1929).

FAMILY RENEWAL AND REBURIAL

Emotional reassurance to descendants and local officials was a critical aspect of the Walton Family Cemetery project, as was the rescue and meticulous documentation of the threatened osteological remains. After confirmation by the state archaeologist that the disturbed burials were in fact in a historic cemetery, the Office of the Chief State Medical Examiner and the Connecticut State Police willingly relinquished their statutory involvement. Similarly, the Town of Griswold's Office of Selectmen appreciated the State Historic Preservation Office's periodic updates as to the rescue archaeology, allowing local officials to respond more effectively to concerned community members. The town's health officer also welcomed the professional coordination and shared osteological knowledge about his community. Keeping community officials properly informed was imperative for establishing a professional working relationship. For instance, the town's health officer concurred with the Office of State Archaeology's evaluation that the cemetery's age obviated modern reinterment requirements for coffins and concrete vaults, the cost of which would have posed significant difficulties for reburial. Adjoining neighbors and local residents were sympathetic to the professional archaeological removal of the burials upon reassurance from the archaeological community that all osteological remains would be reburied.

FIGURE 3   The modern descendants of the Walton family came together to pay their final respects to their historical forebears in the reinterment ceremony held at a local church. (Nick Bellantoni)

As rescue archaeological studies were proceeding, concurrent research in the town land records revealed a 1757 property transfer that associated the cemetery with the Nathaniel Walton family. The state archaeologist, who in Connecticut bears the responsibility for notifying possible descendants, coordinated with the Griswold Historical Society and the Connecticut Genealogical Society to identify surviving relatives of this old New England farming family.

Walton family members were eventually contacted in Massachusetts, New York, Maryland, Nevada, Arkansas, and California. At first, family members were distressed that their historic family burying ground had been disturbed and was further endangered by sand-and-gravel mining. However, as discussions continued, family members came to understand and appreciate that the intent of the Office of State Archaeology was to handle the osteological and cultural remains in a respectful and professional manner, that the family's input was both encouraged and vital, and that the situation offered a rare opportunity to gain insights about their early New England ancestors. Family members volunteered genealogical information, photographs, and even hair samples so that the contemporary genetic record could be compared with ongoing DNA analysis of the skeletal remains.

In the fall of 1992, a reburial ceremony was conducted for the eighteenth- and nineteenth-century Walton family members who had been archaeologically rescued from their historic resting place (Figure 3). Since archival evidence demonstrated that the Walton family had belonged to the First Congregational Church in the Town of Griswold, current church members graciously hosted a reception for Walton relatives who attended from as far away as Nevada. At the invitation of the First Congregational Church, the state archaeologist shared a preliminary analysis of the historic and archaeological data with family, friends, and church members. The Rev. Michael Beynon performed a traditional Puritan recommittal ceremony at the nearby town-owned Hopeville Cemetery. The reburial in this historic cemetery was arranged by the town's First Selectmen. Skeletal remains were arranged according to the archaeological excavation records such that the integrity of rows, body orientation, and relative positions were re-established.

The Walton Cemetery project triggered a number of very sensitive and emotional concerns from a diverse constituency. The property owner, town and state officials, archaeologists, community residents, family members, and religious representatives participated and shared in the decision-making process regarding the respectful removal and subsequent reburial of the Walton family remains. Connecticut statutes provided the administrative guidelines, while the archaeological community offered the sensitivity, diplomacy, and professionalism required for dealing with both the endangered osteological population and their surviving descendants and other interested parties.

REFERENCES

Barber, Paul. 1988. *Vampires, Burial, and Death: Folklore and Reality.* New Haven, Conn.: Yale University Press.

Clark, George A., Marc A. Kelley, J. M. Grane, and M. Cassandra Hill. 1987. "The Evolution of Mycobacterial Disease in Human Populations." *Current Anthropology* 28: 45–51.

Harper, Ross. 1992. "Material Culture Identifications: Walton Family Cemetery." Manuscript on file with Office of State Archaeology, University of Connecticut, Storrs.

Hawke, David F. 1988. *Everyday Life in Early America.* New York: Harper and Row.

Kelley, Marc A., and Leslie E. Eisenberg. 1987. "Blastomycosis and Tuberculosis in Early American Indians: A Biocultural View." *Midcontinental Journal of Archaeology* 12: 89–116.

Kelley, Marc A., and Marc S. Micozzi. 1984. "Rib Lesions and Chronic Pulmonary Tuberculosis." *American Journal of Physical Anthropology* 65: 381–86.

Mann, Robert W., William M. Bass, and Lee Meadows. 1990. "Time since Death and Decomposition of the Human Body: Variables and Observations in Case and Experimental Field Studies." *Journal of Forensic Sciences* 35: 103–111.

McWeeney, Lucinda. 1992. "Walton Family Burial Ground." Report Prepared for the Connecticut Office of State Archaeology. Manuscript on file with Office of State Archaeology, University of Connecticut, Storrs.

Noel Hume, Ivor. 1982. *Martin's Hundred: The Discovery of a Lost Colonial Virginia Settlement.* New York: Dell.

Owsley, Douglas W. 1990. "The Skeletal Biology of North American Historical Populations." In *A Life in Science: Papers in Honor of J. Lawrence Angel,* edited by Jane E. Buikstra, 171–90. Kampsville, Ill.: Center for American Archeology.

Perkowski, Jan L. 1989. *The Darkling: A Treatise on Slavic Vampirism.* Columbus, Ohio: Slavica Publishers.

Phillips, Daniel L. 1918. *Griswold Connecticut Cemeteries: History and Inscriptions 1724–1918.* Unpublished manuscript. Slater Library, Griswold, Connecticut.

——. 1929. *A History, Being a History of the Town of Griswold, Connecticut, from the Earliest Times to the Entrance of Our Country into the World War in 1917.* New Haven, Conn.: Tuttle, Morehouse and Taylor Co.

Roberts, Charlotte, David Lucy, and Keith Manchester. 1994. "Inflammatory Lesions of the Ribs: An Analysis of the Terry Collection." *American Journal of Physical Anthropology* 95: 169–82.

Rumford, Beatrix T. 1965. *The Role of Death as Reflected in the Art and Folkways of the Northeast in the Eighteenth and Nineteenth Centuries.* Master's thesis, State University of New York, Oneonta, New York.

Sledzik, Paul S., and Nicholas F. Bellantoni. 1994. "Bioarchaeological and Biocultural Evidence for the New England Vampire Folk Belief." *American Journal of Physical Anthropology* 94: 269–74.

Sledzik, Paul S., and Peer H. Moore-Jansen. 1991. "Dental Disease in Nineteenth Century Military Skeletal Samples." In *Advances in Dental Anthropology,* edited by Marc A. Kelley and Clark S. Larsen, 215–24. New York: Wiley-Liss.

Stetson, George. 1898. "The Animistic Vampire in New England." *American Anthropologist* 9: 1–13.

Wright, Dudley. 1973. *The Book of Vampires.* New York: Causeway Books.

15

The Homegoing

Michael Alan Park

Mike Park is a biological anthropologist at Central Connecticut State University. He is a prolific writer with a remarkable ability to communicate through his textbooks the important lessons of the discipline to nonanthropologists.

Points to consider when reading this article:

1. Why were the archaeologists concerned that they might not find Henry Opukahaia, even though his grave was marked?

2. How were the skills of archaeology applied in the disinterment of Henry Opukahaia?

3. How were the skills of **forensic anthropology** applied in the disinterment of Henry Opukahaia?

4. How do we know that the archaeologists really found Henry Opukahaia?

We often think of archaeology as taking place in distant and exotic locales. We imagine archaeologists spending years searching for lost cities, cutting narrow trails through tropical jungles, and revealing the vine-encrusted steps of long forgotten temples.

Stereotypes generally do have some truth at their core. Some archaeologists do, indeed, search for years for their prehistoric quarry in locations distant from their homes or universities. However, the roles played by archaeologists, biological anthropologists, and anthropologists in general, are many and diverse—often incredibly so. My friend, colleague, and sometimes co-author Mike Park is a biological anthropologist whose dissertation research was not focused on the ancient hominids of Africa or the genetic analysis of a tribe of South American Indians. Mike's research and Ph.D. dissertation focused, instead, on the fingerprints of members of a religious commune in western Canada, the Hutterites.

With his expertise in biological anthropology, Mike was called in to assist on a project even closer to home. In this instance the "site" was never lost in the first place and was just a short car ride from Mike's house. The combined skills of the archaeologist, who excavated the site, and the biological anthropologist allowed for a long overdue "homegoing."

On a hot July afternoon in 1993, I found myself standing over an open grave in a peaceful hillside cemetery in the small Connecticut town of Cornwall—waiting for a colleague to unearth the remains of a native Hawaiian who had lain interred there for 175 years.

A few weeks before, Nick Bellantoni, the Connecticut state archaeologist, had phoned me with a fascinating story, one I had never heard, although I had lived in the state for twenty years. In 1808, a sixteen-year-old Hawaiian named Opukahaia (Oh-poo-kah-hah-EE-ah) escaped the tribal warfare that had killed his parents

and younger brother—reportedly before his eyes—by becoming the cabin boy aboard a Yankee sailing ship, the *Triumph*. Two years later, sailing by way of China and the West Indies, he landed in Connecticut where he was taken under the care of the president of Yale University. He learned English, took the name Henry, and converted to Christianity, becoming a Congregationalist. He is said to be the first Christian Hawaiian. In 1817 he helped build a missionary school in Cornwall. His dream was to return to Hawaii (then known as the Sandwich Islands) and bring his new faith to his people.

Henry's dream was never realized. On February 17, 1818, at the age of twenty-six, he died during a typhoid fever epidemic that swept through Connecticut. His vision, however, helped inspire the missionary move-

Published here with permission of the author.

ment that would profoundly change the history of the Hawaiian Islands—including a role in their annexation by the United States in 1898. Henry's grave in Cornwall became a shrine both for the people of his adopted town and for visiting Hawaiians, who would leave offerings on his headstone. The inscription on the stone reads: "Oh, how I want to see Hawaii! But I think I never shall—God will do right. He knows what is best."

Then, in the fall of 1992, Deborah Liikapeka Lee, a descendant of Henry's family, awoke from a dream convinced that Henry wanted to return to his homeland. A family association garnered the necessary funds and legal documents, and the next summer Henry's "homegoing" took place. And this is where anthropology comes in.

Old New England cemeteries vary in the precise placement of headstones relative to the bodies beneath them. Moreover, the acidic, often wet New England soil is unkind to organic remains. The recovery, removal, and accurate identification of whatever remained of Henry Opukahaia required the methodologies of archaeology and forensic anthropology. Nick wanted my help with the latter—making sure anything recovered was indeed Henry. He also wanted my help, it turned out, in moving several tons of stone.

First in 1818, and then with modifications later, Henry's tomb had been carefully and lovingly assembled by the people of Cornwall's Congregational Church. They had placed a large horizontal headstone or ledger (the only one of its kind in the cemetery) on a pedestal of fieldstones and mortar several feet high. When we arrived, the headstone was covered by offerings—shells, flowers, candy, and coins. We removed and boxed these and then carefully separated the stone from the pedestal, locking it away in the cemetery sexton's tool shed. We dismantled the pedestal, carefully labeling and diagramming the position of each stone because the portion of the tomb above ground was to be rebuilt by a stone mason. Under the pedestal, and going down about 3 feet into the ground, we uncovered, as we dug, three more layers of fieldstones that acted as a foundation for the monument above and as protection for the coffin and remains we hoped were still below. All the stones were removed, labeled, and set aside. When we were into a layer of sandy soil about 52 inches down, Nick worked alone in the excavated pit, delicately scraping away the dirt inch by inch with a trowel and a brush.

Late on the second day of our excavation, a dark stain became visible in the soil. The wooden coffin itself had long since decayed, but the dark shadow of its six-sided outline could be seen. At that point we began to despair of finding much else. Indeed, the Hartford funeral home that was to prepare the remains for reburial had provided us only with a metal container about the size of a single file cabinet drawer. The family had been cautioned not to expect much.

But then something truly exciting came to light. It was a small portion of the wooden coffin lid, preserved (even to the inclusion of some black paint) possibly by the action of metals from the brass tacks that had been driven into it in the shape of a heart. This was not an uncommon practice for that time period in New England. Inside the heart shape, more tacks spelled out "H.O.," "ae" (from a Latin phrase for "age at the completion of life"), and the numerals "26"—Henry's initials and age at death. After another hour of careful scraping and brushing, Nick's trowel grazed something hard, and within a few minutes the apparent remains of Henry Opukahaia saw the light of day for the first time in 175 years.

To our surprise, the skeleton was virtually complete. The elaborately constructed tomb and the sandy soil with good drainage had kept the bones dry enough for excellent preservation. Apparently, a regular coffin was going to be needed for Henry's eventual reburial after all.

Nick carefully freed each bone from the soil and identified it as he handed it up to me (Figure 1). I confirmed the identification, and the bone was checked off by one of our colleagues from a list of the 206 bones of the normal adult human skeleton. Each bone was wrapped in acid-free paper to prevent any surface damage and then placed in the metal box, which barely managed to accommodate all the bones. We all worked with surgical gloves because harmful pathogens have been known to persist even in old remains, and Henry had died of an infectious disease. (Later in our investigation we ran out of gloves and ignored the caution, but with no ill effects.)

Everything to this point clearly indicated we had recovered Henry's bones, but verification was still necessary. As we identified, recorded, and wrapped each bone, we compared important diagnostic bones with what we knew of Henry from written descriptions and a single drawn portrait. The skeleton was clearly that of a male and, at least at my brief first glance, seemed to conform to that of a person in his late twenties. Henry had been described as being "a little under six feet." We did not have precision measuring instruments with us in the field, but using my own six-foot-one stature as a gauge, I held several of the arm and leg bones up to my limbs and guessed that they belonged to someone a few inches shorter.

As Nick brushed the dirt away from the skull (saving it for last), the face of Henry Opukahaia emerged—the very image of his portrait. The skeleton is more

FIGURE 1 Biological anthropologist Michael Park is handed one of Henry Opukahaia's bones by forensic archaeologist Nick Bellantoni. Together, the work of biological anthropology and forensic archaeology helped in the task of bringing Henry Opukahaia home. (Courtesy William F. Keegan)

than just a bony foundation for the body's soft tissues. The bones themselves are living tissue, connected in many ways to muscles, blood vessels, nerves, and skin. The shape of the outer body is reflected in the skeleton, and vice versa. With training, one can "see" the face of a person in the bony visage of the skull. The skull in the grave, with its prominent nose, high forehead, and heavy, squared jaw was clearly that of the man in the portrait.

We spent two more days with Henry, this time in the garage of the Hartford funeral home. With the bones laid out in anatomical orientation on a gurney, we were able to conduct a more thorough scientific analysis, cleaning, photographing, measuring, and describing the bones. The family graciously gave us their blessing to do this.

Henry's skeleton was indeed surprisingly complete. The only bones missing were the hyoid, a horseshoe-shaped bone in the throat, and five finger bones. The coccyx (tail bone) and xyphoid process (the pointy bone at the bottom of the breastbone) were badly decomposed and identifiable only by the place in which we found them relative to the other bones. Other than

that, the only damage was some deterioration of the back and underside of the skull and to some of the cervical (neck) vertebrae. We hypothesized that Henry's head may have been laid on a pillow, which retained moisture that speeded decomposition.

The size and robusticity of the bones (as well as the perfect match with the portrait) all identified the skeleton as that of a male. The cranium had the typical male traits of brow ridges, a sloped forehead, a protruding, square chin, and rounded upper borders on the eye sockets. The angle at the back of the jaw (the gonial angle) was about 120 degrees — relatively large for males, who more typically have angles close to 90 degrees — and the mastoids (the bony humps behind the ears) were small for a male.

The pelvis, however, was unequivocally male. Essentially, everything about a female pelvis is wide and broad (an obvious adaptation to pregnancy and childbirth), whereas corresponding features of a male pelvis are narrow. The pelvis before us was as good and as typical an example of a male pelvis as any of us had seen.

There are several skeletal traits used to determine age at death. They are all based on changes that take place with regularity in the development of portions of the bones. The latest change that has *already* taken place, and the next change in the chronological order that has *yet* to take place, mark the minimum and maximum age at which the individual died. In Henry's case, the ends of all the long bones, which initially develop separately from the shafts, were almost all completely fused to form a single bone. The exceptions were the crest of the pelvis and the end of the collar bone where it meets the breastbone. Fusion was still taking place at these sites. This indicated an age at death of between eighteen and thirty.

The internal surfaces of the pubic bones (where the pelvic bones meet in front) change appearance at different ages. Henry's matched the standard for an average age of twenty-eight. Similarly, the front ends of the ribs undergo regular changes, and Henry's indicated an age range of nineteen to thirty-three, with a mean of 25.9. All these data coincided well with his documented age at death of twenty-six.

Traditionally, the closure of the cranial sutures has been used as a common method of determining age at death. It is based on the fact that the cranial vault begins as four separate bones that fuse, along suture lines, at certain ages. The method, however, has fallen from favor because there is too much individual variation. Henry's sutures were a case in point. At twenty-six all his major suture lines should have been open or in the process of fusing. In fact, they had all prematurely closed. Some sites were completely obliterated, a condition only seen in the very elderly. There is no indication why this occurred in Henry, nor is there any evidence that it caused any problems sometimes related to premature closure, such as cranial deformation.

There are a number of formulas for estimating overall stature from the measurement of one of the major long bones. Applying four of these to Henry's skeleton gave us an average stature estimate of five-foot-eight—a bit shorter than "a little under six feet"—but these estimates do not take into complete account differences in individual proportions. Henry could have been a bit taller than these calculations indicate.

Henry's skeleton displayed only a few abnormalities. The joint where his jaw met his cranium (the temporomandibular joint) was oddly shaped and noticeably worn. He may well have had some discomfort at this joint during his life. Both hip joints, where the femur articulates with the pelvis, were also oddly shaped, but here there was no indication that this condition caused him any pain or malfunction. Both joints were similarly shaped, and there were no other abnormalities of the bones involved.

Henry's right ribs, numbers 3 through 10, however, showed a striking and very noteworthy condition. On the inside surface between the head of the ribs, where they attach to the vertebral column, and at the angle where they curve toward the front of the body, we observed an ashy, porous texture. On rib 7, this abnormal texture was 44 mm long. This condition is called osteomyelitis, and it occurs in about one percent of cases of typhoid fever, usually in precisely the area where we observed it on Henry's ribs. In the midst of our scientific investigation, this observation served to remind us of the nature of the subject of our study—another human being whom we had come, in only a few days, to know very well indeed.

Toward the end of our analysis, a coffin arrived from Hawaii. It was a fairly plain wooden box but was covered in a layer of koa wood, which is native to the islands. The family requested that we lay out Henry's bones in the coffin in correct anatomical orientation. To do this we lined the bottom of the coffin with heavy foam rubber into which we cut spaces to hold each bone. The family kindly agreed to let us place the wrist, finger, ankle, and toe bones together in four bundles at the ends of the arms and legs. Cutting individual spaces for all those bones would have been quite time consuming.

The following Sunday about 200 people, including those of us who had helped exhume Henry's remains, gathered at the Congregational Church in Cornwall for a "homegoing" celebration. A local Congregational minister, himself a native Hawaiian, spoke over Henry's coffin, which was surrounded by ti leaves, flower and yarn leis, and bouquets of anthuriums. Henry's portrait faced the congregation. The next day Henry Opukahaia was flown home to Hawaii, taken by canoe to Kealakekua Bay on the "Big Island" where he had first boarded the *Triumph* in 1808, and, finally, buried in a cemetery overlooking the bay.

Except for two days of labor under the hot summer sun (and perhaps cutting those spaces in the foam rubber), this was not a particularly difficult endeavor. The archaeological and forensic applications and analyses were fairly straightforward. But in the Cornwall church that Sunday, as we lined up in front of Henry's coffin for photos and the family warmly thanked us for our help, I knew this was one of the most rewarding bits of anthropology I would ever participate in.

Note: Thanks to Nick Bellantoni for including me in the project, and for jogging my memory on some of the details for this article.

I AM AN ARCHAEOLOGIST

Warren Perry

(Photo by Arthur Simoes)

Growing up in the south Bronx of New York City during the 1940s and '50s, my primary concern was survival. In my little corner of the universe, practical issues dominated my early years—staying out of jail, staying alive. I dropped out of high school to support my wife and children, and I joined the military. During this period, I lost my wife to drugs.

After being discharged, I used my GI Bill to attend Bronx Community College where I majored in history, with a specialization in African Americans. (There were no course offerings in anthropology at Bronx Community College.)

Upon graduation I won a Ford Foundation Scholarship for minorities and enrolled at New York University. I came to New York University as an older, nontraditional African American student, and a single parent. I was quite dissatisfied with the history department's neglect of African American studies and studies of people of color in general.

My first encounter with anthropology and archaeology occurred as an undergraduate at New York University during the 1970s. I clearly recall this huge class for introduction to anthropology—more than one hundred people in a large lecture hall. I found the lectures too technical and difficult to follow, but the readings—wow! I learned about human evolution and concepts such as holism, ethnocentrism, and the like. More important, I was introduced to both past and present peoples and cultures I had never imagined. I had assumed that industrial drudgery had always existed everywhere. This course provided insights into the human species and deeper understanding of things that are fundamental to all humans through time and across space. Books such as Evans-Pritchard's *The Nuer,* Conrad Arensberg's *The Irish Countryman,* Brian Fagan's *Men of the Earth,* and Robin Fox's *Kinship and Marriage* revealed different ways to see and understand human social relations and community organizational principles. My desire for a genuine understanding of humans in all their diversity was inflamed.

I began to enroll in other anthropology classes. In physical/biological anthropology I learned how we became human and developed culture, language, and society. In anthropological linguistics I learned of the diversity of human languages and how languages are related historically and how they change through time. In archaeology I learned about the diverse kinds of ancient peoples and cultures and societies that existed globally.

Although I was intrigued by all the subfields of anthropology, for me archaeology provided the perfect balance of physical and intellectual labor. Furthermore, I became aware that there were virtually no archaeologists of color in the discipline. This was evident in the absence of an African American archaeology and the absence of a non-Western perspective in interpreting the archaeological record (materials and sites). Over time it also became apparent to me that the analysis

and interpretation of archaeological materials was dependent on the questions archaeologists ask, and this, in turn, depends on their theoretical position. I felt that I could contribute to an understanding of the past by raising questions and concerns of the heretofore marginalized voices of African Americans. This inspired me to pursue studies of African and African American archaeology and history; class and state formation and social inequality; theories of power, class, race, gender, and ethnicity; and ideological influences on archaeological interpretation. These research questions are now the focus of my work.

After completing my B.A. in anthropology from New York University, I went on to receive my M.A. in anthropology from Hunter College, City University of New York, and my Ph.D. in anthropology with a specialization in archaeology from the Graduate School and University Center, City University of New York.

Today I possess rare credentials for any archaeologist. I am one of only four African Americans in the United States with a Ph.D. in archaeology and one of only a few archaeologists of any nationality with expertise in African and African American archaeology.

The geographic focus of my work is Africa and the African diaspora in the Americas. I have conducted research in historical archaeology in both southern Africa and the United States, focusing on the impact of colonialism and capital penetration and forms of resistance to these processes. As well, I have interests in diversity issues and multicultural education.

I am currently an assistant professor of anthropology at Central Connecticut State University. I teach courses in African Archaeology, African American Archaeology, Dimensions of Diversity and Inequality, General Introductory Anthropology (four field), Historical Archaeology, Introduction to Archaeology, Peoples and Cultures of Africa, Archaeology of the State, and Urban Archaeology. In my capacity as a teacher I try to present these issues both enthusiastically and passionately.

As associate director of archaeology for the African Burial Ground Project in New York City, under a grant from the United States General Services Administration, I am engaged in analyzing the archaeological materials from this eighteenth-century cemetery, which contained 427 bodies and the artifacts (personal possessions) of the first generation of African captives in New York City. My responsibilities include analysis and interpretation of site stratigraphy; horizontal and vertical mapping; artifact identification, distribution, and significance; and coordination of other project consultants and staff. I am also responsible for producing a bibliography of relevant mortuary sites as well as preparation of a final report.

The African Burial Ground Project includes both national and international research teams of natural and social scientists from Africa and the United States who have expertise in the African diaspora. In addition, the project has an Office of Public Education and Interpretation (OPEI). OPEI's primary roles are to inform the public on and involve them in the research.

The research for the African Burial Ground Project is being conducted primarily at the Foley Square archaeological laboratory in New York City, at the biological/physical anthropology laboratory at Howard University in Washington, D.C., and at Central Connecticut State University.

Activist archaeologists involved in this project must publish articles about their research in both academic and public forums. In addition to writing about the African Burial Ground Project, I continue to write about my research in southern Africa.

As an African American scholar, I have come to recognize that an active commitment to teaching and to students does not end in the classroom. It entails obligations beyond the academy, expanding into the community and into the social institutions of the surrounding society. For example, one of my professional missions is to interest and recruit minority students into anthropology and archaeology. In a shrinking world riddled by racial intolerance, all people have a special need to develop a sensitivity to the majority of the world's cultures. We need to understand the prevalence of institutionalized racism and the historical contexts that contribute to the maintenance of these conditions. Teachers of color can facilitate this awareness and also provide the added benefit of serving as role models for "minority" students and white students as well. I believe that anthropologists can make our special knowledge public through public lectures, skills training for community people, and local and public appearances that forge relationships between educators and communities.

I am involved in a number of local anthropological and archaeological research projects in the United States, Africa, and the Caribbean that have to do with African diasporic studies and that involve the local communities. Community engagement is crucial for public accessibility to academic skills and knowledge, and for accountability and responsibility of educators to the communities they serve. It is gratifying to be involved in the exciting challenges of bridging my community work with scholarly research and teaching, and to know that I have been able to provide new research and career opportunities for my students and the communities that I serve. I love my job as an archaeologist and would not want to do anything else.

PART 3

A Useful Past:
Archaeology in the Modern World

In the introduction to this reader I commented on the commonly held belief that archaeology is arcane or esoteric, with no real-world applications. In the standard stereotype archaeologists are globetrotting vagabonds who search for ancient treasure and loot fabulous tombs of their artifacts. There is no real-world use for this kind of nonsense, although it makes for entertaining theater. In reality, the vast majority of what archaeologists excavate isn't "treasure" in the ordinary sense of that term. King Tut tombs and Priam Treasures are few and far between. Instead, most of what we dig up is garbage in the literal sense: food remains, waste products from manufacturing processes (for example, unusable flakes of stone produced when stone tools are made), or broken bits of tools that have been used up and worn out. Most of what we dig up is not treasure at all but stuff ancient people cared so little about that they simply tossed it on the ground, in a trash pit, or on a pile of other garbage.

Beyond the mundane nature of the vast majority of material archaeologists regularly excavate, it should be added that much of this material has not been intentionally hidden away by ancient people. Most of what we excavate are objects that have simply been abandoned and subsequently covered up through any combination of some entirely natural processes. **Alluviation,** the deposition of silt by flooding rivers, and soil formation through organic decay are two such natural processes. One glib, rather unromantic, but not inaccurate definition describes archaeology as "the study of other people's garbage." It is crucial to point out, however, that this stuff of everyday existence, this "garbage," is enormously important precisely for what it is — it is the direct material evidence of common everyday life in the ancient past.

Archaeologists focus on the **material remains** of human behavior, whether those material remains are fabulous works of art destined for museum cases or the desiccated, preserved remnants of ancient human feces. Both of these objects — and everything in between — represent sources of information about ancient humanity and are of great scientific value or significance. Archaeologists spend a not inconsiderable proportion of our time and energy devising methods for finding and recovering such material evidence and, especially, for analyzing these remains for any insights they can provide about the behavior and histories of our ancestors.

This focus on other people's garbage puts archaeologists in a unique position to make a significant contribution to the issues that surround our own *modern* refuse and its disposal. Why is that important? Trash and trash disposal are major issues facing the modern world. Cities and towns across the country have established recycling programs for consumer waste, and the location of new disposal sites is hotly debated. More than any other discipline, archaeology has developed and refined the analytical tools needed for the study of garbage. So when it comes to collecting and analyzing data about modern trash disposal, recycling, landfills, trash dumps, and biodegradability, it should come as no surprise that archaeologists trained to study ancient trash have led the way in the study of modern garbage. The newly minted science of **garbology** is peopled by scientists who, for the most part, have been trained as archaeologists.

Much of what constitutes the **archaeological record** — the garbage of ancient people — reflects directly on the technology of past peoples. Ancient people made tools, weapons, items of adornment, and so forth, and applied their technological skills when making these objects. In an effort to better understand the technological capabilities of the ancient people being studied, archaeologists become expert in these ancient technologies, learning to fire pots, smelt metals, and make stone tools just as people did in the past. Remarkably, there are instances in which ancient people solved technological riddles or developed specific strategies for manipulating their world that can provide us with practical solutions or strategies that work better than our modern approaches. In presenting "A Useful Past," I have also included articles that discuss the practical application of ancient technologies or approaches revealed through archaeological analysis.

16

Food Waste Behavior in an Urban Population

Gail G. Harrison, William L. Rathje, and Wilson W. Hughes

Gail Harrison is an expert in human nutrition and the chair of the Department of Community Health Services at the University of California at Los Angeles. Formerly, she was associated with the University of Arizona College of Medicine, Department of Family and Community Medicine.

William Rathje is a well-known archaeologist who has written extensively on the Maya civilization. He also is the founder and director of the Garbage Project. He is, in a word, Mr. Garbology.

Wilson Hughes is the co-director and one of the original members of the Garbage Project.

Points to consider when reading this article:

1. How were the data collected for the analysis of food waste?

2. The authors call trash "nonreactive." What does that mean, and what is the advantage of a nonreactive data set?

3. About how much food waste was generated by each family in Tucson for each year of the study?

4. How is what Harrison, Rathje, and Hughes do considered archaeology?

Archaeology has been defined as the study of "other people's garbage." In at least one sense, however, this is too limiting a definition. Why should we restrict ourselves to "other people"? Archaeology is also defined as the study of the material remains of human behavior. This broader definition imposes fewer limits; here, archaeologists are not restricted to any time period in particular, or to any specific cultures. In fact, by this definition, we can conduct an archaeology of 2.5-million-year-old human ancestors in Africa, 10,000-year-old Native American hunting camps, 5,000-year-old Meso-potamian city-states, seventeenth-century Pilgrim settlements, the abandoned trash dump in your town, and even the garbage resting at the bottom of your trash can. And people do conduct archaeology at each of these kinds of sites.

Many of our modern problems relate to food and other resource shortages in some parts of the world while, ironically, other areas are beset with problems related to an overabundance of material wealth (and what to do with all that stuff when it's used up). It should not be surprising that the expertise of archaeologists has been called on to address the issue of garbage, which is, after all, our database, regardless of how old — or young (and whether it still smells bad or not). Archaeologist William Rathje is the long-time director of the best known attempt to apply archaeological research to the modern world. The insights provided by his project have significant implications for debates about recycling, waste toxicity, and the environmental impacts of disposable versus reusable diapers and styrofoam drinking cups (this research was even quoted in a pamphlet distributed by McDonald's Corporation a few years back).

From *Journal of Nutrition Education*, vol. 7, no. 1, 1975. Reprinted with permission of the Society for Nutritional Education.

Growing awareness of the finite limits of natural resources under the pressure of an exploding population has made it necessary to look at human utilization of food resources in a new light. The concept of efficiency—ecological and economic—has assumed a new priority in nutrition policy and planning. At the household level, economic inflation has made efficient use of food resources more obviously important to more consumers than it has been in the past.

Recent analyses of the U.S. food production system[1,2] have made it clear that food production in this country is extremely energy-intensive, and that the U.S. food system is reaching the point at which further investments of energy-intensive technology may produce only marginal increments in output. Notably absent from such analyses, however, is an evaluation of the extent, nature, and effects of food waste. No doubt some waste of food is inevitable in any system of production, distribution, and consumption, but little is known about how much waste of food takes place, why, or how much might be avoided.

Food waste in the field and in storage and transportation has been recognized as a significant factor in affecting the availability of food supplies.[3] It has been estimated that up to 40% of the total grain crop in some areas of the developing world may be lost through spoilage or other damage in the field, in storage, and in handling and processing. Opinion varies as to the potential for reducing such losses.[4]

Food waste at the household or consumer level has been studied even less. The fact that household food waste in industrialized countries is substantial has been often remarked upon but seldom documented. The U.S. Department of Agriculture, which conducts household food consumption surveys in the United States, has long recognized the need for reliable data on food waste. In the late 1950s, USDA undertook some studies of household food waste using records of weighed food waste kept by volunteer respondents.[5] These studies utilized small, nonrepresentative samples, and the authors noted that the behavior of the respondents was changed by participation in the study. Even so, caloric loss from waste of household food supplies in these studies ranged from 7 to 10% of total calories.[6]

A problem in studying food waste is that the concept of waste is fraught with moral implications in our culture. Few Americans like to admit that they unnecessarily waste food, and mere participation in a study of waste behavior is sure to bias results. What is needed, then, is a **nonreactive** measure—a means of estimating food waste which does not affect the behavior of the subjects.[7] We propose that the methods of archaeology may be useful in this context.

HOUSEHOLD REFUSE AS A NONREACTIVE MEASURE OF BEHAVIOR

The Garbage Project of the University of Arizona has been studying household refuse in Tucson, Ariz., for two years. The project is archaeological in background, theory, and method. Archaeologists have traditionally studied refuse and the remains of material culture in order to make inferences about ancient civilizations—their ways of life, social structures, and utilization of the environment. The Garbage Project is based on the assumption that the methods and theory of archaeology may offer useful perspectives for dealing with contemporary problems of resource utilization.[8]

The project is accumulating data on a wide variety of resource management behaviors including recycling behavior and purchase of food, drugs, household and personal sanitation items, and other consumables. As a method for studying food utilization patterns and waste behavior, the study of household refuse offers two significant advantages.

First, it is a nonreactive measure of behavior. What goes into the trash can is evidence of behavior which has already occurred. It is the evidence of what people *did*, not what they *think* they did, what they think they should have done, or what they think the interviewer thinks they should have done. In this way, the study of household refuse differs from accepted methods of collecting data on household-level food consumption patterns,[9,10] all of which suffer from problems of **reactivity**—distortion of the behavior itself or the recall of the behavior.

The study of household refuse has its own, but different, limitations as a measure of food utilization patterns. In no way can the evidence of food input to the household, as reflected by packaging or other items in the garbage, be used as a measure of nutritional adequacy or of quantitative consumption of food by the individual household. Garbage disposals, meals eaten away from home, feeding of leftover food to household pets, fireplaces, compost piles, and recycling of containers all introduce biases into the data acquired from the trash can. However, these biases all operate in one direction—they decrease the amount of refuse. Thus garbage data can confidently be interpreted as representing *minimum* levels of household food utilization and waste. On this basis, population segments can be compared and changes over time observed.

A second major advantage to the study of household refuse is that it is inexpensive, relatively easy to do, and requires no time or active cooperation on the part of the subjects. The logistics of a study of household refuse should not be minimized (the Garbage Project requires the efforts of a full-time field supervisor, even at present sample size), but compared to other methods of monitoring food consumption and nutritional behavior, to which the study of refuse may offer a supplement, the study of household refuse is relatively simple. Data collection can be accomplished by workers with relatively little previous training; and there is little need for special equipment or facilities. This is a major departure from traditional epidemiological methods which usually demand a high level of subject input.[11] As a result, household refuse may be studied in a community on an ongoing basis or at frequent intervals in order to detect short-range changes in food utilization behavior.

METHODOLOGY

The Sample

The city of Tucson is an urban community of slightly under 450,000 inhabitants located in southern Arizona. It is characterized by rapid growth in population. The two major ethnic groups are Anglos (whites) and Mexican-Americans, with the latter comprising 27.1 percent of the population in 1973; the proportion of elderly individuals is relatively high, with 12% of the population aged 65 or over.[12]

The sampling unit for the Garbage Project was the census tract. Tucson's 66 urban census tracts were grouped into seven clusters derived from 1970 federal census demographic and housing characteristics. Factor analysis was used to derive groups of significantly associated census variables, and cluster analysis was then used to order census tracts into clusters based on their association with these derived factors of census variables.[13] Data from 13 census tracts in 1973 and 19 in 1974, drawn to be representative of the seven census tract clusters identified by statistical analysis of the data, form the basis for this report.

Data Collection

Refuse was collected for the project by Tucson Sanitation Department personnel from two randomly selected households within each sample census tract, biweekly in 1973 and weekly in 1974. Refuse was collected for a four-month period (February through May) in 1973 and again for the same period in 1974. Addresses were not recorded, in order to protect the privacy and anonymity of sampled households. Specific households were not followed over time; that is, a new random selection of households was done each time refuse was collected. Data from all collections in a given census tract were pooled; thus data analysis is based on the census tract as the unit sampled. Total refuse studied includes the equivalent of that from 222 households in 1973 and 350 in 1974. Households were not informed that their garbage was being studied, although there was local newspaper, radio, and television publicity on the project at frequent intervals with emphasis on procedures taken to protect the anonymity of sampled households. Thus far community reaction to the project has been overwhelmingly supportive.

Fifty student volunteers sorted, coded, and recorded the items in the refuse working at tables provided in the Sanitation Department maintenance yard. After sorting and recording, all items in the refuse were returned to the Sanitation Department for deposit in the sanitary landfill. While the students were not paid for their participation in the project, they had the option of receiving academic credit for archaeological field experience, since they gained experience with the methods and theory of field archaeology while working on the project. Student workers were provided with lab coats, surgical masks, and gloves, and were given appropriate immunizations. In almost three years of the project's operation, there have been no illnesses attributable to garbage work.

Items found in the refuse were sorted into 133 categories of food, drugs, personal and household sanitation products, amusement and entertainment items, communications, and pet-related materials. For each item, the following information was recorded onto precoded forms: Item code; type (e.g., "ground chuck" as a type of "beef"); weight, as derived from labeling; cost; material composition of the container; brand; and weight of any waste. Fifty-two of the category codes referred to food items.

Waste was defined as any once-edible food item except for chunks of meat fat. Bone was not included, nor were eggshells, banana or citrus peel, or other plant parts not usually deemed edible. Food waste was further classified into two categories: *straight waste* of a significant quantity of any item (for example, a whole uncooked steak, half a loaf of bread, several tortillas), and *plate scrapings*, which represent edible food but which occur in quantities of less than one ounce or are the unidentifiable remains of cooked dishes. Potato peels were classified separately, and are not included in "straight waste" for purposes of this paper. It is our guess (yet to be investigated) that "straight waste" may be more susceptible to directed change than is the type of waste we have classified as "plate scrapings."

For purposes of this report, the total weight of a given food item coming into sampled households, as derived from labeling on associated packaging materials which are discarded into the trash can, is termed "input" of that food item. It must be kept in mind that these "input" figures are minimal, and their deviation from actual household food utilization of a type of food item is variable depending on the characteristics of the given households sampled.

RESULTS AND DISCUSSION

The following data summarize the evidence of food utilization and waste patterns for the entire sample for the time period specified. (Analysis of the data according to the socioeconomic characteristics of the individual census tracts is presented elsewhere.[14])

1. The refuse analyzed showed that sampled households waste a significant proportion of their food resources. In 1973, 9.7% of the total food input, by weight, was wasted; in 1974, 8.9% was wasted. (The downward trend was not statistically significant.) Actual waste, of course, was higher since 21.3% of the households in sampled census tracts have garbage disposals in good working order[12] and probably grind up a great deal of their food waste. We are currently undertaking a study which will allow us to estimate the effect of differential use of garbage disposals on the food waste found in garbage cans. These data on waste do not include milk or other beverages, since beverage waste usually goes down the drain; thus, weight of beverages including milk was eliminated from the input figures for calculation of the above percentages.

2. In 1973, straight waste accounted for 55.3% of the food waste and in 1974 it totaled 60.6%. (The change is statistically significant at p <.001 using the difference-of-proportions test described by Blalock.[15]) Thus although the percentage of total food wasted remained stable from 1973 to 1974, the percentage of straight waste versus "plate scrapings" increased significantly.

3. There were some changes between 1973 and 1974 in evidence of utilization and waste of specific food groups (see Tables 1 and 2). The total input of meat, poultry, and fish was significantly smaller in 1974 than in 1973 (normalized to the same sample size). The percentage of these animal protein foods which was wasted (total waste/total evidence of input, by weight) showed a sharp and statistically significant drop from 12% in 1973 to less than 4% in 1974, mainly due to a decline in the rate of waste of beef from 9% in 1973 to 3% in 1974. We find this interesting for two reasons. One is that the high 9% waste of beef occurred during the beef shortage in the spring of 1973. It is possible that during the shortage consumers were overbuying or purchas-

ing unfamiliar cuts or quantities which could not be used efficiently. The change in beef waste is also interesting since there was front-page local newspaper coverage of the Garbage Project, reporting the high level of beef waste (and only beef was mentioned) just at the start of the 1974 data collection period. We don't know whether the publicity had any effect on waste behavior but believe that controlled investigations should be carried out to determine whether heightened awareness of waste behavior could have any effect on actual behavior.

Vegetable input decreased between 1973 and 1974 (again, normalized to the same sample size), but vegetable and fruit waste increased. Waste of fresh vegetables accounted for most of the increase. In both years, vegetable and fruit waste made up a larger percentage of straight waste than of the evidence of household input of food. Input of grain products increased from 1973 to 1974, but proportional waste of grain products decreased. In both years, grain products made up a larger percentage of straight waste than of evidence of household input, the waste being for the most part due to waste of bread.

Sweets and packaged foods in both years made up a smaller percentage of straight waste than of household input. Perhaps the most remarkable change in input occurred in packaged and convenience foods: TV dinners, take-out meals, canned stews, soups, and sauces. Evidence of household input of these items increased by over 30% between 1973 and 1974. The only explanation we can offer is to point out that the percentage of households in Arizona in which two persons held jobs increased sharply in the same period from 14% in November 1973 to 21% in March 1974. With more households with two adults in the labor force, the consumption of convenience foods might be expected to rise.

4. The cost of the food waste we observed is high. Extrapolating average household waste (total food waste, divided by the number of household equivalents in the sample) over a full year and figuring at June 1974 prices, Tucson's annual food waste bill may run between 9 and 11 million dollars. For an average household over a year, the cost of waste was between $80 and $100 of edible food (see Table 3). The biggest contributors to the cost of waste were beef and other meats (in spite of the decline in waste, beef waste is expensive), cheese, fresh vegetables and fruits, take-out meals, bread, and pastry.

Extrapolating from our data to the estimated 110,000 households in Tucson, we estimate that

TABLE 1   Item Percentage of Total Household Input Evidence and Waste

	1973		1974	
Item	% of total input evidence	% of waste—excluding leftovers	% of total input evidence	% of waste—excluding leftovers
Selected protein foods*	19.56	21.74	18.50	11.84
Vegetables	24.40	34.77	19.85	38.62
Fruits	13.64	14.25	15.26	17.26
Grain products	11.23	14.68	14.8	15.8
Packaged goods	4.53	4.28	7.41	5.89
Sugar and sweets	10.10	5.74	9.72	6.55
Other	16.54	4.64	14.46	14.04

*Meat, fish, poultry, eggs, cheese, and nuts.

TABLE 2   Percent of Food Items Wasted*

	Percent of item wasted	
Item	1973	1974
Selected protein foods (meat, fish, poultry, cheese, and nuts)	12.09	3.44**
Vegetables	7.65	10.47**
Fruits	5.61	6.09**
Grain products (excluding pies, cakes, and other sweet pastries)	7.02	5.73
Packaged foods (TV dinners, take-out meals, packaged soups, stews and sauces)	4.96	4.28
Baby foods	3.01	2.42
Fats and oils	1.39	1.08
Dairy (excluding liquid milk)	.92	.73
Spices	.77	4.49
Dips, whips	4.07	1.54
Sugar and sweets (including sweet pastries)	3.04	3.63

*Waste (weight) as percent of total input (weight).
**Significantly different from 1973 value at p <.05.

Tucson was likely to throw out 9,538 tons of edible food in 1974. It may be easier to grasp the significance of this waste if we focus on one item. The average sample household threw away 1.5 ounces of meat, fish or poultry (straight waste) in each garbage collection. That comes to 5.1 tons each time the garbage is collected in Tucson, which is twice a week. Using 1965 USDA data, we can estimate that a two-person urban household may consume about 9.4 pounds of meat, poultry, and fish each week.[16] Tucson's waste in one week would provide a week's worth of meat, poultry or fish for over 2000 such households or a year's worth for 42 two-person households.

5. The quantitative estimates of food input to households derived from packaging materials in the garbage are similar to the quantitative estimates of food consumption for similar households achieved by the USDA household food consumption surveys.[16] If we extrapolate for a year from the evidence of food input by weight in the average Garbage Project sample household, we estimate that the food input in our sample averaged 1.069 tons of food per household in 1973 and .9763 ton in 1974. The median household size in the census tracts in our sample is two persons.[12] If we add together the quantitative estimates for all food categories for the two-person urban

TABLE 3   An Extrapolation of the Cost of Waste/Household/Year*

	1973	1974
Beef	$20.80	$5.20
Other meat	4.58	5.10
Poultry	1.98	1.45
Cheese	3.11	3.86
Fresh vegetables	11.32	12.06
Canned vegetables	1.80	1.25
Frozen vegetables	1.29	.95
Fresh fruit	6.18	7.34
TV dinners	.82	1.01
Take-out meals	4.68	7.90
Soups, stews, etc.	.39	.31
Bread	5.12	4.21
Noodles	.24	1.58
Chips, crackers	1.54	1.28
Candy	1.36	.81
Pastry	5.93	6.83
Baby food	.50	.27
Potato peels	2.18	.92
Total	$73.82	$62.33
Total with plate scrapings:	99.14	82.91
Plate scrapings at 34¢/lb.	25.31	20.58

*Calculated by multiplying average quantities wasted per garbage pickup times the number of pickups a year (104) times current (7 June 1974) averaged Tucson prices.

household in the Spring, 1965 USDA household food consumption survey,[16] we get a total of .9752 ton of food—extremely close to the estimates obtained in our sample by observation of household refuse.

Although the categories of food are not strictly comparable in all details, it is interesting to compare Garbage Project data for the two years with the percentage of total household food consumption obtained in the 1965 USDA survey for urban households[16] (see Table 4). To the extent that the comparison can be made, it appears that people in Tucson in 1973 and 1974 were consuming somewhat less of some animal protein foods, less fruit, and more grain products, sweets, and fats and oils than the USDA sample was in 1965. The overall similarity of the food input pattern shown in Table 4 with the independent USDA household food consumption data is an encouraging indication of the validity of refuse data as an index of food utilization patterns on the community level.

CONCLUSIONS

These preliminary data show that the study of household refuse offers a simple, inexpensive, and nonreactive means of monitoring food utilization and waste behavior on the community level. The data accumulated to date clearly indicate that food waste is a significant factor in food resource utilization and should be seriously considered by nutrition planners and educators.

REFERENCES

1. Pimentel, D., Hurd, L. E., Billotti, A. C., Forster, M. J., Oka, I. N., Sholes, O. D., and Whitman, R. J. 1973. Food production and the energy crisis, *Science,* 182:433.

2. Steinhart, J. S., and Steinhart, C. E. 1974. Energy use in the U.S. food system, *Science,* 184:307.

3. Woodham, A. A. 1971. The world protein shortage: prevention and cure, *World Rev. Nutr. & Dietet.,* 13:1.

4. Berg, A. 1973. *The Nutrition Factor: Its Role in National Development.* Washington, D.C.: The Brookings Institution.

TABLE 4   Percentage of Total Household Food Input

	Food groups as percent of household food consumption by weight, USDA, urban households Spring 1965	Food groups as percent of total evidence for food input, by weight, Garbage Project	
		1973	1974
Selected protein foods*	26.1	19.6	18.5
Vegetables	25.3	24.4	19.8
Fruits	18.3	13.6	15.3
Grain	11.6	11.2	14.8
Sugar and sweets	6.0	10.1	9.7

*Meat, fish, poultry, eggs, cheese, and nuts.

5. Adelson, S. F., Asp, E., and Noble, I. 1961. Household records of foods used and discarded, *J. Am. Dietet. Assn.*, 39:578.

6. Adelson, S. F., Delaney, I., Miller, C., and Noble, I. T. 1963. Discard of edible food in households, *J. Home Econ.*, 55:633.

7. Webb, E. J., Campbell, D. T., Schwartz, R. D., and Sechrist, L. 1966. *Unobtrusive Measures: Nonreactive Research in the Social Sciences.* Chicago: Rand McNally.

8. Rathje, W. L. 1974. The Garbage Project: A new way of looking at the problems of archaeology, *Archaeology*, 27:236.

9. Young, C. M., and Trulson, M. F. 1960. Methodology for dietary studies in epidemiological surveys II. Strength and weaknesses of existing methods, *Am. J. Publ. Health*, 50:83.

10. Pekkarinen, M. 1970. Methodology in the collection of food consumption data, *World Rev. Nutr. & Dietet.*, 12:145.

11. Marr, J. W. 1971. Individual dietary surveys: purposes and methods, *World Rev. Nutr. & Dietet.*, 13:105.

12. Bal, D. G., O'Hora, J. H., and Porter, B. W. 1974. *Pima County ECHO Report*, Tucson, Arizona, Pima County Health Department.

13. Tyron, R. C., and Bailey, D. 1970. *Cluster Analysis.* New York: McGraw-Hill.

14. Harrison, G. G., Rathje, W. L., and Hughes, W. W. 1974. Socioeconomic correlates of food consumption and waste behavior: the Garbage Project. Paper presented at the annual meeting of the American Public Health Association, New Orleans, La., Oct. 21, 1974 (unpublished).

15. Blalock, H. M. 1960. *Social Statistics.* New York: McGraw-Hill.

16. *Dietary Levels of Households in the United States, Spring, 1965: Household Food Consumption Survey, 1965–1966*, Report No. 6, USDA/ARS, Washington, D.C.: U.S. Department of Agriculture.

17

Into the Unknown

William L. Rathje and Cullen Murphy

William Rathje continues as the director of the Garbage Project in its latest incarnation, examining directly the great trash dumps of the United States. Cullen Murphy is the managing editor of the Atlantic Monthly.

Points to consider when reading this article:

1. Why in the world would an archaeologist elect to dig in a modern landfill or trash dump?

2. What did the researchers in the Garbage Project assume they would find in terms of the significance of styrofoam and other nonrecyclables in modern landfills?

3. What did they actually find was the most important contributor by volume to modern landfills?

4. What do the authors recommend be done to deal with the crisis that has resulted from filling up and closing down landfills?

Like all new parents, my wife and I agonized about the many choices we needed to make in deciding how best to care for our young kids. One of those choices may not seem so important, although for some reason it looms large in my memory: cloth or disposable? Diapers, of course. Like the choice offered in the supermarket checkout line — paper or plastic — the cloth or disposable choice made by millions of people every day might be expected to have an enormous effect on the environment. But just how large is this impact? Is the convenience of the disposables overridden by their presumably much greater consequences for the environment? Aren't the parents of young children being incredibly selfish, putting their petty concerns over society's great need to eliminate nonrecyclable, nonbiodegradable products?

How do we know how much precious space is wasted in landfills by nonbiodegradables such as plastic, disposable diapers? We can't know the answer if we don't look. Enter the archaeologists.

Anyone who has made the trip along the upper gullet of the New Jersey Turnpike as it disgorges traffic toward the George Washington Bridge is familiar with the Hackensack Meadowlands. This vast glacial fen runs roughly from Newark, New Jersey, to Nyack, New York, parallel to the Hudson River, and is separated from Manhattan by the Hudson and the long, craggy spine of the Palisades. The southern approach to the Meadowlands is heralded by a grim landscape of chemical plants and refineries, licks of flame dancing beneath the hazy gray of the sky. Across the Meadowlands are twisted roadbeds at what seem to be arbitrary and unnecessary heights. Below, small pools and channels can be glimpsed among the tall reeds, and there are moments even now, as a turn in the road affords a certain view, when the awesome sweep of this wetland in its nativity can be imagined still.

Such moments, of course, are rare. More commonly the eyes take in the massive mounds of garbage, some of them fifteen stories high, that have been dumped in the Meadowlands — blanketed in some cases by a film of dirt, and picked over every second of the day by a scavenging of gulls. More than a hundred communities once dumped their garbage into the Meadowlands, and garbage dumps cover three square miles of it. Almost all of this garbage was deposited in the days before measures were routinely taken to prevent or minimize seepage (as is now mandated by federal regulations). While systems to vent methane gas and control leachate exist at a few of the Meadowlands repositories, most of whatever is leaking out of the vast majority of them is leaking right into the water — into the Hackensack River, eventually, and then into New York Harbor. All but one of the Meadowlands dumps are

From chapter 4 of *Rubbish! The Archaeology of Garbage*, by William Rathje and Cullen Murphy, 1992. Reprinted by permission of HarperCollins Publishers, Inc.

now shut down (the last covers a mere seventeen acres) but the damage has been done. The mounds may not be permanent eyesores—skillful landscaping has beautified many such sites—but their contents could foul the area for decades to come.

The Australian archaeologist Rowland Fletcher calls the largest monuments that any society builds for itself MVSes—Monstrous Visual Symbols. Fletcher has noted that over the centuries, as a society's motivating ideals undergo change, so do its MVSes: from, say, temples and cathedrals to bridges and skyscrapers. The Hackensack Meadowlands are a potent reminder that the largest MVSes in American society today are its garbage repositories. Archaeologists believe that the biggest prehistoric MVS in the New World is the Pyramid of the Sun, at Teotihuacan, which was built in Mexico around the time of the birth of Jesus. Its volume is 75 million cubic feet. The garbage dumps in the Meadowlands exceed that volume many times over, as do most big-city landfills. In the San Francisco Bay area, the volume of the Durham Road landfill has already reached 150 million cubic feet; it has been built from the municipal solid waste of three moderate-sized towns over a period of only fifteen years. Fresh Kills, of course, is many times larger still. These MVSes may not be Chartres, but they are not without a certain grandeur. Many are surrounded by low brush which snags the thousands of thin plastic bags of various hues that blow from the dumping site, and at dawn the sun lights this perimeter in vibrant color.

Landfills are fitting symbols of many of the developed world's twentieth-century preoccupations—and they are great wellsprings of mythology as well. It is somehow fitting that the Hackensack Meadowlands Development Commission chose in 1989 to lodge a garbage museum in the environmental center at DeKorte State Park, which covers a two-thousand-acre tract of not-quite-pristine wetlands that abuts a ridge of dumps. One striking floor-to-ceiling exhibit through which visitors are able to walk is a bright, cavernous jumble of trash. The structure is the work not of a sanitation professional but of a thirty-year-old artist from Newark, Robert Richardson, whose intentions included making visitors feel that garbage was about to engulf American society. "They'll feel that the garbage climbing up the walls is overwhelming and at some point might fall over," Richardson told a reporter. "That's good."

To most visitors the contents of the display no doubt seem visually synonymous with the contents of American garbage in general, and thus with the contents of a typical landfill. Look: There are the empty boxes of Brillo and Tide, the plastic jugs and protective foam cartons, the disposable diapers, the bottles and cans, the fast-food packages—all of these things, assuredly, items that do get thrown away, that one does

find in garbage and in landfills. But the popular perception of garbage sometimes does not accord fully with reality. If a worker from the local department of sanitation were invited over to the garbage museum at DeKorte State Park and asked to point out to visitors how the garbage he has to deal with every day differs from the garbage displayed in Robert Richardson's construction, he might note, to begin with, that there seems to be no dirt mixed in with this garbage, and yet each day's deposits in a real landfill are tucked in with a layer of dirt. He might note that there is no construction and demolition debris, and no food and yard waste or, indeed, organic waste of any kind—no grease-soaked newspapers, no discarded trays of kitty litter, no sewage sludge. (He would, of course, understand *why* there was no organic waste at the museum; it is for the same reason that verisimilitude is kept at bay in colonial Williamsburg.) Our visiting sanitation worker might note that there is a good deal more plastic on display at the garbage museum than you would actually find in most landfills, and a lot less paper. He might note that none of the garbage appears to have been crushed, even though most garbage in a real landfill looks as if it has been run over by a forty-two-ton compactor, which it often has. And he might conclude with the obvious observation that the garbage on display gives off no smell—perhaps venturing to remark, and speaking as a connoisseur, that the bouquet of a well-managed sanitary landfill, though it hangs more thickly than more desirable atmospheres, is not entirely unpleasant.

How wide the gap may be between garbage myth and garbage reality surely varies from one specific issue to another, but there is probably no issue relating to garbage where a gap does not exist. In the Meadowlands garbage museum a life-sized, three-dimensional tableau depicts a twentieth-century American family blithely throwing away plastic cups and sheets of aluminum foil; instead of faces, the display's human figures have mirrors, inviting visitors to see themselves in similar situations. Those mirrors are apt symbols of much of the conventional wisdom about garbage, which often simply reflects the misinformation that people bring to the subject. The result, inevitably, is a closed system of fantasy and shortsightedness that both hampers the effective disposal of garbage and leads to exaggerated fears of a garbage crisis. A growing body of research findings from Garbage Project landfill digs and other investigations has begun to provide redress.

The Garbage Project began excavating landfills primarily for two reasons, both of them essentially archaeological in nature. One was to see if the data being gleaned from garbage fresh off the truck could be cross-validated by data from garbage in municipal landfills. The second, which derived from the Garbage Project's origins as an exercise in the study of formation processes, was to look into what happens to garbage after it has been interred. As it happens, the first landfill excavation got under way, in 1987, just as it was becoming clear — from persistent reports about garbage in the press that were at variance with some of the things the Garbage Project had been learning — that an adequate knowledge base about landfills and their contents did not exist. It was during this period that news of a mounting garbage crisis broke into the national consciousness. And it was during this period that two assertions were given wide currency and achieved a status as accepted fact from which they have yet to be dislodged. One is that accelerating rates of garbage generation are responsible for the rapid depletion and present shortage of landfills. The other is that, nationwide, there are few good places left to put new landfills. Whether these propositions are true or false — they happen, for the most part, to be exaggerations — it was certainly the case that however quickly landfills were being filled, the public, the press, and even most specialists had only the vaguest idea (at best) of what they were being filled up *with*. Yes, think tanks and consulting firms have done some calculations and come up with estimates of garbage quantities by commodity, based on national production figures and assumptions about rates of discard. But until 1987, when the Garbage Project's archaeologists began systematically sorting through the evidence from bucket-auger wells, no one had ever deliberately dug into landfills with a view to recording the inner reality in minute detail.

The Garbage Project was not without some slim archaeological precedent, which dates back to the summer of 1921. While writing up his now-famous dig at Pecos Ruin, on the headwaters of the Pecos River in San Miguel County, New Mexico — a study based on stratigraphic excavation techniques, which established the culture sequence among native peoples in the American Southwest — the pioneering archaeologist Alfred Vincent Kidder worked at Phillips Academy, in Andover, where he was a member of the department of archaeology. Kidder, the first American archaeologist to recognize the significance of stratigraphic layers in ancient ruins and ancient rubbish, became intrigued by a large trench that was being cut through the town of Andover's garbage dump to hold a multicommunity sewer pipe, and he spent a considerable amount of time at the work-site, down in the trench. He was able to see clearly in the strata the transition in light fixtures from whale-oil lamps to light bulbs. He was much taken with Milk of Magnesia bottles, because unlike many bottles the brand name was embossed on the glass, making for easy identification. Just about all archaeological excavations turn up objects whose purpose can-

not be determined (these objects, it sometimes seems, always end up being thrown into the catchall category "religious paraphernalia"), and the Andover dig was no exception: Kidder found a large number of mysterious pieces of flat, rusted iron, some twelve to fourteen inches long. "I couldn't imagine what they were," Kidder would later write. "I took one of them and Madeleine [Kidder's wife] didn't know what they were, and I showed them to my mother, who was visiting us at the time. She said, 'Oh, those are corset bones. When your corset wore out we used to roll it up and tie it with a string and throw it in the rubbish.' They were made of metal. The whalebone ones had gotten to be so expensive that no one used them anymore."

Kidder's brief, serendipitous peek inside the Andover dump has become the stuff of archaeological lore — from the Garbage Project's point of view, it holds a status equivalent to Wilhelm Konrad Roentgen's serendipitous discovery of X rays, in 1895, at the Royal University of Wurzburg, or Alexander Fleming's accidental discovery of penicillin, in 1928, at St. Mary's Hospital, in London — but for more than six decades, strangely, no one followed Kidder's lead.

The first landfill excavated by the Garbage Project, in April of 1987, was the Vincent H. Mullins landfill, in Tucson (the landfill is named, appropriately, for a sanitation supervisor who in the early 1970s had delivered fresh garbage samples to Garbage Project crews). In the years since then, eight other landfills around the United States have been opened up and explored. The landfills were selected to represent varying climates and levels of rainfall, varying soils and geomorphology, and varying regional lifestyles; the garbage deposited in these landfills has been accumulating in some cases for more than forty years. As of mid-1991 the sample included two landfills in Arizona (Mullins in Tucson and the Rio Salado landfill in Tempe, both unlined; average annual rainfall, eleven inches; sandy soils used as cover; garbage deposited since 1952). There were two in California, at the southern end of San Francisco Bay (the Durham Road landfill, in Fremont, and the Sunnyvale landfill, in Sunnyvale, both unlined; average annual rainfall, twenty-three inches; gritty, loamy soils used as cover; garbage deposited since 1964). There were two in the Chicago suburbs (the Greene Valley landfill, in Naperville, and the Mallard North landfill, in Hanover Park, lined and unlined, respectively; average annual rainfall, twenty-nine inches; average annual snowfall, thirty-eight inches; dense clay soils used as cover; garbage deposited since 1970). There were two in the vicinity of Naples, Florida (the Collier County landfill, in the Everglades, and the Naples Airport landfill, on the south side of the airport, lined and unlined, respectively; average annual rainfall, eighty inches; sandy, loamy soils that must be trucked in used as cover; garbage deposited since 1974). And there was one in New York City (the Fresh Kills landfill, unlined; average annual rainfall, forty-three inches; average annual snowfall, twenty-eight inches; no soil cover used because the landfill is in operation twenty-four hours a day; garbage deposited since 1948). Additionally, in the pursuance of specific projects there have been unlimited excavations at two other U.S. landfills, both in Tucson.* Several major excavations lie ahead. The fond ambition of the Garbage Project's staff is to be able one day to add to this list of excavated sites a garbage-dumping ground outside of London that has been in continuous use since at least the fifteenth century.

In terms of their environmental context, the differences among these landfills are extreme. In the Arizona desert the riverbeds are dry for three-quarters of the year, and then run in torrents during the late summer rainy season. In semitropical Florida, alligators sun themselves within sight of landfills and even bask in the leachate ponds. What is striking, however, is the extent to which the contents of these landfills seem to be relatively uniform from one part of the country to another. During its nine U.S. landfill excavations the Garbage Project retrieved 206 samples from sixty-five auger wells (up to eighty feet deep) and numerous backhoe trenches (dug to a depth of twenty-two feet), and exhumed a total of 28,426 pounds of garbage; the wells and trenches at each landfill were placed to ensure a representative sampling by date of refuse deposition. When commodity categories are compared from one landfill to another, the variance turns out to be negligible. For example, by weight the amount of rubber retrieved from the Mullins, Durham Road, and Greene Valley landfills fell in all cases at between 0.4 and 0.6 percent of the total weight of the refuse samples taken at each place. In all nine landfills textiles varied between 2.1 and 3.6 percent of refuse weight. The similarities extended to paper, plastic, and metals—indeed, to every category available. (Some of the slight differences that did exist, such as the somewhat lower proportion of paper in California's garbage than in that of Illinois, reflect different rates of recycling from place to place.) The lack of much variance is a reassuring indication that the Garbage Project's findings with respect to landfill content are dependable.

One key aim of the landfill excavations was to get some idea of the volume occupied by various kinds of garbage in landfills. Although many Garbage Project studies have relied on garbage weight for comparative purposes, volume is the critical variable when it comes to landfill management: Landfills close not because they are too heavy but because they are too full. And yet reliable data on the volume taken up by plastics, paper, organic material, and other kinds of garbage once it has been deposited in a landfill did not exist in 1987. The Garbage Project set out to fill the gap, applying its usual sorting and weighing procedures to excavated garbage, and then adding a final step: a volume measurement. Measuring volume was not a completely straightforward process. Because most garbage tends to puff up with air once it has been extracted from deep inside a landfill, all of the garbage exhumed was subjected to compaction, so that the data on garbage volume would reflect the volume that garbage occupies when it is squashed and under pressure inside a landfill. The compactor used by the Garbage Project is a thirty-gallon cannister with a hydraulic piston that squeezes out air from plastic bags, newspapers, cereal boxes, mowed grass, hot dogs, and everything else at a relatively gentle pressure of 0.9 pound per square inch. The data on the garbage volume that emerged from the Garbage Project's landfill excavations were the first such data in existence.

What do the numbers reveal? Briefly, that the kinds of garbage that loom largest in the popular imagination as the chief villains in the filling up and closing down of landfills—fast-food packaging, expanded polystyrene foam (the material that coffee cups are made from), and disposable diapers, to name three on many people's most-unwanted list—do not deserve the blame they have received. They may be highly visible as litter, but they are not responsible for an inordinate contribution to landfill garbage. The same goes for plastics. But one kind of garbage whose reputation has thus far been largely unbesmirched—plain old paper—merits increased attention.

Over the years, Garbage Project representatives have asked a variety of people who have never seen the inside of a landfill to estimate what percentage of a landfill's contents is made up of fast-food packaging, expanded polystyrene foam, and disposable diapers. In September of 1989, for example, this very question was asked of a group attending the biennial meeting of the National Audubon Society, and the results were generally consistent with those obtained from surveys conducted at universities, at business meetings, and at conferences of state and local government officials: Estimates at the Audubon meeting of the volume of fast-food packaging fell mainly between 20 and 30 percent of a typical landfill's contents; of expanded polystyrene foam, between 25 and 40 percent; and of disposable diapers, between 25 and 45

---

*... [F]our garbage sites in Canada have also been excavated, all of them in Ontario. They are the Burlington landfill, in Burlington; the Brock West landfill, in Pickering; the Oakville landfill, in Oakville; and the West Mall dump, in Etobicoke. A total of three tons of garbage was sorted at the four sites. Most of the data remain unevaluated.

percent. The overall estimate, then, of the proportion of a landfill's volume that is taken up by fast-food packaging, foam in general, and disposable diapers ranged from a suspiciously high 70 percent to an obviously impossible 125 percent.

Needless to say, fast-food packaging has few friends. It is designed to be bright, those bold reds and yellows being among the most attention-getting colors on a marketer's palette; this, coupled with the propensity of human beings to litter, means that fast-food packaging gets noticed. It is also greasy and smelly, and on some level it seems to symbolize, as do fast-food restaurants themselves, certain attributes of modern America to which modern Americans remain imperfectly reconciled. But is there really all that much fast-food packaging? Is it "straining" the capacity of America's landfills, as a 1988 editorial in *The New York Times* contended?

The physical reality inside a landfill is, in fact, quite different from the picture painted by many commentators. Of the more than fourteen tons of garbage from landfills that the Garbage Project has sorted, fewer than a hundred pounds was found to consist of fast-food packaging of any kind — that is, containers or wrappers for hamburgers, pizzas, chicken, fish, and convenience-store sandwiches, plus all the accessories, such as cups, lids, straws, sauce containers, and so on, plus all the boxes and bags used to deliver food and other raw materials to the fast-food restaurant. In other words, less than one-half of one percent of the weight of the materials excavated from nine municipal landfills over a period of five years (1985–89) consisted of fast-food packaging. As for the amount of space that fast-food packaging takes up in landfills — a more important indicator than weight — the Garbage Project estimate after sorting is that it accounts for no more than one-third of one percent of the total volume of a landfill's contents.

What about expanded polystyrene foam — the substance that most people are referring to when they say Styrofoam (which is a registered trademark of the Dow Chemical Corporation, and is baby blue in color and used chiefly to insulate buildings)? Expanded polystyrene foam is, of course, used for many things. Only about 10 percent of all foam plastics that were manufactured in the period 1980–89 were used for fast-food packaging. Most foam was (and is) blown into egg cartons, meat trays, coffee cups (the fast-food kind, yes, but mainly the plain kind that sit stacked upside down beside the office coffee pot), "peanuts" for packing, and the molded forms that protect electronic appliances in their shipping cases. All the expanded polystyrene foam that is thrown away in America every year, from the lowliest packing peanut to the most sophisticated molded carton, accounts for no more than 1 percent of the volume of garbage landfilled between 1980 and 1989.

Expanded polystyrene foam has been the focus of many vocal campaigns around the country to ban it outright. It is worth remembering that if foam were banned, the relatively small amount of space that it takes up in landfills would not be saved. Eggs, hamburgers, coffee, and stereos must still be put in *something*. The most likely replacement for foam is some form of coated cardboard, which can be difficult to recycle and takes up almost as much room as foam in a landfill. Indeed, in cases where cardboard replaced foam, it could often happen that a larger volume of cardboard would be needed to fulfill the same function fulfilled by a smaller volume of foam. No one burns fingers holding a foam cup filled with coffee, because the foam's insulating qualities are so effective. But people burn their fingers so frequently with plastic- or wax-coated cardboard coffee cups (and all cardboard hot-drink cups are coated) that they often put one such cup inside another for added protection.

As for disposable diapers, the debate over their potential impact on the environment is sufficiently vociferous and complex to warrant its own chapter. . . . Suffice it to say for present purposes, though, that the pattern displayed by fast-food packaging and expanded polystyrene foam is apparent with respect to diapers, too. People *think* that disposable diapers are a big part of the garbage problem; they are not a very significant factor at all.

The three garbage categories that, as we saw, the Audubon respondents believed accounted for 70 to 125 percent of all garbage actually account, together, for only about 3 percent. The survey responses would probably have been even more skewed if respondents had also been asked to guess the proportion of a typical landfill's contents that is made up of plastic. Plastic is surrounded by a maelstrom of mythology; into the very word Americans seem to have distilled all of their guilt over the environmental degradation they have wrought and the culture of consumption they invented and inhabit. Plastic has become an object of scorn — who can forget the famous scene in *The Graduate* (or quote it properly)? — no doubt in large measure because its development corresponded chronologically with, and then powerfully reinforced, the emergence of the very consumerist ethic that is now despised. (What Mr. McGuire, a neighbor, says to Benjamin Braddock is: "I just want to say one word to you. Just one word. Are you listening? . . . Plastics. There is a great future in plastics. Think about it.") Plastic is the Great Satan of garbage. It is the apotheosis of the cheap, the inauthentic; even the attempts to replace or transform plastic — such as the recent ill-fated experiments with "biodegradable" plastic . . . seem somehow inauthentic.

There are legitimate causes for concern about plastic, particularly with respect to its manufacture. For the moment the issue is the volume of plastics in landfills. Two statistics have received wide circulation. The first, which appears repeatedly in the press, is that while plastics may make up only 7 percent of all municipal solid waste by weight, they make up some 30 percent of municipal solid waste by volume. This 30 percent figure has a history: It comes from a report published by, and available (for $300) from, the International Plastics Consultants Corporation (IPCC), based in Stamford, Connecticut, a group that was set up to promote the recycling of plastic. The IPCC's methodology for estimating the volume in landfills occupied by plastics begins by accepting the Franklin Associates' materials-flows assumptions and their weight data on various garbage categories. To estimate the volume of various categories of garbage after such garbage has been crushed and compacted, the researchers obtained from the pertinent trade associations and businesses whatever data they had on the bulk density (that is, the volume per unit weight) of items that have been squashed and baled for transport, usually for shipment to recycling facilities.

There were, of course, a few problems. While the bulk density of some types of paper items, such as newsprint and corrugated cardboard, could be evaluated with a certain precision, because these items get recycled and records are kept, the IPCC had to assume that the bulk density of nonrecycled paper items for which they had no data, such as cereal boxes, paper towels, and tissues, was the same as that of recyclable paper. Similarly, the IPCC had to assume that the bulk density of all nonrecycled plastics, from toothbrushes to tables, was the same as the bulk density for the kinds of recyclable plastic for which it had data—primarily PET (polyethylene terephthalate) plastic soda bottles, the kind that most soft drinks now come in. And, of course, there being no trade associations for yard waste, food waste, and many other kinds of garbage, the International Plastics Consultants Corporation had to settle for reasonable estimates of the bulk density of all these garbage categories. The IPCC ended up by concluding that plastics made up 27 percent of a typical landfill's contents, a figure that in news reports was then rounded up to 30 percent.

The second estimate that one encounters with some regularity for the volume of plastics in landfills is 20 percent. The provenance of this figure is a 1988 Franklin Associates study of landfill constituents by weight and volume. This figure is inflated because Franklin Associates (as its researchers readily admit) excluded the huge category "construction and demolition debris"—which accounts for about 12 percent by volume of a typical landfill's contents—from their es-

timation of the total landfill pie, thereby reducing the size of the pie and magnifying the relative proportions of the other constituents. The problem with construction and demolition debris, insofar as Franklin is concerned, is the same one faced by the IPCC: no one keeps records on it. There is no trade association for construction and demolition debris in Washington, and, because local communities are not normally responsible for collecting and carting away such debris, as they are other kinds of garbage, very often not even haphazard documentation exists. And besides, the federal government does not technically consider construction and demolition debris to be municipal solid waste (though it ends up in municipal landfills). For these reasons construction and demolition debris was simply left out of the picture. By Franklin's account, not one ounce of construction and demolition debris—not one cinderblock, two-by-four, or rebar rod—has technically entered American landfills during the past thirty years.

The Garbage Project's methodology has not been quite as sophisticated as that of Franklin or the IPCC: Garbage Project personnel simply measured by weight and volume everything exhumed from sample municipal-solid-waste landfills. The results differ from the Franklin and IPCC numbers. In landfill after landfill the volume of all plastics—foam, film, and rigid; toys, utensils, and packages—from the 1980s amounted to between 20 and 24 percent of all garbage, as sorted; when compacted along with everything else, in order to replicate actual conditions inside a landfill, the volume of plastics was reduced to under 16 percent.

Even if its share of total garbage is, at the moment, relatively low, is it not the case that plastics take up a larger proportion of landfill space with every passing year? Unquestionably a larger number of physical objects are made of plastic today than were in 1970 or 1950. But a curious phenomenon becomes apparent when garbage deposits from our own time are compared with those from strata characteristic, of, say, the 1970s. While the number of individual plastic objects to be found in a deposit of garbage of a constant size has increased considerably in the course of a decade and a half—more than doubling—the proportion of landfill space taken up by these plastics has not changed; at some landfills, the proportion of space taken up by plastics was actually a little less in the 1980s than it was in the 1970s.

The explanation appears to be a strategy that is known in the plastics industry as "light-weighting"—making objects in such a way that the objects retain all the necessary functional characteristics but require the use of less resin. The concept of light-weighting is not limited to the making of plastics; the makers of glass bottles have been light-weighting their wares for decades, with the result that bottles today are 25 percent lighter than they were in 1984. (That is why bottles in landfills are likely to show up broken in the upper, more-recent, strata, whereas lower strata, holding garbage from many years ago, contain many more whole bottles.) Environmentalists might hail light-weighting as an example of source reduction. Businessmen embrace it for a different reason: sheer profit. Using fewer raw materials for a product that is lighter and therefore cheaper to transport usually translates into a competitive edge, and companies that rely heavily on plastics have been light-weighting ever since plastics were introduced. PET soda bottles had a weight of 67 grams in 1974; the weight today is 48 grams, for a reduction of 30 percent. High-density polyethylene (HDPE) milk jugs in the mid-1960s had a weight of 120 grams; the weight today is about 65 grams, for a reduction of more than 45 percent. Plastic grocery bags had a thickness of 30 microns in 1976; the thickness today is at most 18 microns, for a reduction of 40 percent. Even the plastic in disposable diapers has been light-weighted, although the super-absorbent material that was added at the same time (1986) ensures that even if diapers enter the house lighter they will leave it heavier than ever. When plastic gets lighter, in most cases it also gets thinner and more crushable. The result, of course, is that many more plastic items can be squeezed into a given volume of landfill space today than could have been squeezed into it ten or twenty years ago.

This fact has frequently been met with skepticism. In 1989, Robert Krulwich, of the CBS network's "Saturday Night with Connie Chung" program, conducted a tour of the Garbage Project's operations in Tucson, and he expressed surprise when told about the light-weighting of plastics. He asked for a crushed PET soda bottle from 1989 and tried to blow it up. The light plastic container inflated easily. He was then given a crushed PET soda bottle found in a stratum dating back to 1981—a bottle whose plastic would be considerably thicker and stiffer. Try as he might, Krulwich could not make the flattened container inflate.

One item that has not been light-weighted during the past few decades is your typical daily newspaper—the messenger that repeatedly carries warnings about the garbage crisis. A year's worth of copies of *The New York Times*, for example, weighs about 520 pounds and occupies a volume of about 1.5 cubic yards. A year's worth of *The Times* is the equivalent, by weight, of 12,480 empty aluminum cans or 48,793 Big Mac clamshell containers. It is the equivalent, by volume, of 18,660 crushed aluminum cans or 14,969 crushed Big Mac clamshells.

Newspapers epitomize the part of the garbage problem that gets the least amount of attention: paper. During the 1970s futurists and other writers, perceiving the advent of an electronic society, heralded the new paperless workplace, the new paperless culture. "One of the most startling features of the Computer Revolution," Christopher Evans wrote in *The Micro Revolution* (1979) "is that print and paper technology will appear as primitive as the pre-Caxtonian hand-copying of manuscripts seems to us. In sum, the 1980s will see the book as we know it, and as our ancestors created and cherished it, begin a slow but steady slide into oblivion." Predictions like that one were never quite believable even in their heyday, when the consequences of the advent of copying machines were already apparent. It is obvious by now that computers, far from making paper obsolete, have made it possible to generate lengthy hard-copy documents more easily than ever before. A computer with a printer is, in effect, a printing press, and there are now fifty-five million of these printing presses in American homes and offices, where twenty years ago there had been only typewriters. With respect to paper, advancing technology is not a contraceptive but a fertility drug. For one thing, as technology in general has become more and more sophisticated, with more and more components, the engineering specifications needed to describe complex systems have necessarily become more and more voluminous. One environmental consulting group recently publicized the assertion that if all the paper stored on a typical American aircraft carrier were removed, the ship would rise three inches in the water. Garbage Project researchers have been unable to substantiate that claim, but it is definitely the case that, prognostications to the contrary, paper has managed to hold its own among the components of the U.S. solid-waste stream. Edward Tenner, an executive editor at Princeton University Press, recently observed: "The paperless office, the leafless library, the inkless newspaper, the cashless, checkless society—all have gone the way of the Empire State Building's dirigible mooring, the backyard helipad, the nuclear-powered convertible, the vitamin-pill dinner, and the Paperwork Reduction Act of 1980."

For all the competition since the 1950s from plastic, metal, construction-and-demolition debris, and non-paperaceous organics, paper's contribution to a landfill's contents has remained relatively even, at well over 40 percent. Newspapers alone may take up some 13 percent or more of the space in the average landfill—nearly as much as all plastics. Paper used in the packaging of consumer goods has grown in volume by about a third since 1960. Non-packaging paper—computer paper, stationery, paper plates and cups, junk mail—has doubled in volume. The volume of discarded magazines has likewise doubled, to about 1.2 percent—about as much as all the thrown-away fast-food packaging and expanded polystyrene foam combined.

One noteworthy contributor to a landfill's paper content is the telephone book. Dig a trench through a landfill and telephone books can be seen to stud some strata like currants in a cake. They are thrown out regularly, once a year; in the city of Phoenix, that means almost twelve pounds of phonebooks annually (one yellow pages and one white pages) for every business and household. And their expansion in number seems to know no bounds. First there are the normal "Baby Bell" phonebooks published by the seven regional phone companies, often two or three of them per household in a city of average size. Then come the many competing brands of Yellow Pages published by rivals to the Bell system companies: Reuben H. Donnelly and GTE Directories are biggest, but there are some two hundred other yellow pages publishers. And then there are phonebooks that target specific businesses, or senior citizens, or juveniles, or members of different ethnic groups. Miniature, paperback book–sized phonebooks have recently appeared for people who have car phones, to ride beside them on the front seat. In most cases phonebooks are made of paper of such low quality that recycling is difficult, although some end uses do exist.

The avalanche of paper, like everything else about garbage, needs to be seen in perspective. Paper is not inherently a bad thing. There are many uses for paper that end up *limiting* the generation of garbage. The skillful packaging of food products, to give just one example, cuts down markedly on the wastage of foods. But for all paper's virtues, an inarguable fact remains: If garbage volume is ever to be significantly reduced, paper is the foe that must be faced. The task of getting some control over paper is made all the more necessary by the fact that paper and many other organics . . . tend not so much to degrade in landfills as to mummify. They do not, in other words, take up appreciably less and less space as time goes by.

The following chart, which contrasts the findings of a 1990 Roper Poll with recent Garbage Project data, helps to summarize the difference between mental and material realities with respect to landfills. The percentages in the Roper column indicate the proportion of respondents identifying a particular item as a major cause of garbage problems.

	Roper (%)	Actual volume in landfills (%)
Disposable diapers	41	<2
Plastic bottles	29	<1
Large appliances	24	<2
Newspapers	11	~13
All paper	6	>40
Food and yard waste	3	~7
Construction debris	0	~12

Misperceptions such as these are not harmless. They can lead to policies and actions that are counterproductive.

In commemoration of Earth Day, 1990, the New York Public Interest Research Group launched a campaign against the use of certain highly visible and famously odious forms of garbage, such as fast-food containers, aseptic packaging (juice boxes), and disposable diapers, and it urged members of allied environmental groups to spread the word "through newsletters and other publications." One can appreciate the good intentions—as well as the irony of the means of communication employed.

18

Dawn of a New Stone Age in Eye Surgery

Payson D. Sheets

Payson Sheets is an archaeologist at the University of Colorado who specializes in the archaeology of Mesoamerica. He is also well known in the field of lithic replication, the analysis of stone tools by the experimental re-creation of these artifacts.

Points to consider when reading this article:

1. What inspired Payson Sheets to make stone tools for use in modern surgical procedures?

2. How do you imagine Don Crabtree's surgeon reacted when Crabtree suggested the use of stone blades instead of steel scalpels in his operation?

3. What did the surgeon think after using the stone blades?

4. Why did the stone blades work so well?

I can barely imagine the look on the face of Don Crabtree's doctor when Crabtree, one of the American pioneers of **lithic replication**—the study of prehistoric stone tools by trying to make them—presented his physician with the following offer. In 1975 Crabtree was in need of surgery and requested that his surgeon use not the commonly supplied commercial stainless steel scalpels but obsidian blades of Crabtree's own making.

Obsidian is a naturally occurring, usually black, volcanically produced glass. Ancient people the world over recognized the enormous cutting power of obsidian and used it whenever it was available to make spear points, arrowheads, knives, and scraping tools. Though people today may use "stone age" as a derogatory adjective, ancient people and archaeologists know something those people don't: stone-edged blades, especially obsidian blades, are exquisitely sharp.

Remarkable as it may seem, Crabtree convinced his physician to use obsidian blades in his surgery. The surgeon was so impressed by their performance that he used them again when some follow-up surgery was needed on Crabtree.

Payson Sheets was a student of Crabtree, and this episode apparently inspired him to look further into the use of an ancient technology in the context of a modern operating room.

O ccasionally, archaeological findings can be applied to today's world and improve modern life. Archaeologists have rediscovered prehistoric crops and agricultural technologies that are no longer used but have considerable value for contemporary society. Ancient remedies, too, have been found that can help cure illnesses. This is an account of the rediscovery of an ancient technology for making stone tools that died out centuries ago but has an unexpectedly important potential for improving modern medical treatment.

Beginning in 1969, as a young graduate student, I participated in the Chalchuapa Archaeological Project on the edge of the Maya area in El Salvador. Beyond supervising several project excavations, I was responsible for the analysis of the ancient stone tools—composed mostly of obsidian (volcanic glass)—as part of my doctoral dissertation. In my work I discovered that most previous studies classified stone tools by their shape. I did likewise, but I also wanted to contribute something different, so I kept looking for a new angle from which to analyze the Chalchuapa stone artifacts.

In 1970 I excavated a workshop at Chalchuapa where I recovered the remains of ancient obsidian tool manufacture. From the workshop debris I figured out the various techniques, and their sequence, that had been used by the ancient Maya knappers to make

From *Archaeology: Discovering Our Past,* edited by Robert Sharer and Wendy Ashmore, 1996. Reprinted with permission of Mayfield Publishing Company.

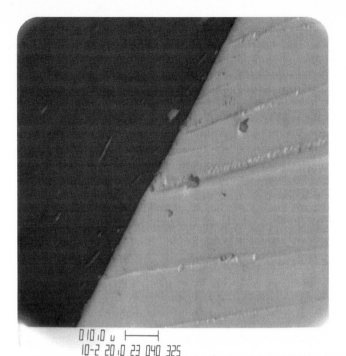
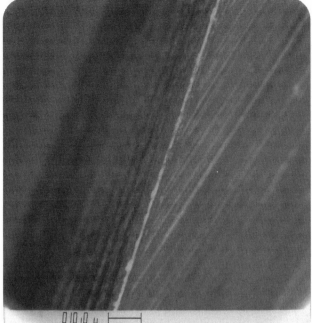

FIGURE 1   Magnified to approximately 400 power, compare the edge of a fresh, steel razor blade (left) and an unused obsidian blade (right). At this level of magnification, the steel edge, among the sharpest produced by modern metallurgical technology, is flat and dull when compared to that of the obsidian blade, produced by an ancient lithic technology. (Courtesy of Terry del Bene)

chipped stone tools. I also identified errors made during this process and how the ancient craftsmen corrected them. These data provided the new angle I was looking for—an analysis based on the ancient tool-making technology. The reconstruction of past behavior, within the structure of the obsidian tool industry, was the first step in developing modern surgical blades based on an ancient technology.

The following year I attended Don Crabtree's training program in lithic technology so that I could learn how to make stone tools. I learned to duplicate the ancient Maya technology including how to make tools and cores by percussion (striking the stone with strong blows to detach flakes) and long, thin obsidian blades by pressure (slowly increasing force applied to a core to detach flakes). Don suggested that the replicas of the ancient blades would be excellent surgical tools and that I should experiment with the technology to see if I could make scalpels that would be acceptable to surgeons. But I was unable to follow up these suggestions; after writing my dissertation, earning my Ph.D., and finding a teaching position at the University of Colorado, I embarked on a new research project in the Zapotitán basin of El Salvador. But by 1979 the guerrilla warfare in El Salvador made the area too dangerous to continue research, so I then had the time to

explore the possibility of adapting obsidian blades for modern surgical use.

Meanwhile, Don had gone ahead and provided a dramatic demonstration of the obsidian blade's utility in surgery. Since he had undergone two thoracic operations in 1975, he had made obsidian blades for his surgeon to use. The operations were very successful, and his surgeon liked the obsidian blades for their ease in cutting and the improved healing of the incisions.

But before obsidian scalpels could find wide use in surgery, a series of problems had to be resolved. The first problem was to determine how sharp the obsidian blades were and how they compared with the various scalpels already used by surgeons. The answers came from examining the edges of obsidian blades, other kinds of stone (chert and quartzite), razor blades, and surgical scalpels under the tremendous magnification of a scanning electron microscope (SEM).

The results showed that the dullest edge belonged to a percussion flake made of chert. The quartzite flake was much sharper, having an edge 9.5 times sharper than the chert flake. I had expected the stainless steel surgical scalpel to be sharper than the razor blade, but the results were the opposite. The scalpel was only 1.5 times sharper than the quartzite flake. The razor blade, a standard Gillette stainless steel double-edged blade, was 2.1 times sharper than the surgical scalpel. This was a surprise to me, but not to surgeons, who often use razor blades for operations by adapting them with "blade breakers," small devices that snap razor blades into segments for surgical use.

Most significantly, the obsidian blade was far sharper than any of these edges. Depending on the edge being measured, the obsidian was *100 to 500 times sharper* than the razor blade and thus was 210 to 1050 times sharper than the modern surgical scalpel!

By 1980 I was ready to see if there was any application in modern surgery for such sharp cutting edges. After calling several prominent eye surgeons, I reached Dr. Firmon Hardenbergh of Boulder, Colorado. The more I described the astounding sharpness of the obsidian edge, the more interested he became. He decided to use one of these blades for eye surgery. The results were quite successful, for the sharper edge did less damage to the tissue and the cleaner incision facilitated healing. And, very importantly, there was less resistance to the blade, so the eye moved far less, allowing the surgeon to make a more accurate incision.

Since that time obsidian blades have been used in other kinds of operations. Healing was usually faster, scarring was reduced (sometimes dramatically so), and often the pain during recovery was reduced or almost eliminated. Once the full research and development program for eye surgery is completed, Dr. Hardenbergh and I plan to modify the blades for use in general surgery and in specialized applications such as plastic surgery and neurosurgery.

We needed to compare the use of obsidian and steel scalpels. We did this by experimental cutting of muscle tissue with both kinds of blades and then examining the incisions with the SEM. The differences were dramatic. The metal blades tore and translocated large amounts of tissue, leaving the ragged edges of the incision littered with displaced chunks of flesh. The obsidian cut was strikingly crisp and clean.

We have improved the blades greatly from their early form in 1980; they are now more uniform in shape and are fitted with well-formed plastic handles. But they still must be made by hand, replicating the ancient Maya technology. The next step will be to engineer a transformation from a traditional handicraft to a modern manufacturing system. Because shapes of cores vary, each blade has to be individually planned and detached, and each blade varies in length and shape. This technology is not adequate for manufacturing large numbers of standardized surgical scalpels.

Part of the manufacturing problem has been solved by designing a metal mold into which we pour molten glass, producing uniformly shaped cores. This process also eliminates the impurities and structural imperfections present in natural obsidian, and it allows us to vary the glass chemistry to maximize desirable properties such as color and edge toughness. We have also designed a machine to detach the blades from the core, and this device is being tested and refined. These improvements in manufacturing have resulted in more consistent blades, but more work needs to be done to fully automate the process and produce precisely uniform obsidian surgical scalpels every time.

Once the blades are in production and are readily available to surgeons, they will have the advantage over even the sharpest scalpel presently used, the diamond blade. Based on present tests, our obsidian blades are just as sharp as diamond blades—in fact they are up to three times sharper. But diamond blades are extremely expensive, costing several thousand dollars apiece, and they are tiny, with only 3 mm of cutting edge. Obsidian scalpels will cost the surgeon only a few dollars each, and the blades can be as long as needed. Fortunately, the ancient Maya have shown us the way not only to sharper and cheaper scalpels, but to surgical instruments that have very real benefits for the patient in reducing trauma, scarring, and pain. In these ways the past has provided a very real improvement to the present.

19

Using the Past to Protect the Future: Marking Nuclear Waste Disposal Sites

Maureen F. Kaplan and Mel Adams

Maureen Kaplan is an archaeologist with field experience in the Near East. Her interest in using archaeological information as a basis for designing long-term markers began in the early 1980s. She contributed to the report, Expert Judgment on Markers to Deter Inadvertent Intrusion into the Waste Isolation Pilot Plant, Sand 92–1382, November 1993.

Mel Adams is a senior scientist at Lockheed, Martin, Hanford. He has long been involved in nuclear waste disposal. He also is an amateur archaeologist with a keen interest in the Native American petroglyphs of Oregon.

Points to consider when reading this article:

1. How can archaeology contribute to the protection of future generations from the long-lived wastes we are producing today?

2. Why can't we assume that people in the future will be able to read the warnings we place in plain English on markers warning of radiation danger?

3. What well-known archaeological monuments do the authors use as models for the ancient marking of sacred places?

4. What kinds of large-scale markers do the authors suggest to warn future people of danger? What kinds of small-scale artifacts do the authors suggest to warn future people of danger?

Human beings are both blessed and cursed with consciousness. We are probably the only beings with a knowledge of our own mortality, recognizing the limited span of our lives and that there will be a time when we will be gone—and the world will muddle along without us.

How humans have dealt with this terrible truth is an interesting question. One might argue that the great monumental works of our species, from Stonehenge to the pyramids to twentieth-century skyscrapers, were built, at least in part, to achieve a sort of cultural immortality through our works. We as individuals may succumb to the inevitable march of time, but we can rest in peace assured that no one will forget us because we built things that will last forever.

In studying these monuments that were intended to remind generations far into the future of the awesome power of now ancient cultures, archaeologists attain a perspective useful in the late twentieth century. Today, our industrial societies produce wastes so toxic and long-lasting that they will effectively never be safe. How do we, in the present, make certain that a place will be forever marked in such a way that all future people will know—not that we were powerful or clever but that they should *stay away*? Finally, we in the industrialized world are attempting to deal with those wastes, to secrete them away so they will not be a threat to our health or the health of our children. But how do we mark these places so that no matter how far we look into the future, no matter the language spoken or the culture followed, our descendants (or will they be extraterrestrial visitors?) will know to leave this place? Archaeologists can help answer this important question.

In today's nuclear age, the safe disposal of nuclear waste is naturally on the minds of both the public and the scientific community. A major concern is the possibility of human disturbance of the disposal site at some time in the future. One relatively simple approach to preventing this is *marking* the site to inform potential intruders of its contents and dangers. In designing the best possible marking system, archaeology is playing an important and revolutionary role. Because archaeology deals with man-made monuments and messages that have survived for extended periods of time, scientists are turning to the past to learn what allows information to survive and to incorporate this knowledge in the design of marking systems for nuclear waste disposal sites.

Archaeological guidelines in fact have been the focus of research performed by The Analytic Sciences Corporation (TASC) for the U.S. Government Office of Nuclear Waste Isolation (ONWI) in Columbus, Ohio, and with Rockwell Hanford Operations (Rockwell) in Richland, Washington. For the last five years the project for ONWI concentrated on the problem of the disposal of "high level wastes"—the spent fuel from power reactors or what remains after the reusable uranium and plutonium have been removed. No permanent site for the disposal of these wastes has yet been chosen, but for most areas under preliminary study, burial is envisioned to take place in a deep mine (450 to 550 meters). This will then be resealed, so that intrusion would require a culture with a level of technology similar to our own.

For Rockwell, work concentrated on a design for disposal sites for the radioactive wastes located at the Hanford Site, a 1500-square-kilometer area in southeastern Washington near a bend in the Columbia River. Established in 1943 as a national security area for plutonium production, it now operates under the Department of Energy. In 1968, 311 square kilometers were set aside as an Arid Lands Ecology Reserve, and during the 1970s the area north of the Columbia River was designated a wildlife refuge. As the name of the ecology reserve indicates, the Hanford Site is located in a desert-like region, a shrub-steppe grassland with an average annual rainfall of 116 millimeters that does not percolate very deeply into the soil.

Environmental conditions are important for understanding past nuclear waste management practices at Hanford, many of which were established decades ago. Only a tiny portion of the site area (less than 0.01 percent) was set aside for waste disposal. Prior to 1970, in these areas low activity liquid wastes from the reprocessing of irradiated fuel were allowed to percolate into the soil at the bottom of deep trenches or similar engineered structures. The higher activity wastes were held in single-shell concrete tanks with metal linings.

(Tank wastes have recently been dried to minimize the amount of material that could leak into the soil once the tanks fail.) Solid wastes, such as contaminated trash, tools and equipment, were buried in trenches during this period. Since 1970, these early disposal practices have been improved or discontinued, but Rockwell is still wrestling with the question of disposing of the pre-1970 material. A draft environmental impact statement (EIS) has been prepared and is under public review for the final disposition of the wastes at the Hanford Site.

Over the years, safety analyses for the disposal of highly radioactive wastes have resulted in the realization that an otherwise effective disposal system can be circumvented by human interference, such as deep drilling or growing deep-rooted crops. In light of this, the draft regulations proposed in 1982 by the Environmental Protection Agency (EPA) state that "the disposal system shall be identified by the most permanent markers and records practicable to indicate the dangers of the wastes and their location." The EPA regulations propose 10,000 years as the most effective time period. (Radioactive materials decay over time, unlike most chemically toxic wastes.)

In using archaeology to design the most permanent markers practicable, three steps were taken. First, we analyzed some ancient markers or monuments, and then we identified the factors in the marking system. Finally, we used archaeological data to develop accelerated testing procedures for proposed materials. The ancient monuments were chosen to represent a variety of cultures and climates, so that the monuments and their survival are not keyed to a particular culture, and to ascertain the effect of climate on survival. We also chose monuments that were at least 1,000 years old, that is, monuments that showed an ability to survive for at least one millennium.

The Fourth Dynasty pyramids at Giza, Egypt, are an obvious starting point. They have already survived nearly half the EPA's suggested 10,000-year time frame. The purpose of the pyramids, who built them, and their contemporary condition are accurately described by several later historians including Herodotus, Pliny the Elder, and the twelfth-century Arab, Abd el Latif. Even without this information, the sarcophagi within the pyramids and the texts on the walls of the later Sixth Dynasty pyramids would proclaim their funerary purpose.

Arguing against the use of a pyramid type of marker is the fact that the pyramids have survived because of their massive size, and that each pyramid marks only a single spot. We hope to delineate a whole area, and building a pyramid to cover its entire surface is impractical. If a smaller pyramid were to be built, saying "do not dig here," drilling could occur next to it without contradicting the warning.

Stonehenge in England was the second ancient marker investigated. This magnificent monument on Salisbury Plain is the culmination of nearly a millennium of use and remodeling, and is an example of a man-made marker that has lasted for nearly 5,000 years in a moist climate. Stonehenge may be very useful for a marking system because of the redundancy of its standing stones, which are much more efficient in delineating an area than the pyramids. The use of multiple components means that the plan of an area can be reconstructed even though some of the components are missing. Stonehenge has lost approximately one-third of its stones, yet there is no debate about its plan. But unlike the pyramids, there is no contemporary written information associated with Stonehenge, which has severely limited our understanding of the monument.

The situation is quite different at the Acropolis in Athens, for which we have surviving contemporary texts. We know, for example, that Pericles (died 429 B.C.) was the prime mover in the decision to rebuild the Acropolis on a monumental scale after peace was made with Persia. There has never been any doubt that the major buildings of the Acropolis had a religious purpose. Today, the Acropolis is an excellent example of ancient monuments that have suffered far more from the hands of man than from the ravages of nature. Acid rain is dissolving the marble sculptures and buildings. The caryatids on the Porch of the Maidens of the Erechtheion have been replaced by casts. The steel bolts and girders of the early 1900s that replaced the old iron ones are weakening and expanding as they corrode. This extra stress has led to cracking of the marble in which the steel is embedded. In some places this has created an immediate danger of collapse—a solemn warning to those who propose technologically advanced materials that have not had the chance to undergo the test of time.

The Great Wall of China is another monument that has lasted for over 2,000 years. Built by the order of Qin Shi Huang Di, the wall was begun in 221 B.C. and completed in 210 B.C. Construction methods differed along its 1,850-mile length, depending on the local building materials. In the east, where stone was plentiful, a foundation of rubble was laid without mortar. The wall was built of dry, tamped earth (*terre pise*) and the upper level was covered with brickwork. In the later Ming period (A.D. 1368–1644), granite foundation stones as large as 4.25 by 1.25 meters were used. The rubble or earthen core of the walls was faced with either brick or stone. Farther west, the wall cuts across wide expanses of loess soil, with little stone for building. The very fine loess was mixed into a slurry and poured between frames to create the wall, which was faced with stone or brick when possible. In several areas, two strips of loess were removed, leaving a rampart of earth. Stone was used again in the westernmost segment.

During its history the Great Wall has been breached and repaired but never forgotten. Its history is contained in a body of literature ranging from poems about its beauty to tales of the horrors endured by the conscripted laborers who built it. Because it was built with bricks, the Wall has needed continual maintenance over its lifetime. For the Rockwell project, it is important to note that the Wall received this care because it served a purpose for the rulers of the country. The marking system for the Hanford disposal site will also serve a public, protective function. Although it will be designed to need as little maintenance as possible, the Great Wall indicates the possibility that the marking system could be updated and repaired by future generations, should this be required.

We also turned to the Nazca lines, a collection of lines, geometric forms, and semi-naturalistic figures found on the desert floor near the town of Nazca in southern Peru (see A. Aveni article in *Archaeology* July/ August 1986). The Nazca lines are drawn on an enormous scale. Single lines may run more than 10.5 kilometers, and one cleared trapezoid measures nearly 800 by 100 meters. The lines are made possible by a set of geological circumstances. Wind erosion across the desert floor carried off the dusty surface soil, leaving behind a "pavement" of pebbles and boulders. Over time these stones developed "desert varnish," a brownish-black coating of iron and manganese oxides formed by the *in-situ* decomposition of the rock. Formation of this varnish is very slow, and may have begun as far back as the Pleistocene period about 10,000 to 30,000 years ago. The underlying soil, however, remained pale in color. Picking up a stone exposes the light-colored soil underneath it, and picking up a row of stones creates a light-colored line. Obviously these lines are a frail phenomenon and undergo rapid degradation when people drive or walk over them. Since many tourists now attempt to see them, they are deteriorating rapidly. Still, the Nazca lines are an example of the potential survivability of even a fragile phenomenon in a suitably remote location.

The last marker we investigated was the Serpent Mound in Ohio, an embankment of earth in the form of an uncoiled serpent. Archaeologists speculate that the Serpent Mound was built by the Adena Indians (800 B.C.–A.D. 100). In its present state of restoration, the Serpent Mound consists of two parts, the serpent and an oval shape in front of its mouth. A small mound of burned stones lies in the center of the oval. The length of the serpent is 380 meters, and its height, generally 1.25 to 1.5 meters, tapers until the tail terminates in a bank about 0.3 meters high. The core is made of stone and clay. For our purposes, the Serpent Mound is an example of what *not* to do. Obviously, the serpent form meant something to the builders, but the meaning has been lost to us. We may take this as a warning that marking a site with symbols or pictures alone may not be sufficient to convey all the information to future investigators. The Serpent Mound has no parallel in the United States. Likewise, there may be only one high-level waste repository in this country. Developing a unique symbol for a possibly unique high-level waste repository could be futile, since the symbol would have no points of reference or comparison for its future viewers.

How do we summarize the lessons learned from ancient markers? Foremost is the importance of contemporary written records to the future understanding of any of those monuments. Languages will change, and we cannot predict which of those in contemporary use will be readable or recognizable several millennia from now. Still we must include written messages to insure the possibility of reconstructing the information at some future time. It appears that only language—as opposed to pictures and symbols—may be capable of carrying higher levels of information and details. Symbols may be of use only in the relative short-term, when their cultural contexts are still understood. For example, if we see an uninscribed statue of a woman wearing a helmet and carrying a shield, we still recognize it as Athena, goddess of wisdom. But the use of symbols with associated texts will give generations in the far future the possibility of regaining the meaning of the symbol. The combined use of pictures and languages is also likely to create a symbiotic effect in recovering the intended information. In other words, the marking system should incorporate symbols, pictures and languages to convey its warning and information.

We have also learned that the materials that survive are natural ones—earthworks and stone. This is not an effect of the technological level of the cultures that built the monument; metals were in common use when most of these ancient markers were built. But there are metals which, although certainly durable, are unlikely to survive because of their intrinsic value; they show a disturbing tendency to be recycled. The Parthenon once bore a set of bronze shields erected by Alexander the Great and an inscription by Nero (A.D. 54–68), which we know about only from the written records and the holes left by the mounting pins. Archaeological evidence is important for indicating the difference between "survivability" and "durability" of materials.

The Nazca lines indicate that the primary emphasis of the marking system should be on detectability at eye level. There is also a subtle relationship between the size and placement of the individual components and the size of the entire monument. Stonehenge, the Acropolis, the pyramids, and the Serpent Mound can all be taken in at a single glance. The patterns and forms of the monuments are immediately perceptible. The inability to perceive a monument in its entirety may hamper the investigator's ability to understand it. This phenomenon may explain why the stone circle of Avebury, which is far larger than Stonehenge, is less widely known. The component parts of Avebury are small compared to the scale on which they are set, and it is easy to stand in one part and not realize that the remaining section of the monument exists. We can see that the components of the marking system must be scaled to a size and placed in such a manner that one person standing on the site recognizes the overall pattern.

Using the information from ancient monuments, we can draw up a preliminary marking system for a nuclear waste disposal site. Its primary feature is a series of monoliths ringing the perimeter of the disposal site. The placement of these monoliths should allow an investigator to stand at one monolith and see the next one on either side. Each monolith will be inscribed with a series of symbols, pictures, and languages to convey a warning and information about the site. A sufficient number of monoliths should be used so that the placement pattern can be identified even if some are lost. Repeating the information on every monolith provides the system with a great deal of redundancy, which allows us to be able to lose a few monoliths without jeopardizing the ability of the system to convey information.

For Rockwell, small subsurface markers are included in the design in addition to the large surface markers. The barrier designs are such that a house with a basement could be built on top of the barriers without reaching the wastes. Any construction on the site, however, is not a desirable situation, so three layers of subsurface markers are included in the proposed barrier designs. The first layer is meant to work its way to the surface by erosion, root action or animal action. These markers are meant to be found before any serious human intrusion into the barrier occurs. They are modeled in principle on the ubiquitous potsherds that allow an archaeologist to tell when a site was occupied even before excavation begins. The two lower levels of markers provide extra security should the first set be ignored or overlooked.

Archaeological information has also been used to suggest materials and sizes for the various components of the nuclear waste site. Stone is suggested for the perimeter monoliths. Since marbles, limestones and sandstones are already deteriorating in today's acid rain, they are not acceptable. The types of stone mentioned *least* in conservation literature are those which are hard, compact, nonbrittle and relatively homogeneous, such as granite and basalt. While these are difficult to work, they are also more difficult to deface. The form of the monolith should be tapered to shed water and make it more difficult to reuse. Its surface should be polished so that water cannot collect in the numerous small crevices and pits of an unfinished surface. A raised band around the edge will protect the inscription from severe wind erosion. To draw on another ancient example, the façade of the Treasury at Petra in Jordan is probably in better condition than any other façades at the site because it is recessed into the cliff wall.

As for size, we propose a guideline of at least twice human height; objects this size are more commonly left at the site rather than transported to a museum. For an upper threshold, the largest stones at Stonehenge are 7.6 meters and stand six meters above the level of the plain. Like the stones at Stonehenge, the surface markers should be monoliths; the one-piece construction minimizes surfaces where corrosion can begin and makes it more difficult to disassemble and reuse the marker.

For the subsurface markers, there is an additional factor to consider. They must be sufficiently distinguishable from the surrounding barrier materials to be noticed by an unobservant intruder. For these markers, stone is set aside in favor of pottery, which with its nearly 8,000-year history has withstood the test of time. Oxides can be mixed into a light-firing body to create eye-catching colors. We propose that the subsurface markers be made in yellow and magenta, the colors of the radiation warning signs currently in use world-wide. The designs are impressed so that even if the glaze fails, the information can still be obtained. A disc or lenticular shape with a 12-centimeter diameter and one centimeter at its widest point is proposed.

The messages to be placed on the markers are still in the development stage. The preliminary design has the front of the monolith bearing two symbols as well as text. One symbol is the radiation warning trefoil, which has been in international use for nearly three decades and spans several cultures. Another symbol, developed on the basis of international driving signs, shows a person digging at a barrier mound and a diagonal line across it. This is an attempt to convey the concept of "do not dig here." The front of the surface monolith would also bear the message "Danger. Radioactive Waste. Do Not Dig Here." This message is repeated in the six languages of the United Nations and the language of the Yak'ma Indians, the native inhabitants of the Hanford region. We do not know, nor can we predict, which language will be recognizable in the future. But as in the case of the Rosetta Stone, where three languages appear together, we will significantly increase the likelihood that one of seven will be recognizable. When the French engineers found the Rosetta Stone they could read the Greek immediately, and the

FIGURE 1   A prototype of a warning message intended to alert future generations to avoid a place where nuclear or chemical wastes have been stored.

hope is that one of our seven languages will be understood, and will help to decipher the repeated message in the other six.

One side panel of each surface marker will be devoted to a larger explanation of the site and its wastes, again repeated in seven languages. A sample text for the Hanford Site could be: "This area contains disposal sites for long-lived radioactive wastes. Each disposal site is marked by a raised mound of earth and rock. These mounds are designed to keep water, animals and humans away from the dangerous material. Do not build houses on the mounds. Do not dig for water within the area outlined by these markers. The soil below the mounds does not cause immediate sickness or death. Disturbing the mounds may cause exposure of humans to radioactivity which may result in cancer and death. Illness may not occur until several years after exposure. These disposal sites were built by the United States Government in (date   )." The other side panel will be devoted to a pictorial description of the Hanford Site, a drawing showing each surface marker and barrier mound.

The subsurface markers will bear a subset of the information presented on the surface markers. Prototype markers have been tested for resistance to environmental stresses. The reverse side bears the radiation warning symbol and the message "Do Not Dig Here. Hazardous Waste Below." The obverse bears the "Do Not Dig" pictograph. Although only one language appears on each subsurface marker, the same message appears in multiple languages on the larger surface markers. In this way, we hope that each group of markers will reinforce the other.

Another part of the Rockwell project involves the use of archaeological information to identify degradation mechanisms for the marker materials. We know that the prime agent of stone decay is water, and two minor agents are wind erosion and stress relief. The criteria for the surface marker stone include hardness, which lowers susceptibility to wind erosion; to reduce the effects of wind-blown particles, the inscriptions on the marker will be recessed. Stress relief is due to quarrying operations that remove confining stresses on the rock and cause it to expand to its original, pre-stressed condition. This can lead to microcracking, and in extreme cases to buckling. These effects can be mitigated by storing the stone blocks for a few months before they are worked into final shape.

Water can degrade stone in several ways. As we know, acid rain is already dissolving many limestones and marbles. Freezing is detrimental when the water within the rock expands to the point of fracturing it. Salt action is extremely destructive, even to rocks resistant to other forms of decay. A testing cycle that incorporates these causes of stone decay has been developed for the surface markers. Since the efflorescence and subflorescence of salts (the formation of crystals on or just below the surface) also cause the deterioration of pottery, the subsurface markers are likewise subjected to this testing cycle. The review of archaeological data has resulted in the design requirement of excellent drainage around each surface marker to minimize salt intake. It may also be desirable to immerse each marker in water to leach out entrapped salts before it is placed at the disposal site.

Our research has made it abundantly clear that a carefully thought-out marking system will be required for a high-level waste repository, wherever it is built. A marking system will be required at the Hanford Site if the on-site option is chosen for the final disposition of wastes. All of this research by Rockwell is being performed to assess the viability of this on-site option; it is not a decision to implement it. And archaeology continues to assist in the task of designing the most permanent markers. While none of the designs are final, archaeological data can still offer considerable information for this all-important task—nothing less than using the past to protect future generations from today's deadly wastes.

20

Archaeology in Social Studies: An Integrated Approach

Heather Devine

A public education officer with the Archaeological Survey of Alberta when this article was written, Heather Devine is currently a doctoral candidate in history at the University of Alberta, specializing in Canadian Native History and American Indian Policy.

....

Points to consider when reading this article:

1. Why should archaeology be part of the social studies curriculum in elementary and secondary schools?

2. Archaeological sites are precious and fragile historical resources. Can inexperienced students, especially young ones, safely participate in archaeological fieldwork? How might they be able to get hands-on experience without damaging the resource?

3. What is **experimental archaeology,** and how might this aspect of the discipline be incorporated in a social studies curriculum?

4. The author states that archaeology can provide a "voice to the ordinary people of long ago." What does she mean by that?

A history student I know has taken a number of my archaeology courses (he has, in fact, minored in archaeology) and is pursuing a career in education. This student is just now fulfilling his student teaching requirement at a local high school. He is also looking to the not-too-distant future, concerned about the job market and wondering how he can sell himself to a local school district as a good choice (the *best* choice) to fill an open position they might have in their social studies program.

He is a bright young man, a serious student with an obvious commitment to learning and teaching, but it's a tough job market. He will be up against many other applicants, some of whom are as dedicated and as committed as he. What makes him different? What gives him a leg up on the competition of mostly history majors? We have discussed this at some length, and I think his strength as a candidate for a social studies teaching job rests, at least in part, in his background in archaeology and anthropology.

In this article Heather Devine provides a valuable argument for the inclusion of archaeology in the standard social studies curriculum in elementary and secondary schools. It also is a good rationale for why my student is a good choice for a high school social studies program. Along with the time framework of archaeology, which is far broader than that of written history, the archaeological record is more democratic. Written history has been, at least until the fairly recent past, rather exclusive, usually focusing on the wealthy and powerful. Archaeology is inclusive, focusing equally on the lives of haves and have-nots, kings and slaves, generals and privates, the uplifted and the downtrodden. This broader perspective my student can bring to the classroom reflects the great usefulness of archaeology to a social studies program.

....

From *The History and Social Science Teacher*, vol. 24, no. 3, 1989.
Reprinted here by permission of Althouse Press.

Ask a student or teacher what "archaeology" brings to mind and a variety of answers will be provided; Indiana Jones, the Atocha treasure, the pyramids of Egypt, the temples at Chichen Itza. But what about L'Anse Aux Meadows? And Head-Smashed-In Buffalo Jump? We rarely hear about archaeological sites in Canada; indeed one might think that no archaeological research is conducted here in Canada. We are even less inclined as educators to give it much prominence in our Social Studies programs. We perceive archaeology as an esoteric, even exotic, pastime having little to do with the real world.

Educators will argue that the demands of the core program are gradually eliminating instructional hours normally devoted to electives. They will note that they do not have the expertise to teach archaeology, and that there are few, if any, relevant instructional materials which lend themselves to integration with the core program. Finally, educators will introduce the issue of accountability and question the relevance of archaeology content when so many other topics need to be discussed in school. In short, teachers must have a strong case indeed to devote a week or two to the study of archaeology content.

ARCHAEOLOGY IN EDUCATION: A RATIONALE

Why study archaeology? Archaeology is often perceived as an esoteric discipline which, although fascinating, has little real utility in the modern world. How does archaeology contribute to our understanding of humanity?

First of all, archaeology satisfies innate curiosity about the past. We marvel at the pyramids and wonder how such an engineering achievement was possible. We argue about the origins of humankind, citing the Bible or Charles Darwin to support our views. We wonder whether people in the past shared the same hopes and fears, troubles and pleasures as people today. Archaeology helps to answer these questions by "putting a face" on ancient humanity through the evidence left behind.

Archaeology also serves an important historical function. It is our only means of charting the prehistoric past. Because the term "prehistory," loosely defined, means "before written records," we are totally dependent upon archaeological investigation for our knowledge of any ancient society that did not leave a written record of events. For indigenous peoples such as North American Indians, Australian Aborigines, and African Bushmen, archaeological excavation is perhaps the only means of reconstructing the ancient (and more recent) roots of their cultures. The few existing historical records and oral accounts do not begin to provide a complete record of the aboriginal cultures that proliferated over thousands of years.

Archaeology serves yet another historical purpose. Not only does archaeological research provide prehistoric information, but it also serves to supplement and validate historical records we already have. Historical records cannot be viewed as totally accurate and complete depictions of life in the past. Historical records tend to document major events and the lives of prominent people. History is also inherently biased. The accuracy and completeness of any historical document is always influenced to some degree by the personal values and interests of the writer, the social context in which the document is written, and the facts available to the writer at the time.

Archaeological research provides information concerning daily life in the past that historical accounts may exclude. In doing so, archaeological data serves to provide a "voice" to the ordinary people of long ago — the labouring classes, women, ethnic and racial minorities — all groups which, until recent years, have been largely underrepresented in historical literature and who have had little involvement in the writing of history.

ARCHAEOLOGY AS A SOCIAL STUDIES TOPIC

Archaeology can be a vehicle for the intrinsic instructional goals of Social Studies curricula. As a Social Studies topic, archaeology is a useful tool for achieving value, knowledge, and skill objectives.

Archaeology is a social science. It studies culture in general and the evolution of cultural processes in particular. The study of past lifeways shows how these value systems change over time. Social science is nonjudgmental; we compare cultures not to determine the superiority of any one culture but to show how a variety of influences cause some lifeways to develop differently. In a multicultural society such as ours, understanding how diverse cultures develop helps us to understand why cultures conflict today.

Archaeology also fosters respect for our surroundings. Our physical environment is composed of both natural and man-made resources. Any discussion of the stewardship of our environment should stress that while we need to preserve non-renewable natural resources such as oil and gas for future generations, we must also strive to protect non-renewable heritage resources, whether they be historic buildings or archaeological sites. Archaeologists work to preserve our human past, and a learned appreciation and support of their activities not only helps to preserve our heritage but also stresses the importance of intrinsic values which contribute to the overall quality of life which we enjoy.

Few educators would support the notion that archaeology content is more important than the study of mathematics or science or history. Traditionally, archaeology is a rather minor topic area in Social Studies, and archaeology topics are taught to satisfy specific knowledge goals in the curriculum (e.g. to understand different methods of studying the past, as part of a study of native peoples). But all educators look for innovative, instructionally sound methods for motivating students and delivering core content. It is in this realm — the area of instructional technique — where the potential of archaeology content has largely been overlooked.

In classrooms across Canada, teachers are searching for ways to successfully incorporate a number of subject disciplines in a thematic context. Instructors are attempting to provide opportunities to master different concepts and apply them to practical, real-world situations. Teachers want to promote qualitative instructional goals such as creativity and teamwork without sacrificing knowledge and skills. The multidisciplinary nature of archaeology implicitly satisfies all of these concerns and thus provides the strongest rationale for its inclusion in the curriculum.

An archaeology unit is an excellent way to foster inquiry skills, particularly those employed in the empirical and social sciences. Hypotheses are established and then tested through systematic excavation; conclusions are based on inferences derived from facts gleaned from excavation and historical, ethnographic, and scientific information. Hypothesis formation and testing is an integral part of archaeological activity, and as a result archaeology is a useful tool for the development of thinking skills.

Archaeology activities also help in the delivery of mathematics and science content. Actual or simulated archaeological survey and excavation require students to utilize metric measurement, graphing and drawing to scale. Aspects of biology and geology — plant identification from pollen analysis, identification of animal bones, the study of soil formation and mineral analysis — can all be touched upon in an archaeology unit.

Language arts and fine arts can also be incorporated into the study of archaeology. Indeed, there are already some elementary language arts texts that incorporate units devoted to archaeological themes (e.g. the "Timespinners" unit in *Reading and How*, by J. McInnes, et al, Nelson Networks Series, Nelson Canada, Scarborough, 1985). The replicative experiments which are a part of archaeological research (e.g. pottery production, tool manufacture) serve equally well as a means of presenting hands-on activities in arts and crafts.

Archaeology is a participatory activity. Archaeological excavation requires active physical and mental commitment on the part of the students involved. Archaeological digging makes special demands on students in terms of stamina, precision and patience. Archaeology projects move pupils outside of the school and into the community. They compel the pupil to work cooperatively with classmates and members of the public. Most students, regardless of their academic potential, can derive a great deal of satisfaction from archaeology activities, and in doing so learn a surprising amount of material in a relatively painless fashion.

Activities in archaeology offer students a multidisciplinary approach to social investigation which is of benefit to both themselves and the community of which they are a part.

FIELD TRIPS

Field trip activities should be an integral part of any unit dealing with archaeology. Such visits could include trips to undeveloped archaeological sites on public or private land, excursions to archaeological digs in progress, or tours of historical interpretive centres and museums with an archaeological component (e.g. artifacts on display, archaeological features on-site).

Teachers must prepare in advance for field trips to archaeological sites, particularly undeveloped archaeological sites. Permission must be obtained from the landowner prior to taking students to archaeological sites on private property. The site should be visited in advance and the terrain and archaeological features noted. Then the instructor should prepare a structured field activity for students to complete during their visit to the site. Such an activity might consist of sketching rock art features, mapping tipi rings, burial mounds, or shell middens, or locating visible archaeological features (e.g. cellar depressions) using maps. Teachers are advised that often a visitor will not recognise archaeological features unless they know exactly what they are looking for. If instructors feel uncomfortable identifying and interpreting the archaeological features at a site, they might consider contacting a regional archaeologist or a member of a local archaeological society for assistance.

If students learn nothing else from a field visit, they should understand the need to protect archaeological sites. Students will benefit from a pre-visit discussion of the site and a review of basic archaeological terms. Students should also be advised of proper field etiquette. There should be no littering, no disturbance of livestock, and all gates must be closed after entering or exiting.

Do not, under any circumstances, excavate, disturb, or remove artifacts from sites. If loose surface debris (e.g. bones, stone flakes, metal objects) is picked up and examined, it should be replaced in the exact location where it was found. What may seem to be a piece of loose garbage could be an important artifact. Archaeologists analyze artifacts on the basis of their original proximity to other artifacts at an archaeological site. Therefore it is essential that artifacts remain in as undisturbed a state as possible. In many provinces, surface collection of artifacts is illegal. Teachers are advised to consult the provincial laws governing historical resources for further information.

A trip to an archaeological dig in progress is always a useful experience. Sometimes it is difficult to visualize exactly what it is that archaeologists do. A field trip allows students to see first-hand the different steps involved in archaeological excavation and analysis. Occasionally there is also an opportunity to work as a volunteer excavator (see "Excavation Activity," below).

A "designated" archaeological or historical site is one which is administered by a municipal, provincial, or federal body and one which has some degree of on-site interpretation, ranging from interpretive signage to a facility complete with exhibits and interpreters. If a designated archaeological site exists in your region, by all means take your class there. Most interpretative facilities offer school programming that complements topic areas covered in provincial curricula. If the facility has a strong archaeological component, hands-on activities such as archaeological dig simulations, prehistoric tool production, or artifact study may be offered. Often it is more convenient for the teacher to utilize these resources than to spend the time and money required to offer the same activities in the classroom setting. These facilities already have the necessary equipment, materials, and trained staff to sponsor the activity.

Museum visits are also desirable, particularly if there are no archaeological or historic sites nearby. Many larger museums offer tours and hands-on activities for students. Younger pupils (K-3) may have the opportunity to handle artifacts in the context of a discovery room activity. Teachers are advised to contact local museums to determine what archaeological materials are available for examination. Some museums circulate outreach kits of facsimile artifacts.

EXCAVATION ACTIVITY

From time to time there are opportunities for students to work as volunteer labourers at archaeological sites. Some archaeological digs, such as those administered by the Toronto Board of Education Archaeological Resource Centre are run specifically for student participants. In most cases, however, student volunteers are accepted at archaeological digs on an *ad hoc* basis. Teachers should be aware that many archaeologists will not permit students under 18 years of age to excavate except under special circumstances. In most cases there are only one or two volunteer positions available for students, and the details must be cleared with the supervising archaeologist in advance. As with other field trip activities, student participants should be familiarized with the site, its history, the kinds of artifacts they are likely to encounter, etc. They should be advised on proper attire for excavation activity and prepare mentally for work on the dig. Archaeological excavation is often dirty and can be physically tiring. It can also be quite tedious. A person can excavate all day and not recover a single artifact. When artifacts are discovered, meticulous measurements and notes must be taken. Patience is a virtue in archaeological work.

Most archaeological excavation activity takes place in the late spring, summer, and early autumn, depending on weather conditions. To find out about regional archaeological projects requiring volunteers, contact your local amateur archaeological society or provincial archaeological regulatory agency (see "Resources for Archaeology in Education," below).

Do not attempt an excavation of an actual archaeological site unless it is under the supervision of a qualified archaeologist who has a permit for such work! This caution applies to survey and surface collection as well. If an excavation activity is desired, a simulated excavation can be planned and executed in the classroom setting. Or, students can visit an interpretive facility or museum that provides the opportunity to participate in simulated digs.

Often budget or time constraints prevent field trip excursions to archaeological sites. However, simulated excavation activities can be offered in the school setting. For instructions on planning simulated archaeological digs, contact interpretive facilities and museums with an archaeological program, regional archaeological resource management agencies, local amateur societies, or anthropology publications geared to educators (see "Resources for Archaeology in Education," below).

Some thoughts to keep in mind when planning a simulated dig:

- Plan your excavation well in advance. Choose artifacts with care, and place the items in your simulation unit according to the concepts you are teaching and the site you are creating.

- Whenever possible, use the tools used by archaeologists: trowels, line levels, tape measures, etc. All of these items are inexpensive and readily available at hardware stores.

- Stress precision in excavation. Make sure that students take accurate measurements of artifacts in the excavation unit before they are removed from the simulation unit, and that this information is recorded on an excavation form. Ensure that archaeological digging tools are used correctly and that artifacts are identified and analyzed using classification and inferencing skills.

- Keep in mind that a maximum of four students can work comfortably at a one metre by one metre unit at any given time. Have more than one unit available, and/or rotate students to ensure that all students have an opportunity to dig.

EXPERIMENTAL ARCHAEOLOGY

Archaeologists are interested in determining how artifacts were created and used because this information provides insights into aspects of technological development and **diffusion**. Experimental archaeology involves the researching of traditional techniques for tool construction and use and experimentation in the manufacture and utilization of tool replicas. Pottery construction, flintknapping (the process of chipping tools from stone), food processing, and weapons manufacture and use are all examples of experimental archaeology activities. Many of these activities, such as pottery manufacture and food processing, can be conducted successfully in the classroom setting. Other activities, such as **flintknapping** or weapon construction, can be potentially hazardous, and may not be appropriate for younger students. Do not attempt these activities with your students unless you are proficient yourself.

Teachers should endeavor to incorporate at least one experimental activity in an archaeology unit. Archaeology, by its very nature, is a hands-on activity. Children find replicative experiments both challenging and enjoyable. More importantly, the use of reproduction artifacts for the recreation of traditional activities of the past serves to minimize the "museum mystique" surrounding artifacts. Quite often we forget that artifacts were not manufactured to be looked at, but were everyday items used and modified by ordinary people. Too often students' sole experience with an artifact consists of passively peering at the item through the glass window of a museum case, where the object sits pristine and isolated, an object to be admired rather than understood. No matter how attractive the exhibit or how well written the display captions, a viewer is unlikely to recognise the skill and patience needed to manufacture and use artifacts from the past. But give a student the opportunity to attempt the traditional methods for manufacturing stone tools, making pemmican, baking bread or molding clay pots, and that individual is likely to re-think his or her notions of life in the past. It is not enough to identify artifacts from early times; what is important is to know how these objects came to be developed, how they were used, and the impact of these objects on day-to-day survival in the distant past.

RESOURCES FOR ARCHAEOLOGY IN EDUCATION

The first step towards integrating archaeology activities into the Social Studies program is to identify a Social Studies concept compatible to archaeological content. Perhaps it is a general topic in Canadian history, such as the study of the western fur trade or early pioneer settlement. Or perhaps you would like to introduce students to the study of hunters and gatherers as part of an examination of culture. From there, you will want to focus on a more specific topic within the broader field to provide students with a case-study situation. Perhaps you will choose to study one particular hunter-gatherer group, or one specific pioneer community. Once you have narrowed your focus, your next task is to locate and compile resource materials. If you are studying a topic area featured in your Social Studies curriculum (e.g. Indian groups of Canada) most of the basic resources listed for the topic should provide you and your students with the background information required to research the topic in more detail. The bibliographical references provided at the end of the textbooks may also provide lists of books and films dealing with the archaeological aspects of the topic you have chosen.

The audiovisual and print materials produced through cultural organizations such as the National Geographic Society and the National Museums of Canada are worthy of note. . . . Interpretive centres at federal and provincial historical sites sometimes provide printed material dealing with classroom-based archaeology activities as a service to schools which cannot take students to their facilities. University and college anthropology and classics departments may also have outreach materials of use to teachers. Periodicals such as *Equinox* and *The Beaver* print archaeology articles from time to time, as do many larger newspapers. Your school librarian will be able to assist you in compiling a classroom reference collection of suitable books.

However, many school libraries have only a limited number of references dealing with archaeology, particularly Canadian archaeology. Beware of pseudo-scientific publications (e.g. *Chariots of the Gods*) which are erroneous interpretations of archaeological information. More useful and trustworthy sources of information are the provincial government bodies which deal with archaeological research and resource management.

ARCHAEOLOGICAL AGENCIES

Each provincial and territorial government has an administrative body responsible for supervising archaeological research and protecting the archaeological resources in its jurisdiction. Most of these organizations have some form of outreach material available to members of the public, ranging from brochures and posters to videotapes and research reports. Teachers are advised that some of this material may not be suitable for utilization by younger students as the reading level can be fairly sophisticated and the content can be highly technical in nature. In most instances teachers will be required to review materials carefully and extract the information required to present archaeology content to students.

Teachers should also contact government archaeological agencies because these organizations maintain links with amateur archaeological societies, university archaeology departments, and independent archaeological consultants — all useful sources of information should teachers need instructional materials, classroom speakers, or in-service instructors.

WORKING WITH ARCHAEOLOGY; A FINAL NOTE

Regulations and fines do not prevent the destruction of archaeological sites. It is through public education that citizens learn the intrinsic value of our historic and prehistoric past. Archaeology in education, therefore, is essential to the investigation, interpretation, and protection of Canada's archaeological heritage.

I AM AN ARCHAEOLOGIST

Lynne Sebastian

I remember the first time my parents came to visit me in the field on an excavation project. They stood quietly on the edge of a partially excavated pithouse that we were bailing out after a heavy rain. As I lifted bucket after dripping bucket of mud and water over my head to crew members on the site surface, my father finally said, "You must all do this for love. They couldn't pay you enough to get you to do this." That pretty well sums it up. I got into archaeology against my better judgment, walking away from ten years of an entirely different career and adopting a physically strenuous line of work for the first time at the advanced age of thirty-one because I found the opportunity to touch the past—to know about life so long ago and in a world utterly different from our own—irresistible.

I was educated as a high school English teacher, but I graduated from college in 1969 in the middle of the first teacher surplus in U.S. history. While job hunting, I took a series of clerical jobs and, quite by chance, was hired to edit archaeology monographs at the Anthropology Museum at the University of Michigan. I showed some aptitude for editing, and as I learned the technical jargon of the field, I found it easy to move from one archaeology editing job to another, eventually arriving at the University of Utah.

While I was working as an editor in the University of Utah anthropology department, two things happened that drew me into that irresistible love for archaeology and brought me to that muddy moment in the waterlogged pithouse. First, one of the professors with whom I worked was elected editor of *American Antiquity*, the journal of the Society for American Archaeology, and he hired me as his copy editor. After years of reading (let's be honest here) dull, dry descriptions of test pits and potsherds, suddenly I was reading cutting edge articles about archaeological theory, method, and synthesis. "Hey," I thought, "there may be something to this archaeology stuff after all!"

Second, I started taking a few graduate courses in cultural anthropology. After years of missing the point of my archaeological officemates' anthropology jokes, I figured I'd be more hip and a better archaeology editor too, if I understood more about the field. Instead of simply achieving those modest goals, I found myself swept up into a whole new way of seeing and understanding the world around me. In anthropology I found tools for analyzing culture and human behavior that made sense to me in a way that literary criticism never had. Suddenly, the patterning revealed in all those test pits and on potsherds was not just dry description but a window into understanding and explaining the past. Although I had to depend on editing to support myself through much of my course work at Utah and later at the University of New Mexico, where I received my Ph.D., I never looked back. I never again wanted to be anything but an archaeologist.

(Photo courtesy of Lynne Sebastian)

Largely because of the excitement I found in my Utah courses in anthropological theory, economic anthropology, and political anthropology, my research interests have always involved attempts to understand social, economic, and political organization in prehistoric societies. My first big field project was a massive excavation program within the pool area of a dam under construction in southwestern Colorado. The prehistoric Pueblo occupation of the area had been relatively brief, but very intensive, and spanned the period during which these farming people were shifting from a dispersed, farmstead or small hamlet pattern of settlement to a pattern of residence in good-sized villages.

As I worked through several summers in that very beautiful part of the Southwest, I thought about those people and how, in the course of a generation or two, they had to solve some very basic problems in social relations and organization. They had gone from an independent, largely autonomous way of life to a life necessarily constrained by the requirements of living in a large group. How did they resolve the conflicts that would have arisen? How did they organize themselves to get community activities done? Who took charge of these organizational efforts, and how did those individuals or lineages achieve and legitimize the social power necessary for leadership?

When I started my work at the University of New Mexico, a major National Park Service research program (headquartered at UNM) was under way in Chaco Canyon in the remote San Juan Basin of northwestern New Mexico. In prehistoric times at Chaco the population continued to increase beyond the village stage characteristic of the Colorado group to the formation of large, architecturally differentiated communities. These communities consisted of massively constructed "great houses," monumental architecture with multiple stories, huge ceremonial chambers, walled plazas, and constructed mounds, surrounded by multiple small villages and connected by a system of formally laid out roads.

As I thought about the Chaco case, the questions that had arisen in my mind while contemplating the emergent villages in southwestern Colorado led to a much broader range of questions about the nature of sociopolitical evolution and the rise of institutional leadership. In its simplest form, my question was: How do societies go from a system where leadership is situational, fleeting, and based on age, kinship, and personal qualities to one where leadership is institutionalized, heritable, and powerful enough to take away people's goods, liberty, or even their lives.

As I completed my course work at UNM and began working on field projects in New Mexico and Arizona for UNM's Office of Contract Archaeology, I kept mulling over these questions about sociopolitical organization in the past, ultimately writing my dissertation on *Leadership, Power, and Productive Potential: A Political Model of the Chaco System.* I loved fieldwork, and even more, I loved the subsequent analyses and write-up phase. I loved to touch handprints still visible in thousand-year-old plaster, to watch the outlines of a community long hidden beneath the drifting sands of the high desert country emerge into the light after so many centuries. And I loved those crystalline moments (which for some reason always seem to happen late in the night) when the gestalt suddenly shifts into place and the analytical puzzle I had been struggling with reveals some tiny piece of that unknown past world with perfect, breathtaking clarity.

So how is it, you might ask, that I have not put a trowel into the ground in more than ten years? Why have I walked away from that seductive, intimate connection with the past that made waterlogged pithouses, sandstorms, nights of sleeping in a tent in subfreezing temperatures, blisters from shoveling, and aches from wheeling endless wheelbarrow loads of dirt all worthwhile? In 1987 I took what I viewed as a short-term job in the New Mexico State Historic Preservation Division, a state agency tasked in state and federal law with working to preserve the historic and prehistoric heritage of our state.

Within a very short time I came to realize, as I never had when working as a field archaeologist, how fragile the archaeological record is and how rapidly it is disappearing under the combined pressures of development, vandalism, and pothunting for pleasure and profit. The need for legal protections, for creative and well-designed excavation programs prior to destruction of archaeological sites by modern development, and for education and outreach to the public about the importance of the past and the nonrenewable nature of archaeological resources is immense and critical.

So ten years later, I'm still here. I worked my way up from being one of the staff archaeologists to being the State Archaeologist to being the Director of the Division and State Historic Preservation Officer. I've committed myself to preserving the remnants of the past for others to explore some day, rather than exploring the past myself, and I know that the rest of my career will lie along the path that I have chosen. Even though I sometimes feel personal regrets over what I've given up, I know that this was the right thing to do. Still, when someone asks me what I do for a living, I always reply, "I am an archaeologist."

PART 4

Helping History:
Setting the Record Straight and
Solving the Mysteries

The goal of archaeology is to understand the past, and in one very real sense, all archaeologists are detectives. Like detectives they collect physical evidence and analyze the remains left by human beings. Unlike actual detectives who conduct their work at the scene of a crime, archaeological detectives conduct their investigations at places where historical events occurred. Here in Part 4 we will examine how, acting as detectives, archaeologists can help fill in the blanks left by the written record through the examination of physical evidence left behind by the people who participated in these historical events.

As detectives of the past, archaeologists can add their expertise to that of historians to provide a more complete picture of historic events. Archaeology can help to illuminate these historical events because, as all historians know, just because people in past times were literate and often wrote accounts of the events that happened in their own lifetimes, we do not by any means today have a perfect understanding of the actual nature of those events. History is not inclusive. Accounts written at the time of an event do not necessarily tell the whole story. Depending on who controls the printing presses, the newspapers, the magazines and, yes, even the radio and television stations in more recent times, a version of history is told, recorded, passed down, and made "official." However, this does not reflect a complete and accurate transcript of what actually occurred. The victors of ancient battles wrote the official accounts of the war; the losers often were silenced and silent.

Napoleon Bonaparte is supposed to have asked: "What is history but a fable agreed upon?" He recognized that the accounts he sponsored detailing his victories on the battlefield were self-aggrandizing, self-serving statements intended to solidify support back home. Perhaps they were also written with an eye to how future people might view this ruler of France. Another great leader, Winston Churchill, said it even more directly. When commenting on his place in history, Churchill was quoted as maintaining, "History will be kind to me for I intend to write it." In a similar manner, slave owners and not slaves wrote the accounts of plantation life. (See Part 2 of this Reader.)

That written accounts may be incomplete or even untrue is the case even when we examine very well-known historical events, the kinds of events that we are all exposed to even in elementary school. Archaeology, with its focus on material evidence—on actual things related to an event, things that can be recovered and analyzed—can help historians gain a more complete picture of events for which most previous information has been literary. Written records may be incomplete, biased, or intentionally inaccurate; the physical record may be incomplete, but it is hardly ever intentionally skewed. Physical evidence of the sort collected by archaeologists can be used to test history, to verify or refute or merely to add details to the official version of events handed down to us. And in some cases, when history provides us with no official version and when the actual nature of the events and the disposition of the historical personages remain a mystery, archaeology can help solve the riddles and allow us to know with varying degrees of certainty what actually transpired.

The articles in Part 4 provide examples of archaeological investigations that have complemented history by adding to our understanding of historical events or that have challenged the official version and caused us to change how we interpret those events. In some instances, archaeology has provided the physical evidence necessary for the solution of historical mysteries when the written record by itself has offered no solution.

21

Post-mortem at the Little Bighorn

Douglas D. Scott and Melissa A. Connor

Doug Scott is an archaeologist with the National Park Service. He has written extensively on the archaeology of the Little Bighorn Battlefield and has co-authored two books on this subject: Archaeological Perspectives on the Battle of the Little Bighorn *and* Archaeological Insights in the Custer Battle: A Preliminary Assessment *(both from University of Oklahoma Press).*

Melissa Connor is a National Park Service archaeologist with expertise in the reconstruction of diet through the analysis of human bone. She was one of the co-authors of Archaeological Perspectives on the Battle of the Little Bighorn.

Points to consider when reading this article:

1. How — and why — can archaeology help us better reconstruct events that occurred during a battle that already has been intensely studied by historians?

2. The human remains left on the battlefield eventually were removed and buried in a mass grave in 1881. Why were bones still found by archaeologists digging in the 1980s at the actual scene of the battle?

3. How does the archaeological analysis of the distribution of artifacts verify the Indian account of the flow of the battle?

4. What new interpretation of the battle is provided by the archaeological evidence?

The Little Bighorn Battlefield National Monument in Montana is an eerie, sad place, memorializing the site of what was either a tragic massacre or a brave victory — it all depends on your point of view.

Other famous battlefields, particularly those from the Civil War, tend to be built up at their margins, with lots of tourist services that, at least in the opinion of some, trivialize these awful spots where the ground was once soaked by the blood of young men. But the Little Bighorn Battlefield is different, looking much as it did when a contingent of more than two hundred U.S. cavalrymen rode into what they presumed to be a manageable contingent of Plains Indian warriors and found, instead, one of the largest accumulations of armed Indians ever recorded. When the smoke from the rifles cleared, all 210 U.S. soldiers were dead, and an unrecorded number of Indians had been killed or wounded.

There is one obvious change visible at the Little Bighorn Battlefield since that awful day in June 1876. Small white marble markers litter the scene. Each one marks the spot where a U.S. soldier fell and died. But, as it turns out, these markers, placed at the battlefield in 1890, are not the only things the army left behind. Artifacts from the battle, including human remains, bullets, and arrows, were also left behind, writing a history of the battle in the hardware of war. This article presents a new vision of the battle based on this evidence.

The anniversary of the Battle of the Little Bighorn falls on June 26, the day 110 years ago when George Armstrong Custer led some 210 men to their death in the Montana Territory. In the years that followed, the story of Custer's Last Stand assumed legendary proportions, while much of the hard evidence of the battle remained unexamined. Then in August 1983, a wildfire scorched four-fifths of the 760 acres of Custer Battlefield National Monument (a cigarette tossed from a car on nearby State Route 212 may have ignited the drought-stricken vegetation), and the National Park

Service, which administers the Monument, enlisted local archeologist Richard Fox to see whether artifacts might be recovered from the denuded landscape. The result has been a full-fledged study by the Midwest Archeological Center of the National Park Service and the University of Nebraska.

Along with Dick Harmon, of the U.S. Geological Survey, and Richard Fox, and aided by many volunteers, we have spent two field seasons encouraging the earth to yield its secrets about this historic battle. We chose to view the battleground as a crime scene, and by using forensic techniques, such as microscopic examination of firing-pin marks on cartridge cases and rifling marks on bullets, we have been able to determine the weapons used by the various participants. These techniques, combined with the standard archeological practice of recording where artifacts are found, have enabled us to deduce the movement of individual firearms over the field of battle, verify cavalry positions, and pinpoint the previously unknown placement of the Indian warriors. Many human skeletal remains were also found, and these tell us of the wounds the men received, as well as the soldiers' general health and condition at the time of death.

The story of the battle begins in 1868, when the Treaty of Fort Laramie was signed with the Sioux and Cheyenne. Among other things, the treaty granted the Black Hills area to the Sioux for "as long as the grass was green and the sky was blue." In the early 1870s, however, rumors spread of gold in the Black Hills, and white miners began slipping into the reservation. In 1874, the U.S. government sent a geological team under Custer to check out these rumors. Gold was among the minerals found, and thereafter there was no stopping the hordes of miners who flowed onto the Indians' land.

The Sioux were disgusted with the government's inability to keep white people from trespassing, especially in the Black Hills, which they considered sacred. As the whites did not seem to be respecting the treaty, many of the Indians saw no reason to abide by its terms and stay on the reservation. Along with Cheyenne from other Indian agencies, thousands of Sioux spent the winter of 1875–76 on their traditional hunting grounds in Montana and the Dakotas, despite a government warning that unless they returned immediately, they would be considered hostile and subject to military action.

In May of 1876, a three-sided campaign was launched to shepherd the Sioux and Cheyenne back to their assigned lands. One column, under Gen. John Gibbon, marched east from Fort Ellis (near present-day Bozeman, Montana). A second column, led by Gen. Alfred Terry and including Custer, headed west from Fort Abraham Lincoln (near present-day Bismarck, North Dakota). The third column departed from Fort Fetterman (near present-day Sheridan, Wyoming) under the command of Gen. George Crook and moved north into Montana. These three units, totaling about 3,000 men, were to meet near the end of June in the vicinity of the Little Bighorn River.

Unknown to Terry and Gibbon, Crook encountered Indians near Rosebud Creek in southern Montana, was defeated by them on June 17, and withdrew his men to Wyoming. Meanwhile, Terry, with some 921 men, mostly cavalry, was moving west up the Yellowstone River to the Little Bighorn. On June 22, the cavalry, led by Custer, left Terry's command to scout ahead.

The 7th Cavalry consisted of twelve companies, each authorized to contain fifty to sixty-four men. In reality, most field units never operated at authorized strength, owing to low budget allotments from Congress, high desertion rates, and men on detached duty. Custer commanded about 715 men, about 160 men under authorized strength. Custer's rank was lieutenant colonel (brevet major general). A brevet rank was an honorific and temporary grade given for special service and as an award for gallantry in action. Custer's second-in-command was Maj. Marcus Reno. Next in line was Frederick Benteen, the regiment's senior captain.

Early on the morning of the 25th, the 7th Calvary was on high ground, with Rosebud Creek behind them to the east and the Little Bighorn about sixteen and a half miles to the west. From a spot subsequently dubbed the Crow's Nest, Custer observed a large Indian camp on the far side of the Little Bighorn. Worried that the Indians might escape, Custer decided to attack and descended westward into the valley. Near the Crow's Nest, Captain Benteen was ordered to take three companies and keep to the south, to block a possible escape route. The pack train, carrying ammunition and guarded by one company, followed Benteen, while the other companies went ahead. At midday, a few miles from the Little Bighorn, Custer again divided his command, ordering Major Reno to take three companies along the river bottom and attack the Indian camp on its southern end. The remaining five companies followed Custer westward along the ridge to the north, preparing to support Reno.

About 3:00 P.M., Indian warriors engaged Reno and his men, forcing them to retreat back across the river and up the bluffs to a defensible position. Meanwhile, Custer must have realized the gravity of the situation as the north end of the Indian camp came into view. About 3:30, Custer's adjutant sent a message to Benteen: "Benteen, Come on. Big village, be quick, bring packs. P.S. Bring pacs [sic]. W. W. Cooke." The messenger, bugler John Martin, was the last to see Custer and the men in his five companies alive.

Summoned by the message, Benteen's forces and the pack train arrived some forty-five minutes later, joining Reno and his men on the hilltop. All were pinned down for two days, fighting to keep their defensive position and wondering when Custer would relieve them. The Indians finally retreated on June 27, when General Terry arrived, joined by General Gibbon's column. Reno sent two men to meet the advancing column, and they found Terry and Gibbon near the abandoned Indian camp. Here, a scout brought the news: Custer and his men lay dead on a ridge above the Little Bighorn.

From that moment until the present, Custer's movements after the messenger left him have been the subject of hot debate. Soon after the battle ended, however, eyewitness accounts began to appear in newspapers across the country. The witnesses were the survivors—the Indians. Weary of army pursuit, the warriors had returned to their reservations, where Indian agents interviewed them. Only then did the warriors learn for certain the identity of the commander they had defeated.

Different versions of Indian accounts of the battle appeared in different papers and journals, and many began to question their accuracy. People suspected distorted reporting by glory-seeking correspondents or faulty translations of Indian words or signs. The Indians, fearing retribution from the army, may also not have told the whole truth. As a result, the Indian accounts were long scorned, although in the past fifteen years, historians who have reviewed them have concluded that the gist of the reports rings true.

The Indians' accounts, collected from survivors up until the middle of this century, state that the camp on the Little Bighorn was established shortly after Crook's defeat at Rosebud Creek, and included the Sioux who had fought in that confrontation. Nevertheless, Custer's arrival apparently took the camp by surprise. As Custer and his men moved north along the ridge, a large contingent of Sioux pressed the attack from the south. A group of Cheyenne and some Sioux also attacked the soldiers from the north and northwest.

At first the shooting was from a distance, but as the soldiers stood their ground, apparently in a V-shaped formation, the intense fire thinned their ranks. It was then that the warriors were able to move in and essentially surround the cavalry. Once many of the soldiers were dead or wounded, the Indians swooped in on those that remained, finishing them off in hand-to-hand combat. Accounts tell of killing wounded soldiers and of stripping the dead of their guns, ammunition, clothing, and other useful items. Some warriors scalped the dead or mutilated their remains, as was their custom in warfare.

In an attempt to make the battleground speak for itself, during the summers of 1984 and 1985 we used the techniques of archeology to unearth thousands of artifacts, despite events that had disturbed the area over the intervening years. After the battle, the Indians removed their dead and wounded, but the dead soldiers lay in the hot Montana sun for nearly three days. When the surviving members of the 7th Cavalry began the onerous task of burying the dead, the bodies were bloated, blackened, and almost unrecognizable. Because there were few shovels or other tools with which to do a proper job, cups, plates, and other available implements were used to mound dirt over the bodies. Afraid that the Indians would return and attack again, the soldiers covered most of the dead with just a little soil and sagebrush.

The powdery soil was not enough to keep coyotes and other scavengers from the graves, and the action of wind, rain, and snow compounded the problem of keeping the men buried. In 1877, the army reburied the exposed bones. All the officers' remains, however, were exhumed and shipped home, except those of Lt. John Crittenden, whose father asked that he be left where he fell. Persistent reports of exposed remains brought the army back in 1879 for another reburial. Finally, in 1881, the army exhumed all the remains from the battlefield and reburied them in a mass grave on Last Stand Hill, near where Custer's body had been found. A large granite marker was placed over the grave that same year.

While the reburial teams stripped the battlefield of its most conspicuous bones and artifacts, many important clues were left to await archeological exploration. We divided our work into three parts. The first was a metal detector survey of the battlefield. Volunteers, often experts in the use of detectors, walked about five yards apart, covering the field. Where their detectors beeped, they flagged the spot. Behind them came a recovery crew that excavated cautiously, searching for the object that had caused the detector to signal, but not moving it out of place. Finally, the survey crews came along to plot each artifact's position on a grid system. This crew also recorded the depth at which the artifact lay and, in the case of bullets and cartridges, noted the orientation and the declination of the piece. Only then was the artifact collected.

The second part of the project was a search in a gully known as Deep Ravine, where twenty-eight men were said to have been buried in place and never subsequently exhumed. At first, we thought that the metal detectors would locate these men, but even after several close examinations, only a handful of scattered artifacts came to light. In 1985, C. Vance Haynes, a geomorphologist from the University of Arizona, volunteered to examine the

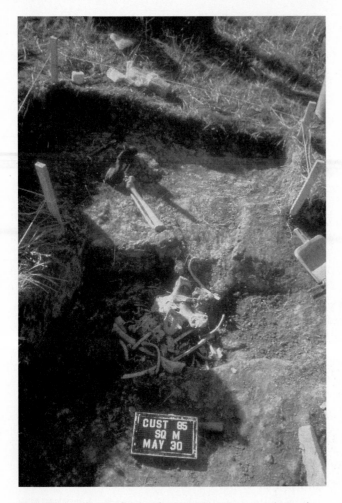

FIGURE 1   The nearly complete remains of a U.S. 7th Cavalry soldier killed in the Battle of Little Bighorn were found by archaeologists excavating in 1984 and 1985 in the vicinity of one of 250 marble markers erected in 1890 where these cavalrymen were thought to have been killed during the battle. (National Park Service, Little Bighorn Battlefield National Mounument)

ravine. Haynes found a deeply buried area that conforms to the historic descriptions of the burial locale; we hope to excavate it in a future field season.

In the third part of our work, we excavated the immediate areas around marble markers that had been placed to commemorate the locations where Custer's men fell. Set in place fourteen years after the battle and more than nine years after the bodies were disinterred and placed in a mass grave, these marble markers replaced wooden ones, many of which had fallen down or been burned by wildfire. Two hundred fifty-one markers dot the main battlefield, yet only about 210 men fell with Custer. One reason to excavate around the markers was to test the appropriateness of their locations.

These three activities—the metal detector survey, the search in Deep Ravine, and the excavations near

the markers—uncovered about 2,200 artifacts, 300 human bones, and 200 bones of horses and other animals. Additional materials (still being analyzed) were collected in 1985 at the Reno-Benteen defense site.

The metal detector survey located hundreds of bullets and cartridge casings. In most cases we could assume that spent cartridges from Springfield carbines and Colt revolvers—the regulation cavalry weapons—had fallen in cavalry positions, and that bullets from these guns had been fired toward the Indians. Conversely, we assumed that bullets found in association with cavalry remains and artifacts came from Indian fire, and that cartridges of the corresponding calibers indicated the Indian positions.

Even before the analyses were complete, we knew that the Indians were much better armed than had been previously documented. The subsequent firearms analyses have identified twenty-five different types of guns used by the warriors. Metal arrowheads were also found, showing that the stereotypical bow and arrow was also used.

Indian arms included army issue Springfield carbines and Colt revolvers. These could have been captured either in the Rosebud skirmish with General Crook's forces or in the valley fight against Reno; some were no doubt taken from Custer's men. Antiquated muzzle-loading firearms were also well represented. Other Indian arms included the .44-caliber Henry, the .44-caliber Model 1866 Winchester, and the .44-caliber Model 1873 Winchester, all repeating rifles. The army did not issue repeating rifles in 1876. The army's single-shot Springfield was not as fast as the repeating rifles, although it was more powerful and more accurate than the majority of the Indian arms.

By using crime laboratory firearms-identification techniques, we could determine how many individual weapons were represented by the archeological artifacts. We estimate that if 1,500 Indian warriors took part in the battle (a conservative number by historical accounts), then about 375 would have been armed with muzzle-loaders and single-shot rifles such as Sharps and Ballards, and about 192 would have been armed with repeating weapons. The rest may have used bows and arrows and a few old pistols and revolvers. Based on these minimal figures, we can conclude that in terms of carbines, Custer's men were outgunned two to one.

There is historical information on the battle that derives from the examination of the battleground at the time of its discovery (including where the bodies of the officers and men were found) and from Indian accounts. Combining this information with the distribution of the recently uncovered buttons, spurs, bullets, and cartridge cases, we are able to make a detailed reconstruction of the battle.

FIGURE 2   An unfired .45 caliber cartridge (government issued) from a model 1873 Springfield Carbine rifle (left) and a .405 grain bullet fired from an army Springfield Carbine (right), both found by archaeologists in their 1984–1985 investigation of the Little Bighorn battlefield. (National Park Service, Little Bighorn National Monument)

The Indian camp that Custer sought to attack contained perhaps 3,000 to 4,000 people, including some 1,500 warriors. The Indians belonged to a number of different bands whose members were affiliated by common language and family ties. The majority were Sioux (Lakota, Teton, Brulé, and Blackfoot), a lesser number of Cheyenne occupied the northern end of the camp, and there were also a few Arapahos. Although camped together for protection, the various bands lacked an overall organization. There were a number of important leaders—Sitting Bull, Crazy Horse, and Gall for the Sioux; Lame White Man and Two Moon for the Cheyenne—but in battle, strategy was determined by individual initiative and charisma, not by a chain of command. According to Indian accounts, Sitting Bull, sometimes thought of as Custer's adversary in battle, did not participate in the fighting but occupied himself with making medicine to strengthen the Indian warriors.

Our reconstruction begins after the messenger left Custer, with the command apparently moving aggressively toward the Indian camp. Encountering Sioux and Cheyenne warriors directed by Gall at about 4:00 P.M.,

Custer moved north and gained high ground at areas now known as Greasy Grass Ridge and Custer Ridge. Here he deployed one company, led by Lt. James Calhoun, in a broad, south-facing arc some 400 yards long. Then, probably to confront a group of Indians attacking from the north and west, Custer took the rest of his men and wheeled north. Leaving Capt. Myles Keogh in charge of a company between himself and Calhoun, Custer deployed his remaining three companies between a high point and a ravine, now called Last Stand Hill and Deep Ravine, respectively.

These deployments formed a broad V-shaped pattern—a classic offensive formation—with the angle to the north, at Last Stand Hill. The cartridge cases attributed to the soldiers are generally in the area of this V. There is very little archeological evidence to document any further troop movement. Although the fight may have been a running one until this final deployment, after this, the units apparently stood their ground.

We determined the soldiers' positions from the presence of spent cartridges from government-issue guns. Bullets fired from the soldiers' guns were found embedded in the ground, often within, or in front of, the

FIGURE 3   Four iron arrow points found by archaeologists in 1984 and 1985 in the vicinity of U.S. Army positions at the Little Bighorn battlefield. The arrows had been shot at the cavalrymen during the battle. (National Park Service, Little Bighorn Battlefield National Monument).

areas in which quantities of Indian cartridge cases were found. Bullets corresponding to the calibers of cartridge cases at Indian positions were found embedded in army positions. A few were associated with human remains.

The most intense Indian fire came from a position about 300 feet southeast of Calhoun's position, where perhaps as many as sixty .44-caliber Henry and Winchester rifles were being fired. A second Indian position, on Greasy Grass Ridge, was southwest of Calhoun's men. A minimum of forty-five guns using .44-caliber rimfire ammunition were fired here, as well as at least seven other types of weapons. Calhoun's men probably were overrun by Indians firing from these two positions.

The only physical evidence we found for any movement among the soldiers' positions consists of some .45-caliber cartridge cases (U.S. Army issue for the Springfield carbine), fired from the same weapons. These were found, first, in the Calhoun position, then scattered along a line toward the Keogh position, and finally, intermixed with cartridges belonging to the Keogh group. Several of Calhoun's men, watching their comrades and then their position fall, must have finally retreated under fire to Keogh's position.

Some Indian weapons fired toward Calhoun's men were also fired toward the cavalry line that stretched from Deep Ravine to Last Stand Hill. This cavalry line was also under attack from the north and west by Crazy Horse, Two Moon, Lame White Man, and other Sioux and Cheyenne warriors. Judging by the numbers

of cartridges that we found, these warriors were not as well armed as those fighting Calhoun's men. Indians joining the attack from the south, after Calhoun's position collapsed, may have added the firepower and numbers needed to overwhelm the cavalry.

The documented movement of a number of Indian weapons indicates that as the battle progressed, the Indians moved upslope toward Custer's final position on Last Stand Hill. Some of the Indians converged at a knoll north and east of the hill to shoot down into the knot of remaining men. We found little evidence that the soldiers fired their handguns. Indian accounts of the battle, gathered many years afterward, state that the soldiers only used their Colts near the end of the battle, when hand-to-hand fighting began, and that after emptying their Colts, the soldiers did not have time to reload before the Indians were upon them. The paucity of Colt bullets and casings among the archeological finds confirms these accounts. The battle was all over sometime between 5:00 and 6:00 in the afternoon.

Our excavations around the markers confirm that most were placed where a soldier fell, as shown by pieces of uniforms, weapons, and human bone found nearby. About thirty-eight pairs of markers (markers placed by twos around the battlefield) usually indicated a single soldier, thus accounting for many of the excess markers.

Although Custer's men were reburied in a mass grave in 1881, we found human remains belonging to at least thirty-two individuals. Dr. Clyde Snow, a forensics expert who is interpreting the remains, says this is not unusual. Whenever untrained people gather up bones, they may overlook small ones, such as hand and foot bones, or not recognize them as human. These were most of the bones we found.

The skull fragments we uncovered showed that the bone had been broken while still green, indicating what Dr. Snow calls "perimortem blunt instrument trauma." An Indian warrior, Black Elk, recounting the final moments of the battle, described how the Indians used hatchets and clubs to finish off the surviving soldiers. While some of the evidence of the trauma we found was undoubtedly induced at the time of death, many of the cut marks and crushed skulls may have resulted from mutilation of the dead, a normal cultural expression of victory for Sioux and Cheyenne warriors. This battle was not exceptional in this regard, but to the soldiers who buried Custer's dead on June 28, 1876, the field was a scene of ghastly and sickening horror.

The excavations around one pair of markers near the Deep Ravine yielded many bones from one individual, some uniform buttons, bullets, and a metal arrowhead. Taking this data, the relative placement of the artifacts, and a little imagination, we could put together the following scenario. The soldier was about twenty-five years old and robust—probably strong for his 5'8" stature. He wore regulation coat and pants and was hit by a bullet from a .44-caliber repeating rifle. The bullet was associated with a few rib bones, suggesting the shot was to the chest and may have been the mortal wound. Whether the man was dead or dying, someone also shot him in the head with a Colt revolver. When the Indians overran his position, they crushed his skull with a war club and hacked at his front and back with knives. The Indians did not remove his uniform for cloth; perhaps it was too bloody to be worthwhile.

So far the archeological data support much in the Indian accounts of the battle and contradict none of them. As the analysis of the material collected in 1985 progresses, we will learn more details of Custer's fight, as well as what happened to Reno and Benteen. The archeological finds provide historians with a new resource in the study of the battle. By itself, each button, bullet, or cartridge may seem unimportant, but both the Indians and the cavalry left behind arrangements of artifacts that reflected their fighting styles, their ideas of leadership, and their concepts of battle.

The Battle of the Little Bighorn epitomized the clash of cultures—the Native American versus the Euro-American—that differed in hundreds of ways, including perceptions of land ownership, treaties, and boundaries. It may not have been of strategic importance in military history, but it did affect the course of this struggle. In the years preceding the battle, individuals sympathetic to the Indians' plight had determined government dealings with them. If the debacle at the Little Bighorn did nothing else, it galvanized the anti-Indian forces in the U.S. government, influencing official policy toward the Plains Indians until nearly the close of the nineteenth century.

22

Victorio's Escape:
GPS and Archaeology Recount the
Tale of an Apache Battle

James Wakeman and Karl Laumbach

James Wakeman is a surveyor at New Mexico State University.
Karl Laumbach is an archaeologist at the private firm Human Systems Research.

Points to consider when reading this article:

1. What is GPS?

2. How did the application of **GPS (Global Positioning Satellite)** technology assist in the reconstruction of the battle between the Apache and the U.S. Cavalry?

3. How did the researchers pinpoint the location of the combatants in this battle that occurred almost 120 years ago?

4. How did Victorio and the warriors he commanded escape the trap laid for them by the Ninth Cavalry?

As mentioned in the introduction to this book, there is a cliché that states, "history is written by the winners." The point, of course, is that the defeated, if they survive, are more interested in saving their lives than in writing the story of their survival. Besides, the victors usually control the books, the printing presses, and the radio and television stations. They are rarely in the mood to afford the vanquished an opportunity to tell their side of the story through these ordinary channels.

The archaeological record, however, makes no such distinction between the conquerors and the conquered. The material record is oblivious to such transient considerations. All material ends up in the ground eventually—some of it preserves and some of it does not. That which is left can be recovered and analyzed in an effort to tell the accurate story of what happened in a given time and place, regardless of who "won" the skirmish.

This is the story of an actual battle that took place on April 6, 1880, not even 120 years ago, between a group of Apache warriors and soldiers from the Ninth Cavalry deep in the desert of New Mexico. The Apache were surrounded and certain to meet their deaths or be captured by the Buffalo Soldiers. Yet, certain as it seemed, this is not what happened. The Indians, led by their war chief Victorio, managed—miraculously—to escape the trap set by the soldiers. Cutting edge archaeology is revealing the solution to the mystery of Victorio's escape and allowing both the victors (in this case, the Apache) and the defeated (the U.S. Cavalry) of this story an equal say in its telling.

As a band of Apache, under the direction of Chief Victorio, crouched in the fading light, more than 70 Buffalo Soldiers—Companies D and F of the Ninth Cavalry—moved into Hembrillo Basin. The previous day, a scouting detachment had skirmished with

35–50 Apaches in the canyon. Then, on April 6, 1880, the scouts had spotted a pair of warriors on a low-lying ridge.

When he received these reports, Capt. Henry Carroll ordered an immediate attack on the position. Not until his troops had secured the ridge did he realize his peril. His exhausted command suddenly faced more than 100 Apache warriors. There was little to do but try to hold them off until Companies A and G arrived with reinforcements.

From *GPS World*, October 1997. Reprinted with permission from Advanstar Communications, 859 Willamette St., Eugene, OR 97401.

Under the cover of darkness, the warriors moved closer. Suddenly, there was a rush of activity as Victorio's men attacked. The 20 soldiers holding the northeast ridge pulled their .45-caliber Colt pistols and met the surge with an intense volley of gunfire, the roar of their guns echoing from the darkened bluffs of Hembrillo Canyon. Then, on a crest above the basin, two columns of reinforcements appeared. Cornered and outnumbered, with more cavalry on the way, Victorio was sure to be defeated. Somehow, though, he managed to slip out of the basin and lead his people to temporary refuge in New Mexico's Black Range Mountains.

By combining sketchy historical battle accounts with archaeological evidence recovered in the basin, researchers recently reconstructed the previous scenario. Although they do not know exactly how the encounter at the skirmish line developed, the researchers were able to clearly define a line by geographically locating .45-caliber pistol cartridges representing 20 different guns.

Deploying the latest technologies—including GPS, geographic information systems (GIS), computer-aided design (CAD), and forensic ballistics analysis—the team of archaeologists from Human Systems Research, Inc. (HSR, a nonprofit research organization in Las Cruces, New Mexico), surveyors from New Mexico State University (NMSU), and volunteers from a local metal-detector club determined the alignment of spent shells. The configuration of the .45-caliber shells revealed that desperate soldiers drew their pistols in close battle during this two-day encounter in the southern New Mexico desert.

Their work was part of an ongoing project that began in the spring of 1994 with the goal of reconstructing the events of this critical, but poorly documented, battle in the American Indian Wars. To accomplish this task, the team mapped the area, recording the battlefield's topography. By combining historic records with geographically referenced data about recovered artifacts, they reconstructed the ensuing events and created three-dimensional models to validate hypotheses about offensive and defensive firing positions, helping them to visualize the combatants' positions.

The research is scheduled to be complete in 1998 and will be used to help preserve this uncommonly pristine historic site and document the battle's history.

VICTORIO'S PEAK

For many historians, this pivotal battle holds much mystique, representing a military master's formidable skill. Acknowledged as one of history's premier guerrilla fighters, Chief Victorio led his tribe against the Ninth Cavalry in defiance of the U.S. government's order to take his people from their homeland and onto a reservation. A superior strategist and beloved leader, Victorio stood—from the 1850s until his death in 1880—as the last chief of the Chihenne (or Warm Springs) Apache.

Victorio's powers were at their peak when the battle in Hembrillo Basin occurred. Until recently, however, little was known about how the battle progressed and how Victorio was able to guide his tribe to safety.

Then, in 1989, while documenting rock art in Hembrillo Canyon for the U.S. Army, a group of HSR archaeologists stumbled across the battlefield. Located inside the Department of Defense's (DoD) U.S. Army White Sands Missile Range boundaries, access to the site had been restricted since the 1940s. Prior to that time, the area had scarcely been visited because of its remote location. Consequently, the battlefield had remained essentially untouched for more than 109 years.

Before visiting the site, archaeologists Karl Laumbach (from HSR) and Bob Burton (from White Sands Missile Range) searched local archives and discovered the memoirs of Lt. Thomas Cruse, who had participated in the battle. With his description of the encounter, they traveled to the site, where they soon located spent cartridges and breastworks, or temporary fortifications. With their interest piqued, they combined forces with NMSU surveyors James Wakeman, Michael MacInnis, and Christine Ochs to embark on a quick trip to map the site and analyze battle details based on topography. At this stage, the fieldwork's scope—mapping topography—was fairly narrow, as researchers were unfamiliar with the site. The team got more than it bargained for, however, eventually finding enough artifacts to virtually reconstruct the entire battle scene.

TACTICAL TOPOGRAPHY

At an elevation of 5,500 feet, the rugged Hembrillo Basin encompasses more than 3,000 acres of harsh desert etched by a network of steep arroyos, or water-carved ravines. This chiseled landscape is broken by sharp peaks and limestone uplifts rising nearly 7,000 feet.

Much of the battle took place in these arroyos and on a series of 6,000-foot ridges that provide a commanding view of the basin. Because defensive and offensive positions are often dictated by topography, the researchers knew the landscape held clues to the battle.

Mapping Methodology

The battlefield's extent was as yet unknown, so the first mapping task in 1993 consisted of preparing a rough topographic map of the battle site region. The archaeologists used this map, combined with other sparsely written reports by battle participants, to ascertain what specific topographic features were important. For example, an uplift called "Victorio's Ridge" seemed to fit the Army's account of the Apaches holding a high point to the south after reinforcements arrived. In this manner, the researchers developed hypotheses about how the action ensued and how Victorio escaped.

But, mapping the terrain to accomplish this task forced the team to face the region's harsh environment and rugged conditions every day. Rattlesnakes lurk in the craggy limestone outcroppings, which are often overrun by painful catclaw (mimosa) shrubs and only occasionally interrupted by scatterings of juniper firs. Two- to four-person university mapping crews had to drive two and a half hours over this desolate and rocky landscape just to reach the battlefield. Because military restrictions prohibited the team from camping on site, five hours of each work day was spent simply coming and going. This challenging work environment demanded a great deal of dedication, especially considering the effort was all volunteer.

To create the topographic maps, researchers selected GPS and three-dimensional modeling software as their primary tools.

The team decided carrier-phase GPS was too expensive. Instead, they adopt a combined strategy of code-phase GPS and radial electronic distance-measuring (EDM) surveys, occasionally employing **pace-and-compass maps**. Surveyors used a six-channel, L1, codeless receiver with an external antenna in a backpack and a second-order, permanently fixed base station at NMSU—65 miles away.

Surveying the Scene

Directed by HSR's on-site archaeologist Billy Russell, MacInnis used the GPS mapping system to line map the study area. As he walked the ridges, MacInnis recorded points at intervals ranging from 15 seconds to 1 minute, depending on the terrain. In three days, he mapped approximately 100 lines and recorded nearly 8,000 points. Back at NMSU's Department of Surveying, he downloaded the rover data and corrected them to achieve the desired 2–5 meter accuracy.

While continuing the line mapping in late 1994, archaeologists discovered a surprising number of artifacts. They also learned that the site was much richer and extensive than previously believed. This, they decided, called for a more accurate and detailed survey than could be obtained using code-phase GPS. If they were to reconstruct the battle, they would need to refine the inaccuracies of the initial mapping.

Soon, plans were under way to begin more detailed mapping using radial EDM techniques.

CLUES IN THE CATCLAWS

The project's next phase, mapping the location of artifacts, began in the spring of 1995. The surveyors established an EDM control network based on local DoD second-order monuments. They conformed the GPS to the EDM work, obtaining more GPS points and making many radial ties to the line-mapping data at definable intersections. They subjected the ties to coordinate transformations and least-squared analyses to accomplish a "best fit" for the data.

The team began mapping artifacts while obtaining further topographic data with the EDM. Because the arroyos are generally filled with dense vegetation and their steep walls often preclude EDM visibility, the team refined and retained the GPS data for these ravines. The ridges, however, lent themselves to EDM shots, which helped to refine the more critical elevation data. Unfortunately, this part of the survey had its downsides. To obtain the EDM shots, surveyors often had to pack their equipment through the dense catclaw and up steep slopes to gain a high vantage point. The setups for these shots usually lasted the entire day, exposing the operator to relentless wind while the rodman sacrificed skin and clothing to the catclaw.

During this phase, the archaeologists also began to analyze available U.S. Geological Survey 1:24,000-scale maps alongside the GPS-based **topographic line maps**. They compared the topographic factors with military accounts of Carroll's position to determine where actual engagements might have occurred. By closely examining surrounding geographic features, such as the subtle limestone uplifts, they determined where the attacking Apaches might have taken cover. Combined, these many factors helped them to select sites that would likely yield battle artifacts. This enabled them to direct the metal-detector volunteers to search in the right locations.

Shell Seekers

The team had engaged the volunteers—including Joe Allen, Bob Sproul, and Jan Peterson—to conduct an in-depth site search. To locate shell fragments and other artifacts, these crews, totaling more than 50 volunteers, caravanned to the site on weekends, often putting in 16-hour days.

The archaeologists structured the metal detection by defining corridors across the battlefield and directing the volunteers as they moved. Volunteers walked abreast 5–10 meters apart, depending on the density of the catclaw, which forced everyone to wear pants and long-sleeve shirts regardless of the weather.

During this two-year phase, this clothing restriction was fine for the winter months, when temperatures could drop to 40°F. But during the summer, when the temperatures sometimes soared to 110°F, it was often difficult to decide what was harder to bear—the thorns or the sweltering heat!

While searching, the team paid special attention to obvious military crests (raised areas that could protect a fighter). When a volunteer found an object, he or she intensively scanned the area with the metal detector to determine whether the find was a solitary artifact or one of a cluster—evincing a static firing position or a line of firing positions. Archaeologists following the metal detectors marked each artifact's location by attaching a flag to the brush or stone nearest the item. Then, they recorded the item type and condition on a standard paper form.

The archaeologists photographed each artifact where it lay. They then attached a numbered aluminum tag to a 10-inch nail and drove it into the rocky ground before removing the find. They also created a sketch map that would enable the surveyors to relocate the item later and verify its location in the computerized maps they planned to create back in the office.

The surveyors accompanied the archaeologists back to the site and obtained EDM (and later in the project, real-time kinematic [RTK] GPS) locations for the recovered items. They recorded these points in a field data collector and a 486 laptop personal computer.

As the flags began to cluster, they visibly defined the various areas within the battlefield. The crew assigned each area an alpha code (Area A, B, C, and so on) and mapped the artifacts by number and code-area designations. Of the more than 1,000 artifacts eventually recovered, approximately 850 were cartridges. These consisted of .45-70, .50-70, .44, and .45-60 caliber, as well as a variety of rimfire pistol shells.

Additional items included Apache jewelry, cavalry tack remnants (curry combs, horseshoe nails, and so forth), and cavalry uniform remnants. The team postulated that one small grouping of shirt buttons, found in an area sheltered from hostile fire, may have marked where a wounded man was treated. They found only one metal arrowhead, indicating that the bow-and-arrow was not extensively used during the fight.

After gathering and mapping the artifacts, the archaeologists bagged, labeled, and cataloged them, entering the data into a computerized database.

A SMOKING GUN

Because the team inferred the combatants' positions based on the caliber of the cartridges, as well as military accounts of the action, it was critical that they be able to determine what caliber of gun was firing from any given location. To accomplish this, in May 1996, the team enlisted the help of Doug Scott, archaeologist for the National Park Service Midwest Archaeological Center in Lincoln, Nebraska. Scott had previously applied his pioneering method of forensic firing pin and extractor mark analysis to determine the source of cartridges collected from the Little Bighorn Battlefield—the scene of Custer's defeat at the hands of the Sioux and Cheyenne in 1876.

Scott's technique is based on the fact that each gun leaves a distinctive firing pin and extractor mark on the cartridge. By painstakingly examining the cartridges under a microscope, Scott can use these marks to effectively distinguish between individual weapons of the same caliber.

To eliminate bias, Scott performed his shell casing analysis with no information regarding where the artifact was found. He recorded his results in a report, identifying the objects by their unique artifact numbers, and sent the report and the items back to the team.

From a Bullet to a Battle

After receiving Scott's analysis, the team related the artifacts back to their GPS-surveyed locations. The clustering of the shells became clearly visible on the maps, enabling the researchers to track the movement of individual guns (see Figure 1).

Data from the cartridges have so far revealed that the .50-70 shells represent 31 separate 1866 model Springfield rifles, eight 1868 model, Springfield rifles, three Remington rifles, and three Sharps rifles.

Historians had originally assumed that because the Army often issued older weapons to its Indian allies, the Apache Army scouts had carried the Springfields. But, analysis of gun locations on the battlefield suggests that most of these were, in fact, carried by the Chihenne and their Mescalero Apache allies. The cartridges from these rifles were tracked from the attack on Carroll's position to a ridge where Victorio directed a brilliant rear guard action while retreating to the south.

The .44-caliber rimfire cartridges represent three separate Henry or 1866 model Winchesters. The trail left by these latter weapons clearly showed Victorio's warriors moving closer to the embattled troopers during the fight, bolstering the hypothesis of the skirmish put forth at the beginning of this article.

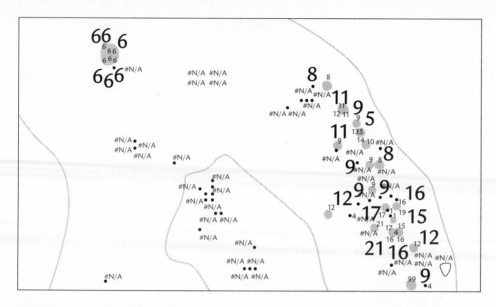

FIGURE 1   Map indicating the location of bullet cartridges found by archaeological survey, documenting the battle and Victorio's escape. Numbers represent individual weapons from which the cartridges were derived. (*GPS World*)

Devil in the Details

The more the archaeologists discovered about the battle, the more excited they became about the possibility of understanding exactly how the events in Hembrillo Basin had transpired. The project had grown substantially, with a larger area being mapped and more artifacts discovered than ever anticipated. Also, because the data sources had varied through the years, the project required increasing efforts to correlate the data and eliminate inconsistencies.

The expanded scope also demanded improved accuracy to control the data on which developing theories were being based. Fortunately, improvements to GPS technology had kept pace with the project's increasingly stringent requirements.

In 1997, the team began using RTK GPS to obtain 1-centimeter accuracy. To conform the early GPS-based line-mapping data with the RTK data, the researchers applied statistical methods, such as moving averages constrained to EDM data. That is, the surveyors took EDM shots near or on line-mapped features and used them as "control" points for the line-mapped data.

During the final field phase, researchers focused on rectifying identification problems, topographic inconsistencies, and mapping the last of a seemingly unending array of artifacts. To complete the correction work, Wakeman, Laumbach, and Botsford visited the site with maps, lists of questions, and an eight-channel, P/Y-code, RTK GPS receiver. One person operated the survey equipment, while the other two worked to help rectify inconsistencies and logged information in a handheld data collector.

Because the observation time with the RTK equipment ranged between 2 and 30 seconds, the team was able to cover a much bigger area in a shorter time than before, surveying more than 900 acres in five days.

BATTLEFIELD LEGACY

In 1997, researchers began to merge the data collected during the previous four years. This final phase helped them with their ultimate goal of reconstructing the 100-year-old battle by relating the artifacts, ballistics information, Army records, positioning data, and individual historical accounts to the topography.

This phase is extremely computer intensive. The graphics file contains more than 85,000 digital objects, including points, text, lines, and three-dimensional terrain renderings and line-of-sight analyses of the firing positions. The database file contains catalog numbers (a critical registry of archaeological artifacts), code areas, artifact numbers, comments, descriptions, and information about cartridge caliber, gun manufacturers, and individual gun identification. All data are georeferenced in a **GIS** according to their GPS-obtained coordinates.

A Military Model

To reconstruct the battle, the team flowed this vast data store into a three-dimensional modeling program. The models have already yielded some interesting preliminary findings (Figure 2). For example, the team

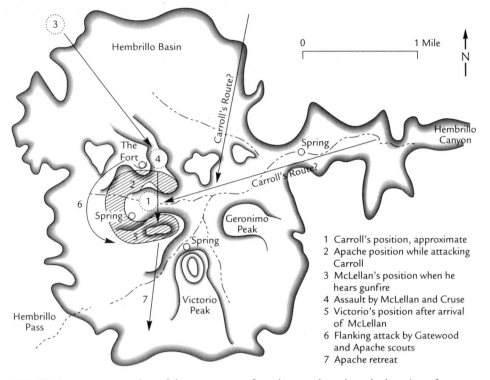

FIGURE 2   A reconstruction of the movement of combatants based on the location of cartridges and bullets — and a determination of their association with particular guns — as they were recovered on the battlefield. (**GPS** World)

knows that the weapons used in the battle had an effective and maximum range of 150 and 500 yards, respectively.

Once researchers determined a firing position, they used a variety of commands to delineate its effective and maximum ranges. Analyzing a profile of the gun's firing range helped them to discover what areas on the battlefield were vulnerable to that particular weapon. The three-dimensional lines defined by a weapon's ballistics, combined with the topography analysis, also indicated where military crests could have sheltered a combatant.

Strategic Specifics

Troop concentrations and cartridges revealed strategies used during the battle. For example, by analyzing the cartridges and line-of-sight information, the researchers corroborated a hypothesis that Victorio had used a high ridge (present-day "Victorio's Ridge") to the south as an effective rear defense after the support cavalry arrived on April 7.

A line of pistol cartridges found near the top of a ridge in Area F revealed that a heated, rapid-fire skirmish had occurred as the beleaguered Buffalo Soldiers fought off an Apache onslaught. Individual firing posi-

tions surrounding the area indicated that the Apaches had superior numbers when they flanked the pinned-down cavalry.

As the reconstruction enters its final phases, researchers will be investigating individuals' progress through the battle. Three-dimensional renderings of these analyses, from the combatants' point of view, will enable the team to create a highly personalized interpretation of this event. HSR will use the models as part of its educational outreach, demonstrating the application to students, military historians, and American Indian War buffs.

INTO THE WILDERNESS

When this project began, researchers did not even know the battlefield's location. The only accounts of the encounter came from Sixth Cavalry officers, who played up their part of the fight with little mention of the valiant Buffalo Soldiers. Researchers had no knowledge of Capt. Carroll's movements at the beginning of the encounter and certainly no idea of the battle's scale or Victorio's strategy.

But by using GPS, along with a battery of software and surveying equipment, the team has ascertained the scale and topographic complexity of the battlefield and begun to "write" this historic account, which explains how Victorio made his escape.

Early in the morning on April 7, as the skirmish between the Buffalo Soldiers and the band of warriors ensued, Capt. Carroll's reinforcements arrived from the east and a company of the Sixth Cavalry, along with Apache Scouts, arrived from the west. Victorio suddenly faced a pincer movement by three separate columns of more than 400 U.S. troops and allies. The end appeared near.

But, Victorio quickly devised a new strategy that would allow him to elude his pursuers and save his people. He led his Apache warriors in retreat to what is now called Victorio's Ridge.

Holding the high ground, Victorio's warriors pinned down the Buffalo Soldiers and reinforcements alike, buying time for the Apache women and children to escape. Col. Hatch (commander of the Department of New Mexico) who was supposed to have arrived from the mountains to the south, had instead withdrawn from that area when a courier reported that Carroll was trapped. In doing so, Hatch opened the door for Victorio's escape.

Victorio's second in command was Nana (pronounced "Nanay"), a hardened warrior more than 70 years old. As Victorio held the Army troops in check, Nana led the women and children to safety through a saddle on the basin's southern extreme. At one point,

the fleeing tribe hid in an arroyo and watched as Hatch's command rode past.

Finally, a combined flanking action commanded by Lt. Charles Gatewood and his company of White Mountain Apache scouts, combined with a frontal attack by another company, forced the Chihenne to abandon the ridge and slowly withdraw. During the retreat, though, Victorio maintained both the high ground and a front that was, according to Army officers' later statements, almost two miles wide, eliminating the possibility of a flanking maneuver.

Six hours after the reinforcements arrived, the last Apache left Hembrillo. The troops and their mounts were too exhausted to follow. Victorio led his tribe across the Jornada del Muerto ("Walk of the Dead Man")—a forbidding expanse of waterless desert west of Hembrillo Basin—and disappeared into the Black Range Mountains.

Unfortunately, Victorio's escape only hastened the end for the Chihenne. The U.S. Cavalry, humiliated and criticized for allowing the Apaches to escape, pursued them relentlessly in the succeeding months. In October 1880, troops trapped the Chihenne at Tres Castillas in northern Mexico. The cavalry killed more than 78 Apaches, including Victorio, taking their scalps for the bounty offered by the Mexican government. Sixty-eight women and children were taken prisoner. Only 17 Chihenne escaped.

23

Donner Party Archaeology

Donald L. Hardesty

Don Hardesty is an archaeologist at the University of Nevada. He has written an extremely interesting book on the topic of this article titled The Archaeology of the Donner Party *(University of Nevada Press).*

Points to consider when reading this article:

1. What do the sites excavated by Donald Hardesty represent? Who do we think lived or camped at those spots?

2. Do any of the artifacts recovered provide any particular insights into the people who lived in these sites?

3. What does the archaeological evidence tell us about the diet of those people who wintered over in the excavated campsite?

4. Was there any direct archaeological evidence that supported the historical accounts of cannibalism?

The story of the Donner Party, a group of eighty-seven emigrants heading by wagon train to California in 1846, is the historical equivalent of a terrible automobile accident on the interstate. Certainly you have noticed how passing cars will slow down, seemingly so their horrified yet curious occupants can get a glimpse of the terrible human tragedy being played out on the shoulder of the highway. The Donner Party story is like that. We are, at once, both repelled and drawn to the incident.

The story is awful yet poignant. It is the tale of a community of human beings challenged in the most extreme way imaginable, lost in the mountains, buffeted by the worst snowstorms in a century, trapped without food for days, weeks, and even months. Half of the party died. Many of the deceased were otherwise healthy, adult men in the prime of their lives, their energy spent in the effort to will their wagons along an untested trail to the winter camp where they succumbed. Surprisingly—or perhaps not—adult women and their children survived disproportionately. Your odds of surviving the ordeal were much improved if you were a woman, and remarkably so if you were traveling with family to tend and to be tended by.

And then there is the cannibalism. By all accounts of the survivors and their saviors, some survived the winter by eating the flesh of their dead companions. We are both revulsed by the notion of people subsisting by eating their comrades, and yet, at the same time, we stand in awe of those whose will to live allowed them to do so, and to transcend this terrible truth to go on with their lives in California. The winter camp of the Donner Party is now an archaeological site—actually, a series of sites. Its excavation by archaeologist Donald Hardesty provides us with a window into the cabins where this drama was played out.

D**uring** the twenty-five years following the opening of the California Trail by the Bidwell-Bartleson party in 1841, several hundred thousand emigrants traveled overland to what was to become the American West. The earliest emigrants to use the trail tried several alternate routes and shortcuts. Among the best known of these was the Hastings Cutoff. In 1846, Lansford Hastings, a California lawyer and the author of a popular emigrant guidebook, promoted a new trail as a shortcut to California. The cutoff left the main Oregon-California Trail just west of South Pass, went south past Fort Bridger in the present state of Wyoming, down through the Wasatch Mountains and across the Great Salt Lake Desert to the Humboldt River, where it connected once again with the main California Trail. The Hastings Cutoff was used by several emigrant parties between 1846 and 1850 before it was abandoned.

From *Overland Journal,* vol. 10, no. 3, 1992. Copyright Oregon-California Trails Association.

Without question, the best known of these was the Donner party.

On 20 July 1846, a group of emigrants joined together just west of South Pass in present Wyoming to take the Hastings Cutoff. George Donner was elected captain of the wagon train. Although intended to save time, the cutoff, along with bad decisions, bad luck and conflict within the group, greatly delayed the party's trip along the trail. Wagons and goods had to be abandoned, and five of the party of eighty-seven perished along the trail. Those remaining did not reach California's Sierra Nevada until late October of 1846 and were trapped in the mountains by early winter storms. Despite several escape and rescue attempts, the emigrants were forced to spend several months in two winter encampments. The Murphy cabin, the Breen-Shallenberger cabin and the Graves-Reed cabin made up one encampment at the east end of what is now Donner Lake. The second encampment, approximately five miles to the northeast, was the Donner family camp. Not until 21 April 1847 did the last member of the Donner party leave the camps. Only forty-seven survived the ordeal, some of whom may have done so by cannibalizing the dead. Probably because of the alleged cannibalism and human suffering, the Donner party has become one of the major symbols of the extreme hardships faced by emigrants of the American westward movement.

Written accounts of the tragedy appeared in newspapers and periodicals shortly after the rescue, and C. F. McGlashan's *The History of the Donner Party* was published in 1879. The accounts and histories are based mostly on information contained in contemporary letters and journals kept by Donner party members or by rescue parties, on later reminiscences of some of the survivors and on several secondary sources.[1] Not much more is likely to come from the written record. George Stewart, in the preface to the 1960 edition of *Ordeal by Hunger,* observes that there is likely to be no additional information about the tragedy "unless some miracle of excavation at Alder Creek should bring to light the diary which Tamsen Donner is said to have kept."[2]

However, some new information that is independent of the written accounts may be contained in archaeological remains of the Donner party. As early as the 1870s C. F. McGlashan and some of the survivors of the tragedy dug into the two mountain campsites. Fragments of "old porcelain and chinaware . . . readily distinguished by painted flowers, or unique designs enameled in red, blue, or purple colors" were unearthed at a depth of one to six inches in the floor of the Breen-Shallenberger cabin.[3] A cooper's inshave, an iron wagon-hammer and a whetstone with the initials "JFR" (James Frazier Reed), along with round headed pins and a tin box that had once contained hemlock

were dug up at the Graves-Reed cabin in 1879. Other artifacts dug up at the lake camp included glass tableware, buttons, fishhooks, gun flints, mirrors, and "bolts, nails, screws, nuts, chains, and portions of wagon irons."[4] George Stewart also mentions that on 12 November 1935 he "did some excavation at [the site of the Donner family camp], finding at two places layers of charcoal deposits about four inches below the present ground-level."[5] The site of Murphy's cabin apparently was not disturbed by these early attempts at archaeology. McGlashan, for example, writes that he did not dig into the Murphy cabin site because the "marsh grass . . . firmly resists either shovel or spade."[6]

None of these early attempts, of course, took advantage of **controlled stratigraphic** excavation and other methods used in modern archaeology. These methods include the careful observation and documentation of the **soil matrix** (layer) in which the physical remains are found, the **provenience** (location) of the objects and what objects were found together. Accurate three-dimension maps of the physical remains then can be prepared and interpreted.

Within the last decade, there have been three archaeological studies of the Donner party sites using modern methods. In 1984, the site of Murphy's cabin was excavated by the University of Nevada, Reno, in cooperation with the California Department of Parks and Recreation and sponsored by the National Geographic Society.[7] In 1986, the Antiquities Section of the Utah State Historical Society excavated and recorded the remains of several wagons thought to have been abandoned by the Donner party in the mud flats of the Great Salt Lake Desert.[8] The most recent archaeological study took place in 1990 at the Donner family camp on Alder Creek, the second of the two mountain camps.[9] This project was conducted by the University of Nevada, Reno, in cooperation with the Tahoe National Forest.

ARCHAEOLOGY OF THE DONNER WAGONS— 1986 EXCAVATION

Written accounts suggest that four Donner party wagons were abandoned in the Great Salt Lake Desert sometime between 31 August and 2 September 1846. The archaeological record of what has been interpreted as the Donner wagon site includes "wagon wheel ruts, identifiable stains of metal wagon parts such as wheels, wooden wagon parts, extensive concentrations of charcoal, animal remains, and a scattering of small early to mid-nineteenth century artifacts. . . ."[10] Five wagons, four of which belonged to the Donner party and another to the 1850 John Wood party, are known from documentary accounts to have been abandoned at this place on the mud flats. One of the sites with unusually wide wheel tracks and remains of an abandoned cache of goods appears to be the place where James F. Reed's large "pioneer palace" wagon was abandoned and later retrieved by Reed; none of the other wagon sites, however, could be identified precisely. The 184 identifiable artifacts recovered from the Donner wagon site are mostly fragments of firearms, tack and animal equipment, wagon parts and clothing.

THE ARCHAEOLOGY OF MURPHY'S CABIN— 1984 EXCAVATION

Of the three log cabins at the Donner Lake camp, Murphy's, which was closest to the lake, was the most unusual. It was built against a large granite rock that was used as one of the walls and as a chimney. The sixteen members of the Murphy, Foster and Eddy families lived in this cabin; other people, however, moved into and out of the cabin during the winter. Murphy's cabin appears to have been abandoned sometime in late March or early April of 1847. What happened to the cabin afterward is known only generally. It may have been burned in June of 1847 by Gen. Stephen Watts Kearny's Mormon Battalion. The battalion's men are reputed to have interred some of the scattered human remains in a mass grave inside the cabin.[11] Without question, the cabin had been destroyed by 1872, when the *Truckee Republican* reported on 7 May that "all the [Donner] cabins have been burned down or carried away by relic collectors."[12] In the late 1870s, the site of Murphy's cabin was located by C. F. McGlashan after visits to the site with some survivors of the tragedy. In 1879, six logs were still in place at the cabin but the last log was removed in 1893 and the fragments placed in 5,000 vials and sold.[13]

Not much is known from written accounts about the architectural details or layout of Murphy's cabin. The size is unknown, but contemporary accounts and later recollections suggest that it had a flat roof covered with animal skins, canvas and tree branches; it may have had either one or two rooms. The 1984 archaeological study provided additional data about the cabin and what happened there.

First, the discovery of the thin organic layer with artifacts, charred wood, charcoal and ash that marked the dirt floor suggests the size and shape of the cabin. It was rectangular, about twenty-five feet long and eighteen feet wide and oriented approximately northeast-southwest along the face of the big rock. What about the layout of the cabin's interior space? No archaeological evidence of more than one room was located. At the base of the big rock, a hearth "hot spot" marked by a dense concentration of charcoal, ash and burned

bone was located. The hearth appears to have "wandered" across the base of the boulder during the winter; the rock face and an opening through the roof would have been used as a chimney.

Second, more information about construction details was acquired from the excavation.[14] Although parallel to the big rock, the cabin was longer than the rock and extended outward beyond the face of the rock wall. Postmolds located at the ends of both short wall extensions suggested that "cribbing" had been used to tie otherwise floating wall ends to the large rock. Cribbing was a common nineteenth-century log cabin construction method used in similar situations and involved driving vertical posts on both sides of horizontally-laid wall logs. Furthermore, the roof log on the northwest side appears to have been placed flush against the curved rock wall and to have been cradled in two prominent notches located about eight feet up on the face.

Third, this 1984 excavation also refuted the common belief that the cabin floor contained human remains in a mass grave prepared by a detachment from Gen. Stephen Watts Kearny's Mormon Battalion on 21 June 1847. No archaeological evidence of a grave was found.

Finally, the Donner party is remembered, at least in part, for the alleged practice of cannibalism of the dead at the mountain camps and during escape attempts by some of the survivors. Murphy's cabin is one of the places where cannibalism supposedly occurred. Patrick Breen recorded in his diary on 26 February 1847 that "Mrs. Murphy said here yesterday that [she] thought she would commence on Milt [one of the dead teamsters] and eat him."[15] A rescue party led by James Reed seemed to confirm the event three days later by finding the mutilated body of the teamster at the door of the cabin. Several small bone fragments recovered by the 1984 excavation were identified as human by radioimmunoassay methods used by Dr. Gerold Lowenstein of the University of California Medical School in San Francisco. Unfortunately, the remains are so fragmented that the practice of cannibalism at the cabin could not be confirmed.

ARCHAEOLOGY OF THE DONNER FAMILY CAMP—1990 EXCAVATION

The 1990 excavation at the reputed site of the Donner family camp on Alder Creek was intended to shed light on another controversy in the history of the Donner party. Bringing up the rear of the wagon train as it moved up the Truckee Canyon, the twenty-one members of the George and Jacob Donner families and their teamsters were stopped by a broken wagon axle. The group included six men, three women and twelve children. By the time the wagon had been repaired, the early winter storm hit, and the group was unable to catch up with the main body of the party. On 3 November 1846, the Donner family established a camp about five miles from the lake camp. Written accounts suggest that the family and their teamsters lived not in cabins but in three tents and crude, brush shelters.[16]

Most authorities believe that the site of the Donner family camp is on Alder Creek. The Alder Creek site is based on C. F. McGlashan's nineteenth-century interviews with survivors of the Donner party and with members of rescue parties. In 1879, McGlashan and several other citizens of Truckee, California, visited the Alder Creek site with Nicholas Clark, a member of the second rescue expedition who spent three weeks at the camp in the winter of 1846–1847.[17] In 1921, the site was visited by P. M. Weddell of San Jose, California, a Donner buff who had interviewed McGlashan and received instructions from him about the location of the site.[18] Weddell placed wooden signs on trees marking the location of the trail taken by the Donner party and at the site of the Donner family camp. In 1927, both Weddell and McGlashan visited the site, and McGlashan verified the marked location of the camp; the wooden markers are still in place.[19]

The Alder Creek site, however, has been somewhat controversial. Other emigrant parties traveling along the California trail between 1845 and 1850 appear to have taken a route up Truckee Canyon that leaves the river in the vicinity of present Verdi, Nevada, goes around the north end of the Verdi Range through Dog Valley, then turns southward and goes across the Little Truckee, on past Prosser Creek continuing directly back to the Truckee River at about the center of what today is the town of Truckee.[20] No emigrant diaries suggest a diversion off the main Dog Valley road that would have gone up Alder Creek and down Trout Creek. Why would the Donner family have departed from the commonly used trail and taken a deviant route that rises an additional 600 feet over more mountainous and difficult terrain when they were already exhausted?[21] Or, if they did take the commonly used Dog Valley route, why would they establish a camp at least a mile off the trail? The camp, therefore, must have been closer to the Dog Valley road along which most emigrant parties traveled.[22]

In 1990, the University of Nevada, Reno, conducted archaeological studies at the Alder Creek site marked by McGlashan and Weddell to help resolve the dispute over the location of the Donner family camp. The first excavations took place at the reputed sites of the shelters in which the George Donner and Jacob Donner families lived, but nothing except modern trash was found. At this point, metal detectors were used to sur-

vey the surrounding area. After a period of fine-tuning for local conditions and after finding a large number of modern pulltabs from aluminum cans and .22 cartridge casings, two metallic hot spots were located. Excavations at the hot spots turned up artifacts and other archaeological remains that could be dated to the Donner party time period. The two hot spots, in fact, are only 100 to 150 feet from the two shelter sites marked by Weddell.

Archaeological remains recovered from the hot spot next to the Jacob Donner shelter are the most abundant and suggest the kinds of domestic activities that would be associated with one of the winter shelters occupied by the Donner family. Indeed, the remains are quite similar to those found at the site of Murphy's cabin. Included are fragments of ceramic tableware and glass bottles, musket balls, buttons, charred and calcined bone fragments. The site is difficult to interpret because of extensive mixing by rodents. Furthermore, the excavation has not located a hearth, such as the one at Murphy's cabin, which would give the best evidence for a shelter site. Future excavation at the site may locate a hearth; however, the concentration of bone and charcoal marking the hearth most likely has been dispersed by rodents to the point that its integrity has been lost completely.

The second hot spot is in the meadow west of the George Donner tree and includes few artifacts or other material remains related to domestic activities. Bone, charcoal, ceramic tableware, glass bottles and other domestic artifacts, for example, are completely missing. The **artifact assemblage,** however, includes wagon parts, oxen shoes, cut nails, percussion caps, musket balls and two coins—an 1830 United States Liberty penny and an 1839 farthing from the Isle of Man. The site may mark the location of one of the Donner family wagons, and the artifact assemblage represents the debris from material possessions packed in the wagons. One of the more interesting questions to be asked of the hot spot is whether or not it is the site of the shelter lived in by the teamsters. The physical evidence of the domestic activities expected to take place in a shelter is sparse; however, the apparent absence of domestic artifacts may be misleading. The occupation of the teamsters' shelter was less intense and shorter than the other shelters; therefore, less trash was likely to have been left.

ARTIFACTS FROM THE THREE DONNER PARTY SITES

The artifacts from the Donner party sites are representative of the material culture being transported overland by emigrants traveling on the California Trail in the late 1840s. Unfortunately, most of the Donner party's possessions were discarded along the way, salvaged from the mountain camps by rescue parties during the winter of 1846–1847 or picked up by any number of visitors after the camps were abandoned. Written accounts of the trip across the Great Salt Lake Desert and the Humboldt Sink, for example, document the loss of heavy and bulky artifacts, including household furniture and boxes of books. To the extent that the Donner wagon sites have been identified correctly, the 1986 excavation in the Great Salt Lake Desert by the Utah Historical Society provides a glimpse at what was left behind.

Most of the identifiable artifacts at the Donner wagon site are associated with firearms (including musket balls, percussion caps and gun flints), tack and animal equipment, wagon parts and clothing. A few household artifacts and hand tools such as augers and grass hooks also are represented in the assemblage.

Most of the household artifacts are food and toiletry containers such as glass medicine bottle fragments, a glazed stoneware bottle or jug handle and a hotel china salt dish. Personal items such as jewelry and tobacco pipes are missing entirely. If interpreted as the remains of the abandoned Donner wagons, the artifacts provide an interesting comparison to the mountain camp remains. (Perhaps the largest number of artifacts at the Donner wagon site and the Donner family mountain camp are in some way associated with wagons or animal transportation.) Wagon hardware, oxen shoes and cut nails are the most common in both assemblages. Only a few transportation-related artifacts, however, are in the Murphy cabin assemblage. Other comparisons among the three sites are to be found in the artifacts used as household furnishings, armaments, personal adornment and symbols.

HOUSEHOLD FURNISHINGS

The emigrants in the Donner party carried with them many items intended to be used to set up new households in California, and many of the artifacts recovered from the excavations at the two mountain camps reflected this domestic baggage. The artifacts included fragments of ceramic tableware, table utensils, cobalt blue glass bottles, iron cooking pots and stoneware jugs. Most of the ceramic tableware came from the Donner family camp on Alder Creek. George Miller of the University of Delaware examined the Alder Creek assemblage and reached the conclusion that the ceramic tableware is typical of styles introduced in the mid-1830s and the early 1840s. No older styles are represented, suggesting either that new tableware was

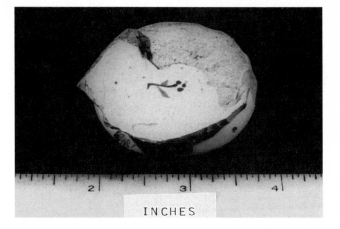

FIGURE 1   The base of a ceramic cup recovered in the archaeological excavation of the Donner family campsite on Alder Creek (now Donner Lake) where the immigrants were trapped during the most trying time of their ordeal. (Donald Hardesty)

purchased when the owners moved to California or that their households were set up after 1835. Both decorated and undecorated white ware plates, muffin plates, cups and saucers are included in the assemblage. All of the decorated plates have unscalloped blue shell edges with shallow, repetitive molded patterns. Decoration of this kind made its appearance in the 1840s and continued to be produced through the 1850s. The decorated cups, saucers and bowls in the assemblage are sprig painted—small and widely spaced hand-painted floral designs in apple-green, red, blue and black. Advertisements for sprig painted tea, table and toilet wares appear as early as 1831. The earliest sprig painted wares are French porcelains, but the Staffordshire potters took up sprig painting in the early 1840s. In general, the ceramics recovered at the site were the least expensive decorated tea and table wares on the market at the time. No examples of even cheaper wares, undecorated creamware, known to exist at the time, were located by the excavation.

ARMAMENTS

By far the most abundant artifacts recovered from the three Donner party sites are associated with armaments. Written accounts of the party mention a six-shooter, a pepper box pistol, rifle, muzzle loader, caps, bullets and a powder horn. A single barrel brass pistol and flintlock were reputedly found at the sites in the nineteenth century. McGlashan mentions that gun flints were found at the Breen-Shallenberger and Graves-Reed cabins, and three were recovered in the 1984 excavation at the site of Murphy's cabin. But without question the largest number of firearm-related artifacts are musket balls. The size of the balls range from .64 caliber to birdshot, but most of the balls are either in the .50 to .59 caliber range or in the .16 to .22 caliber range. Percussion caps from what was cutting edge firearms technology at the time were recovered from the Alder Creek and Donner wagon sites but not from Murphy's cabin.

CLOTHING, PERSONAL ITEMS AND SYMBOLS

The two mountain camp assemblages include a variety of artifacts used as clothing, personal items, ornaments and symbols. No such items were recovered from the desert wagon sites. Several brass, glass, iron and pewter buttons from garments were found at both mountain camps, along with a few fragments of clothing and shoes. Personal ornaments included a brooch with a blue glass setting, a silver-plated dangling earring or pendant and several beads. The twelve beads in the Murphy cabin artifact assemblage were glass; spherical, conical or donut-shaped; colored red, light blue, white or amethyst; and were manufactured by molding, pressing or winding. Several clay tobacco pipes also were discovered, including white kaolin Dublin clay pipestems and a gray ceramic pipe bowl with two grooves and rows of repeated circles.

Two artifacts from the winter camp sites have been interpreted as personal symbols. Perhaps the most interesting of these is a religious medal recovered from the Murphy cabin site. The medal was examined by Richard Ahlborn of the National Museum of American History at the Smithsonian Institution, who found it to be stylistically similar to those made in the United States between 1825 and 1875 and used by Roman Catholics. Such medals were stamped out from a base metal and then plated with tin or silver. According to Ahlborn, "the representation of Jesus, encircled by the inscription "SWEET HEART OF JESUS HAVE MERCY ON US," and of His mother, encircled by "BLESSED VIRGIN MARY PRAY FOR US" are typical in both gesture and sentiment of the mid-nineteenth century. These representations somewhat anticipate the popular sacred-heart themes, as they did not become official Catholic dogma until about 1875."[23]

Another personal symbol recovered from the Donner family camp in 1990 is a brass American eagle with a shield and arrows. This symbol appears to be part of a United States army uniform insignia "worn on the Infantry dress shako from 1821 to 1851 and on the 1855 Light Artillery dress shako, until 1872."[24] Whether the emblem might have been left behind by General Kearny's Mormon Battalion during their trip

FIGURE 2   A Roman Catholic religious medal found in the archaeological excavation of the Murphy family cabin. It is marked by the phrase, "BLESSED VIRGIN MARY PRAY FOR US." (Donald Hardesty)

through the camp in 1847 is an interesting, but conjectural, question.

COINS

Without question the two most exciting artifacts located by the Donner party excavations are coins. Two were found at the Alder Creek site in 1990—an 1830 United States Liberty head penny and an 1839 copper farthing from the Isle of Man. John Denton, the only person in the Donner party known to have come from England, was traveling with the George Donner family and may have been working as a teamster. In her reminiscences, Virginia Reed Murphy describes Denton as about thirty years old and a gunsmith and gold-beater from Sheffield, England, who perished on the way out of the mountains with the first relief party. What, if any, connection John Denton had with the Isle of Man is unknown.

ANIMAL REMAINS

In addition to artifacts, several animal bone and teeth fragments were recovered from the three Donner party sites. The faunal remains at the Donner family mountain camp are in the process of being analyzed; however, preliminary studies of the 306 identifiable animal remains at the Murphy cabin site and the fifty-seven at the Great Salt Lake Desert wagon site allow some conclusion. Both include the remains of domestic cow and mule. Cattle, probably oxen, are the best represented animals.

Mostly lower limbs from a minimum of three individual animals were identified at each of the two sites. Perhaps the most interesting, and the second most common, animal remains recovered from the Murphy's cabin site have been identified by Amy Dansie at the Nevada State Museum as bear. If this identification is correct, the archaeological record confirms the written account that William Eddy, one of the cabin's residents during the winter of 1846–1847, killed an 800 pound grizzly bear.

CONCLUSIONS

In conclusion, then, recent archaeological studies at the three Donner party sites have begun to tap a new source of information about what is probably the best known event in the history of the California Trail. To date, the studies have added architectural details of Murphy's cabin and refuted the common belief that there was a mass burial of Donner party victims inside the cabin. Perhaps more important, however, is archaeological confirmation that the Donner family camp is indeed on Alder Creek, well off the most commonly used emigrant route of the 1840s. In addition, the 1990 field season identified two clusters of archaeological remains that may be sites of shelters at the camp. Together these studies have shown that the systematic examination of the archaeological record can help write Donner party history; however, it also is clear that much more work remains to be done.

NOTES

1. Edwin Bryant, *What I Saw in California* (Philadelphia, PA: D. Appleton, 1848).

   Edwin G. Gudde, *Bigler's Chronicle of the West* (Berkeley: University of California Press, 1962).

   Eliza P. Donner Houghton, *The Expedition of the Donner Party and its Tragic Fate* (Chicago, IL: A. C. McClurg and Company, 1911).

   C. F. McGlashan, *History of the Donner Party* (Truckee, CA: Crowley and McGlashan, 1879).

   Virginia Reed Murphy, *Across the Plains in the Donner Party, 1846* (1891). Reprinted (Olympic Valley, CA: Outbooks, 1977).

   David Morris Potter, ed., *Trail to California: The Overland Journal of Vincent Geiger and Wakeman Bryarly* (New Haven, CT: Yale University Press, 1962).

   James Frazier Reed, "Narrative of the Sufferings of a Company of Emigrants in the Mountains of California, in the Winter of '46 and '47," *Illinois Journal* (Springfield, IL: 9 December 1847).

   J. Quinn Thorton, *Oregon and California in 1848* (New York: Harper, 1849).

2. George R. Stewart, *Ordeal by Hunger,* 2nd edition (Boston, MA: Houghton-Mifflin, 1960), p. vii.

3. McGlashan, *History of the Donner Party,* 14th edition (San Francisco, CA: A. Carlisle and Company, 1927), p. 258.

4. Ibid., p. 258–259.

5. Stewart, *Ordeal by Hunger,* p. 304.

6. McGlashan, *History of the Donner Party,* 14th edition, p. 260.

7. Donald L. Hardesty, "Archaeology of the Donner Party Tragedy," *Nevada Historical Society Quarterly* Vol. 30, 1987, p. 246–268.

   Susan Lindstrom, *An Archaeologically and Historically Based Rendition of the Murphy Cabin* (Truckee, CA: Donner Memorial State Park, 1986).

8. Bruce Hawkins and David Madsen, *Excavation of the Donner-Reed Wagons* (Salt Lake City: University of Utah Press, 1990).

9. Donald L. Hardesty and Susan Lindstrom, *Archaeology of the Donner Family Camp* (Nevada City, CA: Tahoe National Forest, 1990).

10. Hawkins and Madsen, *Excavation of the Donner-Reed Wagons,* p. 131–132.

11. Thomas Swords, Report of a Journey from California by the South Pass to Fort Leavenworth in 1847, 30th Congress, 2nd session, House Executive Document No. 1, Serial Set No. 537, 1848.

    Daniel Tylor, *A Concise History of the Mormon Battalion in the Mexican War* (Chicago, IL: Rio Grande Press, 1964), first published in 1881.

12. *Truckee Republican,* 7 May 1872.

13. C. F. McGlashan, *The Location of Site of Breen Cabin* (Oakland, CA: Privately Printed, 1920), p. 7–8.

14. Lindstrom, *Rendition of the Murphy Cabin.*

15. Stewart, *Ordeal by Hunger,* p. 267.

16. Ibid., p. 84.

17. P. M. Weddell, "Location of the Donner Family Camp," *California Historical Society Quarterly,* March 1945, p. 75.

18. Ibid.

19. Ibid.

20. Harold Curran, *Fearful Crossing* (Reno, NV: Great Basin Press, 1982).

    Charles Graydon, *Trail of the First Wagons Over the Sierra Nevada* (Gerald, MO: Patrice Press, 1986).

W. Turrentine Jackson, *Historical Survey of the Stampede Reservoir Area in the Little Truckee River Drainage District* (San Francisco, CA: National Park Service, 1967).

Dale Morgan, ed., *Overland in 1846: Diaries and Letters of the Oregon-California Trail* (Georgetown, CA: Talisman Press, 1963).

21. Charles Graydon, *The Emigrant Trail in the Vicinity of the George Donner Campground* (Nevada City, CA: Tahoe National Forest, 1989).

22. Ibid.

23. Richard Ahlborn, Personal Communication, 1985.

24. Sidney B. Brinckerhoff, *Metal Uniform Insignia of the Frontier U.S. Army 1846–1902* (Tucson: Arizona Historical Society, Museum Monograph Number 3, 1972), p. 14.

24

The Tsar of All the Russias

William R. Maples

Dr. William R. Maples was a very well-known forensic scientist who participated in many famous cases. Before his recent death, Maples was curator of the C. A. Pound Human Identification Laboratory at the Florida Museum of Natural History and a fellow of the American Academy of Forensic Sciences.

Points to consider when reading this article:

1. Those who took part in the execution of the tsar and his family hoped to eliminate any evidence of their deed. Did they succeed?

2. What role was played by forensic anthropology in the identification of the remains of this royal family?

3. Why is there a mystery associated with the tsar's daughter Anastasia?

4. Were Anastasia's remains among those identified by forensic scientist William R. Maples?

Make no mistake, the animated feature movie *Anastasia* was an enjoyable hour-and-a-half of entertainment. Of course, to enjoy the movie you had to ignore some glaring historical inaccuracies. In the film there is little to indicate that the regime of Tsar Nicholas II, Anastasia's father, was one of the most brutal and des-potic ever to plague a country. The wealth and power of the tsar and his family were virtually unlimited, and the poverty and powerlessness of the Russian people were extreme. The communist regime that replaced the monarchy may have been cruel and brutal in its own way, but it cannot be said that it replaced a democratic, fair, or even very popular system. Anastasia was not a little girl when the revolution deposed her father and crushed the monarchy, as the movie would have us believe. She was already a pampered teenager, more than seventeen years old.

That the tsar and his family were killed by the new communist government of Russia was never in doubt; some of those personally involved in carrying out the execution bragged too loudly for too long to maintain the supposed secret of the fate of the royal Romanov family. However, questions of exactly how it was carried out and where were left open. The new government in Moscow despised and feared the members of the royal family when they were alive, and feared them almost as much after they had been killed. The communist regime could countenance no martyrs who might inspire a counterrevolution, so the remains of the family were destroyed, but not perfectly. In 1979, more than sixty years after the Romanovs were killed, their bones were discovered, and twelve years after that, in 1991, they were recovered. And now, in 1998, they have been returned and buried in St. Petersburg, the traditional burial site for Russian tsars.

The world will never know what we did with them. . . .
  —Peter Voikov, Soviet ambassador to Poland, 1935

It was a sunny day on the edge of Siberia when I climbed the stairs to the second floor of the Forensic-Medical Examination Bureau, where the skeletons were kept. The bureau was located in Ekaterinburg, eight hundred miles from Moscow, deep in the Ural Mountains. A city of dreadful fame, Ekaterinburg is the Golgotha of Soviet Communism. Here, in the basement of a house that has since been destroyed, was carried out one of the most fateful mass executions in this century.

In Ekaterinburg, on the night of July 16–17, 1918, Tsar Nicholas II, the last of the Romanovs, was summoned downstairs with his whole family to a basement room in the so-called "House of Special Designation," a mansion requisitioned from an engineer named Ipatiev. Waiting for him was a Bolshevik death squad led by Commander Jacob Yurovsky.

Near midnight a decree of execution was read out to the amazed royal family and their servants: Tsar Nicholas, the Tsarina Alexandra, their frail hemophiliac son Alexei, their four daughters, Olga, Tatiana, Marie and Anastasia, the family doctor, Sergei Botkin, a cook named Kharitonov, a footman named Trupp and a maid named Anna Demidova—eleven people in all.

Yurovsky had not finished speaking when the first shots exploded in the narrow room. Thrown backward by the force of bullets, the Tsar spun around and fell dead. His family and retainers fell with him, in a blizzard of lead. The roar of a Fiat truck engine, running loudly outside the back door, helped mask the homicidal racket. Twenty minutes later the corpses were carried out into the summer night, where they vanished, seemingly forever.

"The world will never know what we did with them," boasted Peter Voikov, a Bolshevik official at Ekaterinburg who was ambassador to Poland when he uttered these words, seventeen years later.

On July 19 the local *Ural Worker* newspaper announced that the Tsar was dead:

EXECUTION OF NICHOLAS, THE BLOODY
CROWNED MURDERER
SHOT WITHOUT BOURGEOIS FORMALITIES
BUT IN ACCORDANCE WITH OUR NEW
DEMOCRATIC PRINCIPLES.

But no mention was made of his family, and for nearly three quarters of a century the exact details of the massacre remained a Soviet secret. Despite the most zealous searches by pro-Tsarist investigators immediately after the shootings, the corpses of the Tsar and his family were not unearthed. Only a single finger, apparently belonging to a woman, together with scattered burned and molten personal effects, turned up in the recesses of an abandoned mine twelve miles outside of the city.

Now, unexpectedly, from a bog on the outskirts of Ekaterinburg nine more or less complete skeletons had come to light in a shallow grave, along with fourteen bullets, bits of rope and a shattered jar that once contained sulfuric acid. Could these be the remains of the Romanovs? I and my colleagues had been invited by the Russians to come halfway around the world to try to answer this question.

The nine skeletons were identified only by number. Five were female, four male. Of the five females, three were young women, only recently grown to maturity. All the faces were badly fractured, every single one. This fact made reconstruction of facial features risky or impossible, but it also conformed to the accounts of the assassinations: that the faces of the victims were smashed in with rifle butts to render them unrecognizable.

All of the female skeletons had dental work. None of the males did, though we knew from historical records that Dr. Botkin had a denture plate in his upper jaw, which was later extricated from the mud of the Four Brothers Mine by the White Army investigators. Sure enough, one of the males had a few teeth in his lower jaw, no teeth at all in his upper jaw, and probably wore false teeth in life.

The enamel surfaces of the teeth showed the signs of acid etching. The outer tables of the cranial vaults were eroded away by acid also. A single broken jar that had once contained sulfuric acid was also found among the remains. This, too, agreed with accounts of the killings. A receipt for 400 pounds of sulfuric acid, requisitioned shortly before the murders, still exists in Russian archives. I have seen copies of this receipt with my own eyes.

In all, fourteen bullets were recovered from the grave, along with the remains of one hand grenade detonator. All the bullets were 7.62, 7.63 or 7.65mm, about the equivalent of .32-caliber bullets. The Russians told us they believed nine of the bullets came from Nagants, four came possibly from a Browning and one from some other gun, possibly a Mauser. These bullets had almost certainly lodged in the bodies at the time of death, but twelve of them had gradually come loose as the remains decomposed. The Russians told us that loose teeth had also been found in the shallow grave, mixed in among the bones.

Three bodies, Numbers 2, 3 and 6, had through-and-through gunshot wounds to the head. Another body, No. 9, had a stab wound in the breastbone that could have been made by a bayonet. It is important to remember that not every lethal wound, whether it be a bullet or a knife thrust, will leave a mark on the skeleton underneath, even when the ribs and vertebrae are recovered intact, which was certainly not the case here.

• Body No. 1 was identified by its pelvis as a fully grown female. The skull was missing its facial bones. There was a gold bridge of poor workmanship on the mandible—not very expensive dental work. But the most revealing detail turned up in my examination of the ankle joints. These showed an extension of the joint surfaces, as if the woman had spent many hours crouching or kneeling, perhaps while she was scrubbing floors or doing other menial work. On the basis of these joints, together with the overall composition of the group, I believe this skeleton belonged to the Tsarina's maid, Anna Demidova.

• The [next] skeleton [2] belonged to a mature man with a very flat, sloping forehead. I believe it is that of Dr. Sergei Botkin, the physician who watched over the young Tsarevich Alexei, who died with the family, and whose photograph in life closely matched the shape of this forehead. The skull had no upper teeth, and Botkin's dental plate had been found by White Russian investigators over seventy years earlier at the mouth of the Four Brothers Mine. The skull had a gunshot wound from a bullet that entered the left frontal bone in the upper left corner of the forehead and exited through the right temporal area.

• Body No. 3's skeleton belonged to a young adult female with a bulging forehead, in her early twenties when she died. It has been tentatively identified as belonging to the young Grand Duchess Olga. The shape of the head agrees extraordinarily closely with lifetime photographs of Olga. Half of her middle face, the facial bones between the tops of the eye orbits and the lower jaw, was missing. She clearly was completely grown, and the roots of her third molars, her "wisdom teeth," were fully developed. Regrettably the bones of the legs were not intact; they had been cut into sections after being dug up but before we arrived on the scene. As a result, they could not be used for height estimates. Instead we used bones from the arms to estimate the female's height. Though arm lengths are not as reliable as leg lengths, we arrived at a height estimate of 64.9 inches. Dr. Levine found extensive amalgam fillings in her teeth, a trait shared by the other two young females. It is very likely they were fond of sweets, in life.

In Body No. 3, the bullet entered under the left jaw, broke the jaw, went through the palate behind the nose and exited through the frontal bone of the skull. Such a trajectory could come from a gun placed under the chin and fired up, or from firing at a body already lying on the floor. The exit wound was very neat, drilled in a near-perfect circle. The top of the skull showed signs of acid etching.

I will pass over Body No. 4 for now, and return to it later, for reasons that will become apparent.

• Body No. 5 belonged to a woman in her late teens or early twenties. Half of her middle face was missing, a pattern of damage already seen in Body No. 3. Dr. Levine and I agreed that she was the youngest of the five women whose skeletons lay before us. We concluded this from the fact that the root tips of her third molars were incomplete. Her sacrum, in the back of her pelvis, was not completely developed. Her limb bones showed that growth had only recently ended. Her back showed evidence of immaturity, but it was nevertheless the back of a woman at least eighteen years old. We estimated her height at 67.5 inches. The Russians told us that a bullet had been found in a lump of adipocere near this body. We believe this skeleton is that of Marie, who was nineteen years old at the time of the murders.

• Body No. 6 belonged to a young woman who was nevertheless fully grown. Her dental and skeletal development fell neatly between that of Bodies 3 and 5. There was no evidence of recent growth in her limb bones. Her sacrum and pelvic rim were mature, which made her at least eighteen. On the basis of her limb bones, we put her height at 65.6 inches, right between the other two young females. More important, her collarbone was mature, making her at least twenty years old. The Grand Duchess Tatiana was twenty-one years and two months old at the time of the shootings, so this skeleton agreed very closely with the historical record.

Body No. 6 had a gunshot entrance wound high on the back left side of the skull, and an associated exit wound just in front of the right temple. The minimum diameter of the entrance wound was 8.8mm, which would be consistent with the .32-caliber handguns used in the assassinations. A slug from a .32 is 7.6mm in diameter. This young woman had been shot in the back of the head.

So: 3, 5 and 6 were Olga, Marie and Tatiana, in that order. Where was Anastasia? None of these three young female skeletons was young enough to be Anastasia, who was seventeen years and one month old the night of the shootings. Our Russian hosts believed that Body No. 6, the midmost of the three young females, was the long-lost Anastasia. Alas! We had to disagree, based on the growth patterns of the teeth, pelvises, sacra and long limbs of the three skeletons before us. The Russians had labored manfully over Body No. 6, attempting to restore its facial bones with generous dollops of glue, stretched across wide gaps. They had been forced to estimate over and over again, while reassembling these fragments, almost none of which were touching each other in the reconstruction. It was a remarkable and ingenious exercise, but it was too fanciful for me to buy: Anastasia was not in this room.

Another piece of evidence was the height of the skeletal remains. This young woman was roughly the same height as the other two young women whose remains were discovered in the mass grave. In photographs of Anastasia taken with her sisters a year before her death, she is shorter than Olga and noticeably shorter than Tatiana and Marie.

There are no photographs of the royal family in the months immediately preceding the shootings. Could Anastasia have undergone a "growth spurt" in those months before the shootings? Could she have suddenly "caught up" with her sisters in stature? It is extremely unlikely.

In September 1917, only ten months before the shootings, while she was under house arrest in Tobolsk, the Tsarina Alexandra wrote in her diary: "Anastasia is very fat, like Marie used to be—big, thick-waisted, then tiny feet—*I hope she grows more. . . .*" (My italics.) Though the quote is rather vague, it seems to indicate clearly that Anastasia was not yet as tall as her sisters, and might be expected to grow taller.

I will pass over Body No. 7 for the moment, and return to it presently.

• The skeleton of Body No. 8 was very fragmentary and was grievously damaged by acid. It belonged to an adult male in his forties or fifties. The maxilla (upper jaw) of Body No. 8 was not recovered. The mandible was recovered, but it had lost its remaining teeth at death. The area immediately above the eye orbits, where our eyebrows are in life, was noticeably flat. The owner of this skull, when alive, had a flattened profile. From the hip and pelvic remains, this skeleton was clearly male. He does not appear to have been very big. One ulna was fractured and later healed. I believe this to have been the skeleton of the cook, Ivan Mikhailovich Kharitonov, mainly by a process of elimination that I will explain later.

• The skeleton of Body No. 9 belonged to a big, heavy-boned man over six feet tall, who was beginning to show evidence of aging. The back of the skull was missing. The teeth were worn. There was a stab wound, probably by a bayonet, through the breastbone from front to back, but I am convinced this particular breastbone does not belong to this set of remains. For the rest, the robust size of the skeleton agrees well with descriptions we have of the footman, Alexei Igorevich Trupp, who was part of the Tsar's entourage at Ekaterinburg.

We have now discussed Bodies 1, 2, 3, 5, 6, 8 and 9. Let us return to Bodies 4 and 7, in reverse order.

• Body No. 7 was in some ways the most important of all that were found in the pit. It belonged to an older woman whose rib cage may have been damaged by bayonet thrusts—the bones were not well enough preserved to allow me to say this with certainty. But it was not these that commanded our attention. Rather, it was her amazing and exquisite dental work. My colleague, Dr. Levine, initially thought the two silvery crowns in the lower jaw were aluminum "temporaries." They weren't. To his astonishment, he found they were made of platinum. When we took flash pictures of this skull, the gleaming platinum crowns coruscated brilliantly in the sudden light. Dr. Levine also discovered beautiful porcelain crowns in this skull's jaws, along with wonderfully wrought gold fillings. It was stunning dental work, extremely costly and cunningly contrived.

It was this rich dental work, so precious-metaled it was far beyond the means of all but the richest Russians, that convinced the men who initially excavated the mass grave that here, at last, were the remains of the royal family. The Tsarina Alexandra mentions visiting the dentist several times in her diaries, and it is well that she did. The Bolshevik assassins despoiled the Tsarina of her jewels, but they could not take her teeth; and these beautiful tooth crowns spoke eloquently even in death. Taken together with the scattered bullets, the bits of rope and the smashed jar of sulfuric acid, these teeth were a powerful signal to the excavators that they were dealing with the grave of the Tsar and his family.

• Body No. 4 I believe to be the skeleton of Tsar Nicholas II. It belonged to a middle-aged man of fairly short stature. The skeleton possessed a clearly male pelvis. The skull had a very broad, flat palate that is consistent with the mouth shape of the Tsar in photographs taken before he grew his beard. It had a jutting brow line, and so did the Tsar: the curving, protruding supraorbital bones are consistent with photographs of Nicholas taken during his life. The hipbones showed the characteristic wear and deformation produced by many hours on horseback, and we know the Tsar was an ardent horseman.

The only jarring note was struck by the extraordinary, rotten condition of this skeleton's teeth, and the complete absence of dental work. There was not a single filling in any of the remaining teeth. All these were worn to gray nubbins. The lower jaw showed clear inroads of peridontal disease. The owner of these teeth was long overdue for dentures. Why didn't he get them? As Tsar, he could surely afford a good dentist!

I believe Nicholas must have had a horror of dentists and, because he was Tsar, no one could force him to visit one. Rank has its privileges, and among them is the liberty to let your teeth go to rack and ruin if you desire. Was the Tsar a coward before the dentist's drill? Did he have a horror of physical pain? His jaws seemed to say so. Is it speculating too far, to glimpse in these rotten, neglected teeth a vivid, concrete symbol of the Russian royal family in those final years, falling to pieces, but nevertheless unwilling to take the necessary, painful steps needed to repair the damage and save themselves? Perhaps, perhaps not.

I picked up the skull and held it in my hands, staring at it intently. It was a gray thing with a crushed face. A dark void yawned in the middle of its features, below the eye sockets and above the jaw. Blows of terrific force had shattered its features. I was haunted by the line in George Orwell's *Nineteen Eighty-Four*, a nightmarish view of the future based partly on the already famous brutality of the Soviet state: "*If you want a picture of the future, imagine a boot stamping on a human face—forever. . . .*" The Tsar's skull was grievously mutilated, the remains perfectly consistent with his fate. He was among the first, and certainly the foremost, victims of Bolshevik savagery.

In 1993 there was a dramatic new development in the story of the royal bones. DNA tests carried out in Great Britain have matched a blood sample from the British royal family with the DNA recovered from the Russian skeletons, with a 98.5 percent degree of certainty. Dr. Mary-Claire King at the University of California, Berkeley, has worked on samples we brought back and has confirmed what the British had reported.

DNA (deoxyribonucleic acid) is the substance that contains the genetic code that makes each human being unique. There are two types of DNA present in each living cell, nuclear DNA and mitochondrial DNA. The first type, called nuclear or genomic DNA, is quickly lost during heating or decomposition in human remains. It will linger longer in a dried sample of blood, or semen on clothing; but by the time human remains have begun to decompose, it is virtually impossible to isolate nuclear DNA anymore. Bacteria swarm in the remains, flies move in and pollute the body with their DNA, and what is left is a messy hodgepodge that is useless for nuclear DNA sampling.

Fortunately, the second type of DNA, mitochondrial DNA, lies not in the nucleus but outside, in the cell itself. This substance is present in the female ovum and in the tail of the male sperm, but when the sperm fertilizes the egg at the moment of conception, the tail of the sperm breaks off. Thus the mitochondrial DNA of the male is lost, and only that of the female is passed on to each of the offspring. And it is passed on without variation, from one generation to the next. Every single child has the mitochondrial DNA of its mother, who has the mitochondrial DNA of her mother, and so on. Changes in mitochondrial DNA are extremely rare, and happen on the order of once every three to four thousand years. That is the wonderful thing about mitochondrial DNA. It stays the same in a family for generation after generation and is passed on through the female line. It can endure in our bones for hundreds of years, if they are not cremated.

In the case of the Romanovs, we can easily go back to Queen Victoria, who has been described as the grandmother of Europe's royal families. Queen Victoria, like any mother, passed her mitochondrial DNA on to her offspring. And one of her daughters passed that same mitochondrial DNA on to her offspring, one of whom was Alexandra, the wife of Tsar Nicholas II. And Alexandra passed her mitochondrial DNA on to all her children. Similarly Alexandra's sister, Princess Victoria of Hesse, passed it on to her children, one of whom was the mother of Prince Philip, the Duke of Edinburgh, and his sisters. Therefore the mitochondrial DNA found in the blood of Prince Philip would be identical to that of Queen Victoria and the Tsarina Alexandra. It only remained to carry out the necessary tests.

These were performed in July 1993 near London. Prince Philip submitted a sample of his blood and its DNA was extracted. At the same time, Pavel Ivanov, head of the DNA unit at the Russian Academy of Sciences, brought a sample of the Romanov bones to Great Britain. There, using a technique called PCR or polymerase chain reaction, a small sample of DNA was extracted from the bones and grown in a culture.

There are only four nucleotides that make up all mitochondrial DNA: cytosine, adenine, thymine and guanine, known as CATG for short. In mitochondrial DNA there are 16,569 base pairs of nucleotides, arranged in a ring. A computer printout of a DNA sequence looks like a diabolically complex code, based on just four letters in neat columns, repeated again and again in slightly varying order for page after page. Luckily we do not have to scrutinize all 16,569 pairs. We can focus on certain "hyper-variable regions," made up of a total of just 608 base pairs. Computers are of great help in matching up the hyper-variable regions. When the results for the hyper-variable regions in two DNA samples match up at these crucial checkpoints, you can be virtually certain they are the same.

This is what happened when Prince Philip's blood DNA was matched up with the Romanovs' bone DNA. Dr. Peter Gill of the Forensic Science Service of the Home Office said the probability that both samples contained the same DNA was "almost 99 percent." Taken in conjunction with the compelling physical skeletal evidence, the results are clear and unequivocal. Short of the Last Judgment, when the dead shall rise up and be cloaked anew with flesh, and all our doubts are scheduled to be resolved in the twinkling of an eye, we may say that the mystery of the Romanovs is solved as nearly as it is likely to be. Nevertheless we recommended in our report that the site around the pit be carefully excavated and searched for the remains of the two bodies Yurovsky said he burned. I believe such a dig might well turn up the calcined remains of Anastasia and Alexei.

"Anna Anderson" went to her grave in 1984, claiming she was Anastasia. Her body was cremated and this removed the last possibility of establishing the truth or falsity of her royal pretensions. Cremation destroys utterly all organic components of bone. No known technique can recover any DNA from cremated remains. There are supposed to be hair samples taken from Anna Anderson but these are cut hair, not rooted hair. The shafts of human hair are largely composed of dead material, devoid of significant amounts of DNA. Only hair plucked by the roots from the scalp can be tested for DNA with any real hope of success. There are some tissue samples from Anna Anderson's body, in a hospital where she underwent surgery in life. To date, legal difficulties have prevented testing these samples for their DNA.

A commission in Russia will hear our team's conclusions, and I believe the British DNA work to be the final word in resolving this old mystery. It is my understanding that the Romanov remains will be interred in St. Petersburg, which was once, briefly, known as Leningrad.

25

Archaeology in the Search for Amelia Earhart

Thomas F. King and Richard E. Gillespie

Tom King is an archaeologist with deep roots in the historic preservation movement and extensive experience conducting archaeological excavations on Pacific Islands. Ric Gillespie is the founder and director of The International Group for Historic Aircraft Recovery (TIGHAR).

Points to consider when reading this article:

1. How can archaeology help solve the mystery of the disappearance of Amelia Earhart?

2. What artifactual evidence is presented that Amelia Earhart and Fred Noonan did not crash and die in the ocean but made it to land and survived, if only for a short time, on a small Pacific island?

3. Has definitive evidence been found that they survived the loss of their airplane?

4. What kind of archaeological evidence would be necessary to prove beyond a reasonable doubt that Amelia and Fred survived on Gardner (Nikumaroro) Island?

It is difficult for those of us who have grown up in an era where airflight is quite ordinary to imagine the challenges that faced the early aviators—people like Charles Lindbergh and Amelia Earhart.

Lindbergh was the first pilot to fly a plane solo across the Atlantic Ocean. Amelia Earhart's challenge was, if anything, even more daunting. Her goal was to become the first woman pilot to fly a plane around the world. Earhart, accompanied by her navigator Fred Noonan, took off from Oakland, California, on May 20, 1937, flying east to Tucson, Arizona, in the first leg of her attempt to circumnavigate the globe. It actually was her second attempt to set this record. Her previous try had ended in a near tragedy. On March 17, 1937, she had also started in Oakland, but flew in the other direction, west, across the Pacific to Hawaii. During her takeoff in Hawaii for the second leg of the trip, she suffered a crash that seriously damaged the aircraft—and could have ended her life.

The second attempt was, at least initially, more successful. Earhart flew the plane, a Lockheed Electra 10E, from Oakland to Tucson, then on to Miami, across the Atlantic, then over Africa and much of southern Asia, on to Australia, and then to Lae, New Guinea. Amelia and Fred left New Guinea on July 1, hoping to arrive back at their starting point, Oakland, for a celebration on July 4, Independence Day. The Pacific is an enormous ocean, and they would have to stop on Howland Island for refueling. They never made it to Howland.

Most believe that Earhart simply ran out of gas and crashed into the ocean, never able to locate the tiny spot of land cresting above the waters of the vast Pacific. Maybe so. But is it possible that Amelia Earhart found another harbor, another place to land? Can archaeological evidence place Amelia's Lockheed Electra, or perhaps even Amelia herself, on Gardner (Nikumaroro) Island? What follows is the story of a valiant attempt to solve this sixty-year-old mystery: What happened to Amelia Earhart?

O n July 2, 1937, America's famous female aviation pioneer Amelia Earhart disappeared while attempting a round-the-world flight. Earhart's disappearance captured the imagination of the nation, and has been the subject of vigorous speculation ever since. The Earhart Project of The International Group for Historic Aircraft Recovery (TIGHAR) is an attempt to apply rigorous research methods—notably including those of archaeology—to solving the Earhart mystery.

TIGHAR is a small non-profit group whose purposes include promoting the preservation of historic aircraft and using physical evidence to study questions of aviation history. The Earhart Project is only one of TIGHAR's research projects, but it has become a compelling one. It illustrates how archaeology can be applied to unravelling historical mysteries. It also illustrates how archaeology can, and indeed must, work in concert with a wide range of other disciplines to achieve its goals.

THE FACTS

Earhart and her navigator, Fred Noonan, began their attempt at a round-the-world flight flying east from Oakland, California. Their aircraft was a twin-engine Lockheed Electra 10E. By the end of June they had reached Lae, New Guinea. From Lae they jumped off on the first of July for the 2600-mile journey to Howland Island. Howland, a speck of a coral island under U.S. jurisdiction about 1500 miles southwest of Hawaii, had a runway and facilities for refueling. The Coast Guard cutter *Itasca* was lying off Howland prepared to help guide Earhart and Noonan in using radio navigation procedures. Noonan was a highly experienced aerial navigator who had worked with Pan American to pioneer its clipper routes across the Pacific.

Through a series of errors, *Itasca* and the Earhart plane never achieved two-way communication, but *Itasca* did record numerous messages from Earhart, some estimated to have been from no more than about fifty miles out. However, Earhart and Noonan never arrived at Howland. The U.S. Navy launched a search using the battleship U.S.S. *Colorado*, the aircraft carrier U.S.S. *Yorktown*, and other vessels, but no trace of the Electra was found.

THE THEORIES

Over the years, two "theories" have been prime candidates for public acceptance as to Earhart's fate. The "crashed and sank" school holds that the Electra simply ran out of gas and crashed in the ocean. The "spy" school holds that Earhart was in fact spying on the Japanese, or at least that they thought she was, and that they captured and executed her. A number of other theories, such as the "captured by aliens" school and the "alive and living in Bayonne" school, are less credible.

In 1988, TIGHAR was approached by two veteran aerial navigators, Tom Willi and Tom Gannon, with a "new" theory. Research later showed it to be the oldest theory of all—proposed to the Coast Guard by technical experts in 1937, but not thoroughly investigated at the time. In brief, the proposition is that Noonan, following accepted practice at the time, navigated to a line established by celestial observations that should have passed through Howland Island, but could not tell whether he was north or south of the island. There is no land for thousands of miles north of Howland, while to the south lie the Phoenix Islands. The rational thing for Earhart and Noonan to do, therefore, would have been to fly south along the line. If they had hit the line south of Howland they obviously would not have ended up there—as, of course, they did not—but they would have wound up in the Phoenix Islands.

NIKUMARORO

For various reasons, the island known in 1937 as Gardner Island is a prime candidate for an Earhart/Noonan landing in the Phoenix group. At the time, Gardner was part of the British Gilbert and Ellice Islands Colony; today it is part of the Republic of Kiribati, and bears the name Nikumaroro. In 1937 it was uninhabited, as it is today. From 1938 to 1963 it was colonized by Gilbert Islanders, today known as I Kiribati—the last addition to the British Empire before the sun set on the Empire during World War II. Although Navy float planes from U.S.S. *Colorado* flew over the island in search of Earhart—and reported "signs of recent habitation"—the search did not extend to the ground. Radio signals purporting to come from the Earhart plane were traced to the vicinity of Nikumaroro by radio direction finders, but were dismissed as the products of hoaxes. Nikumaroro has become the primary focus of TIGHAR's research into the Earhart disappearance. Our goal is to find unequivocal physical evidence that will establish, once and for all, what really happened to Earhart, Noonan, and the Electra 10E.

The TIGHAR proposition is that Earhart and Noonan flew along their line of position south of Howland Island, and landed on Nikumaroro. They broadcast radio signals that were dismissed as hoaxes, and were not seen by the *Colorado* pilots in their brief overflight of the island. They died on the island, and their remains, and those of the Electra, may still be there. We reject the "spy" theory for several reasons—notably that there is no credible evidence to support it, that the Japanese had nothing to spy on in the area in 1937, and that any overflight of Japanese held territory by Earhart and Noonan would have occurred at night if they had the fuel to make it occur at all. We disbelieve the "crashed and sank" theory because it fails to account for the post-loss radio signals and it gives too little credence to Noonan's navigational abilities.

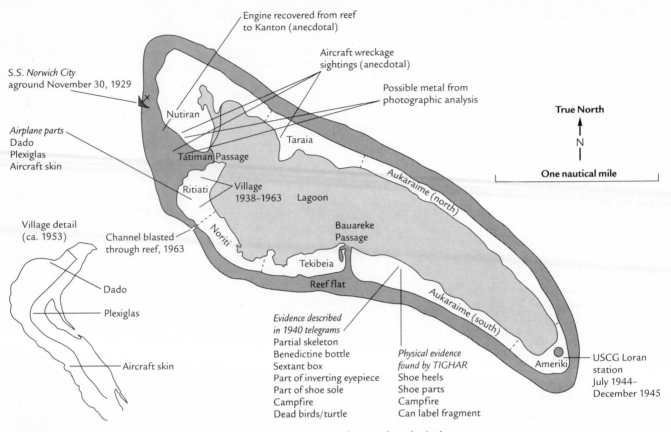

FIGURE 1   Outline of Gardner Island, now known as Nikumaroro, where archaeological evidence suggests Amelia Earhart and her navigator Fred Noonan may have crash landed in her unsuccessful and ultimately tragic attempt to circumnavigate the Earth. (Ric Gillespie)

Our proposition is just that, however—a proposition. So we set out to test it, using archaeology and other methods.

NIKU I EXPEDITION: 1989

On our first expedition to Nikumaroro we were painfully naive. We half expected to find the Electra sitting in some obscure location under a tree, or in easily locatable pieces on the reef. We also anticipated being able to move around the island with relative ease—after all, the island is only three miles long and a mile wide, including its lagoon. In fact, survey work was very difficult. The island is heavily cloaked in a dense, nasty shrub called Scaevola, and temperatures routinely ran in excess of 100 degrees Fahrenheit. The waters around the island are infested with sharks, and the reef drops off steeply from a shallow flat to over 2000 feet in depth.

After some initial reconnaissance, we attempted to survey closely spaced transects through the dense foliage. This quickly proved infeasible; the Scaevola was simply too dense and difficult to cut through. We nec-essarily fell back on a less formal method—inspecting every place we could get to, but not trying to cut through the more impenetrable vegetation.

Metal detectors were used in locations where it appeared that soil deposition could have buried airplane parts or other evidence. Meanwhile, a team of divers inspected the reef flat and the reef face down as far as they could go—about 120 feet.

The results of the first year's work were puzzling and disappointing. The divers found virtually nothing. The land team found airplane parts, but nothing intact, and the parts were not at all where we had expected them. Rather than being out in the bush where a plane might have been abandoned or crashed and never seen and reported by the colonists, the plane parts were in the remains of the village itself. They were mixed up with a great deal of non-aircraft aluminum and other technological debris that could be confused with airplane parts. The U.S. Coast Guard had maintained a Loran (navigation) station on the southeast end of the island during part of World War II, and when it was dismantled much of what made it up had come to the village.

The village itself was much more highly organized than we had expected. Rather than an informal alignment or two of thatched huts, as we had expected, it was organized along three meter-wide roads around a dead-square parade ground, in the center of which was a thick, fallen flagstaff.

The roadways were neatly lined with upright coral slabs, and extended away from the parade ground past the landing a quarter mile away and into the bush to the southeast. Around the parade ground itself were large concrete platforms that had supported substantial wood and thatch buildings. The largest of these was the "Rest House"—we had a photo of it in a report on the colony. It had been a handsome thatched structure with two wings on a central bay, and had been the residence for the colonial officer-in-charge, Gerald Gallagher.

Gallagher had been second-in-command of the Phoenix Islands Settlement Scheme (PISS) to Harry Maude, who at 95 is still writing about the central Pacific at his home in Australia, and who has been an invaluable help to us. Harry had come up with the idea of the "PISS" to relieve population pressures in the southern Gilbert Islands, though recently he has acknowledged a political motive as well—to outflank the Americans who were looking hungrily at the Phoenixes as possible landing places for transpacific flying boats. Gallagher was a charismatic leader, much respected by the people of the colony, but he had died tragically on Nikumaroro, shortly after returning from leave in Fiji in September of 1941. At his request, he had been buried in the parade ground on Nikumaroro, at the base of the flagpole. Here we found his grave, covered by a monument modeled on that of Robert Lewis Stevenson in Samoa.

The airplane parts we found in the village that first year included some rather nondescript pieces of aluminum, a large aluminum box that turned out to be a navigator's bookcase from a PBY, and a "dado"—a piece from the interior of an airplane that covers the cables in the space along the edge of the flooring. The dado perfectly matches pieces that were in Earhart's plane, and appears to be of non-military origin; in fact, military craft of World War II vintage did not have dados.

There were many graves in the village, marked in the traditional way of the I Kiribati with low platforms surrounded by standing coral slabs. We found one grave quite a distance from the village, however, in an area called Aukaraime by the colonists. It was a small grave—too small to be the grave of an adult unless the bones were redeposited in it, in disarticulated form. This grave, through serendipity, was to play a very important role in our research.

THE KILTS STORY

TIGHAR's historical research had unearthed a 1963 article in the *San Diego Union,* about an ex-Coast Guardsman named Floyd Kilts. Kilts had taken part in dismantling the Loran station on Nikumaroro, and was convinced that while there, he had learned what really happened to Amelia Earhart. According to Kilts, he had been approached by "a native," who through an interpreter had told him a remarkable story. In the early days of the island's settlement, the colonists had found the skull of a man and the skeleton of a woman, with "women's shoes, American kind, size nine." They had taken these to "the Irish magistrate," who had gotten very excited because he thought they might be the remains of Earhart and Noonan; he had put them in "the island's four-oared boat" and headed for Fiji to turn them over to the authorities. But before getting there, he had gotten pneumonia and died, whereupon the "natives," who Kilts said were "superstitious as hell," had thrown the bones overboard.

There's lots of obvious nonsense in the Kilts story. There never was an Irish magistrate on Nikumaroro, dead or alive. Nobody would be fool enough to try to row from Nikumaroro to Fiji, a distance of almost 900 miles, except under extreme duress. But like the Homeric epic of the Trojan War, there were things about the story that rang true. While there was no Irish magistrate, there was, of course, Gallagher, and further research showed that his nickname had been "Irish." There was a four-oared boat, used as a lighter between the shore and supply ships. Gallagher had died, though upon his return from Fiji, on the island, not in a boat on his way *to* Fiji. Kilts, unfortunately, was dead, and the *Union* reporter could not remember anything about his interview with him.

We speculated endlessly about what the Kilts story might mean. If bones had been found, and had been associated in the minds of the colonists with the tragic death of their much-respected administrator, what would they have done with them? It didn't seem likely that they would have thrown them in the water; this could make for unquiet ghosts. Burial seemed more likely, in a remote grave on land belonging to no one. Land like Aukaraime.

NIKU II EXPEDITION: 1991

The evidence was thin but tantalizing, and it was enough to justify TIGHAR's backers in supporting another expedition. A major target in 1991 was the grave at Aukaraime. With the permission and oversight of the Kiribati government, TIGHAR planned to excavate

FIGURE 2   Members of the TIGHAR team, Veryl Fenlason (left) and Kenton Spading, employ a device that uses electromagnetic readings to detect disturbed earth that might, in turn, indicate the presence of buried remains here on Nikumaroro. Using archaeological procedures, the team has found some tantalizing hints that Amelia Earhart may have landed here at the end of her unsuccessful attempt to circumnavigate the world. (Courtesy of Ric Gillespie)

the grave and see if it contained the redeposited bones of Earhart and Noonan.

We were amazed at the changes that had taken place in the island. A major storm had swept in sometime in 1990, and had badly eroded the shoreline adjacent to the village. The site where the dado had been found could not be relocated, but while inspecting the village area the team came upon a large piece of aircraft aluminum that the storm had apparently washed out of the ground. It more closely matched the Electra than it did any other aircraft type known or suspected to have been in the neighborhood. A piece of control cable and other airplane parts were also found. But the village was not the focus of investigation.

The grave was, and it was carefully, laboriously, excavated. And it was found to contain the bones of a young child. We replaced the bones and reconstructed the grave just as we had found it. We had tested and rejected a hypothesis, which is what scientific archaeology is all about, but no one could be said to be happy about it.

In the traditions of the I Kiribati, Nikumaroro is the home of Nei Manganibuka, a powerful and benign spirit. Manganibuka is associated with the buka trees (*Pisonia grandis*) that covered the island before the colonists cleared it for coconut planting, and that still clothe the land called Nutiran on the northwest end. Over the years we have come to believe that Manganibuka looks out for us on the island, and she certainly did during the refilling of the grave. The expedition doctor, Dr. Tommy Love, was leaning against a tree and tying his boot when a hermit crab, which populate Aukaraime by the thousands, turned over a leaf at his foot. Under the leaf was the heel of a shoe.

We immediately laid out a grid over the area, cleared the loose vegetation, and did a detailed search of the ground. This resulted in the recovery of a shoe sole in many small pieces, another shoe heel (from a different shoe), a grommet, a medicine bottle and a thermometer.

The first of the heels was a Cat's Paw replacement heel. The BiltRite shoe company, which now owns Cat's Paw, identified it as a replacement heel dating from the mid-1930s. The sole was from a blucher oxford style shoe.

Going back to photographs of the Earhart flight, we found one showing Amelia climbing into the Electra, with her foot on the wing. Photo-enhancement showed that her shoe was a blucher oxford type, and that it had a new heel. Comparing the size of the shoe with the known distance between rivets in the wing, we could determine that the shoe was about size 9 or 10.

So even though we had not found the bones from the Kilts story, we *had* found something that closely matched the shoes—"woman's shoe, American kind, size 9."

The other focus of Niku II was a search of the deep reef face, down to 2000 feet, using a robotic submersible operated by Oceaneering International. Once again, though, the underwater survey drew a blank.

ERIC BEVINGTON

TIGHAR is a good-sized organization, and between expeditions we were able to draw on our diverse membership for volunteers to do documentary research, studies of aerial photos, oral historical studies, and a wide range of technical analyses. We found and interviewed veterans of the Coast Guard Loran station, located and examined extensive colonial records, sent a specialist to interview the survivors of the colony, now living in the Solomon Islands. A surprising number of aerial photos were located, showing the island at various times from the late 1930s to the present, and these were closely studied. Recovered artifacts were matched with known parts of the Electra, and with every other kind of plane reported to have been in the vicinity. Records of every Naval squadron that had operated in the area during World War II were inspected, with special attention to records of crashes. Navy flyers were interviewed who had visited the island during the War. Perhaps the most important source of information in the years following Niku II, though, was an unexpected one: Eric Bevington.

Bevington was another ex-civil servant who had served in the Gilbert Islands before World War II. Now retired and living in the south of England, he had been with Harry Maude on the first exploratory visit to Niku-maroro, in October of 1938, only about three months after Earhart's disappearance. We had no idea he was alive, until in 1990 he published his recollections in a little book titled *The Things We Do for England, If Only England Knew* (Laverham Press, Salisbury, Wilts, 1990). A TIGHAR team was immediately on a plane for England.

Bevington proved to be an alert, vigorous, and knowledgeable informant, who kindly shared with us his diary as well as his verbal recollections. One thing he reported was that on their first day on the island, he and a group of I Kiribati had walked most of the way around the island (a considerable undertaking). In the course of this walk, he had noted "signs of recent occupation," which resembled a place "where someone had bivouacked for the night." He couldn't remember more specifics, but he did remember that he had showed the site to Maude the next day. He also was able to point out the spot on a map. It was Aukaraime.

NIKU III-PRELIMINARY: 1996

The third expedition was a very brief one, only four days on the island, including the sea voyage up from Fiji. Its primary focus was a water catchment facility that had been reported on the windward southeast side of the island by ex-Coast Guardsmen, and subsequently detected in modern aerial photography. We were successful in finding the facility, but also found clear evidence that it had been constructed by the colonists.

Once again, we took a brief look at the village, and once again came up with airplane parts—more aluminum and a piece of plexiglas that precisely matches that used in Earhart's plane. On the other hand, it does not match the thickness or curvature of plexi used in any other plane reported in the area.

NIKU III: 1997

The repeated discoveries in the village—during informal surveys peripheral to the main focus of work—convinced us that a much more detailed, systematic inspection was in order, so this was one of the major thrusts of the Niku III expedition in early 1997. Another focus was the lagoon, where a detailed sample survey would be carried out using electromagnetic sensors and divers. The third focus of attention was Aukaraime, where more surface survey, electronic prospecting, and test excavation were planned. In the village we hoped to do detailed work in at least two sites—a complex of old equipment and other material identified in contemporary documents as the village carpenter's shop, where control cables and other airplane parts had been found, and a house site we called "John Manybarrels' house" for its numerous rusted 55-gallon drums. This was where the plexiglas had turned up during the 1996 Niku III expedition.

By this time we had developed a rather detailed—perhaps overly complicated—hypothesis about what had happened to Earhart and Noonan. Along the east side of Baureke Passage, on the west end of Aukaraime, there's an area that's routinely overwashed by storm surges, and hence is pretty flat and clear of vegetation. Old air photos indicate that it was clear in 1937, with a high buka forest fringing its eastern edge. We speculated that Earhart could have landed on the open flat, and then taxied under the bukas to keep from frying in the tropical sun. Bukas are high enough, and wide enough, to have shielded the Electra from the eyes of the *Colorado* pilots. From the pilots' reports, we calculated that they had spent only about ten minutes over the island; if Earhart and Noonan were back in the bush for some reason, they might not have had the time to get out and attract attention. So, we proposed, the search missed them, they pitched camp at Aukaraime, and there they eventually died of thirst, starvation, exposure, the effects of injuries, or some combination of factors. The plane, we thought, might have remained in place long enough for the colonists to salvage some pieces from it before being washed over into the lagoon by one of the storm surges that keeps the "landing field" clear. It was this salvaged aluminum, we hypothesized, that wound up at places like John Manybarrels' house, taken there to make tools and handicrafts.

As it turned out, John Manybarrels' produced a good deal of airplane aluminum, most of it in small, rectangular pieces that were apparently on the way to being made into ornaments or perhaps fish lures. Several were clustered together with pieces of pearl shell and a glass bead. Another site nearby, "Sam's Site," produced even more aluminum; we mapped and studied Sam's Site because we kept running into airplane parts when we walked across it on the way to Many-barrels'. Time and weather ended up precluding study of the carpenter's shop.

Underwater work once again came up blank. This was by far our most detailed underwater survey, and was directed at the portion of the lagoon that seemed most likely as the place the Electra would have wound up if it were washed in from the "landing field." We were able to cover only about two percent of the lagoon area, however, and the plane could certainly have floated well beyond our search area.

At Aukaraime, we laid out a grid system of four-meter squares centered on the place where the Cat's Paw heel had been found, and began slinging away the coconuts and palm fronds that covered it. As we cleared the ground, we scanned it visually and then swept it with the electronic sensors. Meanwhile we got down on hands and knees and began turning over the small fragments of vegetation that covered the ground, looking for anything we might find.

The electronic sensing revealed one rather vague underground anomaly, which we probed with two test pits. Nothing at all was found. One small metal ring, perhaps some kind of washer or eyelet, was found in searching the ground. Otherwise, Aukaraime appeared to be a bust. On the last day we could work there, though, Kris Tague, who was in charge of the work, decided that we needed to probe the exact spot where the heel had been found. So another test pit was laid out, and digging immediately exposed a concentration of charcoal and wood ash. When we excavated this we found that it was a roughly circular concentration about fifty centimeters in diameter and ten centimeters thick, lying just under the surface of the ground. Screening around this feature revealed a fragment of partly burned paper that appears to be the label off a can or jar. It bears the words "___rower Produce" and a picture of leaves that resemble those of a banana plant. We're now researching can and jar labels, to see if we can find out where this one came from, how old it is, and whether it might have been on something that Earhart is known to have had on board.

Upon our return from Niku IV we catalogued all the artifacts and have subjected many of them to vari-ous kinds of analysis. It now appears that none of the aluminum from Niku IV can be related to Earhart's Electra. We have subjected the contents of the ash and charcoal feature (which we brought back complete) to water separation and done a preliminary analysis of the charcoal. It appears more likely to have come from buka wood than from coconut, suggesting that the fire that produced it burned before 1941, when Aukaraime was cleared and planted in cocos.

Meanwhile, a number of new clues have come from other sources—some of them quite exciting. We now have firsthand reports of airplane wreckage on the reef, and documentary confirmation that the colonists did find human bones, apparently on Aukaraime, and did deliver them to Gallagher, who sent them to Fiji. We are actively pursuing these and other leads.

CONCLUSION

Archaeology is one of several research disciplines that we're employing in pursuit of the truth about the Earhart/Noonan disappearance. It has been important to us because it has allowed us to record and understand the context of our discoveries, which is fundamental to understanding the discoveries themselves. It is also an important part of applying rigorous scientific practice to our work, which has never been done in previous Earhart studies. Other students of the mystery have dismissed Nikumaroro because they have assumed the Colorado's search to have been comprehensive; we know it was not. Proponents of the "spy" school have asked so many leading questions of so many people on Saipan and in the Marshall Islands that it is now impossible to sort out truth from fiction among the oral accounts. We are trying to do better—to generate testable hypotheses and then to use rigorous methods to test them. Archaeology is one of the methods we use, and a very important one.

But archaeology won't do the job by itself. It has to be coupled with other disciplines. In this case we're employing oral history, historical research, materials research, photointerpretation, biology, forensic anthropology, the working experience of pilots, navigators, and aircraft designers, and specialists in everything from antique food containers to satellite imaging. In the case of the Earhart search, as in most complex pieces of historical research, an interdisciplinary effort is needed, and archaeology is a key component in that effort.

I AM AN ARCHAEOLOGIST

Robert Stewart

Professional archaeology is my second career. I grew up in Everett, a suburb of Boston dominated by heavy industry and New England's coal distribution facilities. Before becoming an **industrial archaeologist** I worked as an engineer in the process and manufacturing industries for thirty-five years. My childhood experiences destined me for a career in engineering and technology and set the stage for a second career as an industrial archaeologist.

The availability of coal encouraged development of illuminating gas plants and the construction of New England's only blast furnace. The radiance of molten pig iron in the night sky and the bouquet of coal tar by-products wafting over the neighborhood dominate my most cherished childhood memories. The town's most prominent landmark was a small mountain of sulfur stored outside Monsanto's sulfuric acid plant. Today a good part of the old hometown is a Superfund site, a toxic waste site for which the federal government has established a fund to pay for its cleanup.

Further direction in my career path came from my fifth grade teacher, Miss Peabody. She inspired her students to see excitement and adventure in the discovery and exploration of the world immediately around them. This included an oil refinery, coke ovens, mills, and factories.

When I was nine, I organized my first expedition into a historic industrial site. My brother and I explored the remains of an illegal distillery about a quarter-mile from our house. It had been a major source of bootleg hootch throughout prohibition. Somehow the revenue agents didn't manage to smash the stills and close the place down until 1932, and the ruins were still in good condition by 1942. Curiosity about the booze-making process led to studying how the place had worked. Developing proficiency in process analysis was to become an important skill in both my careers.

My present work centers on the investigation, analysis, interpretation, and recordation of historic industrial and maritime sites. Railroads and bridges also are within my scope of interest. A major part of my research takes place in the field—measuring, sketching, photographing, and analyzing extant buildings, structures, and large artifacts. In performing this work, I've surveyed the depths of coal transport systems under an abandoned power plant and some tunnels in the New York subway system. I was a member of a team that photodocumented the structure of a 350-foot-high hammerhead crane at the Philadelphia Naval Shipyard. Projects have led me from the powder magazines and engine rooms of a century-old warship to the cavernous innards of NASA's historic wind tunnels. My work on railroads required recordation of archaic nineteenth century manually operated signal and switch control towers and the world's first electrical generating plant built exclusively for railroad use. I've squirmed into the greasy machinery pits of old bascule

(Photo by Marta Shearin)

bridges to analyze gear mechanisms and delineated an early nineteenth century rope-making process. During these projects, I've recorded oral histories with working people. This diverse group has included World War II women shipyard workers, railroad employees, coal handlers, watchmakers, and commercial fishermen. I do scholarly research in specialized engineering or patent libraries or in government archives. My reports often include valuable old photographs and documents from local historical societies. Aerial photographs, land records, insurance maps, corporate journals, and registers often provide useful information for my projects.

Technology and its effect on culture has always fascinated me. I grew up in an extended family of skilled workmen, machinists, carpenters, and a pattern maker. My uncles worked in steel mills, gun factories, gas plants, and machine shops. I'm very comfortable in a blue collar environment among the workers who produce much of the nation's wealth and keep the productive power of the world humming. Technology changes rapidly, and the people who are closest to it generally do not write about it. I believe their stories need to be told and their technology recorded. The desire to interpret history through examination of industrial sites and artifacts using the techniques of archaeology was an understandable consequence of my background and work experience.

The study of old machines and obsolete processes led me to a degree in archaeology and contact with faculty members who shared a passionate interest in industrial archaeology. It's a field where I can usefully apply a working lifetime of skills in a new area. I imagine my chief source of motivation is an insatiable curiosity about technology and how it influences our culture.

I spend about 40% of my time in fieldwork, primarily documenting sites, photographing structures with a large format camera, and measuring them. Library research takes about 20% of my effort. Processing photographs, delineating industrial artifacts, organizing material, and writing and publishing reports takes up the remaining time. I deliver several lectures each year at professional symposia or museums.

Most of the funding for my research is a consequence of The National Historic Preservation Act of 1966. That act and subsequent legislation requires input from state historic-preservation officers before federally funded construction projects can proceed. As a result, the federal government is now the chief source of funding for archaeological research conducted in the United States. State regulations customarily require many private developers to pay for and file cultural resource reports before the bulldozers roll.

The documents for many engineering and industrial sites are maintained in the Historic American Engineering Record (HAER) collection. A division of the National Park Service, HAER directs the production of **site reports** for deposition in the Library of Congress. Site documentation to HAER standards is a frequently selected option to soften the adverse impact of federally funded projects. The standards require written documentation, photographs, and measured drawings. The Library of Congress provides technical specifications so that all material can be easily integrated into their archival collections.

I work with prehistoric and historic archaeologists who need a consultant in industrial archaeology. I also work for HAER and private clients. These clients provide grants and contracts to carry on my work, which is proving to be an engrossing and useful second career.

PART 5

If the Present Were an Archaeological Site

There have been a number of attempts—primarily humorous, but informative nonetheless—by archaeologists and others to imagine what future archaeologists might make of the material record of our own present. For example, Robert Nathan's (1956) book, *The Weans,* presents a world some five or six thousand years in the future where African archaeologists are attempting to understand the ancient and extinct culture that once ruled the "Great West Continent." This greatly ancient civilization is called the "Weans" because it is believed, on the basis of inscriptions found on their crumbling monuments, that they called their land the "We" or the "Us" to distinguish themselves from the rest of the world. Nathan's Weans are, of course, a clever, thinly veiled reference to the society of the United States (U.S., get it?) in the mid-1950s.

Along with being entertaining, these exercises approach some important issues in archaeological epistemology and, at the same time, allow us to evaluate modern life through the lens of a mythical archaeologist from the future. In a sense, the theme here is the reverse of that presented in Part 1 of this reader. There, the question is, "Can the study of the past provide insights into the study of the present?" Here the question is, "Can the 'archaeological' study of the present provide insights into our study of the past?"

In virtually all of the fantasies in which some future archaeologist attempts to analyze our modern material culture, they get it mixed up. It is a running joke in archaeology that when we are clueless concerning the function or meaning of some recovered artifact, we often fall back on the explanation that the object in question must surely have been "ceremonial" in intent. In the archaeological fantasies you are about to read, this is a common thread. Perhaps it is true—it is certainly instructive. When archaeologists encounter the ordinary or mundane in ancient societies, we may be too quick to ascribe some unwarranted ceremonial significance.

Part of the problem here is that archaeologists do not just excavate individual objects, we recover artifacts in spatial contexts. In other words, we pay attention to where objects are found and what is nearby. We excavate sites so carefully and

159

meticulously and keep accurate records of where everything is found because archaeological sites are far more than the sum total of their constituent parts. An inventory of artifacts found at a site is only part of the database. Where each object was found in relation to each other object tells us how these objects were used together to accomplish some task. The very same flaked stone object may have been a weapon for hunting big game animals, a weapon of war, or a ceremonial grave offering to a deceased hunter. When such objects are found outside of their original contexts — for example, when the artifact was disposed of in a communal trash pit or if it was removed from a site by an artifact collector who made no record of its context of discovery — determining function can be quite difficult. The same will be true for future archaeologists who attempt to understand the function of piles of rusting, compacted metal (crushed automobiles) or the interrelationships among items excavated at landfills.

It is useful to be reminded of such difficulties in archaeological interpretation of the past, especially those resulting from the problems inherent in having members of a particular cultural group in a particular time period (primarily Western scientists in the present) attempting to explain the lifeways of ancient people with very different cultures. The articles in Part 5 provide an important cautionary lesson.

26

The Mysterious Fall of Nacirema

Neil B. Thompson

*Neil B. Thompson was the director of the Program of American Studies at
St. Cloud State College in Minnesota when he wrote this article.*

Points to consider when reading this article:

1. Who were the Nacirema?

2. How do future archaeologists interpret "racs"?
    What do they propose their function was in the
    ancient culture of Nacirema?

3. What, in reality, were the behaviors called
    "swarm dances" by students of Nacirema culture?

4. How accurate is the description of Nacirema
    culture? Even if it is not accurate, what insights
    are provided in the interpretation presented in
    the article?

Archaeology deals with some very serious and significant issues, as can be clearly seen in the articles already
presented in this reader. The energy crisis, giving a voice
to those silenced by traditional history, and the modern
challenge of waste recycling certainly are all both serious and significant.

You should not, however, get the impression from
this that archaeologists are all serious — all of the time.
Every once in a while, an archaeologist — or a nonar-
chaeologist with a love and appreciation for the disci-

pline — steps back from his or her analysis of potsherds,
bones, tombs, or monuments and considers the following question: What if someone were to apply the same
forms of analysis that we perform on those potsherds,
bones, tombs, and monuments to our own, twentieth-
century American culture?

Neil B. Thompson performed precisely this archaeological exercise in 1971. Thompson didn't need to start
from scratch here; in fact, an exercise in cultural anthropology of a group called the "Nacirema" (read it
backwards) was published in 1956 in the journal of
the American Anthropological Association (written by
Horace Miner). Miner analyzed common, everyday behaviors of modern American life, behaviors that we
all take for granted, view as natural, and assume that
everybody must practice. In Miner's anthropological
study, medicine cabinets, oral hygiene practices, and
even use of a bedpan in the hospital are viewed as the
interesting and exotic behaviors of an alien culture.
Thompson does the same here, acting not as an ethnog-
rapher but as an archaeologist attempting to understand the now extinct Nacirema culture on the basis of
the material objects they (we) left behind.

The revival of concern in the recently extinct culture of
the Nacirema is, to say the least, most interesting, and
perhaps reflects an increasing state of concern for our
own society. (Aspects of the Nacirema culture were first
described by Horace Miner in "Body Ritual Among the
Nacirema," *American Anthropologist* (1956) 58:503–507.)
The use of a multidisciplined approach in deciphering
this puzzling culture is gratifying, for it is only by
bringing all our methodological techniques to bear on

the fragments of evidence in our possession that we
will be able to rationally study and understand the history of this apparently vigorous but short-lived culture.

Through exploratory digs by our archeological expeditions, we are able to say with some confidence that
the Nacirema were the dominant group in the complex
of North American cultures. Although the Nacirema
left a large number of documents, our linguists have
been unable to decipher any more than a few scattered
fragments of the Nacirema language. Eventually, with
the complete translation of these documents, we will
undoubtedly learn a great deal about the reasons for
the sudden disappearance of what, from the physical
evidence, must have been an explosive and expansive

From *Natural History*, November 1971. Reprinted with permission.
Copyright the American Museum of Natural History 1998.

culture. For the present, however, we must rely upon the physical evidence we have uncovered and analyzed in order to draw any conclusions concerning its extinction.

When we examine the area occupied by these people in a single overview, it is immediately apparent that the Nacirema considered it of primary importance to completely remake the environment of the lands they occupied. On studying the fringes of their territory, particularly their penetration of the Cree cultural area to the north, one is struck by the energy that they expended on this task. Trees, if in large enough numbers and size to influence the appearance of the landscape, were removed. In treeless regions, hills were leveled and large holes were dug and partially filled with water. In a few areas the Nacirema imported structural steel with which they erected tall, sculpturesque towers. Some of these towers were arranged in series, making long lines that extended beyond the horizon, and were linked by several cables running through the air. Others, particularly in the northern fringe area, were erected in no discernible geometric pattern and were connected by hollow pipes laid on the surface of the earth.

When one views areas normally considered to be within their cultural suzerainty, one sees evidence of similar activity. Most trees were removed. In some areas, however, trees were replanted or areas were allowed to reforest themselves without assistance. Apparently, the fetish against trees went by fits and starts, for the Nacirema would sometimes move into a reforested area and again remove the trees.

Most of the land, however, was kept clear of trees and was sowed each year with a limited variety of plants. Esthetic considerations must have led to the cultivation of plants poisonous to human life because, while the products of the cropland were sometimes used as food, few were consumed without first being subjected to long periods of complicated processing. Purifying chemicals, which radically changed the appearance and the specific weights of the seeds or fibers, were added. These purification rituals were seldom performed in the living quarters, but rather in a series of large temple-like buildings devoted to this purpose. A vast hierarchy of priests dressed in white (a symbol of purity) devoted their lives to this liturgy. Members of another group, the powerful ssenisub community (whose position will be explained later), constantly examined the efforts of the first group and, if they approved, would affix to the finished product one of several stamps, such as "ADSU" or "Doog Gnipeekesuoh." Still a third group, the repeekkoobs, accepted and recorded on permanent memorial rolls the gifts of the general population to their priestly order.

On a more limited territorial basis, the Nacirema spent great time and energy constructing narrow ribbons, called steerts, across the landscape. Some steerts were arranged in connected patterns, and in regions with a great concentration of people, the patterns, when viewed from the air, increased in size and became more elaborate. Other ribbons did not follow any particular pattern but aimlessly pushed from one population center to another. In general, their primary function seems to have been to geometricize the landscape into units that could be manipulated by a few men. The steerts also served as environmental dividers; persons of a lower caste lived within the boundaries of defined areas while those of the upper caste were free to live where they chose. Exploratory digs have shown that the quality of life in the different areas varied from very luxurious to poverty stricken. The various areas were generically referred to as ottehgs.

The task of completely altering the appearance of the environment to fit the Nacirema's ideology was given such high priority that the ssenisub community completely controlled the amassing of resources, manpower, and intelligence for this purpose. This group, whose rank bordered on that of a nonregimented priestly caste, lived in areas that were often guarded by electronic systems. There is no evidence to suggest that any restraints — moral, sociological, or engineering — were placed on their self-determined enterprises.

For a period of about 300 solar cycles (a determination made on the basis of carbon-dating studies), the Nacirema devoted a major part of their effort to the special environmental problem of changing the appearance of air and water. Until the last 50 solar cycles of the culture's existence, they seemed to have had only indifferent success. But during the short period before the fall of the culture, they mastered their art magnificently. They changed the color of the waters from the cool end of the spectrum (blues and greens) toward the warm end (reds and browns).

The air was subjected to a similar alteration: it was changed from an azure shade to a uniform gray-yellow. This alteration of water and air was effected by building enormous plants in strategic locations. These are usually found by our archeologists in or near large population centers, although, as success rewarded the Nacirema's efforts, they seem to have built smaller plants in outlying areas where environmental changes had not yet been effected. These plants constantly produced a variety of reagents, each appropriate to its locale, which were then pumped into the rivers and lakes or released into the atmosphere in the form of hot gases. The problem of disposing of the many by-products of this process was solved by distributing them among the general population, which retained them as venerated or decorative objects in their living quarters for a short time, then discarded them in huge middens that were established near every population center.

In regions where colder temperatures apparently prevented the reagents from changing the color of the water sufficiently, the Nacirema, near the end of their cultural explosion, built special plants that economically raised the water temperature to an acceptable level for the desired chemical reaction.

The idea of a man-made environment was so pervasive that in some areas, notably in the provinces called Ainrofilac and Anaisiuol, the Nacirema even tried to alter the appearance of the ocean currents. In these regions they erected steel sculptures in the sea itself and through them released a black and slick substance, which stained the waters and the beaches. This experiment, however, was relatively unsuccessful since the stains were not permanent and the Nacirema apparently never mastered a technique for constantly supplying the reagent.

Early research has disclosed the importance of ritualistic observance among the Nacirema. In support of these observations, we should note the presence of the quasi-religious Elibomotua Cult, which sought to create an intense sense of individual involvement in the community effort to completely control the environment. This pervasive cult was devoted to the creation of an artistic symbol for a man-made environmental system.

The high esteem of the cult is demonstrated by the fact that near every population center, when not disturbed by the accumulation of debris, archeologists have found large and orderly collections of the Elibomotua Cult symbol. The vast number of these collections has given us the opportunity to reconstruct with considerable confidence the principal ideas of the cult. The newest symbols seem to have nearly approached the ultimate of the Nacirema's cultural ideal. Their colors, material, and size suggest an enclosed mobile device that corresponds to no color or shape found in nature, although some authorities suggest that, at some early time in the development, the egg may have been the model. The device was provided with its own climate control system as well as a system that screened out many of the shorter rays of the light spectrum.

The object was designed to eliminate most sounds from the outside and to fill the interior with a hypnotic humming sound when the machine was in operation. This noise could be altered in pitch and intensity by manipulation, through simple mechanical controls, of an ingenious mechanism located outside the operator's compartment. This mechanism also produced a gaseous substance that, in a small area, could change the appearance of the air in a manner similar to the permanent plant installations.

In the early stages of the symbol's development, this was probably only a ritualistic performance since the production plant was small and was fueled by a small tank. This function, however, may have been the primary reason for the cult's symbol: to provide each family with its own device for altering the environment by giving it a private microuniverse with a system of producing the much desired air-changing reagent.

The complete machined piece was somewhat fragile. Our tests of the suspension system indicate that it was virtually immobile on unimproved terrain; by all of our physical evidence, its movement was restricted to the surfaced steerts that the Nacirema had built to geometricize the landscape.

We are relatively certain that a specially endowed and highly skilled group of educators was employed to keep the importance of these enclosed mobile devices constantly in the public eye. Working in an as yet unlocated area that they referred to as Euneva Nosidam, these specialists printed periodical matter and transmitted electronic-impulse images to boxlike apparatus in all homes.

While some of the information was aimed at describing the appearance and performance characteristics of the various kinds of machines, the greatest portion of the material was seemingly aimed at something other than these factors. A distinguished group of linguists, social psychologists, and theologians, who presented the principal symposium at our most recent anthropological conference, offered the hypothesis that the elibomotua symbols, also known as racs, replaced the processes of natural selection in the courtship and mating rituals of the Nacirema. Through unconscious suggestion, which derived from Euneva Nosidam's "mcnahulesque" materials, the female was uncontrollably driven to select her mate by the kind of elibomotua he occupied. The males of the culture were persuaded to believe that any handicap to masculine dominance could be overcome by selecting the proper cult symbol. In this way, the future of the race, as represented by Nacirema culture, was determined by unnatural man-made techniques.

The symposium was careful to point out that we have not yet uncovered any hard evidence to show whether or not this cultural trait actually had any effect on the race or its population growth. We have found, however, one strange sculpture from the Pop Loohcs depicting a male and female mating in an elibomotua's rear compartment, indicating a direct relationship. The hypothesis has the virtue of corresponding to the standard anthropological interpretations of the Nacirema culture—that it was ritual ridden and devoted to the goal of man's control of the environment.

Further evidence of the Nacirema's devotion to the Elibomotua Cult has been discovered in surviving scraps of gnivom serutcip. Some of these suggest that one of the most important quasi-religious ceremonies was performed by large groups who gathered at open-air shrines built in imitation of a planetary ellipse and called a kcartecar. There, with intensely emotional reactions, these crowds watched a ritual in which powerful gnicar racs performed their idealized concept of the correct behavior of the planets in the universe. Apparently, their deep-seated need for a controlled environment was thus emotionally achieved.

The racs did not hold a steady position in the planetarium, but changed their relationship to the other racs rather frequently. Occasionally a special ritual, designed to emphasize man's power over his universe, was enacted. On these unannounced occasions one or more of the planet symbols was destroyed by crashing two of them together or by throwing one against a wall. The emotional pitch of the worshipers rose to its highest level at this moment. Then, on command of the high priest of the ceremony, all the gnicar racs were slowed to a funereal speed and carefully held in their relative positions. After an appropriate memorial period honoring man's symbolic control of the universe, the machines were given the signal to resume their erratic speeds and permitted to make unnatural position changes.

We can only speculate on the significance of this ritual, but it seems reasonable to conclude that it served as an educational device, constantly imprinting in the individual the society's most important values.

Many of the findings of archeological explorations suggest that these symbols of universal power took up a large portion of the time and energy of the Nacirema society. Evidence indicates that a sizable portion of the work force and enormous amounts of space must have been devoted to the manufacture, distribution, and ceremonial care of the devices. Some of the biggest production units of the economy were assigned this function; extensive design laboratories were given over to the manipulation of styles and appearances, and assembly lines turned out the pieces in serial fashion. They were given a variety of names, although all of those made in the same time period looked remarkably alike.

Every family assumed the responsibility for one of the machined pieces and venerated it for a period of two to four solar cycles. Some families who lived in areas where a high quality of life was maintained took from two to four pieces into their care. During the time a family held a piece, they ritually cleansed it, housed it from the elements, and took it to special shrines where priests gave it a variety of injections.

The Nacirema spent much of their time inside their elibomotuas moving about on the steerts. Pictures show that almost everyone engaged, once in the morning and once in the evening, in what must have been an important mass ritual, which we have been unable to decipher with any surety. During these periods of the day, people of both sexes and all ages, except the very young and the very old, left their quarters to move about on the steerts in their racs. Films of these periods of the day

show scenes analogous to the dance one can occasionally see in a swarm of honeybees. In large population centers this "dance of the racs" lasted for two or three hours. Some students have suggested that since the swarm dances took place at about the time the earth completed one-half an axial rotation, it may have been a liturgical denial of the natural processes of the universe.

Inasmuch as we are reasonably certain that after the rite most of the adults and all of the children left the racs and were confined inside man-made structures variously called loohcs, eciffos, tnalps, or emohs and, when released, went immediately to their racs and engaged in the next swarming, the suggestion may be apropos. The ardent involvement of the whole population from ages 6 through 65 indicates that it was one of the strongest mores of the culture, perhaps approaching an instinctual behavior pattern.

It should also be mentioned that, when inside their racs, people were not restricted to their ottehgs, but were free to go anywhere they chose so long as they remained on the steerts. Apparently, when they were confined inside a rac, the Nacirema attained a state of equality, which eliminated the danger of any caste contamination.

These, then, to the best of our present state of knowledge, were the principal familial uses of the Elibomotua Cult symbols. After a family had cared for a piece long enough to burnish it with a certain patina, it was routinely replaced by another, and the used rac was assigned to a gallery keeper, who placed it on permanent display in an outdoor gallery, sometimes surrounded by trees or a fence, but usually not concealed in any way. During their free time, many persons, especially those from the ottehgs of the lesser sorts, came to study the various symbols on display and sometimes carried away small parts to be used for an unknown purpose.

There seems to be little doubt that the Cult of the Elibomotua was so fervently embraced by the general population, and that the daily rituals of the rac's care and use were so faithfully performed, that the minute quantities of reagent thus distributed may have had a decisive effect on the chemical characteristics of the air. The elibomotua, therefore, may have contributed in a major way toward the prized objective of a totally man-made environment.

In summary, our evaluation of both the Nacirema's man-made environmental alterations and the artifacts found in their territories lead us to advance the hypothesis that they may have been responsible for their own extinction. The Nacirema culture may have been so successful in achieving its objectives that the inherited physiological mechanisms of its people were unable to cope with its manufactured environment.

27

Lost Vegas

Ivor Noël Hume

Before his retirement, Ivor Noël Hume was the chief archaeologist at Colonial Williamsburg in Virginia. Noël Hume has long been one of the leaders of and one of the most prolific researchers in historical archaeology in the United States.

Points to consider when reading this article:

1. How would archaeologists of the future interpret an extraordinary site like Las Vegas?

2. Would an archaeologist from the future get a skewed perspective of American life if his or her research was focused on a large, atypical site like Las Vegas?

3. What's the lesson here for present day archaeologists excavating sites from the actual past?

4. What changes have taken place in the architecture of Las Vegas hotels since this piece was first published?

Las Vegas is appalling, bizarre, and fascinating all at the same time. The glitz, the lights, the Elvis impersonators, the sheer otherworldliness of it all is rather disorienting.

Now imagine that you are some future or alien archaeologist and, of all places, the ruins of the ancient holy city of Las Vegas become the focus of your research. Las Vegas as the symbol or emblem of all American culture—it is a frightening concept. Can we learn something about archaeological analysis by examining this obviously atypical place as if it were an archaeological site? Just as important, can we learn something about our own society by attempting to step outside our cultural landscape and view our most popular adult playground through the microscope of a scientist outsider? Can we have some fun doing it? Archaeologist Ivor Noël Hume certainly has some fun in this masterful archaeological analysis of America's adult fantasyland.

Most of the world's great civilizations have been tagged with a place or period remembered for its depravity: the People of the Plain would have been forgotten had they not had their Sodom (not to mention their Gomorrah) vanish in a rain of fire and brimstone. Rome had her Pompeii, and the British colonists in the Americas had Port Royal, Jamaica—until the morning of June 7, 1692, when an earthquake sent much of it sliding into Kingston Harbor. France, of course, has Paris in any period, and the United States has Las Vegas.

Sodom has yet to be found, but the ruins of Pompeii buried in the eruption of Vesuvius in A.D. 79, have been the subject of archaeological excavation for more than two hundred years. Divers have probed the silt-buried remains of Port Royal, and the recovered artifacts attest to the town's prosperity if not to its debauchery. What, we may ask, will be the legacy of Las Vegas if its ruins lie buried in the dry Nevada desert for several centuries?

"Does anybody really know what the palace at Las Vegas looked like?" asks an archaeology student at Nairobi University in the year 2403.

The professor projects three-dimensional pictures of fragmentary pseudoclassical statuary and crumbling cinder block tracery onto a wall-sized screen. Excavations, he says, have revealed basements filled with rusting machinery believed to have been lighting and climate controls. The bases of concrete columns heavily weathered by blown sand suggest that the ruins stood for many years before the desert covered them with sediment.

"What about coins?" asks another student. "If Las Vegas was a gambling center, there ought to be coins."

From *Horizon*, May 1979. Reprinted here by permission of the author.

The lecturer nods. Dollars of silver were found in the lowest levels, he explains, but the coins found higher up had all fallen apart. In 1965 the United States mint stopped making silver coins and turned to a cheaper "clad" coinage comprised of outer layers of copper-nickel bonded to an inner core of pure copper. The core quickly corroded in the ground, and the coins literally fell to pieces. Such coins were characteristic of the "live for today" philosophy of that decadent period, the professor adds.

Several students shake their heads, unable to understand so crass a culture, while at the back a girl (who will probably fail the course) doodles rings around the quaint names written on her pad: Bugsy Siegel, Mayer Lansky, Jimmy Hoffa.

Archaeologists interpret the past through the different artifacts found in successive layers of the ground. What's on top is usually more recent than what's underneath. But unless a town is torn down every time it undergoes a cultural change, its evolution is not so clearly defined. The new rises alongside the old, with the products of several periods coexisting, at least for a while. So it is with the four great cultural epochs of Las Vegas, hereafter defined as Vegas I, II, III, and IV.

Time, fact, and fiction were inextricably caught up in Nevada's spinning wheels, but the bald outline of Las Vegas's mushroom growth is clear enough. The gold found in Six Mile Canyon in 1859 led to the building of Virginia City, that most notorious of all the gold rush mining camps. Catering to its unruly inhabitants, the Nevada legislature legalized gambling in 1869. In the space of twenty years, the state's cornucopia, the Comstock Lode, yielded more than $50 million in gold and silver, but it was a different Comstock whose influence was to affect the next chapter of Nevada's history. The antivice campaigning of Anthony Comstock, coupled with the temperance movement and growing Mormon influence, pushed the state's legislature into repealing the gaming law, a prohibition that lasted until 1931.

The Mormons who founded Las Vegas in 1855 remained aloof from the good life as defined by the gentiles of Virginia City, and it was not until 1909 and the arrival of the railroad that the town's character began to change. In 1930, Secretary of the Interior Ray Wilbur's dedication of the Hoover Dam heralded a six-year project and the arrival of an army of government-paid workers with cash in their pockets and nowhere to spend it (this in the depths of the Great Depression). With gambling again legalized, 1931 saw half a dozen gaming houses open in Las Vegas. Clustered close to the railroad station on Fremont Street, they were a small beginning, and the resident Mormons prayed they would stay that way.

Ten years later, a Los Angeles hotel operator, Tommy Hull, built the first casino-motel west of town on the highway now named Las Vegas Boulevard but universally known as the Strip. Hull called his place El Rancho Vegas and thus introduced the first major change in the town's cultural history. This was the one that archaeologists will know as Vegas I, Western B — Western A being the sand-and-sweat, pioneer period from 1855 to 1931 and Western B the tit-n-tinsel pastiche that early kings of the Strip promoted.

In 1941, a mile down the highway, another Western B emporium went up; they called it the Last Frontier Hotel. That was the year in which a dapper little man with a taste for checked jackets stopped by to look the town over and liked what he saw.

Benjamin "Bugsy" Siegel had a winning smile that belied his reputation as lead salesman for the products of Murder Incorporated. It was Siegel who persuaded his boss, Mayer Lansky, to underwrite land purchases along the Strip and to build a hotel-casino that would outdo the already flourishing gambling center at Reno. With some reluctance, Lansky's partners agreed, and in 1946 Siegel built the hotel he called the Flamingo. It marked the first breach in the cultural wall of Vegas I, Western B.

By today's standards the hotel was unbelievably modest. A single pink flamingo topped a column rising all of ten feet above the single-story building across whose entrance a simple neon sign proclaimed "Lounge, Restaurant, Casino." In the driveway a dozen wire-framed light bulbs (muted heralds of a billion bulbs to come) bordered a small bed of evergreens. All around Siegel's oasis, empty desert stretched bleakly toward distant mountains. But he could see further, and Siegel assured his partners that in ten years Las Vegas would become the world's gambling mecca.

No one remembers why Siegel called his hotel the Flamingo, and it is mere speculation that he associated the bird with a watering place. Nevertheless, the oasis concept was soon to take root, providing Las Vegas with its second cultural phase, the Islamic or Arabian Nights era of Vegas II. Bugsy Siegel never lived to see it. His Flamingo lost money, and, like most gamblers on a losing streak, his costly efforts to recoup only dug his hole deeper. In June 1947, while Siegel waited in his mistress's Los Angeles living room, outside, hidden in the bushes, persons unknown adjusted their sights. Thus did the task of steering the Flamingo to solvency pass into the warm hands of Siegel's partner, the balding and steely-eyed Gus Greenbaum.

Siegel's vision became flashy reality between 1947 and 1955 when the friends of Mayer Lansky built the hotels and casinos that made Las Vegas famous. They were the giants of the archaeological transition from

Vegas I-B to II: the Desert Inn, Sands, Dunes, Sahara, and (still anchored in the western desert) the Thunderbird, since renamed the Silver Bird. Not fitting the theme at all was the Riviera, which found itself in trouble from the start. Gus Greenbaum had saved the Flamingo, and so in 1956 the old firm brought him out of retirement to salvage its $10 million investment. But Greenbaum had lost his touch. The Riviera continued in the red, and, in December 1958, he and his wife were found in their Phoenix home with their throats cut.

The Islamic-era Vegas II reached its flamboyant apex in the 1960s with the building of the Aladdin Hotel. By then fundamental changes had taken place, changes having nothing to do with restaurants disguised as Bedouin tents or cigarette girls in harem pants barely disguised at all. In 1966 the Howard Hughes organization moved in, and three years later the state of Nevada publicly permitted trade corporations to buy and build hotels. The image of a mobster behind every cactus was fading, though the shadow of Jimmy Hoffa was to add a new and questionable dimension.

Although the El Rancho Vegas hotel (cornerstone of the town's Western B period) burned down in 1960, its influence lingered on; through the Islamic period, though centered largely in the downtown area, it was exemplified by such hotels as the Golden Nugget, Horseshoe, and Lady Luck. Vegas III, the Greco-Roman era, began in 1965 and was the brain child of onetime ceramic tile manufacturer, Jay Sarno, whose ambition was to leave the world a building that would "be exciting and give pleasure." He gave it Caesar's Palace—main street America's vision of Imperial Rome, cypress avenue, fountains, mosaics, columns, statuary, and all. The Carrara marble statues borrowed from the works of Michelangelo and several other sculptors from the third century B.C. to the nineteenth century A.D. are seen against a background of blue and gold mosaic, a facade of Sarno-classical grandeur impressive enough to have made Nero sing and Caligula clap his bloody little hands.

Sarno was the first to admit that "complete authenticity, we don't have." Nevertheless, he gave us a gambling room he called Caesar's Forum and a Circus Maximus to house his really big shows.

He put his lesser lounge entertainment in Nero's Nook and named his best dining room the Bacchanal. Any lesser visionary might have let the coffee shop go at that, but remembering that Judea was part of the empire, Caesar's Palace had its Noshorium—and an Antony and Cleopatra where men's and ladies' rooms ought to have been. But, like the Roman Empire, Caesar's Palace was constantly reaching out for new conquests and fresh ideas—some of them hard for archaeologists to fathom. Thus, in a 1978 palace restroom

coup, Antony was ousted in favor of his Julius, while in honor, perhaps, of Caesar's Gallic conquests, the Noshorium became the Cafe Roma.

Traditionalists, who may have preferred the cluster of standard hotel stores before they became the Appian Way Shops, could still find a drink and a moment of cultural reflection aboard Cleopatra's Barge, which sailed fixedly on in a girdling ribbon of blue-lit water. It was neither the tinkling water nor the authentic rigging that gave the vessel distinction.

Credit for that goes to its figurehead, which lunged out over the heads of passersby. Cast in the form of an Egyptian maiden, whose monstrous mammae (*sans* nipples, to avoid grooving scalps of basketball players) dangled below the bowsprit with all the authority of a set of pawnbroker's balls, the figurehead all but impaled the entrance to Ah Soh's Steak House on the other side of the concourse. Unintimidated by this display of bare classical clout, the Japanese intrusion into the Roman Empire marked the beginning of a new archaeological period: Vegas IV—which, for want of anything better, can be dubbed the Oriental or Ah Soh Era. Into it fits a new landmark, the pagoda-roofed Imperial Palace.

Meanwhile, inside the Flamingo and behind a great wall of plywood, workmen toiled to create something identified on the wall as "The Peking Market" and, in a message even more inscrutable, as "The secret spirits of Doctor Wu." But in spite of all this activity, the Strip may have played its China card. In the space of eleven months, while the Imperial Palace remained unfinished, a gaudy throwback to Vegas I (Western B) sprang like a Death Valley blossom out of a dusty hole in the ground. The Barbary Coast casino opened its doors on March 2, 1979, even before its signs were up or its brickwork complete.

Not all the casino-hotels are as easily filed into cultural slots. The Circus Circus had a faintly Vegas III ring to it—girls in classical tunics apparently off the same peg as Caesar's—but there the similarity ended. The dominant theme was just what it twice said: the big top and its attendant midway. Further up the Strip, the giant MGM Grand was part western, part Islamic, slightly oriental, and just enough Greco-Roman to be gloriously and unabashedly vulgar. Outside, a bronze fountain of heroic proportions spouted water from the nipples of four overweight beauties and from the mouths of dolphins rather oddly gripped between their knees.

Inside, most casinos looked the same. Bathed in the ruddy glow of internally lit slot machines, punctuated by pools of white light over the gaming tables, cultural periods were lost in a world of eternal night. Smoked glass doors banished the day, and no clocks intruded. The time is now; past and future are out of sight, and only the clatter of coins, the rattle of dice, and the mesmerizing flash of checks and cards moving back and forth across fields of green baize were allowed to hold the attention.

Out on the Strip in the sunlight's glare, Las Vegas had a less soothing countenance. Brisk desert winds drove sand into every receptive cranny, and at bus stops and intersections the shattered artifacts by which future archaeologists would judge the Las Vegan cultures littered the sidewalks, Beer bottles, broken glasses, and empty Polaroid packs crunched under foot, while the wind-blown remnants of free tabloid newspapers wrapped themselves around one's legs. This may have been the only place on earth where you could look down and find yourself wearing a double-page spread promoting a brothel, or a front-page view (in florid color) of a slightly contorted girl wearing a smile broader than her garter belt.

From their Olympian view, the class of A.D. 2403 will study the artifacts and conclude that Las Vegas was indeed the American Sodom. It may well be appalled to discover that the town once played host to more than nine million visitors a year—a multitude vastly greater than the visitation to most of the nation's more conventional shrines. The class will be equally shocked to read a document called a "poll" that shows that 40 percent of Las Vegas's visitors went there to gamble, and that only 3 percent claimed to be there on business. Clearly, as the twentieth century ran out, hoopla, not history, was the people's choice.

The conclusions of archaeologists, sociologists, and theologians are often naively simplistic. Pompeii and Port Royal were destroyed by sudden natural convulsions, which, if termed "acts of God," meant that they got what they deserved. In reality, Pompeii was no more immoral than any other Roman resort, and Port Royal was a port. Their inhabitants's mistake lay in failing to read the writing on the wall or, rather, to heed the rumbling in the earth. Rarely does the future learn from the past, and in Las Vegas the endless bacchanal goes on.

After multimillion dollar flood damage in 1975 sent Little Caesar's fishing for Cadillacs, their palace management put out warning signs in low areas of the parking lots: NO PARKING—DANGER—FLASH FLOODS. Around them the cars nestled grill to grill. The signs are gone now; the sun shines—and out in the desert nuclear physicists calculate the odds for a game wherein, one hopes, little is left to chance.

No one is taking bets on whether Las Vegas will become monument in Period V or XIII. Only this is certain: While it lasts, the on-site study of Vegas I to IV offers an unbeatable field trip for any student who can count to XXI.

28

Motel of the Mysteries

David Macaulay

*David Macaulay is a brilliant illustrator and author whose many books illuminate
the workings of humankind's technological achievements.*

Points to consider when reading this article:

1. Who is the fictional archaeologist Howard Carson based on?

2. What has archaeologist Howard Carson actually discovered? What does he think he has found?

3. What lessons should we learn from Howard Carson's hilarious misinterpretations?

4. What really are Carson's "water trumpets," "sacred urn," and "sacred parchment"?

David Macaulay is not an archaeologist. He is an illustrator and author. Through exquisitely detailed pen and ink drawings, Macaulay trains his artist's eye on castles, cathedrals, cities, ships, mills, pyramids, and a host of other technological marvels. His illustrations take these things apart, show how they work, and then put them back together again.

One of Macaulay's earlier books is a bit different from the others. Instead of focusing on technology, *Motel of the Mysteries* is a hilarious send-up of archaeology.

It is some time in the very distant future, and archaeologist Howard Carson has made the archaeological discovery of the century or, perhaps, the millennium (and no, it is not a coincidence that Howard *Carter* was the actual discoverer of the tomb of Egyptian pharaoh Tut-ankh-amun). As you read this excerpt from Macaulay's book, it will become clear that Carson is excavating nothing more than a sleazy twentieth-century motel, though he manages to construe the place as an ancient, sacred necropolis. The book is especially hilarious if you know a bit about the history of archaeology. Some of the lines achieve their humor (at least for archaeologists) by being actual quotes from Howard Carter (he's the real archaeologist, and he really did reply in response to the question, "Can you see anything?" as he first gazed into Tut's Tomb, "Yes, wonderful things.") Reading *Motel of the Mysteries* can be a humbling experience for an archaeologist. But it also is a valuable reminder of the mistakes we can make when we impose a preconceived perspective on the archaeological record. And besides, it's very funny.

The ground below his feet suddenly gave way. He was precipitated headlong downward. When the dust had settled and he had recovered his spectacles, he found himself at the bottom of an ancient shaft, facing the entrance of a long-forgotten tomb. The shaft, probably dug by tomb robbers shortly after the tomb was sealed, had been covered initially by the natural vegetation of the surface. More recently, the whole area had been buried under vast quantities of soil from the adjacent excavation.

Unimpressed and rather annoyed at this inconvenience, [Howard] Carson's first thought was to call out for assistance, but, before he could utter a sound, light from the shaft caught the area around the handle on the tomb door. Upon closer inspection, he discovered that the sacred seal which was traditionally placed on the door following the burial rites was still in place. Staff artists' reconstructions of similar, but always defiled, tombs that had appeared in his most recent *National Geographic* flooded his mind. Thunderstruck, he realized he was on the threshold of history. His entire body trembled as he contemplated the possible significance of his find. The mysterious burial customs of the late twentieth-century North American were finally (and as it turned out, magnificently) to be revealed.

Less than a month later, aided by his companion, Harriet Burton, who "enjoyed sketching," and a

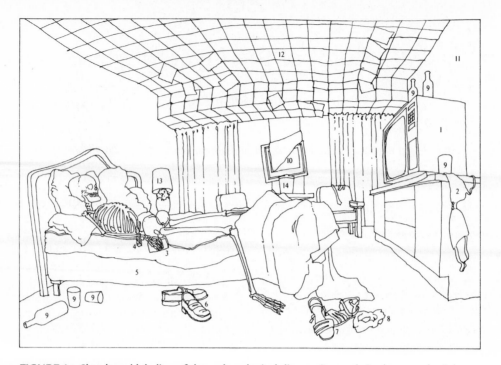

FIGURE 1   Sketch and labeling of the archaeological discoveries made in the outer burial chamber. (David Macaulay)

dedicated group of volunteers, Carson began the first of seven years' work on the excavation of the Motel of the Mysteries complex, and most specifically on the removal and recording of the treasures from Tomb 26.

While Carson paced back and forth in a supervisory manner, Harriet numbered each of the items surrounding the entrance as well as those on the great door. Descriptions of the most significant discoveries are to be found in her diary:

> Number 21, "the gleaming Sacred Seal, which had first caught Howard's attention, was placed on the door by the officials after the burial to protect the tomb and its inhabitant for eternity."
> Number 28, "the Sacred Eye, which was believed to ward off evil spirits."
> Number 18, "the partially exposed Plant That Would Not Die. One of these exquisite plants, which had apparently been grown in separate pieces and then joined together, was placed on each side of the entrance."
> Numbers 19 and 20, "containers in which the sacrificial meal was offered to the gods of eternal life."

Once the exterior of the tomb had been recorded in detail, preparations for entering it were begun. With a steady hand, Carson, who had presumably picked up a few tricks in his time, jimmied the lock. With his helpers peering nervously from a safe distance, he cautiously pried open the door. The creaking of the ancient hinges, in Miss Burton's own words, "cut through the silence like the scream of a ghostly fleeing spirit." Suddenly, to Carson's astonishment, the door stopped

dead. A frantic but successful search for the obstruction revealed a beautifully crafted chain about two thirds up the inside of the door, linking it with the sturdy frame. Clearly this stood as the final barrier between the present and the past. Once the workers had sawed through the chain, they withdrew, and Carson continued to open the great door.

At first, everything was dark. Carson lit a match. Still everything was dark. Carson lit two matches. Still, everything was dark. Attempting to avoid a rather protracted delay, Harriet eased the large spotlight toward the entrance with her foot. As the blanket of darkness was stripped away from the treasures within the tomb, Carson's mouth fell open. Everywhere was the glint of plastic. Impatiently, the others waited for a response. "Can you see anything, Howard?" they asked in unison.

"Yes," he replied . . .

"WONDERFUL THINGS!"

Everything in the Outer Chamber faced the Great Altar(No. 1), including the body of the deceased, which still lay on top of the Ceremonial Platform(No. 5). In its hand was the Sacred Communicator(No. 3) and around its wrist was a flexible golden band(No. 4) bearing an image similar to that of the upper altar. Signs of the ancient burial ritual were everywhere. A variety of garments, including the ceremonial chest plate(No. 2) and shoes designed to hold coins(No. 6), were scattered about the chamber. Various contain-

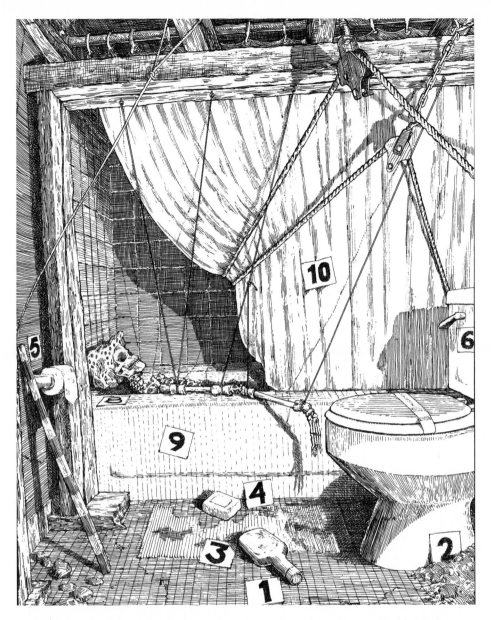

FIGURE 2   Detailed drawing of the fabulous discovery made in the inner burial chamber. (David Macaulay)

ers(No. 9) which had once held libations and offerings stood on the altar and around the platform. A statue of the deity WATT, who represented eternal companionship and enlightenment, stood faithfully next to the platform. To ensure maximum comfort during eternal life, several pieces of beautifully crafted furniture were placed in the room, along with additional garments stacked carefully in a specially designed rectangular pod. Perhaps the single most important article in the chamber was the ICE(No. 14). This container, whose function evolved from the Canopic jars of earliest times, was designed to preserve, at least symbolically, the major internal organs of the deceased for eternity. The Yanks, who revered long and complex de-

scriptions, called the container an Internal Component Enclosure.

Aware that the two pairs of shoes implied a double burial and having seen only one body, Carson immediately began searching for another chamber. By the time he had found the entrance to what eventually became known as the Inner Chamber, Harriet had already catalogued and numbered it. Quivering with excitement, Carson removed his shirt and began the delicate operation of dismantling the door.

Although it seemed hardly possible, the contents of the Inner Chamber were even more dazzling than those already discovered. Harriet immediately began tagging and identifying each item while Howard drew conclusions. As he had predicted, a second body was present, and this one appeared to have been buried with more care and ritual than the first. Wearing the Ceremonial Head Dress(No. 8), it had been placed in a highly polished white sarcophagus(No. 9), which had in turn been sealed behind an exquisite and elaborately hung translucent curtain(No. 10).

The proportions of the sarcophagus had been precisely determined to prevent the deceased from ever sliding down into a fully reclined position. The similar postures of the two bodies led Carson to the conclusion that the proper burial position had the chin resting as much as possible on the chest. Although the outer surface of the sarcophagus was plain, there were two sets of ceremonial markings on the inside. The first consisted of ten parallel rows of slightly raised discs along the floor of the sarcophagus over which the body had been placed. The second was an almost entirely faded line that ran all the way around the walls parallel to

and about ten inches above the floor. Two water trumpets, one about five feet above the other, projected from the end wall facing the deceased. Some of the music required during the final ceremony was produced by forcing water from the sacred spring through the trumpets and out through a small hole in the floor of the sarcophagus. Other music came from the music box(No. 6) situated above the Sacred Urn(No. 2). Articles No. 1 and No. 4 were used in preparing the body for its final journey and No. 5 was the Sacred Parchment, pieces of which were periodically placed in the urn during the ceremony. Carson was overjoyed to find that the Sacred Point was perfectly preserved on the sacred parchment. Very few had previously been uncovered, and none in such remarkable condition. The Headband, which bore the ceremonial chant, and the Sacred Collar (not numbered) were still in place on the Sacred Urn to which they had been secured following the ceremony.

29

Back to the Future:
An Archaeological Adventure

Mary Resanovich

Mary Resanovich is a sixth-grade science teacher at Ben Franklin Elementary School in Yorktown Heights, New York.

***

Points to consider when reading this article:

1. What are the key lessons of this article — for the young students and for anyone attempting to reconstruct an alien culture from their unfamiliar material objects?

2. What aspects of the scientific process do the students learn in this project?

3. What is the purpose of the Convention of Twenty-Fourth–Century Household Archaeologists?

4. How do actual archaeologists attempt to achieve accurate and not such fanciful explanations of the things they recover?

Combine *Motel of the Mysteries* with elementary school kids and you have an idea of the pedagogical approach of teacher Mary Resanovich. School kids are given the assignment of conducting an archaeological analysis of their own material culture.

Imagine it. It's the future. You're an archaeologist and a kid, and your job is to attempt to figure out the function of the stuff in your own house. The only problem, you also have to imagine that you are a member of a different culture and that all the things that are familiar to you are, now, completely unfamiliar. It is a fascinating mental exercise — and a valuable and ingenious use of archaeology in the classroom. How do you analyze and reconstruct culture if you are an outsider, an alien, a bearer of a different set of behaviors and beliefs? What is a telephone, a radio, a can opener, or a toothbrush?

This use of archaeology works on a number of levels because the kids are required not simply to come up with silly or goofy explanations of the objects in their houses but to provide detailed descriptions of these objects, deduce their functions, and then support those deductions. A valuable part of the exercise rests in the fact that they must describe each artifact and explain the reasoning behind their analysis to the "chief archaeologist," who also is completely unfamiliar with the culture of the society being investigated. It is obvious from this article that the kids have a blast, get turned on to archaeology, and begin to think about cultural variation.

***

This is Dr. C, intrepid archaeologist, reporting from some kind of twentieth-century house. It is my most extraordinary discovery yet here at the site of Shrub Oak, in the year 2359. I believe I have found some sort of toe-lint remover!"

This began one of my sixth-grade students' description of her toothbrush. Yes, her toothbrush. Believe it or not, this student received an A on her assignment. Why? Because this student's piece included a specific, detailed description of her toothbrush, including its measurements, what it was made of, where it was found, and how it looked and felt, as well as her most creative inference of how it might be perceived in the future.

Learning to write specific, precise, and detailed observations is often difficult for students. Yet, the ability to observe, measure, and make inferences about the world — as well as the ability to communicate this information both orally and in writing — are the most basic of the science process skills and are the cornerstone of all higher-level science skills.

From *Science and Children,* October 1997. Reprinted with permission from NSTA Publications, copyright © 1997. National Science Teachers Association, 1840 Wilson Blvd., Arlington, VA 22201-3000.

Mastery of such basic skills is outlined in the Science as Inquiry Content Standard of the *National Science Education Standards* (National Research Council, 1996). This standard specifies that students should possess the abilities necessary to conduct scientific inquiry, including the ability to describe their observations and form explanations of phenomena based on what they have observed. Students must also be able to effectively communicate their observations, inferences, and procedures to others.

OBSERVATIONS AND INFERENCES

I begin the school year, as many do, with a review of the basic science skills such as measuring, observing, predicting, classifying, and communicating, with a strong focus on written communication. For the first few weeks, the students work on writing descriptions and observations of various items and phenomena.

I start by having students focus on a different sense each day. One day we listen to something and describe it; another day we taste something (Herald, 1996). After the students write their descriptions/observations, we share and discuss them, looking for similarities and differences. Students then write more detailed observations, culminating in an activity in which they must describe a configuration of Lego blocks so specifically that someone else can replicate it based on their written observations (Scarnati, 1996).

After practicing observations, I introduce the concept of inferences to the class. I try to clarify for my students that observations are based on sensory information. They can be seen, heard, tasted, smelled, or touched. Inferences are educated, logical guesses of what is going on in a system or phenomenon, based on observations. Observations can be quickly confirmed by the senses, while inferences need to be tested. This also correlates with the Science as Inquiry Content Standard, which states that children should be able to see and explain the connections between their observations, or evidence, and their inferences or explanations.

Students practice making observations and inferences using a number of historical objects such as pictures of cave paintings and other ancient art forms and old photographs. Again, we list students' observations and discuss the breadth of their inferences, trying to determine on which specific observations their inferences are based. We then wrestle with the question of which inference is "correct."

This leads into a discussion of the fact that not all inferences are correct; they must be studied and tested. We discuss the constantly evolving, ever-changing nature of science. Students are frequently surprised to hear that what we now believe to be true *may* someday be disproved.

I challenge students to think about what people once believed, but which we now know is not true, such as the concept of a flat Earth or the Earth as the center of the universe. We discuss how new inferences and theories are based on new observational data.

Using a collection of articles from the local newspaper or children's magazines, students look at recent scientific discoveries that have changed our understanding of the world. Last year, we read an article about a new microscopic organism found on the mouthparts of lobsters, which may lead to the creation of a new phylum. Another article discussed a new theory that the Earth's core spins at a different speed from the mantle and crust. This year, I plan to use some articles on the Mars Pathfinder Expedition.

This aspect of the activity brings in two different *National Science Education Standards*. First, it involves the Understandings About Scientific Inquiry Content Standard, which requires that students realize that "The scientific community accepts and uses such explanations until displaced by better scientific ones. When such displacement occurs, science advances" (National Research Council, 1996, p. 148). It also relates to the History and Nature of Science Content Standard, which explains that "Scientists do and have changed their ideas about nature when they encounter new experimental evidence that does not match their existing explanations" (National Research Council, 1996, p. 171).

To demonstrate this concept in a creative way, to give students further practice in writing descriptive observations, and to get their creative juices flowing, I give students a writing assignment inspired by David Macaulay's book *Motel of the Mysteries* (1979), although I *do not* introduce the book itself to the students because it is not appropriate for this grade level.

BACK TO THE FUTURE

Motel of the Mysteries is about an archaeologist of the future who discovers a twentieth-century motel and mistakenly interprets its contents.

Similarly, my students imagine they are famous archaeologists in the year 2359 who have just discovered a twentieth-century house. Their job is to select an object from their own house, write a detailed description of it, and explain, as an archaeologist from the twenty-fourth century who has never seen the object before, what they think its purpose was—but their inference about the object's purpose must be incorrect.

To further illustrate the assignment, I give students a model report to the "Archaeological Institute of the

DR. J. GREENHOUSE MAKES IMPORTANT DISCOVERY

I'm Dr. J. Greenhouse, an archaeologist, reporting from the mountains. I've just made a spectacular discovery here at what used to be Yorktown Heights, New York, at the turn of the twenty-first century.

I am almost certain that my latest discovery is an ancient telephone! The item is a rectangular shape about 17.5 cm long and about 14 cm wide. Its height is 4 cm. The telephone is white with one patch of light gray. The top of the rectangle is slightly curved. Looking at it from the top, the back half of it has little holes that you're supposed to speak into and hear out of.

The telephone has two buttons that say "H" and "M." I'm not sure how the telephone knows if it's hot or mild outside. I guess it's somehow connected to the Weather Bureau.

The next two buttons are an "Alarm," which tells you when your time is up for talking, and "Sleep," which you press when you go to bed so that the ringing phone doesn't disturb your sleep. Each time you press one of these buttons, it goes "Click, click!" Right below these two buttons is some kind of switch about 6 cm long that you push to hear people talk.

At the front of the telephone is a button that is 7.5 cm long that says, "Repeat Alarm." Weird, huh? I guess you use this button to report a fire or other emergency.

On the side of the phone, there's a switch that says "AM" if there is "any message" and "FM" if there is a message "for me"!

The side also has a "Volume" knob that lets you hear the other person better and a "Tuning" knob that tells what number you're calling. This is my favorite part of the phone because it lets you change to another call if you don't like the conversation. Just turn the "Tuning" knob a little and you're talking to another person. Sometimes people are even singing to you! It's amazing what they had back then!

Phone calls in those days must have been very long and exhausting, because every telephone is on a little table next to the bed. It seems that there is a telephone in every bedroom of the house. They come in many shapes, sizes, and colors. They are attached to the wall with a wire to keep them from falling off the table in case you fall asleep during one of those long phone calls with your grandmother.

Well, I have to go now because I just noticed that there's another singing telephone message "FM" (for me).

(If you haven't guessed it by now, it's a clock radio.)

Twenty-Fourth Century" that I have written and a scoring rubric of items their reports should include.

The students' reports should be as detailed as possible and must include all of the following information:

- the object's dimensions,
- what it looks like,
- a description of it using at least one of their senses,
- what materials it contains,
- where at the "dig" it was found (where in their house it belongs),
- and their inference/theories on how it was used in the twentieth century.

Each item is worth two points so that partial credit can be awarded for students who need to add more description.

"ARCHAEOLOGICAL" FINDS

The responses to this activity are incredible. The students show their creativity and think of some wonderful inferred uses. One student identified his hair dryer as a weapon, and since he had found it in a bathroom, he inferred that it must have been used to chase people from that area. The "archaeologist" who discovered the toe-lint remover inferred, rather logically, that it was found in a drawer because "who wants to see your toe-lint removers?" A third student who discovered what she thought was an ancient telephone and answering machine—in reality a clock radio—inferred that "AM" meant "any message" and "FM" meant "for me"! (See box for her complete description.)

Even those students who normally hate to write enjoy this activity. Because they become wrapped up in the activity, the students almost forget that they are practicing the most fundamental skills of science investigation: observing, measuring, inferring, and communicating.

Reading over these assignments is exciting. Following the student's description and trying to identify the object is fascinating. The students recognize this, too, and hoping to stump the teacher, can't wait to see if I have been able to piece together their clues.

When writing comments on the reports, I take on the persona of the director of research "back at the lab." By pretending to be at the lab and not at the "dig site," I make students responsible for describing the object well enough for me to be able to picture it and theoretically rebuild it in the lab. This also allows me to encourage students to write more description in a nonthreatening way. On reports that lack detail, I inform students that "Everyone back at the lab was thrilled by your discovery! We urge you to send us more detail so we can reconstruct this historic object." After the "field reports" are returned, students are allowed to rewrite their work for additional credit, thus encouraging revision and further description.

We follow up the activity by holding an International Convention of Twenty-Fourth–Century Household Archaeologists, where students present their findings to their peers to see if the others can correctly identify their items, or perhaps propose a different possible use. This once again ties into the Science as Inquiry Content Standard, which asks students to recognize and analyze alternative explanations for objects and phenomena. The importance of being an effective communicator becomes especially important during this meeting, when students must be sure that their writing is clear and logical enough to be understood by their peers.

WRITING AND LEARNING

This project is an engaging way to show students how to use science process skills and writing skills. In mak-ing the leap from observation to inference, scientists must think actively and creatively. Furthermore, this creative twist enlivens the process of learning to write in detail. Science is linked with other curricular areas, such as social studies and language arts. Finally, through this writing assignment, students learn to think more openly, explore multiple possibilities, and, perhaps, to question more readily what they observe.

RESOURCES

Bellamy, N. (1996). Putting first things first. *Learning, 24*(5), 45–47.

Herald, C. D. (1996). How I start the school year. *Science Scope, 20*(1), 28–30.

Macaulay, D. (1979). *Motel of the Mysteries.* Boston: Houghton Mifflin.

National Research Council. (1996). *National Science Education Standards.* Washington, DC: National Academy Press.

Scarnati, J. T. (1996). There go the Legos. *Science and Children, 33*(7), 28–30.

I AM AN ARCHAEOLOGIST

Cece Saunders

(Photo courtesy of Cece Saunders)

Growing up with the war movies of the 1950s left me with the intense desire to be John Wayne so I could crawl under the barbed wire and dash through muddy battlefields. This childhood dream was inexorably altered when I realized the marines did not let women play their games and that Margaret Mead had far more fun in the wilds of New Guinea than John Wayne ever had in the war. My lifelong adventure with archaeology was born when I discovered I could combine my earliest love of "trench mud" with the anthropologist's field observations.

For more than sixteen years I have been a **contract archaeologist**—combining fieldwork, research, and interpretations to produce assessments for cultural resource management (CRM) studies. These assessments, or evaluation studies, are required as a function of various **environmental review** procedures on federal, city, and state levels. I consider myself one of those lucky individuals who wakes each morning to work that is "fun" and "just what I want to do." But an understanding of my professional routine must extend beyond images of John Wayne and Margaret Mead and even a later archaeological hero, Indiana Jones. I am in business to support myself. Although my daily activities are integrally involved with **cultural resources** and rely on my graduate training as an archaeologist, many of my working hours are directly related to seemingly nonarchaeological endeavors: writing cost specifications for competitive bids, negotiating contracts with zealous lawyers, and keeping anxious real estate developers or highway engineers informed. Juggling all of these tasks is, for me, a great part of the fun of a small contract archaeology firm.

When Historical Perspectives, Inc. was founded in 1982 as a partnership of two recent master's degree graduates, I directly handled one-half of each facet of every project, digging in the trenches, estimating budgets, doing archival research and report writing, as well as cleaning and cataloguing artifacts. It was not difficult because we had only two or three limited projects at a time. Our first contracts were for small, site-specific developments (one warehouse along the East River in Brooklyn or a five-house subdivision in Connecticut). In the early 1980s we were operating without a well-established, consistent standard, or format, for conducting and writing archaeological evaluations. I was part of the baby boom generation that flooded the field and implemented the CRM guidelines by trial and error.

Although we have continued to maintain a very small office, typically I now juggle fifteen projects in various stages of production that range over several states and in size up to 12,000 acres. We now offer a variety of services in addition to assessments for environmental review procedures, such as archival research, historic structures recordation, and neighborhood and industry histories. However, we do not maintain a full-time staff. Rather, we subcontract specific tasks according to the parameters of each project: project site location (Staten Island, New York, or Hartford, Connecticut), potential resources (extant twentieth-century iron bridge or possible seventeenth-century Dutch village), and experience (monitoring sewer installations or analyzing details of Sanborn Insurance maps).

As of 1997, 85% of the total domestic budget for archaeology was a direct result of CRM, or **compliance archaeology.** Regardless of this statistic and the image of business, and despite the broad range of skills we draw upon, the small firm contract archaeologist is not guaranteed (1) a livable wage or (2) respect in academic circles. CRM tasks are compliance driven and, most important, are rarely undertaken with any degree of happiness by a client, whether that client is a private condominium developer or the federal highway administration. The archaeological component of the environmental review process is perceived by many as "red tape" and creates grumbles and sighs of exasperation if not outright resentment from a deadline-driven construction boss.

If I were just now choosing a career path, I would do it all over again, but I would enter the CRM world with a clearer understanding of necessary job skills and a realistic expectation of the short- and long-term benefits. I would anticipate a broad range of challenges. Let me tell you about a few of them.

Testing and monitoring. "Traveling with a trowel" at low pay and in less than glamorous conditions for short-term projects is usually the first CRM position, or rite of passage. A field crew member digs countless **shovel test pits,** one pit rarely distinguished from another except by slight shades of **Munsell**-coded dirt. I have dug my share of 50 cm x 50 cm pits and still think it is a necessary experience. Ranking right up there in boredom, but also good experience, is monitoring heavy machinery as it chews up loam, sand, and gravel. It just takes intestinal fortitude to tell a backhoe operator that an arrowhead was found in the backdirt and you need to halt his progress.

Thousands of photographs. Although I have balanced on top of fire hydrants and dangled from rusty fire escapes to snap the perfect view of an excavation unit, most of my photographs are taken to document existing conditions, what a site looks like today, which is often bustling with people and whizzing traffic. I have been "escorted" back to my van by a street gang member and warned to get out of the "hood." One innocent snapshot of a Brooklyn rowhouse triggered an onslaught of plainclothes policemen pouring out of what appeared to be just one more average city dwelling. The detectives were renting the rowhouse as a "safe house" in a witness protection program, and photographs were a *no-no.* I take urban photographs surreptitiously because drug dealers don't want to be caught on film and tenants often do not know their building is slated for demolition.

Fun interviews and glimpses of humankind. I have interviewed retired Naval engineers on the routing of sewer lines in waterfront forts and walked recently plowed fields with farmers hoping to pinpoint where the family collection of Indian relics originated. I have interviewed one of the first two African American women to break the World War II hiring freeze at a brass works. She had taken a colorblind aptitude test to prove that African American women could, indeed, handle delicate, small-scale manufacturing operations.

Hours and hours of research in city halls, historical societies, corporate archives, and many obscure, dusty basements. I have poured over corporate company archives to reconstruct damages done to neighborhood buildings by a major pharmaceutical company's first "explosive" experiment during its inaugural year of business (in downtown Brooklyn). Dogged pursuit of bits and pieces of the past has kept me inside the Science and Technology Annex of the New York Public Library, as well as the Map Division and Genealogy Department. The past records of large engineering firms, utility companies, and public transportation and parkland adminis-

trations have proven to be great resources, as have been the small village historical societies and local two-room libraries. The detective work tracking down informants and documents is a treat for me. I have tapped postcard collections and family photo albums. I have sought advice from a porcelain "doll restorer," members of a bottle-hunters club, and my dentist.

Testimony and discussions at public meetings. Chameleon-like, the small firm CRM manager must be as comfortable dressed in a suit at a table with Zoning Board officials as she is wielding the shovel or kibitzing with the soil boring rig crew. As an aspiring actress, I spent much of my high school career on stage. I never imagined that stage presence and acting skills would serve me well as an archaeologist!

A balancing act. I continually walk the tightrope of complying with environmental review requirements (local, state, or federal jurisdiction), keeping the client informed and comforted, and tracking the project budget. It is a business, and the objective is to be profitable. But my ultimate responsibility is to the resource. I have to maintain a balance between reasonable expectations and actions, staying current with applicable laws and their interpretations and the archaeological literature.

Team participation. As more and more urban sites of defunct manufacturing complexes are recycled into new uses, CRM contracts will involve more bricks, asphalt, and abandoned generators than cornfields. Escalating costs in such developed areas argue for expanding techniques that sample subsurface conditions prior to archaeological testing. I work closely with other members of the environmental analysis project team, sharing information that can guide where and whether we test. For example, when the architects need soil data for drainage and foundation design criteria, I ask for continuous tube samples of the first few feet and use copies of the testing logs to get a glimpse of buried strata. The toxic materials scientists alert me to buried tanks and pipelines they have located, and when I find archival evidence of an early gasoline station or buried naphtha tanks, I share the critical information on potential residues.

Dispelling myths. I have often repeated the phrase, "Man never saw a dinosaur" because much of the public thinks the goal of an archaeologist is to find the lost *Rex.* I also disappoint the new acquaintance who stammers: "Gosh, (gee willikers) an archaeologist! What is your most famous discovery?" I feel comfortable extolling the fine points of a rusted pony truss bridge or a derelict factory building or explaining that a handful of Native American points and sherds is truly meaningful. At least *I* am satisfied that my "discoveries" are famous.

PART 6

Forensic Archaeology

Recall any news report where the police or FBI are investigating an unsolved murder where the body was never found. Weeks, months, or even years after the crime was committed, with the trail long since gone cold, a new piece of evidence may be brought to light. Someone, perhaps a neighbor of the victim, remembers seeing a stranger in the woods. Or perhaps a dog, digging gleefully in some loose soil (as dogs are apt to do), comes loping toward his or her master, all bark and wagging tail, with a gruesome prize in its mouth—a human bone. Next, the local police or FBI will descend upon the **site** (I use that common archaeological term consciously) to search for additional clues. The investigators use hardware cloth screens to separate fragmentary evidence from the surrounding soil matrix, and they rely on trowels, dental picks, and brushes to gently move soil away from possible bone remnants. These all are items in the tool kit of every field archaeologist. Archaeologists often are called on by local and national law enforcement agencies to aid in such searches expressly because of our experience and expertise at recovering small, fragmentary bits of evidence from the earth. In a particularly infamous crime committed in Connecticut—the so-called Woodchipper Murder—named for the tool used by the murderer to dispose of his wife's body—an individual trained and experienced in archaeology was called in to use the techniques of our craft in an attempt to recover identifiable remains of the missing wife. A guilty conviction and long prison sentence are both testaments to the usefulness of archaeological techniques in this case. Recovering clues from the scene of a crime or an accident is not unlike recovering clues from the scene of an ancient life. Our skills here are not esoteric; they are directly relevant and useful for the task at hand.

For the same reason, the skills of the archaeologist have come in handy in the search for MIAs in southeast Asia. More than 2,500 American soldiers who fought in the Vietnam War have never been accounted for. For the families, the military, and the country as a whole, closure has been elusive with so many Americans missing and unaccounted for. Archaeologists have been able to contribute their skills in searching for the often meager remains at U.S. military aircraft crash sites of more than twenty-three years ago in the jungles of Vietnam.

The articles in Part 6 exemplify the usefulness of archaeological field and analytical procedures to help solve crimes, or at least to understand the nature of those crimes, and to help recover and identify the remains of missing servicemen and servicewomen.

30

Criminal Investigations:
A Forensic Archaeology Case Study
from Connecticut

Nicholas F. Bellantoni and David G. Cooke

Nick Bellantoni is the state archaeologist of Connecticut and possesses a remarkable ability to get people excited about the past.
Dave Cooke is an avocational archaeologist in Connecticut with extensive field experience.

Points to consider when reading this article:

1. Why was the state archaeologist called in to investigate the desecration of a tomb in Middletown, Connecticut?

2. How was the vandalism at the Chauncey family crypt associated with the discovery of a human skull behind a car wash in Cromwell, Connecticut?

3. How were archaeological field techniques used to analyze the tomb vandalism?

4. How was forensic archaeology used to connect the vandalized tomb with the skull found in Cromwell?

A human **skull** is an uncommon discovery indeed in Connecticut's woodlands, and one that demands explanation. How did the skull in question come to rest, of all places, in the woods behind a car wash in bucolic Cromwell, Connecticut? Was it the remains of a missing person, a victim of some deadly assault, or the accidentally disinterred remains of an ancient Native American?

The skull was brought to Nicholas F. Bellantoni, an expert in identifying bones. The authorities hoped that Nick might be able to give them an accurate assessment of who the person was whose skull seemed to have been unceremoniously dumped behind the car wash. Was it a man or a woman, an older adult or a teenager, a person of European, Asian, African, or Native American descent?

Meanwhile, in nearby Middletown, Connecticut, police had been alerted to an episode of vandalism in a crypt at a local cemetery. Once again, Nick's archaeological expertise at recovery of even small pieces of evidence was called on by the police to investigate the crime scene in the crypt. Treating the floor of the crypt as one might treat an above-ground archaeological site, Nick was able to solve two mysteries at the same time.

Recent state legislation in Connecticut has provided for professional archeological involvement when unmarked burials are accidentally encountered during construction and other land-altering activities or as a result of cemetery vandalism. As a result, the Office of State Archaeology at the University of Connecticut (Storrs) and the State Historic Preservation Office have provided technical assistance to law enforcement agencies throughout the state. Most notably, criminal trespass at the Chauncey family crypt at the Indian Hill Cemetery in Middletown, Connecticut, evolved into a case study where forensic archeological and anthropological techniques were employed to assist municipal police to understand the nature of the vandalism, to provide information on the sequence of criminal events, to sort skeletal remains disturbed during the vandalism, and to restore the desecrated family crypt as near as possible to its original condition.

In August 1991, the state archeologist was notified that a human skull had been discovered in a wooded area behind a car wash facility in Cromwell, Connecticut.

From *CRM*, vol. 19, no. 10, 1996. Reprinted here by permission of the author.

This discovery appeared to be linked to a different on-going investigation that was being conducted by the Middletown Police Department, which requested our technical assistance in identifying this unusual find.

The specimen consisted of a single human **cranium** (the part of the skull that includes the bone face, upper jaw, and vault areas). No mandible or lower jaw was present. The discovery was considered to be "old bone" by the Office of State Archaeology in that it contained little organic matter and exhibited a breakdown of the cortical/periosteal surface. Although the skull was found lying on the surface of the ground in a wooded area, it showed no signs of weathering, bleaching, rodent gnawing, or other marks indicative of exposure. In addition, the skull gave no evidence of soil adherence or plant root development in any cranial **foramena.** Thus, it had been neither buried in the ground, nor exposed to the elements for any length of time. Age, sex, and racial estimates strongly suggested an adult, white female, probably 45 to 55 years old. All dentition was lost **perimortem.** Cause of death or other pathological conditions could not be discerned.

After preliminary analysis by the Office of State Archaeology, the police requested further technical assistance with an on-going investigation of vandalism at a family crypt in a Middletown cemetery. Police investigators had been working the case for a number of months and questioned whether the Cromwell skull could have originated from the Chauncey family crypt at Indian Hill Cemetery. One investigative "lead" involved certain individuals of known satanic cult associations whose motive for the break-in and vandalism would be to obtain a human skull for ritual purposes.

The Chaunceys were a very prominent early New England family, emigrating from England by 1638. The Chauncey lineage includes the second president of Harvard College, the first full-term graduate of Yale College, celebrated ministers, and a co-builder of the Panamanian railroad. The family crypt is architecturally impressive with brownstone arched doorways leading to the 130 square foot interior. Three rows of stacked vaults house 17 members of the Chauncey family dating from 1821 to 1979.

The state archeologist and a team of students and **avocational archeologists** entered the crypt to identify and interpret human remains and material culture disturbed by the vandalism. Four vaults had been clearly violated. The crypt's marble-tiled floor was littered with disarticulated skeletal remains, wooden and cast-iron coffin fragments, burial clothing, casket linen, and hardware from the desecrated burials.

In order to facilitate the recording of the spatial distribution of the human remains and coffin parts scattered within the crypt, a modified archeological grid system was devised. A wooden frame, constructed and elevated by corner posts over the crypt floor, provided pertinent datum points for subsequent field measurements. A gasoline-powered generator and several large flood lights were installed for adequate lighting. Once in place, standard archeological field methods for the recording of human remains and material culture enabled the controlled recording of horizontal and vertical **provenience** in order to determine the spatial orientation and relationship of the vandalized burials.

Skeletal remains of four individuals ranging in age from 2 to 68 years at death were documented *in situ* on the crypt's floor and subsequently sorted in order to develop a sequence of criminal activity and to restore the remains to their appropriate burial vaults upon completion of our investigation. In this process, it was established that the cranium discovered in Cromwell was that of Lucy Alsop Chauncey, who died in 1855 at 56 years of age.

Based on the horizontal and vertical distribution of osteological remains, coffin parts, and funerary remains on the crypt floor, the Office of State Archaeology was able to reconstruct the probable sequence of events for the criminal activities. Skeletal elements for all of the individuals whose vaults had been violated were accounted for in the crypt with the one exception of Mrs. Chauncey's cranium. The degree of decomposition of her post-cranial remains was consistent with that of the cranium and the mandible fit into the temporal-mandibular fossa. The archeological recovery of jewelry and other objects of monetary value as well as the haphazard manner in which human and coffin remains were scattered throughout the crypt appeared to eliminate burglary as a motive for the vandalism. There was no indication of any systematic search for artifacts which one would expect if the vandals were looking for material to sell or collect. While we cannot positively account for what else may have been removed, we are absolutely confident that the cranium that was recovered by the police was removed from Lucy Chauncey's crypt, supporting the contention that satanic cult activity may have been a possible motive.

With the evidence from the forensic archeology at the Chauncey family crypt, Middletown Police arrested a suspect, of known satanic cult involvement, for the robbery of a gun store. This individual was taken into custody in lieu of $10,000 bond following his arrest and was arraigned on four counts of interfering with a cemetery or grave site, one count each of third-degree burglary, first-degree criminal mischief and sixth-degree larceny.

Federal, state, and local law enforcement agencies are recognizing the importance of establishing an investigative partnership with archeologists and anthropologists in their efforts to collect physical evidence from crime scenes whenever human remains are involved. Archeological field techniques have been designed to maximize the information retrievable from a given site where ostensibly very little cultural material remains exist for analysis. The application of archeological research methodologies to a criminal investigation will result in a greater degree of accuracy in the location of physical evidence and the best assurance for the recovery of materials and remains that may otherwise be lost. Archeologists are seldom familiar with criminal investigation procedures and require the supervision of a professional criminal investigator. Likewise, the criminal investigator may not be aware of the sophisticated techniques and analyses archeologists can provide. Archeologists need to familiarize themselves with state and local legislation regarding forensic applications of their work as well as the appropriate state cultural resource managers with mandates to oversee such investigations. Cooperative partnerships between law enforcement agencies and archeologists and anthropologists, like the successful case of the Chauncey family crypt, will result in the improvement of forensic sciences and hopefully, successful prosecutions at the community and state judicial levels.

31

Forensic Aviation Archaeology:
Finding and Recovering
American MIA Remains

Thomas D. Holland and Robert W. Mann

Thomas Holland has served as the curator of the Museum of Anthropology at the University of Missouri. Currently, he is a forensic anthropologist and the scientific director at the U.S. Army Central Identification Laboratory, Hawaii.

Robert Mann worked for five years at the Smithsonian Institution and now is the senior anthropologist at the Central Identification Laboratory, Hawaii.

Points to consider when reading this article:

1. How is forensic archaeology being used to help resolve the MIA issue in Vietnam?

2. What are the duties of the U.S. Army Central Identification Laboratory, Hawaii (CILHI)?

3. What kind of site is most commonly analyzed and excavated by the CILHI?

4. In the case discussed here, how did the forensic scientists know the site was genuine?

It was an awful period in American history. American servicemen and servicewomen were fighting and dying in an unpopular war half a world away in Vietnam. Back home, the streets were filled with people protesting American involvement in a war that seemed unwin-nable, with no clearly articulated goal. Though our technology was far superior to that of the "enemy," the more soldiers we sent, the further away any kind of resolution seemed to be.

Were we on the wrong side of a popular insurrection that reflected the will of most of Vietnam's people? Were we fighting a heroic and misunderstood struggle against an attempt by the Communist world to dominate Southeast Asia? Was Vietnam a domino in a chain of dominoes, all of which would fall after it did? Our confusion was agonizing. Soldiers returned to a nation so confused over its purpose that these sons and daughters of America were resented and even reviled by many.

The final insult to some who served in Vietnam are the MIAs, the 2,500 American men and women who served in the war, never returned, and have never been accounted for. The techniques of archaeology have been applied when the Vietnamese government has seen fit to allow Americans to follow the few leads that are left concerning the disposition of the MIAs. This article describes the result of one such foray. For the MIAs, it seems, this may be the only way we can bring them home.

Forensic anthropologists lend their skills to identifying homicide victims for the Federal Bureau of Investigation, excavating Civil War burials for the National Park Service, and recovering American war casualties for the Department of the Army. Each of these endeavors requires the implementation of scientific principles, including crime-scene investigation, forensic anthropology, aviation archaeology, botany, photography, medicine, ballistics, and law. By combining an ever-evolving multidisciplinary approach, forensic anthropologists at the U.S. Army Central Identification Laboratory, Hawai'i (**CILHI**), are able to resolve the fate of American MIAs.

The relationship between anthropologists and the armed services has been long and productive. In par-

From *CRM*, vol. 19, no. 10, 1996. Reprinted here by permission of the authors.

FIGURE 1 This muddy pond is actually the crater left by the impact of an American B-52 bomber when it crashed during the war in Vietnam. Members of a U.S. search team are shown here mapping the crater as part of their search for remains. (Courtesy of the U.S. Army CILHI Photography Lab)

ticular, forensic anthropology has profited from methods and techniques developed by the Army Central Identification Laboratories for the identification of U.S. war casualties. Historically, the Central Identification Laboratories, under the direction of such notable figures as Charles Snow, Mildred Trotter, T. Dale Stewart, Thomas McKern, and Ellis Kerley, were temporary, mission-specific organizations formed after World War II, the Korean War, and the Vietnam War. Combined, these labs accounted for the identification of thousands of military and civilian personnel, including more than 430 Americans from the Vietnam War. Many of the forensic techniques pioneered in these laboratories continue to be the mainstay of forensic anthropology.

In its present—and now permanent—incarnation, the CILHI is the largest skeletal identification laboratory in the world and is recognized as an internationally-respected leader in human identification techniques and forensic aviation archaeology. Formally established in 1976, the laboratory's expanded charter includes both the recovery and identification of U.S. war dead from all past military conflicts. These identifica-

tions are achieved by traditional methods and techniques, as well as more novel approaches including isotopic analysis, scanning electron microscopy, video superimposition, and most recently, **mitochondrial DNA (mtDNA)** analysis.

A typical CILHI recovery effort consists of locating and excavating an aircraft crash site or less frequently, an isolated burial. The mission begins when a recovery team departs for the host country. With some variation depending on the mission circumstances, a team consists of an anthropologist, who functions as the recovery leader; an Army officer and a senior non-commissioned officer, who oversee the team's logistical needs; a medic; a photographer; a linguist; an explosive-ordnance technician, to handle the ubiquitous unexploded bombs found on old battlefields; and one to six Army graves registration specialists who provide the bulk of the sweat and muscle. If the mission is to recover a crashed aircraft, a team includes an aircraft-wreckage analyst to identify key aircraft components and aircrew-related artifacts such as flight-suit material.

FIGURE 2 Using standard archaeological sifters, members of a joint U.S./Vietnamese team search for physical remains at the crash site of a U.S. F-4 Phantom fighter jet. (Courtesy of the U.S. Army CILHI Photography Lab)

Sites are excavated using standard archeological procedures and are similar in many respects to any CRM-governed site, with two exceptions. First, the CILHI teams work in some of the most remote and dangerous locales in the world, from the jungles of Southeast Asia to the mountains of the Himalayan Chain to the ocean waters of the Pacific Islands. In addition, team members function in an official capacity as quasi-diplomatic agents of the United States. The site is governed by a foreign country (often a country, such as North Korea, that is on relatively poor terms with the United States government) as are the U.S. team members. A recent recovery in western Iraq, for example, was conducted under the watchful eyes (and at times guns) of the Iraqi Republican Guard. Second, since the identification of human remains is a forensic issue, the recovery site must be treated similar to a crime scene; that is, there must be a proper chain-of-custody for any recovered remains and artifacts from the time they leave the ground to their receipt at the CILHI.

The following example highlights how standard archeological procedures, combined with experience and common sense, have led to the recovery and identification of American MIA remains.

EXCAVATION OF SITE IN VIETNAM

One of the CILHI's more complex cases involved the 1972 loss of a U.S. A-7D Corsair aircraft shot down in a remote area of North Vietnam. As there were no American eyewitnesses to the incident, no one could "prove" whether the pilot had ejected from the aircraft or remained in it when it crashed.

In 1994, a preliminary survey team composed of U.S. personnel under the direction of the Joint Task Force-Full Accounting (an umbrella organization charged with accounting for all U.S. war casualties from the Vietnam War) and their Vietnamese counterparts interviewed several Vietnamese informants who claimed that they had found and buried the body of a U.S. pilot in 1972. The survey team located the purported grave of the pilot in an old bomb crater and excavated a 1x2 meter test pit that yielded pieces of flight suit, life support equipment (e.g. oxygen hose), and a few human bone fragments. The team, lacking an anthropologist, closed the site. The human remains were sent to the CILHI, and everything else was forwarded for analysis at the Life Sciences Equipment Laboratory, its adjunct Life Services Artifact Section, and additional support laboratories at the San Antonio

Air Logistics Center, Kelly Air Force Base, Texas, for detailed analysis.

In an unusual twist, one of the pilot's children paid her own way to Vietnam and visited the crash site. She interviewed a villager who allegedly found the pilot's helmet, and with a little persuasion, she obtained the helmet. She knew it was her father's helmet because she found his name written inside it (the FBI later authenticated that the name had not recently been written). Although no sophisticated equipment was needed to see the name, the survey team had overlooked this piece of evidence. That the survey team had missed such compelling evidence prompted further action by the Joint Task Force and the CILHI, and as a result, the CILHI was directed to deploy a full search and recovery team with more specialists, including an anthropologist, to the site.

In the meantime, the laboratories at Kelly Air Force Base had completed their extensive analysis of the pilot's equipment and aircraft wreckage and formulated an opinion based on reproducible evidence. According to the laboratories, the life-support equipment was torn, stretched, and burned in a manner consistent with being in an aircrash. Their preliminary report stated that the pilot was in the airplane when it crashed.

In April and May 1995, a 12-man CILHI recovery team arrived at the crash site to complete what the earlier survey team had begun. Its objectives were threefold: identify the airplane; recover any associated human remains; and recover evidence to confirm or refute the Life Sciences Equipment Laboratory's preliminary determination that the pilot was in the airplane when it crashed.

The first order of business was to re-interview the witnesses. The pilot, according to the man who had found the helmet, had ejected from the airplane before it crashed. The Vietnamese later found the dead pilot, seated in his ejection seat, hanging in a tree a few hundred meters from the crash site. They removed his body, disposed of the ejection seat, and buried his remains in an old bomb crater down the mountain side.

Based on this information, the recovery team excavated the grave in the bomb crater, enlarging the project area to 12x16 meters to account for any disturbance or scattering of remains through cultivation. The team also excavated the area where villagers claimed to have found the ejection seat and lastly, the crash site itself. All three areas were dug to culturally sterile soil. Fortunately for the pilot's family, the team found more human bone fragments (within inches of where the survey team had excavated), the pilot's dog tag, pieces of his flight suit, and life-support equipment from the bomb crater. Although the ejection seat site yielded no material evidence, the recovery team found a piece of the aircraft fuselage near the crash site stenciled with

A7D 223, indicating the aircraft type and serial number. By the time the team closed its field investigations, there was nothing else to be found. All cultural material—evidence, in legal terms—had been recovered. The evidence was then used to reconstruct the circumstances of the shootdown.

Preliminary field analysis of the material evidence from the burial suggested that the pilot had actually ejected before the plane crashed. The Life Sciences Equipment Laboratory's "evidence" of tearing, burning, and stretching could be explained in another way. Specifically, witnesses told the recovery team that the bomb crater had been cleared, burned, and cultivated for many years. Thus, the interpretation offered by the Life Sciences Equipment Laboratory might be incorrect. The tearing and burning could easily have resulted from the activities related to cultivation. The initial survey team didn't have this information, and the Life Sciences Equipment Laboratory's scientists' train of thought didn't entertain such cultural activities as slash-and-burn cultivation.

Anticipating the possibility that the findings of the Life Sciences Equipment Laboratory might be incorrect, the recovery team's anthropologist was careful to document everything found at the grave site. Specifically, he instructed team members to notify him the moment they found bones, teeth, flight-suit material, or a dog tag. Each of these items was photographed exactly as it was found and the anthropologist personally removed them from the ground. The dirt from the dog tag and the piece of serialized fuselage were removed and placed in separate Ziploc bags for further analysis, if so desired. Although the anthropologist didn't know exactly what tests the soil might be subjected to, he was careful to preserve each piece of evidence.

As the case evolved, one piece of evidence that proved critical was the photodocumentation of live, unbroken rootlets growing into the pilot's bones. This evidence served as legal proof that the Vietnamese had not recently "salted" remains in the bomb crater. As a matter of fact, before the excavation was completed, the team anthropologist was asked (by field radio through the U.S. Joint Task Force-Full Accounting office in Hanoi) how he knew the remains had not been recently planted at the site. The "proof," he told them, was the fact that the remains had rootlets growing through them, and along the back of the dog tag. These items had laid in the ground for many months, not weeks. In fact, a more precise age for the rootlets (i.e., the time it took the rootlets to grow to their present lengths based on their species) could later be determined by a botanist. Similarly, a few months later the Life Sciences Equipment Laboratory analyzed the soil adhering to the dog tag and the back of the serialized aluminum fuselage to determine whether these items had originated from the same site. The possibility existed that the Vietnamese had retained these items in some warehouse and salted the site before the recovery team arrived. Soil analysis using EDX (Energy Dispersive X-ray) proved that the items originated from the same area on the mountain.

When it was all said and done, the recovery team had gathered significant evidence supporting the Vietnamese witness' statement that the pilot ejected from the airplane before it crashed. Further, a little cultural curiosity on the part of the anthropologist yielded information overlooked by the initial survey team — namely, that the bomb crater had been cleared, burned,

and cultivated. With this information, the Life Sciences Equipment Laboratory reversed their preliminary hypothesis that the pilot was in the airplane when it crashed. The final report reflected this opinion. CILHI had resolved the contradictory questions by conducting a thorough "crime scene" investigation, and excavation of the grave, ejection seat, and crash sites.

The pilot's remains were later identified using traditional anthropological techniques and mtDNA analysis. Aviation archaeology, combined with forensic anthropology, botany, chemistry, and photography, had been used to solve the mystery of a 23-year-old MIA death.

32

Forensic Archaeology and the Woodchipper Murder

Albert B. Harper

Al Harper is a trained biological anthropologist with extensive experience in archaeological excavation. He also is a lawyer who specializes in forensic evidence. He teaches a course in forensic science at the University of Connecticut School of Law.

....

Points to consider when reading this article:

1. Why did the police call in a forensic archaeologist to help search for the body?

2. What was the archaeologist able to find in the powder produced by the woodchipper? How was he able to find it?

3. What evidence definitively connected the remains from the woodchipper and the missing woman?

4. What mistakes did the murderer make that led to his arrest and conviction?

It is one of the more grotesque scenes in a movie chock full of graphically depicted murder and mayhem. One of the bad guys (the complete psycho) has just killed the other bad guy (the sleaze-ball) and is attempting to dispose of his body using a small woodchipper, the kind you can buy or rent to convert brush or small branches into sawdust and, logically, wood chips. He hasn't quite finished, and his partner's foot is sticking up out of the chipper when the extremely pregnant sheriff catches him in the act.

Fargo was a terrific movie, but, as the cliché goes, truth is often stranger (in this case, even more bizarre) than fiction. A woodchipper figures prominently in one of the most infamous murder cases in Connecticut's recent history. The woodchipper in question was rented, and not one of the little ones seen in the movie. No, this was a large, professional woodchipper of a kind used by loggers that can turn even entire tree trunks into dust in seconds. The murderer thought sure that this woodchipper was up to the task of utterly and completely disposing of all evidence. He didn't reckon on the investigative skills of the archaeologist and forensic anthropologist.

....

Helle Crafts was last seen about 7 P.M. on November 18, 1986, when she was dropped off at her home in Newtown, Connecticut, by a friend and co-worker. Helle, a flight attendant for Pan Am, had completed an international shift and was home with her husband and children for Thanksgiving. Some forty days later, tiny fragments of human tissue and bone, which were later proven to be parts of Helle's head, hands, and feet, were found amidst hundreds of wood chips littered on the shores of the Housatonic River in western Connecticut. The case is most remarkable in demonstrating the scientific capacity of a team of forensic experts to collect, analyze, interpret, and reconstruct an event that a murderer so carefully and craftily tried to obscure.

HELLE'S DISAPPEARANCE

Helle's disappearance was suspicious from the start. She had returned home from an overseas flight and was not scheduled to leave again for several days. Helle had started divorce proceedings against her husband, Richard, but the couple nonetheless continued to reside together.

The night of her disappearance, an early winter snow and ice storm caused power outages in many parts of the state, including Newtown. About 6 A.M. on

....

Published here by permission of the author.

the morning of November 19, 1986, Richard took their three children and the nanny to his sister's home in Westport. He told the nanny that Helle had gone ahead and would meet them there. When they arrived and did not see Helle, Richard said that Helle had taken a flight to visit her mother who lived in Denmark.

Helle's friends were rightly concerned about her unusual absence, but at each inquiry Richard provided an excuse that delayed any additional investigation. Thanksgiving came and passed with no word of Helle. Finally, Helle's friends made their concerns known to Helle's divorce attorney who in turn alerted a private investigator, Keith Mayo, who had previously investigated Richard's amorous adventures, and serious inquiry began. Acting independently, Mayo uncovered a series of unusual events that eventually led the police to undertake the exhaustive investigation that led to the discovery of Helle's remains on the shores of the Housatonic River. Without Mayo's dogged persistence, Richard Crafts, who had beaten a state police polygraph, would have gotten away with murder.

THE FATE OF HELLE CRAFTS

Richard Crafts was an unusually thorough man in everything he did. A commercial airline pilot, Crafts was exacting in the details. He had plotted Helle's demise and disappearance for some time. Helle was scheduled home from her European tour on November 18. Not so coincidentally, Richard had arranged for the delivery of a new dump truck, the cash purchase of a new freezer, and the rental of a large commercial size woodchipper that could devour twelve-inch diameter logs, all for her November 18 homecoming. A series of unplanned events—the delay in delivery of the truck and the unexpected snow storm and power outage—crimped his plan, but only slightly. Crafts made quick arrangements to rent a U-Haul truck capable of towing the woodchipper, paid extra to have the chipper available after the eighteenth, and conveniently used the snow storm as an excuse to get his children and their nanny out of the house until he could complete the deed.

By chance a U-Haul truck towing a large woodchipper was seen by several witnesses along the shores of the Housatonic River during the night of November 20. Crafts was seen at various other locations with the U-Haul and chipper in tow. Armed with this evidence and a search warrant, police and Dr. Henry Lee, director of the State Forensic Lab, searched the Craft's home, finding a bloody mattress cover, several drops of human blood, and many other pieces of evidence that would eventually lead to Crafts' conviction.

It was, however, the evidence found in the wood chips along the river that led to Crafts' arrest for the murder of his wife on January 13, 1987. It was late December when the wood chips alongside the road skirting the Housatonic were discovered. The winter was typical for New England: rain, sleet, snow, followed by more rain, sleet, and snow. The ground was now frozen solid, as were the piles of debris, wood chips, and Helle's remains.

Archaeological excavation is carefully planned and executed research designed to provide complete control of a site's stratigraphy. In contrast, forensic recovery of human remains is often undertaken with due haste and records nothing more than the **provenance** of the body and evidence surrounding it. As Helle's body was not yet viable, the State Police Major Crime Squad constructed a makeshift laboratory, melted the ground with jet heaters, and began the arduous task of sifting through thousands of bits of wood chips. Dr. Bruno Frohlich, a biological anthropologist trained in archaeological methods, recovered many of the tiny fragments of bone using standard archaeological **flotation** methods. Each fragment recovered was assigned a field identification number, noting the location where the fragment was found, and packaged for additional analysis at the forensic laboratory.

Scattered among the leaves and wood chips recovered from the frozen mud on the shore of the Housatonic River were very small pieces of bone, hair, and tissue interspersed in the debris. Additionally, a crown of a human tooth and a lower premolar with a fractured root were also recovered. This was the evidence that was needed to obtain an arrest warrant for Richard Crafts. The police now had a body, such as it was, and evidence that the body had been subjected to very severe forces either before or after death.

ROLE OF FORENSIC ANTHROPOLOGY

The recovery of bone fragments immediately raised the need for a forensic anthropologist to determine whether the bone fragments were human, and if so, to whom did they belong?

The development of forensic anthropology as a subspecialty of **physical anthropology** has been an important trend in anthropology over the past several decades. Originally, the application of physical anthropology to legal issues was a mere sideline of the interests of physical anthropologists. Dr. William Krogman's (1962) book, *The Human Skeleton in Forensic Medicine*, and Dr. Lawrence Angel's work at the Smithsonian Institution for the FBI are hallmarks in the development of forensic anthropology. The foundations to the science were, of course, much earlier, but the disciplinary origins of forensic anthropology can be found in the 1960s and 1970s.

The role of the forensic anthropologist is to determine, first, that the remains are human. All vertebrate species have a skeleton that is adapted to the environment occupied by the species, and each species has a unique skeletal morphology. Although most anyone would surely recognize a human cranium as being human, identification of other bones of the human body can be difficult even for persons trained in medicine.

Once the forensic anthropologist has established that the bones are human, the analysis shifts to deciding class characteristics that might be useful in narrowing a search to a single individual. Usually the analysis first focuses on the age at death, which can be accurately determined in young persons but less accurately as age increases. The forensic anthropologist relies on morphological clues such as the appearance and union of the **epiphyseal bodies,** the development and eruption of the teeth, the metamorphosis of the face of the **pubic symphysis,** the closure of the **cranial vault suture,** and other morphological changes that occur with age.

Next, the forensic anthropologist decides whether the remains are male or female based on the shape of the pelvic bones, the morphology of the cranium, and the size and rugosity of the long bones.

Determining racial ancestry is a more difficult task because of the high degree of variation in the species. All humans are extremely similar, and most of the variation that can be attributed to ancestral origin occurs in the facial skeleton. Under the best of circumstances, the forensic anthropologist is often limited to an assignment of an individual's racial origins to the major continental races and then only with difficulty.

Regression equations relating long bone length to living stature permit reconstruction of body height. Determination of body weight is very difficult without nonskeletal evidence such as clothing.

Once the class characteristics of age, sex, race, and stature are determined, the forensic anthropologist searches for clues that might assist in determining actual identity of the remains. The most common method to detect identify is through comparison of dental records. Comparison of X rays of the frontal sinus or trabecular patterns of the vertebra have been used to provide proof of identity. Osseous pathology, including fractures and arthritis, is useful in providing clues as to the actual identity.

Finally, the forensic anthropologist determines the post-mortem interval. The rate of decomposition of the body depends on environmental circumstances, especially ambient temperature, surrounding the body after death. The post-mortem interval can be accurately determined only in large temporal units.

WHAT WAS LEFT OF HELLE?

The total morphological approach outlined here was impossible to apply in this case. All that remained of the body in the wood chips were sixty-nine tiny fragments of bone, the largest of which was 38 x 14 x 5 mm. Most of the fragments were much smaller, typically 10 x 8 x 4 mm. All were fractured in multiple planes and at multiple angles by an instrument exerting great force. Most of the fragments were rectangular in shape, with the long edge of the rectangle almost invariably cut at a straight, steep angle.

The degree of destruction was enormous and precluded identification of specific bone, species, age, sex, race, or body size for most of the pieces. Remarkably, some pieces—parts of the head, hands, and feet—could be identified as being an adult human female.

Most of the pieces were cortical or compact bone, which is found in the shafts of the long bones. Only two fragments were wholly trabecular or spongy bone located in the epiphyses or vertebra. Importantly, seven fragments could be identified as being part of the cranium because of the unique layering of the cranial bones.

Of the fragments that could be identified as human and from a particular bone, four fragments stand out as most important.

First, part of the ball joint of a human big toe was found, ligament and cartilage intact. The distal articular surface of the first metatarsal was severed in one plane, and the attached articular surface of the proximal phalanx was severed at a right angle to the metatarsal. The ball joint of the foot is a unique human adaptation to upright, bipedal locomotion.

Next, the recovery of the distal phalanx of the left thumb provided the clues that the remains were those of an adult human female. The epiphysis of the phalanx had united with the shaft, indicating skeletal maturity. The small size of the bone, nearly complete but severed into two pieces, was a sign that the thumb belonged to a woman.

Of the several pieces of cranial bone, one piece was especially informative as it was possible to ascertain that the fragment came from the parietal bone of a human. The inner surface of the human parietal is well marked with deep arterial grooves from the blood supply to the meninges of the outer surface of the brain. Moreover, the surface of the inner wall was larger than the surface of the outer table, proving that the fragment had been ripped out of the parietal bone by a force coming from the outside to the inside of the skull. This is important because although a person might survive a severed toe or thumb, no one could survive having a part of the parietal bone forced into the brain.

Finally, three tiny fragments of cortical bone were found not in the pile of wood chips by the river but in association with the U-Haul truck Crafts rented to tow the woodchipper. The three fragments were held together by strands of light brown-blonde human hair.

Many of the fragments were very greasy, and several were attached to bits of decaying nonosseous tissue. This observation suggested that the person had not been dead for a long period of time, perhaps for a few weeks or months at most.

In the final analysis, the sixty-nine tiny fragments of bone demonstrated that the remains were an adult human female, most likely of European origin, whose death had occurred only a short time before the remains were recovered.

IDENTIFYING HELLE CRAFTS

It was remarkable, given the enormous destruction of the skeleton, that it was possible to discern that the tiny bone fragments belonged to an adult, European woman, but this was not sufficient evidence to prove that the remains were those of Helle Crafts.

Here, as in most cases, the team approach to forensic science paid off. Forensic serologists were able to establish that the fragments that could not be identified morphologically were biochemically human. The blood type of the person was "O-positive," as was Helle Crafts.

DNA taken from the small bits of tissue adhering to the thumb and toe fragments was determined to be from the child of Helle's mother and the mother of Helle's children. This evidence was never presented in court because of the potential complication of DNA evidence in an already highly complex case. In 1988 the use of DNA in the forensic context was still quite novel. Under the laws of Connecticut then, introducing DNA evidence would have invoked a lengthy legal battle called a Frye hearing to decide whether DNA typing was generally accepted by the scientific community. A Frye hearing would have unnecessarily diverted the focus of the trial from the real issue of whether Richard murdered Helle.

Besides the blood, bone, and flesh, thousands of blond hairs were recovered from the wood chips, Crafts' car, the woodchipper, and from Crafts' chainsaw, which was found in the Housatonic River with the serial number filed off. Some 2,660 strands of hair were examined and determined to be human Caucasian head hair of blond color. The hair had been tinted and suggested that the owner had been a woman who visited a hair salon.

The real proof that the remains were Helle Crafts came from the remarkable analysis of Dr. Gus Karazulas, the forensic dentist who examined the tooth and crown found in the wood chips. Ordinarily, a forensic dentist will compare known dental records with the entire dentition of the deceased. Dr. Karazulas had a crown to go on. Thousands of X rays later he was able to prove that the crown was identical to the crown Helle Crafts had had made in Denmark.

The tooth, a lower premolar, was also Helle's tooth, and the root had been fractured with a force that Dr. Karazulas had never seen before.

CRAFTS ON TRIAL

As one might imagine, the "Woodchipper Murder" created enormous publicity, so great that the trial was moved across the state. State's Attorney Walter Flanagan carefully orchestrated the story of Helle's disappearance, the discovery of the wood chips, the forensic science evidence, and then Dr. Lee's reconstruction of the murder.

Crafts was defended by Daniel Sagarin whose blistering cross examination and suggestion that the state had framed Richard almost won the day. After three weeks of deliberation, one juror refused to continue, and the case was declared a mistrial.

A mistrial does not ordinarily confer the constitutional protection against double jeopardy. Crafts' second trial, this time without the aid of Sagarin, resulted in his conviction. His conviction was upheld by the Connecticut Supreme Court.

WHAT HAPPENED TO HELLE?

Richard Crafts is the only person who knows what happened to Helle. The crime scene reconstruction by Dr. Lee suggests that after the children had been put to bed, Helle and Richard perhaps discussed the divorce. Helle was wearing a blue nightshirt and was in the bedroom when she was struck with some heavy instrument, perhaps Richard's police flashlight. The blow probably killed her and resulted in the blood splatter found on the mattress and bedroom wall.

At this point Richard began the plan to dispose of her body. First, he placed Helle's body in the freezer, and then he began the process of cleaning up the blood in the bedroom. He moved the incriminating carpet and box spring to a nearby wooded lot, and he hid Helle's car.

After he had the children and nanny out of the house, he continued with his plan. Authorities believe that Crafts took Helle's dead and frozen stiff body to the wooded lot and dismembered her into smaller pieces with his chainsaw. Richard then took her dismembered body to the banks of the Housatonic River where he fed the parts to the woodchipper. Most of the tiny chips of frozen human flesh and bone disappeared into the river. Perhaps some were eaten by local carnivores. Sixty-nine tiny pieces of bone, a crown, and a tooth were all of Helle that was ever found.

Despite Crafts' best, and almost perfect, attempt to get away with murder, he was arrested, tried, found guilty, and sentenced to fifty years in prison. His conviction was the result of the efforts of the forensic science team in reconstructing the events surrounding the disappearance, death, and dismemberment of Helle Crafts.

REFERENCES

Herzog, Arthur, *The Woodchipper Murder,* 1989, Henry Holt, New York.

Krogman, William M., *The Human Skeleton in Forensic Medicine,* 1962, C. C. Thomas, Springfield, IL.

I AM AN ARCHAEOLOGIST

Francis P. McManamon

I am the chief archaeologist of the National Park Service; in this capacity I also serve as departmental consulting archaeologist for the entire Department of the Interior. I also oversee the Archaeology and Ethnography Program of the National Center for Cultural Resource Stewardship and Partnerships in Washington, DC. With this trio of titles, what is my actual job, and how did I get to it?

First, let me describe the work each of my jobs involve. As chief archaeologist of the National Park Service (NPS), I work in the headquarters office in Washington, DC. I serve as the primary advisor to the director of the National Park Service and other senior officials of the organization on activities and issues relating to archaeology. For example, I develop national policies and guidelines for how archaeological sites and collections are treated and I recommend how funds for archaeological investigations should be distributed nationally. Most of my daily work consists of drafting or reviewing documents, participating in meetings, and organizing activities for NPS archaeologists. However, much time is also spent advocating or representing archaeological concerns and interests with other NPS officials involved with historic preservation, park management, resource protection, or visitor services. My job does not involve conducting archaeological field investigations or what normally is considered archaeological research. The National Park Service employs about 125 full-time archaeologists who do undertake or oversee more typical archaeological research involving interpretation and management. Most of these professionals work at one of seven archaeological centers or at regional offices or at national park units.

The programs and projects for which the chief archaeologist is responsible focus on the development of policy, regulations, and guidance for NPS archaeology and the care of archaeological resources in NPS units. One of the activities related to this function involves working with other NPS archaeologists at the headquarters office and throughout the nation to decide how the $2.3 million available for archaeological inventory and recording of NPS archaeological sites is spent. Another activity involves working with other archaeologists to develop a professional handbook describing archaeological methods and techniques to be used for various kinds of archaeological activities undertaken in NPS units.

My second job, as departmental consulting archaeologist (DCA), has a governmentwide scope. The position was originally created in 1927 by the Secretary of the Interior to designate one archaeologist in the Department of the Interior to review applications for Antiquities Act permits and monitor the archaeological and paleontological work carried out under those permits. Jesse Nusbaum, NPS archaeologist in the southwestern United States, was designated as the first DCA. Nusbaum reviewed all Antiquities Act permits and regularly

(Photo by Kate Pierce McManamon)

visited the excavation sites, monitoring how the work was being conducted. In a series of reports to the Secretary of the Interior, he noted difficulties in the enforcement of the Antiquities Act, which prohibited excavation or removal of archaeological resources without the permission of the Secretary, including increasing interest in American antiquities, greater access to archaeological sites due to the automobile, and the likelihood of tourists picking up artifacts as mementos. The issues in these reports of 1929–1931 resound to us in the 1990s, and the looting of archaeological sites and the effects of cultural tourism continue to be of concern.

The job of DCA has shifted and grown since 1927. Rather than reviewing and monitoring archaeological permits, the job today involves working to coordinate archaeological programs administered and carried out by a variety of federal agencies. This often is done through drafting and enforcing regulations and guidelines implementing laws that relate to archaeological resources, such as the Archaeological Resource Protection Act and the National Historic Preservation Act. I also have been assigned a variety of tasks related to the implementation of the Native American Graves Protection and Repatriation Act, such as drafting the regulations implementing the law, providing staff and professional support for the federal advisory committee established by law, and administering grants to Indian tribes and museums.

Finally, I act as manager of the Archaeology and Ethnography Program at the National Center for Cultural Resource

Stewardship and Partnerships. Federal agencies go through reorganizations regularly. The most recent for the NPS involved substantial "downsizing and restructuring" that moved personnel out of the central offices and into field positions. In the reorganization, the NPS combined its headquarters for NPS system archaeology, NPS system cultural anthropology, and the DCA with the Archaeology and Ethnography Program. The program, located in Washington, DC, has a staff of fourteen: seven archaeologists, three cultural anthropologists, three clerks or secretaries, and one editor. In addition, consultants work on program activities regularly as do a number of student interns who spend a semester, a summer, or a year working on different activities. As program manager, I organize and oversee the work of the other professionals in the program office, develop budgets, monitor spending, in consultation with others set program priorities, and ensure that the office runs effectively and smoothly. One area of particular concern during the past several years has been improving public understanding, appreciation, and participation in legitimate archaeological activities.

Working for a public agency as an archaeologist has provided me with a great deal of personal and professional satisfaction. When I began working for a state Historic Preservation Office, the activities I was involved in spanned a wide range: from developing and maintaining the statewide site inventory to reviewing proposals of public projects for their potential impact on archaeological resources to working with local historical commissions on their archaeological issues.

Important archaeological activities are carried out by public agencies at all levels: local, tribal, state, and federal. Some public archaeologists undertake archaeological field projects of one or another sort. Mainly these are site inventory and evaluation studies, although sometimes archaeological excavations are undertaken. Often archaeologists in public agencies work with other professionals to plan agency actions and to ensure that archaeological resources are appropriately considered as part of public projects.

One of the challenges public archaeologists encounter daily is explaining the value of archaeological resources in ways that can be both comprehended and appreciated by nonarchaeologists. Public archaeologists need to be able to communicate with a general, nonspecialist audience. The professional rewards from such effective communication include influencing agency or office actions to improve archaeological interpretation, preservation, or protection—for example, convincing the law enforcement section of an agency to turn more of its attention to apprehending or prosecuting archaeological site looters or vandals. It also is personally rewarding to convey to a group of managers, lawyers, or other professionals a sense of the importance of archaeological resources and the most appropriate way to investigate them. After twenty years of working in public archaeology, I feel that I am directly helping to preserve and protect important remains that will help us learn about America's ancient and recent past.

Glossary

alluviation The accumulation of soil (alluvium) by flooding rivers.

anthropology The holistic and integrative study of humanity in all of its biological and cultural aspects.

Antiquities Act Federal law passed in 1906 that authorizes the president to designate historic landmarks, as well as historic structures and prehistoric sites on federal land, as "national monuments." The law mandates protection of these landmarks, structures, and **sites.**

archaeological record All of the material objects human beings left behind that have been preserved and are recoverable by the archaeologist.

archaeological survey The search for archaeological **sites** through any of a number of procedures including but not limited to **shovel test pitting,** coring, surface inspection, aerial photography, chemical analysis of soil, and magnetic or electrical analysis of the subsurface.

Archaeological Resources Protection Act Passed in 1979, this law extended and clarified the **Antiquities Act** of 1906. Its purpose is to protect archaeological resources and sites on public and Indian lands; it establishes specific and severe penalties for disturbing archaeological **sites** on these lands.

archaeology Study of human groups by analysis of the **material remains** they left behind. Can include an analysis of their documents in **historical archaeology.**

artifact Any object made and used by a human being and recovered at an archaeological **site.**

artifact assemblage The entire grouping of objects made and used by people found in an archaeological **site,** region, or time period.

avocational archaeologist An amateur archaeologist.

biological anthropology The anthropological study of human beings from a biological perspective. Usually includes questions of biological evolution of humanity and biological variation among modern human beings. The same as **physical anthropology.**

bioarchaeology Analysis of the biological entities found at archaeological **sites,** including animal bones, plant remains, and human remains.

CILHI The Central Identification Laboratory, Hawaii. U.S. military facility where forensic scientists, including forensic archaeologists, carry out the task of attempting to recover and identify the remains of U.S. servicemen and servicewomen killed in the line of duty.

compliance archaeology Conducted as a result of federal, state, or local laws that mandate that archaeological **sites** be searched for, excavated, preserved, or protected especially when such sites might be threatened with destruction as the result of construction projects.

contract archaeologist An archaeologist who works in **compliance archaeology** through contracts with municipalities and environmental or historic preservation firms.

controlled stratigraphic excavation Excavating a **site** by peeling back soil layers according to the **stratigraphy** found at the site.

cranial vault sutures The squiggly lines that demarcate the places where the various bones or plates of the **skull** are joined.

cranium The **skull** minus the lower jaw (mandible).

cultural anthropology That part of anthropology that focuses on human culture, that is, the economic, social, political, and ideological aspects of human beings.

cultural resources Aspects of the cultural and human landscape that are viewed as resources for learning and study. Prehistoric archaeological sites, historical houses, and Civil War battlefields are examples of cultural resources.

cultural resource management (CRM) The study, preservation, and protection of **cultural resources.** CRM archaeology is usually conducted to comply with federal, state, or local laws or mandates related to the study, preservation, or protection of **cultural resources** (see also **compliance archaeology**).

cultural tourism Tourism that is inspired by peoples' desire to visit archaeological or historical sites or to encounter a foreign culture.

demographic Related to the vital statistics of a population and including population size, age, longevity, sex ratio, and ethnic background.

diffusion The movement of cultural practices or ideas across cultural boundaries. Also called cultural borrowing.

enamel hypoplasia Microscopic defects in the enamel of adult, permanent teeth that are caused by nutritional deficiencies in the early years of a person's life, long before the adult teeth are visible above the gum line.

environmental review Assessment of the possible impacts on the environment of a proposed construction project. The environment includes water, air, plant and animal communities, as well as the historical or **cultural resources** (historical houses or prehistoric archaeological sites) in a given community or region.

epiphyseal bodies Each of the long bones (for example, the bones of the arms and legs) are made up of three segments when we are born: a shaft (diaphysis) and two end caps (epiphyses; epiphysis, singular). Epiphyseal bodies are these epiphyses or end caps. The epiphyses fuse to the shafts of the bones during growth.

ethnohistory That part of the **historical record** consisting of publications such as explorer journals, travel books, colonist memoirs, or missionary tracts, in which members of a literate cultural group—often Europeans—come into contact with an alien group of people and described them.

excavation The carefully controlled exposure and removal of archaeological material from an archaeological **site.** Careful record keeping of the precise location and depth where each item was found is crucial.

experimental archaeology   The attempt to replicate through a controlled experiment some element of an ancient technology.

feature   Sometimes called a nonportable **artifact,** a feature is a combination of artifacts and/or organic refuse found together, usually demarcating the location where some activity took place in the past. A trash pit, hearth, stone tool making workshop, or even a human burial are features.

flint knapping   Using percussion (with, for example, a stone hammer) or pressure (with, for example, an antler tine or tip) to produce flakes of flint. Flint is a hard, lustrous rock that produces sharp and durable edges and was commonly used by ancient people in the production of stone tools. The more general term "knapping" is used in the production of stone tools from flint as well as other materials.

flotation   Separating archaeological **artifacts** and organic remains from the soil in which they were deposited with the use of standing water. Items with a higher relative density than water (for example, stone flakes) will sink, and items with a lower relative density than water (for example, charcoal or burned seeds) will float.

foramena (foramen, singular)   Natural openings or orifices in bone.

forensic anthropology   The use of anthropology in law; usually, the detailed study of human skeletal remains in the attempt to identify a deceased individual and help solve a crime, most commonly a murder.

garbology   The archaeological study of modern trash, including the analysis of household refuse at its source as well as the **excavation** of trash dumps.

GIS (Geographic Information Systems)   The use of sophisticated mapping computers and attendant electronic databases to analyze the positioning of any geographically distributed phenomenon, for example, archaeological **sites.**

global positioning   Determining an exact location on Earth through the use of **Global Positioning Satellites** (see **GPS**).

GPS (Global Positioning Satellite)   A satellite in geosynchronous orbit used to very precisely locate the observer on Earth. Originally used strictly by the U.S. military for location and targeting, the GPS satellites have now been made available to anyone who needs to pinpoint precisely the location of anything, for example, an archaeological **site.**

historical archaeologists   Archaeologists who focus on cultures with a system of writing. In the United States and Canada, historical archaeologists ordinarily focus on the period after Columbus's voyages and examine sites and documents associated with European, Asian, and African migrants to the New World and their descendants.

historical record   The written record including official documents (birth, school, marriage, death), personal documentation (letters, diaries), and published histories.

hominids   Human beings and our ancestors who walked on two feet. Technically, members of the taxonomic family Hominidae. The first hominids date back to about 4.4 million years ago in Africa.

hunter-gatherers   People whose subsistence base includes hunted wild animals and gathered wild plants; foragers.

industrial archaeologist   Historical archaeologists who focus on the material remains of industrial sites including those related to resource extraction, manufacturing, energy production, and transportation.

in situ   Literally "in place." **Artifacts** or **features** at an archaeological **site** that have not been moved since they were deposited by human beings are "in situ."

Iron Age   Usually used to label the period in human history characterized by the smelting of iron and its use in industry commonly thought to have begun about 3,000 years ago in western Asia and Egypt. The term is of limited applicability because iron tools replaced bronze tools in different places and at different times.

laser transit   Sophisticated sighting device employing a laser that is used in making topographic maps.

Late Woodland Period   Prehistoric time period in eastern North America. The Woodland Period (Early, Middle, and Late) dates from 2,700 years ago to the time of initial European contact. The Late Woodland is generally dated from approximately 1,200 years ago to initial European contact in the early seventeenth century (about 350 years ago).

Late Archaic Period   Prehistoric time period in eastern North America. The Archaic Period (Early, Middle, Late, and Terminal) is dated from after 9,000 to about 2,700 years ago. The Late Archaic is generally dated from 5,000 to 3,400 years ago.

lithic replication   The process in **experimental archaeology** of making stone (lithic) tools in an attempt to copy and illuminate an ancient technology.

material remains   Those physical objects found at an archaeological **site** that have been preserved and can be recovered and examined.

material culture   The things people make and use. Material culture becomes the **material remains** found at an archaeological **site.**

matrix   The surrounding soil in which archaeological remains are found.

midden   Pile or deposit of organic remains (food and other trash) left by ancient people.

Middle Archaic Period   Prehistoric time period in eastern North America. The Archaic Period (Early, Middle, Late, and Terminal) is dated from after 9,000 to about 2,700 years ago. The Middle Archaic is generally dated from 7,000 to 5,000 years ago.

mode of subsistence   Means by which a people supply the material necessities of life, especially food (hunting and gathering, horticulture, agriculture).

mtDNA analysis   Examination of mtDNA (mitochondrial DNA). MtDNA is found in all of an animal's cells and is useful, along with standard DNA, in tracing evolution and in the identification of an individual based on bone, blood, or other body fluid samples.

Munsell   A soil color guidebook that consists of pages of precisely identified and named color chips. Allows for the accurate and consistent identification and recording of soil colors.

National Register of Historic Places A federally mandated and maintained honor role of places (houses, battlefields, mines, bridges, archaeological **sites,** and so forth) deemed historically significant and worthy of recognition and preservation according to an established set of criteria.

National Historic Sites Protection Act Law passed in 1966 that established as a government policy the identification, protection, and preservation of historic sites for their cultural, educational, aesthetic, and inspirational qualities. This law also mandated establishment of the current **National Register of Historic Places.**

Native American Graves Protection and Repatriation Act Federal law passed in 1990 that protects the graves of Native Americans. Prohibits the desecration of these graves and mandates that Native American skeletons and funerary objects housed in museums in the United States be returned to descendant communities for reconsecration and, usually, reburial.

Neandertal (alt. spelling, Neanderthal) Ancient form of humanity. The Neandertals existed approximately 130,000 to 30,000 years ago in Europe and the Middle East. They were anatomically quite distinct from modern humans and likely were not directly ancestral to us.

New Archaeology Refers to a revolution in archaeological method and theory beginning in the 1960s that applied a scientific, deductive approach to reasoning, was ecological in perspective, and applied mathematical and computer models to archaeological questions.

nonreactive behavior Behavior not affected by its scientific analysis. Trash disposed of without the knowledge that it will be examined is nonreactive behavior. The behavior is conducted as usual without any attempt to change it merely because someone will be analyzing it. Compare to **reactive behavior.**

obsidian Naturally occurring volcanic glass that is usually black and translucent at the edges. An excellent raw material used by ancient people for producing extremely sharp-edged tools.

Old Stone Age Paleolithic. Refers to the period from about 2.5 million years ago to about 10,000 years ago.

oral history Traditional stories verbally passed down from generation to generation.

osteological Relating to bone.

pace and compass map Map produced with a compass and by pacing out distances. Usually preliminary to a more sophisticated map using surveying tools like a **laser transit.**

Paleo-Indian Time period and culture in the New World dating from about 11,500 to 9,000 years ago. Often characterized by the use of large stone spear points with channels or "flutes" (as in a fluted column) on both faces to facilitate hafting onto a wooden shaft.

paleoanthropologists Anthropologists who focus on the physical and cultural evolution of ancient forms of humanity.

paleoenvironment The ancient environment including temperature, precipitation, seasonality, and plant and animal communities.

paleopathology The study of ancient pathology and disease. Often the human skeleton exhibits diagnostic traces of pathology (diseases like cancer, arthritis, and tuberculosis; nutritional deficiencies; trauma). Paleopathologists search for such evidence in an attempt to reconstruct the health of an ancient individual or of an entire community.

Pequot War Battle fought in 1637 between the Pequot Indians of southeastern Connecticut and the European colonists of their territory. Of short duration, the war ended when the English colonists burned the main Pequot village, killing more than 400 people.

perimortem Latin for "near to death." Used by forensic anthropologists to describe conditions of the skeleton that originated near to the time of death of the individual, as opposed to "postmortem" features that occurred on the bones after the person's death.

physical anthropology The anthropological study of human beings from a biological perspective, usually including questions of the biological evolution of humanity and biological variation among modern human beings. The same as **biological anthropology.**

potlatch Ceremony held by Northwest Coast Indians in the United States and Canada in which an enormous amount of wealth and goods are freely given away.

potsherds, pottery sherds Broken pieces of pottery.

prehistoric Belonging to a period before the development of a written record.

prehistory The period of the past before the development of a written record.

provenance Source or origin. Also used as a synonym for **provenience.**

provenience The exact location in an archaeological **site** where an **artifact** or **feature** was found.

pubic symphysis Point of articulation between the two halves of the pelvis. The pubic symphysis exhibits a regular pattern of wear during the life of an individual that can be used to determine the age at death.

reactive behavior Behavior that is affected by its scientific analysis. People's responses to a surveyor's questions about their trash disposal habits represent reactive behavior (their responses may be affected by the fact that someone is asking the question and, possibly, passing judgment on them). Compare to **nonreactive behavior.**

shovel test pits Holes excavated with shovels in the initial testing of an area in the search for subsurface archaeological remains. Usually all soil removed in a shovel test pit is passed through hardware cloth screening of one-quarter or one-eighth inch mesh in the search for even very small bits of archaeological evidence. Once a site is found in this way, further subsurface investigation is conducted with smaller tools including trowels, brushes, and dental picks.

site A place where people in the past lived, worked, or carried out a task and left **material remains** of their activities. An archaeological site may have been a city, a village, a camp, a quarry, a cemetery, among many other possibilities.

site report A detailed accounting of an archaeological **site** including a description of its excavation as well as an enumeration and analysis of all materials found at the site and their spatial contexts.

skull The bony container for the brain along with the bones of the face. Includes the **cranium** and the lower jaw or mandible.

soil matrix The surrounding soil in which archaeological remains are found.

spear points Sharp, pointed, usually symmetrical stone weapons ordinarily hafted onto wooden shafts.

Stonehenge Five-thousand-year-old site in the south of England, part of a broad cultural practice of the construction of large stone (megalithic) monuments. The main part of Stonehenge consists of thirty huge, upright stones, each 10 feet tall and weighing approximately 50,000 pounds, arranged in a 100-foot circle. These stone uprights are connected at their apexes with 30 stone lintels, each weighing about 12,000 pounds.

stratigraphic layers Natural layers in the soil or regular, imposed layers by which archaeologists excavate and keep track of the vertical positioning of **in situ** archaeological material.

stratigraphy The layering of soil.

Terminal Archaic Period Prehistoric time period in eastern North America. The Archaic Period (Early, Middle, Late, and Terminal) is dated from after 9,000 to about 2,700 years ago. The Terminal Archaic is generally dated from 3,400 to 2,700 years ago.

test excavation A preliminary **excavation** or sounding to determine the presence of archaeological material, to assess the density of this material, or to determine the **stratigraphy** of a **site.**

test pit A test **excavation,** usually a **shovel test pit,** undertaken to determine the presence of archaeological material, to assess the density of archaeological material, or to determine the **stratigraphy** of a **site.**

topographic map A map showing the terrain of an area.

Upper Paleolithic The final period of the Paleolithic or **Old Stone Age** in Europe dating from 40,000 to about 10,000 years ago.

Index